Administration of Intercollegiate Athletics

Administration of Intercollegiate Athletics

Erianne A. Weight, PhD, MBA

University of North Carolina at Chapel Hill

Robert H. Zullo, PhD

Seton Hill University

Editors

Human Kinetics

Library of Congress Cataloging-in-Publication Data

Administration of intercollegiate athletics / [edited by] Erianne A. Weight, Robert H. Zullo.
  pages cm
 Includes bibliographical references and index.
 1. College sports--United States--Management. 2. National Collegiate Athletic Association. 3. National Association of Intercollegiate Athletics. I. Weight, Erianne A., 1981- author, editor of compilation. II. Zullo, Robert, 1975- author, editor of compilation.
 GV351.A36 2014
 796.043--dc23

ISBN: 978-1-4504-6815-2 (print)

The web addresses cited in this text were current as of April 2013, unless otherwise noted.

Acquisitions Editor: Myles Schrag; **Developmental Editor:** Melissa J. Zavala; **Managing Editor:** Anne Cole; **Copyeditor:** Tom Tiller; **Indexer:** Susan Danzi Hernandez; **Permissions Manager:** Dalene Reeder; **Graphic Designer:** Joe Buck; **Cover Designer:** Keith Blomberg; **Photograph (cover):** © Bill Shettle/Icon SMI; **Photo Asset Manager:** Laura Fitch; **Visual Production Assistant:** Joyce Brumfield; **Photo Production Manager:** Jason Allen; **Art Manager:** Kelly Hendren; **Associate Art Manager:** Alan L. Wilborn; **Printer:** Bang Printing

Printed in the United States of America

10 9 8 7 6 5 4 3 2 1

The paper in this book is certified under a sustainable forestry program.

Human Kinetics
Website: www.HumanKinetics.com

United States: Human Kinetics
P.O. Box 5076
Champaign, IL 61825-5076
800-747-4457
e-mail: humank@hkusa.com

Canada: Human Kinetics
475 Devonshire Road Unit 100
Windsor, ON N8Y 2L5
800-465-7301 (in Canada only)
e-mail: info@hkcanada.com

Europe: Human Kinetics
107 Bradford Road
Stanningley
Leeds LS28 6AT, United Kingdom
+44 (0) 113 255 5665
e-mail: hk@hkeurope.com

Australia: Human Kinetics
57A Price Avenue
Lower Mitcham, South Australia 5062
08 8372 0999
e-mail: info@hkaustralia.com

New Zealand: Human Kinetics
P.O. Box 80
Torrens Park, South Australia 5062
0800 222 062
e-mail: info@hknewzealand.com

E6118

Contents

Preface

The industry of intercollegiate athletics is poised for a renaissance. This book comes to press amid a steady stream of tumult in the media, where headlines are dominated by community-shaking scandals, passionate reform commentaries, league-altering court cases, spiking expenses for facilities and coaches' salaries, conference realignment announcements, and concerns about athletes' health and safety. These media emphases provide a very narrow representation of intercollegiate athletics as being founded on a win-at-all-costs mentality in a multibillion-dollar industry.

However, when one searches beyond the headlines and game-day stadium scenes into the actual corridors of athletics departments, the overtones of scandal and greed quickly fade into the (often luxurious) shadows. Here, we see thousands of administrators working long hours, generally for very modest pay, and striving to facilitate educational growth opportunities for their student-athletes and service to their community.

We also see thousands of student-athletes striving to balance the demands of their complex lives. They often rise from bed far earlier than other college students. They face grueling training sessions at the mercy of coaches who wield power over their time, their bodies, and sometimes even their minds. They attend a full load of classes, often while physically exhausted; participate in additional extracurricular activities required of athletes; and, in many cases, work part-time jobs to help cover their expenses. And they meet these demands in addition to all the demands faced by typical full-time college students while often living under scrutiny from the media, fans, and sometimes even their classmates, professors, and friends.

It is for these athletes that the industry of intercollegiate athletics exists. It is for them that most athletics administrators, coaches, and staff members choose to devote their professional (and much of their personal) lives to facilitating positive life-changing experiences. Indeed, given that athletics is a facet of our educational system—and a department within our colleges and universities designed to provide opportunities for educational growth—it is troubling to witness the growing divergence between the narrow public perception and the general private reality. It is, in fact, heartbreaking to witness the extravagance, hypocrisy, and mentality of the few who perpetuate the ills in the industry and take advantage of the power that can be so easily wielded over a population of extraordinary collegiate athletes.

The revolution that this industry needs is sitting right in front of these words. The revolution this industry needs is you. We need well-trained leaders who understand the purpose of intercollegiate athletics and care about the athletes the educational model should sustain. We need leaders who understand how critical money is to the operation of college sport and who think strategically about how it is disbursed and are selective and innovative in its attainment. We need leaders who passionately strive to fulfill the missions of their universities through faculty–athletics partnerships, who act as responsible stakeholders of their university's brand, and who strive to use the power of athletics to benefit their communities. We need leaders who embrace diversity and understand how valuable, and essential, it is to involve multiple perspectives in critical and everyday decision making. We need leaders who challenge the status quo, challenge the media, prepare for the future, and believe in the transforming power of intercollegiate athletics. If this sounds like a challenge you are up for, then read on, because we need you to be at the forefront of the intercollegiate athletics renaissance that is on the horizon.

To help you prepare to take part in such a transformation, this text provides you with an overview of the daily operations and inner workings of intercollegiate athletics departments. We pair this foundational knowledge with chapter-by-chapter leadership lessons, discussion questions, and learning activities to help you prepare for the active role you will soon play in the industry. The text focuses on larger NCAA-governed institutions but also includes examples of policies and procedures for governance and management structures

eBook available at HumanKinetics.com

that vary depending on the resources and objectives of a school.

A test package and image bank are available for instructors at www.HumanKinetics.com/AdministrationOfIntercollegiateAthletics. The test package includes questions that instructors can use to create customized tests. The image bank includes all of the art and tables sorted by chapter, and can be used to create customized presentations based on specific course requirements and other learning aids for students.

We begin this journey with a historical foundation written by Dr. Ellen Staurowsky, a beloved champion of student-athletes' rights, a former director of athletics, and a leading scholar of intercollegiate athletics. We then move to a discussion of governing bodies with the help of Barbara Osborne, a sport law expert and former senior woman administrator and associate athletics director. The third chapter covers leadership and management principles from scholarly literature infused with personal insights and application examples from intercollegiate athletics from a variety of leaders in the field. Richard Baddour lent tremendous expertise to this chapter in his first semester after retiring from his impactful 15 years as director of athletics at the University of North Carolina at Chapel Hill.

The book then transitions into a chapter-by-chapter examination of subunits within the athletics umbrella, highlighting interdepartmental synergies and opportunities for leadership throughout the athletics organizational chart. These chapters have been carefully crafted by academic and professional leaders in order to provide a foundation from which you can confidently practice, lead, and innovate in this industry that we care about so deeply.

Acknowledgments

When Rob approached me at a NASSM conference several years ago with a clear vision for this book and an amazing foundation already in place, I knew immediately it was a project I wanted to tackle because of the knowledge I would gain and the wonderful companion I would have along the journey. Thus, my primary thanks at the conclusion of this project goes to Rob Zullo, whose passion for the field of intercollegiate athletics and sport management education is continually inspiring. The support of the Human Kinetics' team was also incredible. Myles Schrag, Melissa Zavala, and Anne Cole each went above and beyond in their support, meticulous edits, and thoughtful feedback at every step of the journey. I would like to thank my students, colleagues, and mentors at The University of North Carolina at Chapel Hill, Bowling Green State University, and Indiana University. I have learned so much from each of you and am grateful for the guidance, inspiration, and challenges that inspire me to continually seek knowledge and work to improve every day in every facet of my professional expedition.

I am grateful for the countless professionals who contributed to the content of the book. At the outset, Rob and I determined to have the content of each chapter be driven largely by what practitioners told us they wished they had known, and what they wished their new hires knew. Toward that end, we conducted many interviews and phone calls in order to gather and articulate this valuable information. Special acknowledgement to Richard Baddour and Scott Palanjian, in particular, for their tremendous help in the foundational stages of the text. Their insights, research and encouragement were paramount to this project coming to fruition.

I would like to thank my high school and college track coaches and officials for fueling my passion and paradigm. I would not be in this field, nor would I hold the passion I do for intercollegiate athletics, had I not experienced how wonderful and transformational education through athletics can be. Coaches Jones, Caviness, Boyack, and Archer, thank you for being my mentors, advocates, and teachers.

Finally, I would like to express my gratitude to my incredible parents, Daniel and Linda Allen, for instilling a foundational hunger for education and appreciation of hard work, and for being a constant source of support and encouragement in every aspect of my life; my sisters, Chelsea, Megan, and Lindsay, for being my eternal best friends; my husband, Matt, for being my primary research partner, source of joy, fount of wisdom, and absolute perfect companion in life; and my daughters, Aleah and Lillian, for providing a completely new lens through which to see the world, for making me smile and laugh continually, and for reminding me of what really matters in life.

—Erianne A. Weight, PhD

My motivation in creating this book stems from my time with Drs. Ronald Hyatt, Doug Toma, Myles Brand, Gerhard Lenski, Peter Zullo, and Robert Gruver. Each has served as a tremendous influence both personally and professionally on a continuous basis.

I need to recognize Myles Schrag and his team at Human Kinetics for believing in the proposal and standing by the project through its fruition. You all are unbelievable. Many thanks and appreciation to my students for your daily inspiration, as I am so proud of you and amazed at your successes. Thank you to my colleagues at the University of Virginia, the Virginia Military Institute, the University of North Carolina, Virginia Tech, University of Georgia, Mississippi State University, and James Madison University. A special salute to Claude Felton and Matt Chelap, two amazing friends and mentors, who are the models my students should emulate in terms of professionalism. Thank you to friends, colleagues, and mentors in Professors Dawn Bennett-Alexander, John Billing, Sarah Fields, Billy Hawkins, Fred Mueller, Barbara Osborne, Ed Shields, and David Shonk. You all planted the seeds. I also need to acknowledge Seton Hill University and my wonderful colleagues in the business division, as well as President JoAnne Boyle, President Bibiana Boerio, Sister Victoria Marie Gribschaw, and Provost Mary Ann Gawelek. You truly never work a day in your life if you love what you do.

Much love to my better half, Ashley, who completes me, and to my mother and my siblings who inspire me. Finally, much thanks, appreciation, and eternal gratitude to such a distinguished colleague, Erianne Weight.

—Robert H. Zullo, PhD

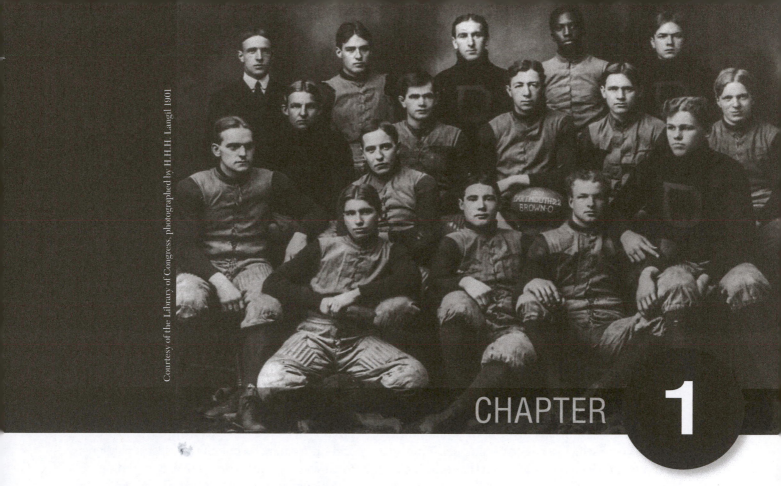

CHAPTER 1

A Brief Historical Perspective on Intercollegiate Athletics

Ellen J. Staurowsky, Drexel University

In this chapter, you will explore

- higher education and student experience in nineteenth-century America,

- the early years of college sport as a student-led enterprise,

- the emergence of the NCAA and the evolution of college sport governance,

- the distinct history of women's college sport as an integrated part of the educational enterprise,

- the role of historically black colleges and American Indian boarding schools in providing athletics opportunities for students of color, and

- concluding thoughts about how these threads combine to form a backdrop for what we understand about college sport today.

HISTORICAL PERSPECTIVES IN THE LIVES OF COLLEGE SPORT ADMINISTRATORS

As a director of athletics, the daily demands of your job loom large. As much good will and enthusiasm as your program has engendered in the community and among constituencies on your own campus (i.e., administrators, alumni, athletes, donors, faculty, fans, media, and parents), you cannot help but notice that there is a constant wave of dissatisfaction manifest in persistent calls for reform, concerns about athlete health and well-being, questions about whether athletes are receiving a legitimate education while pursuing their sports and frustrations with the perceptions that coaches are paid too much and the athletic department is engaged in excessive spending.

In confronting those issues as a leader, what do you educate yourself about and how do you approach these problems? To know an industry is to know what forces have shaped its present and future. The only way to do that is by looking to the past. In college sport, there is a certain reverence for some aspects of history. Traditions as embodied in school colors, the alma mater, certain rituals associated with your particular school and conference, and storied rivalries all speak to connections with the past. At the same time, within the average working day, the scripts that you enact on a daily basis have often been set in motion generations before you ever took over the reins of leadership. Unseen and unknown, they may guide you in directions you are not even aware of. The greater appreciation you have for the historical roots of the college sport enterprise, the more you are able to understand problems as they exist in present day and the more able you will be to identify ways to address those problems. While you do not want to be bound by the past, you also do not want to approach problems from a position of ignorance. Balancing the past, present, and future may be one of the biggest challenges for anyone seeking to lead college sport programs effectively in the 21st Century. To be better prepared, read on.

Poll a dozen people about their perspectives on the value of college sport to higher education and a dozen different answers are likely to be expressed. There will be those who extol the virtues of participation in college sport, the bonding, the camaraderie, the tests of courage and will. There will be others who point to the benefit college sport provides in creating avenues to education, inspiring work ethic, goal orientation, and focus that predicts success in academic settings. And there will be still others who celebrate the capacity of college sport to serve as an anchor for institutional identity, pride in place, a generator for publicity, and a bridge between higher education and broader communities.

Though the value of college sport may be obvious to some, its shape and contours have been forged out of controversy and ongoing calls for reform. Today, the intense media scrutiny that is characteristic of twenty-first-century society highlights an array of issues for Americans to contemplate related to the college sport enterprise. Yet this flurry of broadcast and journalistic analysis bears a remarkable resemblance to concerns expressed generations earlier and dating back as far as 150 years or more. For example, a college president faced with the challenge of attracting a student body and meeting enrollment demands in the early 1900s was as likely to fret then as she is today about the threats posed by athletics to academic integrity. Indeed, more than 100 years ago, Woodrow Wilson, then president of Princeton University and later the 28th president of the United States, observed that the centerpiece of higher education often competed for attention with other offerings that both students and the general public found more alluring: "The sideshows are so numerous, so diverting—so important, if you will—that they have swallowed up the circus, and those who perform in the main tent often whistle for their audiences, discouraged and humiliated" (Wilson, 1909, p. 576).

These tensions were recently revisited by Scott Carlson (2013), who explored the evolution of the "country club" college. At such institutions, administrators invest more and more in "consumption amenities," such as athletics complexes and other kinds of entertainment, that lend the air of a resort community to the experience of campus residential life as a way to maintain market share and garner publicity. In fact, regardless of whether we are talking about small, selective institutions in the least competitive arena of what the National Collegiate Athletic Association (NCAA) refers to as Division III—where athletics is viewed as critical to the overall admissions process because of its power to bring tuition-paying students to campus (Stevens, 2007)—or about large public universities with multimillion-dollar athletics programs that draw more than a hundred thousand fans to football games, the relationship between athletics and academics has rarely been harmonious (Desrochers, 2013).

Indeed, one encounters an almost parallel universe when comparing today's headlines with those that appeared in earlier years when the structure of college sport was being put into place. For example, a diary maintained by Harvard football coach Bill Reid in 1905 indicates the preoccupations that accompanied the job (Smith, 1994). For one thing, the media had to be managed, and deception was not out of the question. In addition, as the highest-paid coach in the country at the time, Reid became the focal point for discussions about excessive coach compensation, much like Ohio State's Urban Meyer (Staurowsky, 2011) or Alabama's Nick Saban today (Brady, Berkowitz, & Upton, 2012).

Reid also shared with Meyer an anxiety born of the job that led to deterioration of his own health. When Meyer took the head coaching job at Ohio State in the fall of 2011, he had been on a hiatus from coaching due to job-related anxiety. He had stepped away from great success in a highly lucrative coaching position at the University of Florida, where his teams had won the Bowl Championship Series (BCS) national championship game in 2005 and 2006 (Buckeye Biography, 2013).

Reid also faced other challenges—such as keeping athletes eligible and managing relationships with faculty—that resonate with current discussions regarding the NCAA's academic reform efforts (O'Neil, 2012) and current investigations into academic fraud (Pickeral, 2012). Reid pondered how to deal with players who exhibited too great a preference for strong drink, womanizing,

and altercations with the law. These themes are all too familiar today, as in the case of a former University of Miami booster who disclosed that he had treated athletes to lavish parties, given them money and jewelry, and arranged sexual favors for them (Robinson, 2011).

In the area of campus politics, Reid undermined university president Charles Eliot's efforts to ban football by going to Harvard's governing board. In the present day, power struggles involving coaches who make more than their presidents (and in some cases more than any other public official in their state) continue to raise concern that college presidents are not in charge of athletics (Staurowsky, 2011).

Despite these similarities, some dramatic differences have also emerged in the evolving American educational landscape. Colleges and universities once dominated by male students are now populated by coeducational student bodies, and on many campuses female students are in the majority. Similarly, racial segregation has given way to integrated campuses. As these changes have occurred, athletics programs have also changed. As a result, grounding our approach to intercollegiate athletics in an appreciation of its historical roots offers insight into how issues arise and develop, what happens when issues remain unresolved, and where potential pathways to progress might be uncovered.

HIGHER EDUCATION AND STUDENT EXPERIENCE IN NINETEENTH-CENTURY AMERICA

In the modern consciousness, it would be difficult to dispute the notion that football serves as the center of the solar system of college sport. In the December 2012 IMG Intercollegiate Athletics Forum (presented by *Street & Smith's SportsBusiness Daily/Global/Journal*), the tone for the two-day discussion of the business of college sport was set when it was announced that "college football owns Saturdays," meaning that college football drew the highest Saturday night ratings among network television programs seven times during the 2012 season (Elfman, 2012). In a further indication of football's status, in the lead-up to the first night

King Football

The term "king football," which has been used to describe the power and money associated with college football, comes from the title of a book written in 1932 by Reed Harris, a student editor of the Columbia University school newspaper. Harris' attacks on football as overly commercial and anti-intellectual eventually resulted in his dismissal from the university. When he was readmitted after an appeal, he declined and wrote the book instead.

As Michael Oriard (2001) reports in his book on the evolution of college football from 1920 to 1950, the expression "king football" was appropriated by others who either decried its vulgarity or celebrated its expression of the boldness of the American spirit. See the cover of Oriard's book in figure 1.1. Here are two *New York Times* headlines from stories dealing with alleged corruption in the college game; the first was published in 1932, the second, nearly 80 years later, in 2011.

King Football: Racket or Sport? (Kiernan, 1932)

The Dangerous Cocoon of King Football (Vecsey, 2011)

Figure 1.1 *King Football* by Michael Oriard.

game of the 2012 season, ESPN hosted an online chat about college football that lasted 25 hours. However, for all of football's dominance today, it was not always this way.

In fact, in the years before the American Civil War, football was decades away from being crowned king, and other sports were pursued as occasional pastimes. Institutions of higher learning were small. Typically, "Old Main," a large central building imbued architecturally with the hopes and aspirations of the founders, housed the administration, served as the location for classrooms, and provided a space for social activities (Dober, 2007). Dormitories offered spartan conditions (Mendenhall, 1993). Fraternity life emerged out of literary and secret societies, and students made their homes in fraternity-sponsored lodges or houses (Birdseye, 1907).

A day in the life of a college student in the 1850s would likely include rising early and attending chapel. A good portion of the morning and early afternoon would be dedicated to lectures and recitations, and the evening would be devoted to studying. The afternoons, however, presented students with free time—time to escape faculty demands and the monotony of a curriculum that was sometimes boring, dry, or unchallenging and instead pursue their own interests and activities (Mendenhall, 1993; Smith, 1988). Often living in rural communities that offered few amusements, students made their own fun and gravitated at times toward the rebellious.

Indeed, though campuses may have been pastoral, the atmosphere often was not. To the contrary, collective student unrest was a hallmark of early campus life (Allmendinger, 1973), and it could be triggered by any of a number of motivations, some of the worst involving bad food (Ireland, 2012). Between 1766 and 1834, for example, Harvard was the site of no less than eight rebellions, which resulted in property damage, physical clashes between faculty and administrators, and mass student suspensions and expulsions (Ireland).

Male students' physical pursuits were also areas of ambivalence and protest. Faculty and college administrator efforts to manage the engagement of male students in sport activities eventually distilled into two complementary but often competing models of sport participation—one being the eventual foundation for the intercollegiate athletics team model and the other being "the collegiate gymnastics model." While male students pursued rough team games such as shinny, a form of hockey that inspired faculty members to ban it as "low and unbecoming of gentlemen and scholars" (Rudolph, 1990, p. 151), gymnast-physicians advocated physical training regimens based on German and Swedish gymnastics to promote overall health and well-being (Soares, 1979).

As a result of that advocacy, schools in the Northeast started to build gymnasiums to support these programs, beginning with Harvard in 1820 (Seidentop & Vandermars, 2011). In 1860, Amherst College added a Department of Hygiene and Physical Education (Sweet, 2011) to address concern about student health and the rise of team sports that were becoming more attractive. As the nineteenth century wore on, however, students balked at the "mechanical," "business-like" approach to movement professed by their instructors (Rudolph, 1990, p. 153). As a result, the tide began to turn. "While pre–Civil War educators thought gymnastics foster[ed] self-control and were superior to most team sports, postwar students began to argue that athletics assuaged the monotony of the industrial-era curriculum" (Ingrassia, 2012, p. 22).

It is something of an irony, then, given the focus educators placed on student health concerns, that intercollegiate athletics owes its start to the exhaustion of a quite serious young man who was wearing himself thin studying for the Junior Exhibition at Yale University in 1852, where he delivered a speech titled "Roma Disrepta" in Latin (Mendenhall, 1993; Whiton, 1901). But so it was. James Whiton had brought honor to himself and his family by placing second in his class that May, missing out on the top spot by a mere fraction of a point. The effort left him "out of sorts," and a decision was made for him to return to New Hampshire with his family to rest and rejuvenate. On that trip home, Whiton met with a business associate of his father's, James Elkins, an agent with the Boston, Concord, and Montreal (BC&M) railroad. In the course of their conversation, the idea for a rowing regatta was born (Mendenhall, 1997; Smith, 1988), and "the assurance of a free excursion and a jolly lark" was persuasive enough to get four teams (three from Yale and one from Harvard) to sign on (Mendenhall, 1993, p. 16).

Patterned after the Oxford and Cambridge regatta in England (Ingrassia, 2012), this one featured three teams from Yale and one from Harvard competing on Lake Winnipesaukee in front of an audience of roughly a thousand spectators. The crowd included a future U.S. president, as well as local dignitaries and politicians, members of the "fairer sex" waving their handkerchiefs, enterprising vendors making the most of the occasion, and curious townspeople (Mendenhall, 1993; Smith, 1988). An original handbill promoting the event (figure 1.2) documents both the expense associated with building the boats and the discipline of the men who crewed them. A training race in the morning was followed by lunch, mineral water, ale, brandy, and cigars—a menu that apparently agreed with the members of the Harvard crew, who went on to victory in the afternoon, collecting a set of silver-tipped black walnut oars for their trouble (Mendenhall, 1993; Smith, 1988).

At a gala dinner and dance later that day, "toasts were drunk, and the oarsmen passed resolutions thanking their hosts and particularly the committee for the treatment they had received" (Mendenhall, 1993, p. 20). Collecting their free passes, they then boarded the BC&M and returned to their institutions, having taken part in an event that, despite one skeptic's prediction that it would be a "frolic without sequel," became a model for other regattas and contributed to the growth of intercollegiate athletics on college campuses (Sack & Staurowsky, 1998).

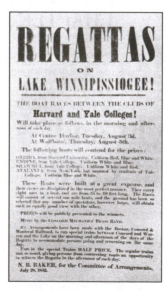

Figure 1.2 **Promotional handbill for the 1852 Harvard-Yale regatta.**

From that point on, as intercollegiate athletics grew, questions arose about who should run them and how they should be run. Through the early part of the twentieth century, intercollegiate athletics for men were run by students in an entrepreneurial fashion similar to the approach taken by James Whiton at Yale. Organizers experimented with a range of financial models—creating student organizations and associations for the purpose of collecting dues to support their athletic endeavors; approaching businesses for sponsorship of teams and events; selling tickets to contests; and promoting fundraising campaigns.

These developments happened alongside the rapid expansion of educational institutions (as a result of the Morrill Land-Grant Acts of 1862 and 1890) into states whose populations had not yet grown enough to support them (Sack & Staurowsky, 1998, p. 19). In this context, institutions faced greater competition for students and increasing pressure to move away from a classical curriculum in favor of programs that focused more on practical skills in order to appeal to an increasingly business-minded public. In turn, college administrators began to use advertising as a means of selling their institutions. "What they needed more than anything was a bridge that could link the high culture of the university with the mass culture of the broader society. . . . In the late 1800s few campus activities could better meet that need than intercollegiate sport" (Sack & Staurowsky, p. 20).

In particular, football—with its flare for spectacle, its assurances of masculine superiority, and its tests of valor, made for and by the sport pages (Oriard, 2001)—assumed a new status among the sports that were taking hold on college and university campuses. Though baseball, basketball, tennis, track and field, wrestling, and other sports also commanded interest among students, football's star was ascending. This development was aided in no small measure by increasing commercialism, which took the form of building stadiums for the purposes of generating gate receipts and drawing large numbers of people to campuses, cultivating media attention, and forging relationships with boosters and sponsors (Smith, 1988; Sack & Staurowsky, 1998). Amid these changes, student leadership would give way to professional coaches hired to bring a scientific approach to coaching and performance. Schools that hired professional coaches, such as Yale and Harvard, would dominate the intercollegiate athletics scene well into the twentieth century—but not without a price to be paid (Smith; Sack & Staurowsky).

While administrators fed the growth of intercollegiate athletics, and student interest carried it forward, faculty members opposed the incorporation of athletics as mass spectacle. They warned of the dangers of increasing commercialism and professionalism and labeled the model a threat to the academic mission of higher education (Chu, 1989). Faculty strongly opposed the recruiting of "tramp athletes" who were "subsidized" (in other words, paid to play) and did not attend classes, as well as the "smash mouth" nature of football, where formations such as the flying wedge set the stage for bloodshed and occasionally death (McQuilkin & Smith, 1993).

Concern about threats to academic integrity, as well as students' health and well-being, served as rallying points around which faculty mobilized to exert influence over college sport during this era. Indeed, according to Barr (1998, p. 5), "the high point of faculty control in intercollegiate athletics" occurred between 1895 and 1914, as they worked to form faculty-led conferences. These efforts contributed to the creation of the National Collegiate Athletic Association.

THE NCAA AND THE FOUNDATIONS OF A COLLEGE SPORT GOVERNANCE STRUCTURE

As faculty attempted to assert their voice against an expanding tide of support from students, alumni, governing boards, and the public, college presidents were caught in the middle—trying to respond to the requirements of institutions with uncertain financial futures while working to mediate disputes on both sides. Meanwhile, slippage in the status of athletics was becoming ever more problematic. The understanding of athletes as unpaid amateurs was subverted by boosters who offered payments under the table. In addition, with a touch of creativity from team loyalists who had deep pockets, athletes were hired into jobs for which they were paid to do nothing (Sack & Staurowsky, 1998). In a

1905 article in *Collier's,* Stanford president David Starr Jordan laid responsibility at the feet of faculty members and declared that the standards of colleges should exist "in fact as well as in name." He elaborated as follows:

> *The professor who neglects his duty to escape the execrations of the bleachers is an accessory in fact to whatever the bleachers may demand. Nine-tenths of the athletic parasites remain through neglect on the part of the individual professors or through the scholarship committees to do their own duty in the matter of upholding standards.*

> David Starr Jordan, president,
> Stanford University, 1905

Professors who understood Jordan's point were organizing and attempting to provide oversight to rein in college sport from the professional and commercial influences that were increasingly taking it away from the mandates of higher education. Most significant, in 1895, a group of faculty members started the process of forming the Intercollegiate Conference of Faculty Representatives, which would later become known as the Western Conference and eventually the Big Ten (Sack & Staurowsky, 1998). In 1898, seven of the eight schools that now make up the Ivy League sought to exert similar control when faculty, students, and alumni from all but Yale attended a conference on college sport reform at Brown University. Seeking to create an interinstitutional governance structure, the participants addressed agenda items that included athletics scholarships, undergraduate and graduate eligibility, summer baseball for pay, commercialism, and the role of faculty in athletics governance (Sack & Staurowsky, 1998).

In 1906, these attempts to control athletics and respond to calls for reform led to creation of the NCAA—the first in a long line of college sport reform efforts that continue today. For a timeline of major athletics reform efforts, see figure 1.3.

Though noble in intent, the report from the 1898 conference at Brown reads as if it were written by people who—despite understanding the high purpose of an amateur approach to college sport—were somehow unaware that commercial forces and the ever-expanding complex of support for college sport were moving it to the center of higher education rather than the periphery. The point was not lost, however, on R. Tait McKenzie, a renowned physician, physical therapist, physical educator, and sculptor who taught at the University of Pennsylvania. In a 1910 address to the NCAA convention, McKenzie mapped out an exhaustive history of 1,200 years of Greek athletics before observing that college sport was dangerously close to abandoning the amateur model and operating at a level of professionalism that marked the end of the Greek athletic model, in which sport was valued for its entertainment appeal (Crowley, 2006).

Faculty efforts did periodically slow the rising tide of professionalism during certain windows of opportunity. For example, at the 1918 NCAA convention, faculty delegates approved a de-emphasis of campus sport in light of personnel and resource shortages related to World War I. They believed that this step would allow them to rein in college sport (Sperber, 1993). A similar moment occurred in 1926, when the American Association of University Professors issued a bulletin decrying excesses associated with college football and the building of

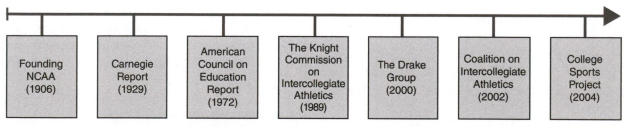

Figure 1.3 **Major athletics reform efforts.**

Reprinted from E. Staurowsky, 2005, *Reclaiming our inheritance as faculty: Understanding academic freedom in relationship to college sport,* Paper presented at the meeting of the North American Society of Sociology and Sport Conference (Greensboro, NC). By permission of E. Staurowsky.

large stadiums, which were perceived as menaces to higher education (Smith, 2011).

Crisis in Football: Player Safety

Another moment of potential opportunity for reform had presented itself during the 1904 football season, which was distinguished by 21 player deaths and more than 200 serious injuries. In response, "muckraking newspapers at the time focused on the brutality and alleged corruption of the game, and editorials began to appear demanding athletic reform" (Sack & Staurowsky, 1998, p. 32). In fact, calls to reform or abolish the game reverberated across the United States, and they found special resonance in the White House.

Moved by public outrage, President Theodore Roosevelt, an outdoor sport enthusiast who extolled the virtues of a strenuous life in response to his own periodic struggles with ill health, took the side of reform. In 1905, Roosevelt convened members of the football power elite who made up the American Intercollegiate Football Rules Committee to discuss the future of the game. When the committee failed to address the problem, a second meeting, and then a third, called by New York University chancellor Henry MacCracken, resulted in the formation of the Intercollegiate Athletic Association of the United States, which in 1912 was renamed as the National Collegiate Athletic Association.

Athlete Eligibility and Amateurism

Despite the fact that football reform catalyzed the formation of the NCAA, the effects of the commercial market were driving the rule-making process even during those first meetings. This reality was evidenced in concerns about fair competition and equal opportunity to share in the profits of what was fast becoming an emerging industry. At the same time, the NCAA, upon its birth, espoused a definition of amateurism borrowed liberally from British universities such as Oxford and Cambridge. Consistent with that standard, members were expected to avoid practices that violated amateurism principles, especially "the offering of inducements to players to enter colleges and universities because of their athletic abilities or supporting or maintaining players while students on account of

their athletic abilities, either by athletic organizations, individual alumni, or otherwise, directly or indirectly" (Intercollegiate Athletic Association of the United States, 1906, p. 33). Member institutions were expected to abide by these rules, though enforcement was left to individual institutions, who were supposed to act in accordance with a code of honor (Crowley, 2006; Sack & Staurowsky, 1998).

Over the years, the NCAA membership continued to define amateurism. Within a decade of the organization's founding, it developed a definition of the amateur athlete. According to Article VI(b) of the 1916 bylaws, an amateur was "one who participates in competitive physical sports only for the pleasure, and the physical, mental, moral, and social benefits directly derived therefrom" (National Collegiate Athletic Association, 1916, p. 118). By 1922, the definition was revised to read as follows: "An amateur sportsman is one who engages in sport solely for the physical, mental, or social benefits he derives therefrom, and to whom the sport is nothing other than an avocation" (National Collegiate Athletic Association, 1922, as quoted in Sack & Staurowsky, 1998, p. 35).

This emphasis on athletic activity as an "avocation" (i.e., diversion or hobby) obscured the fact that male athletes in this era received remuneration in the form of room, board, and other financial compensation to play for college teams. With an enforcement structure that relied on "home rule"—in which individual institutions made their own determinations of how to abide by NCAA rules—schools took liberties. As the NCAA itself notes in retrospect, "'home rule' was both sensible and attuned to the political and philosophical realities of the time, but it carried a built-in tension between the NCAA's commitment to amateurism and its reliance on the member institutions to honor that goal. That 'trust factor' became the root of the Association's early enforcement challenges and it continues as a primary driver of enforcement issues today" (National Collegiate Athletic Association, 2013, para. 3).

Home Rule and the Sanity Code

The NCAA amateur code of the 1920s through the 1940s, which embraced sport participation as an avocation, was rendered unenforceable by factions in the membership and in external publics that did not fully endorse it. The problems arising from this lack of universal agreement about the code were compounded by the fact that home rule left the monitoring of rule violations up to individual institutions. Not surprisingly, this era of college sport was marked by the emergence of an underground economy in which college athletes were paid under the table in the form of jobs, loans, athletics scholarships, and money. In the 1929 Carnegie Report on American College Athletics, which constituted a detailed study of the practices employed by coaches and administrators in running intercollegiate athletics programs at that time, 81 of 112 colleges and universities were found to have offered subsidization (financial support) to athletes because of their ability to compete on teams (Savage, 1929). When publicly questioned about the state of intercollegiate athletics, college presidents would laud the merits of the amateur code even as they overlooked the transgressions happening on their own campuses. Meanwhile, they argued that concerns about hypocrisy in college sport were overblown and merely anecdotal.

Recognizing the need to replace home rule with an effective enforcement mechanism, NCAA members issued an executive regulation in conjunction with the Sanity Code (see sidebar) to create a constitutional compliance committee and a fact-finding committee. The compliance committee was authorized to make rulings about interpretations of constitutional language and to answer inquiries about whether or not certain practices were forbidden by the NCAA constitution. The penalty for an institution that failed to comply with rules was termination of NCAA membership—if approved by a two-thirds vote.

No sooner had the Sanity Code been inserted into the NCAA constitution and the compliance committee put in place than allegations arose that the code was unenforceable. In opponents' views, this half-measure would still allow the underground economy to flourish. In particular, schools in the Southern, Southeastern, and Southwestern conferences took exception to the Sanity Code because they had grown accustomed to offering full athletics scholarships. In fact, they threatened secession from the NCAA.

The crisis continued to mount when the compliance committee announced that twenty institutions were violating rules. Thirteen came off of the list within a year, but the other seven—Boston College, the Citadel, Villanova, Virginia Military Institute, Virginia Polytechnic Institute, the University of Maryland, and the University of Virginia—remained to force the issue. By 1950, schools opposed to the Sanity Code, which they viewed as hypocritical and contradictory to the definition of amateurism, stood their ground, forcing a confrontation at the NCAA convention. When it came time to vote on expelling schools for failing to comply with the Sanity Code, the membership was unable to muster the needed two-thirds majority.

Sanity Code

Efforts by NCAA members to resolve the differing viewpoints about subsidizing athletes eventually led to the passage of the Principles for the Conduct of Intercollegiate Athletics, which later became known as the Sanity Code. The measure was intended as a compromise between Southern schools (e.g., Maryland, Virginia, and the Citadel) that wished to offer athletes full athletics scholarships and Northern schools (e.g., Harvard, Princeton, and Yale) that were opposed to such provisions. The Sanity Code of 1948 conceded the awarding of financial aid for athletic talent but required that awards be need-based, meaning that recipients had to demonstrate financial need. In order to sidestep the fact that athletes were being paid for services provided on the field or court, a clause from earlier constitutions was used to clarify, "No athlete shall be deprived of financial aids . . . because of failure to participate in intercollegiate athletics" (Sack & Staurowsky, 1998, p. 34). This stipulation allowed the awards to be viewed as gifts, thus presumably averting potential problems associated with pay for play.

Thus the experiment of the Sanity Code came to a de facto end, leaving the membership to hammer out another arrangement about the subsidizing of athletes. By 1957, NCAA rules permitted universities to pay athletes room, board, tuition, and fees as an inducement to sign on. Within the rules that governed these athletics scholarships, some vestiges of the amateur ideal continued to operate; for example, an athletics scholarship was to be given to an athlete for four years with the expectation that the award would remain available regardless of the athlete's contribution on the field or court.

In 1972, another change in the rules turned the athletics scholarship into a one-year renewable award, which increased the pressure on athletes to perform. Thus it changed their overall day-to-day relationship with coaching staffs and institutions. Coaches now had the power to terminate scholarship agreements with athletes after one year. Indeed, "within a half century, the concept of amateurism had become a convenient label that the NCAA could arbitrarily define to suit its needs" (Sack & Staurowsky, 1998, p. 47).

Big-Time College Sport and the Influence of Television

From its beginning, college sport has been viewed by its developers and supporters as a form of entertainment. Students enjoyed playing sports, of course, but comparisons between college sport and other forms of entertainment hinged on the capacity of some sports to draw a crowd, garner media attention, and be promoted as events where people wanted to be—and be seen.

The disputes that threatened to break apart the NCAA—over the management of programs and the terms and conditions under which athletes were recruited and compensated in the 1950s—were fueled in part by questions about how television would either enhance or interfere with the money-making potential of football. Under home rule, some schools, such as Notre Dame (three-time national champion in the 1940s) and perennial powerhouse Penn, negotiated television contracts independently in the belief that this new commercial medium offered exposure and financial possibilities not yet fully appreciated (Smith, 2001). The remainder of schools in the East, however, feared that television would negatively affect game attendance; more specifically, they subscribed to the idea that "radio aroused curiosity while television satisfies" (Smith, 2001, p. 60).

Under pressure from the Big Ten and various NCAA institutions, Notre Dame lost its advantage in negotiating its own television deal due to the NCAA's decision to put forward an experimental national television plan designed to control football telecasting nationally. In the experimental year of 1951, Penn notified the NCAA that it would continue with its own plan, only to be labeled a "member not in good standing." With expulsion on the horizon and other schools refusing to play Penn, the NCAA took over national control of football television contracts. In assessing the NCAA's decision at the time, the assistant attorney general of the Department of Justice's antitrust division, H. Graham Morison, commented that "if the colleges commercialize football they must expect commercial rules to be applied to them. If they compete for gate receipts, they should expect to be governed by the laws of free competition" (Smith, 2001, p. 72).

The seeds of discontent sown during this dispute

"Big-Time" College Sport

The term "big-time" is not an accidental or random descriptor of the mass-mediated spectacle of college sport. To the contrary, as Ingrassia (2012, p. 5) notes,

At the turn of the [20th] century, the same time when college football emerged, diverse crowds flocked to entertaining vaudeville variety shows. The companies that sponsored these popular events were dubbed either big-time or small-time, depending on how far they traveled, the size of the cities or theaters where they performed, and the number of tickets sold.

eventually came to fruition in multiple ways. For one thing, the pressure to acquiesce to the NCAA's vision of national television control led Notre Dame president John Cavanaugh to envision a "super conference" of football powers. "Cavanaugh's insights, though not accepted in 1951, eventually were put into practice by the College Football Association [CFA]—a now-defunct group of 63 football colleges formed in 1977 to negotiate television deals—in 1984 and by some of the major conferences in the 1990s" (Smith, 2001, p. 65).

In addition, the anti-trust challenge to the NCAA television policy that had been anticipated by Morison, the assistant attorney general, came in 1984 in the form of a lawsuit brought by the boards of regents of the University of Oklahoma and the University of Georgia. One day after the U.S. Supreme Court found in favor of the boards, the NCAA Division I-A television committee moved to pass a less restrictive plan. Within a month, Notre Dame received a multiyear, US$20 million contract offer from the NBC television network, which it declined. By 1990, however, Notre Dame reached an agreement with NBC that created controversy because of damage done to the CFA's television contract. These events set the stage for the evolution of the Big Ten Network, the Texas Longhorn Network, and the Pac-12 Network and spurred controversies regarding the management of postseason bowl games.

The increased financial independence of the college football powers did not leave the NCAA without significant financial resources. In fact, retaining rights to its postseason men's Division I basketball tournament, the NCAA negotiated its first billion-dollar television deal in 1989 with CBS. By 1995, that agreement doubled in value (Byers, 1995; Dunnavant, 2004).

DEMOCRATIZATION OF COLLEGE SPORT

The democratization of the higher education system in the United States can be traced, in part, through the opportunity for racial and ethnic minorities to play college sport. For example, the Golden Dome and the statue of Mother Mary at the University of Notre Dame came to symbolize a place where the Catholic faith was treasured and

diverse traditions were shared and valued (About ND, 2013). Indeed, Notre Dame became home to students from immigrant families who would not have been admitted to elite schools due to their background and social standing (Sperber, 1993).

Strikingly, the university took root in a state where three of four white males were members of the Ku Klux Klan and where anti-Catholic and anti-immigrant sentiments were a regular part of the world view of most Indianans. These tensions came to a head in a 1924 riot pitting Notre Dame students against members of the Ku Klux Klan, who espoused anti-Catholic views. In this difficult climate, Notre Dame teams played a role in changing attitudes and providing opportunities (Tucker, 2004), and the "fighting Irish" became a representative term for disenfranchised persons seeking a better life in America.

The complicated tensions involved in issues of inclusion and exclusion are seen perhaps most clearly in the contributions made by football teams at American Indian boarding schools, including the Carlisle and Haskell schools. These schools were formed as part of a U.S. government policy intended to solve the "Indian problem" through either assimilation or extermination. In other words, American Indians were either to be stripped of their language, customs, culture, traditions, and dress or face the prospect of imprisonment or death.

The boarding schools themselves were military installations. In them, American Indian children were removed from family and strictly disciplined; thus they suffered the stress and trauma of leaving the security of their homes to make their way in a white world (Bear, 2008). For the role played by American Indian football teams in this difficult situation, see the sidebar titled The Rattling of the Bones.

The cultural spaces of college sport were equally contested for African Americans. Historically black colleges and universities (HBCUs) were often required by law to compete among themselves. As a result, a rich tradition of rivalries developed between these schools, such as Johnson C. Smith University (North Carolina), Grambling State University (Louisiana), Howard University (Washington, DC), Lincoln University (Pennsylvania), Livingstone College (North Carolina), and Tuskegee

The Rattling of the Bones

One of the most famous teams to emerge out of the American Indian boarding school system was the Carlisle Indians, a team credited with introducing innovations into the game, including the forward pass, the flea-flicker, the end-around, and the reverse (Jenkins, 2007). The team included All-Americans Jim Thorpe (Sac and Fox, Oklahoma), Albert Exendine (Delaware and Cherokee, Oklahoma), and Joe Guyon (White Earth and Ojibwe, Minnesota) and compiled a record of 38 and 3. This achievement was even more remarkable considering that Carlisle was one of the most-traveled teams of the time, playing all major games at away venues (Oxendine, 1988).

In a telling 1912 confrontation with the team from the United States Military Academy, Carlisle debuted an offense that had not been seen before and executed it in a way that left the soldiers without doubt as to who had won the day. Carlisle won 27 to 6 in a game described by Carlisle player Gus Welch as the most satisfying contest he ever won, (Jenkins, 2007). Welsh described the experience of the win as "the rattling of the bones." For all of the efforts to assimilate American Indians, the Carlisle teams used sport as a vehicle to preserve their identity and oppose the oppression inherent in the system.

University (Alabama). According to Grundy (2001, pp. 179–180), "officials at black colleges had looked to sports to build race pride and solidarity . . . at the same time [that] athletic contests gave community cultural endeavors a place within the symbolically potent sphere of education pursuits."

For African Americans at previously all-white institutions, their place on college football teams inspired attention, was the subject of periodic racial unrest, and served as a focus of political debate. In addition, from the late nineteenth century through the 1970s, African American players on integrated teams were barred from playing against some teams in the South, who refused to play against integrated teams. Resistance to recruiting African American players by all-white teams led to a migration of African American players further north to schools such as Michigan State in the early 1960s. Gene Washington, a native of La Porte, Texas, has spoken of the decisions that African American players of that era had to make in leaving home to pursue their dream of playing college football:

All the Southern players, we were outcasts from our own states. All of the states where we were from, they would not take black athletes. We bonded at Michigan State because we all had similar stories. We could make a contribution. That was very important to us. We didn't talk about that all the time, but we knew we had something to prove, and this is our opportunity (Rittenberg, 2013).

The notion of white players competing with and against black players on the same field fueled political debate among segregationists, particularly in the South. In 1956, when the Georgia Institute of Technology was slated to play in the Sugar Bowl against the University of Pittsburgh, which included African American star Bobby Grier, Georgia governor Marvin Griffin ignited a student protest when he sought to bar the team from playing. Tech students took to the streets of Atlanta and eventually won a concession that the team could go, but not without the Georgia legislature passing a law banning interracial contests within state boundaries (Watterson, 2000).

As a measure of the talent level in the HBCU football ranks, Jackson State alone had 11 players drafted by the National Football League in 1968 (Oriard, 2009). Over time, however, as segregation gave way, both in higher education generally and on the playing field in particular, the HBCU talent pool was drained, which resulted in long-term negative consequences for those programs. For example, some of the most accomplished HBCU football programs (Grambling, Florida A&M, Southern, and Morgan State) lost prized recruits to schools such as Auburn and Alabama.

WOMEN'S COLLEGE SPORT: ENTREPRENEURS VERSUS EDUCATORS

Rebellion can take many forms. As noted earlier in this chapter, the all-male enclaves of Harvard and Yale in the 1800s were places where students tested authority in physical ways. Sport itself was a form of protest, and interclass conflicts played out on the football field. At Harvard, for example, Bloody Mondays were the scene of violent competitions organized between members of the lower and upper classes to determine who would dominate in the hierarchy of the school. This practice was carried out in blatant defiance of concerns expressed by faculty members and administrators.

Women who sought to be educated were engaging in a rebellion of their own by defying social conventions dictating that women were to be seen and not heard. Indeed, the mere act of going to college raised concerns about female health, as acknowledged in 1875 by L. Clark Seelye, the first president of Smith College:

We admit it would be an insuperable objection to the higher education of women, if it seriously endangered her health. . . . With gymnastic training wisely adapted to their peculiar organization, we see no reason why young ladies cannot pursue study as safely as they do ordinary employments. (Sack & Staurowsky, 1998, p. 55)

This preoccupation with the health of women college students in the late 1800s and into the early years of the twentieth century created an opening for women's sport to take hold in a formally developed women's physical education curriculum. However, just as there was ambivalence about women being educated, so too was there concern about women participating in strenuous physical activity.

Letting go of the belief that a woman's destiny was determined by her biology and that she would forever be thought of as the weaker sex (see sidebar titled The "Weaker Sex") became the substance of discussions about the appropriateness of women participating in sport throughout the twentieth century. Women were also keen observers of what was happening in men's sport. With this perspective, while women physical educators were systematic and careful in challenging prohibitions against strong physical exertion by women, they were not prepared to accept the commercial, professionalized model of men's athletics as the ideal. To the contrary, they were hesitant to lend their support to a system that so blatantly contradicted the educational mission of

The "Weaker Sex"

Because women were cast as the "weaker sex"—frail in both body and psyche—prohibitions were installed to insulate female college students from the supposed potential for harm when devising rules of play for a variety of games. For example, Senda Berenson, director of physical education at Smith College, and Clara Baer, her contemporary at H. Sophie Newcomb College, each set out to adapt the rules of basketball to suit female players. Confronted with the belief that women jeopardized their capacity to have children if they participated in activities that were too physically demanding, Berenson and Baer reworked the dimensions of the court to prevent women from running full court, confining them instead to small sections (offense, defense, middle).

In addition, emphasis was placed on teamwork and passing rather than scoring. Players were discouraged from becoming overly excited or exerting themselves too much; in fact, they were penalized if they bumped into one another, fell down, or were too enthusiastic about the idea of winning. When games were "got up," they were intended to be held in front of all-female audiences—free from any additional pressure that might result if males were present.

These rules have often been interpreted as indicating that women are anticompetitive, but in point of fact they speak to the realities of women's lives at the time. If the women physical educators navigating this delicate territory had advocated too strongly, they themselves might have been out of a job. As for the players, if they had gotten hurt, the games might have been taken away from them.

higher education in its payment of athletes (either formally or under the table), that emphasized winning over education, that opened the door for corruption due to the financial stakes involved, and that led to public scandal.

In 1924, the Women's Division of the National Amateur Athletic Federation issued guidelines for women's sport to "stress enjoyment of the sport and the development of sportsmanship, and to minimize the emphasis placed on individual accomplishments and the winning of championships" (Suggs, 2005, p. 25). Referred to as the Women's Division platform, these guidelines "emphasized that sport for women should be inclusive and based on democratic and educational principles; in balance with other aspects of life; and unmotivated by profit, spectator, or commercial interests" (Sack & Staurowsky, 1998, p. 67). The platform also firmly put forward the notion that women's sport was to be coached by women (Sack & Staurowsky).

The preferred format for women's college sport emerging from the platform was the "play day." In this approach, groups of women from various colleges would converge on one campus to participate in a variety of sports that they had most likely learned in their physical education classes, including field hockey, basketball, and volleyball (Gerber, Felshin, Berlin, & Wyrick, 1974). Women would not, however, play for their own schools but would be placed on mixed teams through a lottery system.

A few progressive institutions—such as Bryn Mawr, Ursinus College, and others in the Philadelphia area—did not subscribe fully to the belief that women should be prevented from playing varsity sports. Ursinus, for example, offered varsity sports for women in 1923. These institutions, however, were clearly in the minority (Sack & Staurowsky, 1998).

By 1957, the Division for Girls and Women's Sport (DGWS) (a division of the American Association for Health, Physical Education and Recreation) acknowledged the necessity of meeting the needs of highly skilled female athletes with competitive opportunities. The opportunities were limited, however, because they "deprived others [girls and women] of the many different kinds of desirable activities which are inherent in well-conducted sports programs" (Sack & Staurowsky, 1998). Still, momentum from the women's movement and the rise of a new feminism in the 1960s chipped away

at the societal hesitation to allow women to participate in varsity competition. As that shift occurred, women physical educators felt increasing concern about how to handle championship competition.

In an attempt to get a handle on the issue, the DGWS created the Commission on Intercollegiate Athletics for Women (CIAW) in 1967. Five years later—in the same year that Title IX of the Education Amendments of 1972 was enacted to protect students from discrimination on the basis of sex in federally funded schools—CIAW became the Association for Intercollegiate Athletics for Women (AIAW). Still seeking to carve out a space for an educationally sound and student-centered model of college sport, the AIAW issued a policy statement in 1974 advocating "separate but comparable sports for female and male athletes" and arguing that the centerpiece of a college sport experience should be "the enrichment of life of the participant" (Holland, 1974, p. 12).

This unique stance on the part of the women's athletics community—which sought autonomy in fostering a model of college sport different from the one already in place for men—ended up serving as a point of contention for those who believed that the requirements of Title IX would not allow such a distinction. Having sought to avoid the pitfalls of men's intercollegiate athletics, the AIAW had cautioned against the adoption of athletics scholarships, believing that they distorted the educational experience of athletes, were prone to manipulation by coaches, and served as the basis of a pay-for-play system. However, under pressure from a lawsuit brought by Fern Kellmeyer (a junior college coach) and female tennis players, the AIAW acquiesced on the issue of athletics scholarships and reversed course in 1973 (Staurowsky, 2012). By 1980, the NCAA effectively took over the AIAW in a power play designed to undermine women's leadership in athletics by moving to offer championships in Divisions II and III. The following year, the takeover was completed when the NCAA committed to hosting women's championships in Division I as well.

As Michelle Hosick (2011) of NCAA News wrote, the decision was a difficult one for those committed to the idea of women forging their own way in college sport. Christine Grant, a former AIAW president who served with distinction for

Christine Grant (1981), former president of the Association for Intercollegiate Athletics for Women (AIAW) and longtime women's athletics administrator at the University of Iowa, remembers what it was like to be at the 1981 NCAA Convention, where the association voted to sponsor Division I women's championships, thus effectively undermining the AIAW. She issued the following statement:

I rise in symbolic opposition to the motion before you.

It is difficult to describe the actions taken in the last three days.

I, and many other women, came here convinced that a desire for mutual accommodation between AIAW and NCAA would far outweigh any thirst for precipitous action.

Obviously, I was in error. Obviously, it was not persuasive to you that by your actions women in athletics—students and professionals—were losing control of their own destinies. Obviously, it was not persuasive to you that it was the conviction of those most closely associated with women's athletic programs that your actions will do untoward damage to those programs. And finally, it is obvious that our appeal to your sense of fair play had little effect upon your actions.

I find it somehow fitting that Father Joyce's same pleas on behalf of football coaches, however, were persuasive to and prevalent in this assembly. [Earlier in the day, Father Edmund Joyce, representing the University of Notre Dame, had spoken on behalf of the football powers arguing against legislation that would have placed financial limits on athletic scholarships (UPI, January 13, 1981)]. I would hope in the future that you might be as considerate of women's athletics, and those involved in it, as you have demonstrated you can be to football coaches.

My three days here have not been pleasant. As 1980 AIAW president, I was privileged to meet a large majority of those directly involved in administering women's athletic programs and female student-athletes. In the last three days, I have seen their hopes and aspirations to chart a new and innovative course for intercollegiate athletics severely damaged. I believe we will all live to regret the actions you have taken. I believe our institutions and our students will suffer in the coming years from the loss of a viable option to NCAA governance.

I am not angry at what has occurred, but I am profoundly sad. Mainly, I'm sad that I have found very little sincere interest in the preferences of the women in athletics, or in seeking a mutually agreeable alternative governing structure for men's and women's athletics. Instead, I and many of the other women who have spoken have sensed aggression and hostility toward our views, and an unbridled desire for the precipitous extension of this association's authority into women's athletics.

You have spoken of options, yet with motion after motion you have assured that women will have no options. The realities of women in subordinate positions and the practicalities of conflicting noncompetitive rules systems have left very little option indeed. You have bought your way into women's athletics with the lure of big money and other luxuries, but you haven't bought it from those most directly affected.

As certainly as I stand before you, you will find that you have also bought the philosophy and expectation of organizational responsiveness that those in women's athletics have held dear. AIAW is not a governance organization, but it is also an idea. And, while I do not know what the future may hold for that organization, I do know that the idea will never die.

many years as the University of Iowa's director of athletics for women, described the impact on AIAW leaders as follows: "We were fighting for our lives. And we lost. It was a very difficult and emotional situation" (Hosick). Speaking to the all-male NCAA membership who was deciding the fate of the women in the AIAW, Grant evoked a sentiment that had been expressed years before by women suffragists. She implored, "This is an opportunity for you to send a message to the leadership of this organization, and to the hundreds of women who cannot speak for themselves, that you will not take the women against their will" (Hosick).

AIAW leaders speaking that day recall being booed, something NCAA officials deny, and finding scraps of paper with mocking caricatures left for them by male delegates. While some believed that separate athletics associations for men and women would not be permitted because of Title IX, there was a sense among AIAW leadership that the NCAA had literally "bought" agreement from some women leaders and that those women had sold out. In other words, some women leaders felt trapped, forced to vote to dissolve the AIAW in the absence of litigation. Others blamed the NCAA and the women who aligned with it. In either case, the NCAA's decision to bring women's athletics under its governance structure led to the merger of men's and women's athletics departments nationwide, which was followed by the demotion of hundreds of women physical educators and administrators. The legacy of that decision and the loss of women's leadership in college sport remains after 30 years.

NATIONAL ASSOCIATION OF COLLEGIATE DIRECTORS OF ATHLETICS (NACDA)

NACDA, founded in 1965, provides athletics administrators with an organization that fosters networking, the exchange of ideas, and professional development. It allows people in senior leadership positions to share their experiences and their expertise about current issues, challenges, and best practices through publications, workshops, and an annual convention. NACDA also includes smaller groups that focus on marketing, development, business, licensing, compliance, academics, media relations, and facility and event management. The

organization also promotes diversity initiatives. Whereas the NCAA convention addresses legislative issues, the NACDA convention better serves individuals within their specific professions in intercollegiate athletics through breakout sessions and guest speakers. The organization addresses issues in NCAA Divisions I, II, and III and in the National Association of Intercollegiate Athletics (NAIA), two-year colleges, and other stakeholders in college sport.

CONCLUSION

With the benefit of a historical perspective, we can better appreciate the origins of key issues in intercollegiate sport and the complexities of potential resolutions. The age of the super conference (meaning the current state of affairs in big-time college sport) for example, was set in motion more than 60, perhaps more than 100 years ago, and the legacy of those early tensions related to the earning power of football persists today. Indeed, the century-old insight of Penn's R. Tait McKenzie, who saw signs of professionalism in the college sport system that grew out of male-only institutions, remains relevant today in light of the continuing escalation of coaches' salaries and the ongoing questions about appropriate compensation for revenue-producing athletes. The "tramp athlete" of yesteryear who did not receive a college degree may have a counterpart in the here and now.

The history also remains relevant on various other fronts. For example, the NCAA's efforts to address issues of diversity and inclusion have been expanded recently to include creating a more welcoming environment for lesbian, gay, bisexual, and transgender athletes. In addition, a 2013 letter of clarification from the U.S. Department of Education's Office for Civil Rights outlines athletics departments' obligation to provide opportunities for disabled athletes. And just as threats to football players' health contributed to the creation of the NCAA in the first place, concerns about traumatic brain injuries among players now threaten the financial viability of the college sport enterprise. With an eye toward these issues and others, this text gives you an opportunity to learn more about the mechanisms in place to govern athletics and to shape the future through a responsive mobilization of creative decision making and problem solving.

Leadership Lesson

Paradigm

A paradigm is a framework of ideas, beliefs, values, and experiences through which an individual interprets and responds to reality. In essence, a paradigm is an individual's world view. As we study the history of intercollegiate athletics in relation to the present and future landscape of the industry, pay attention to the paradigm or framework that you use when perceiving issues involved in intercollegiate athletics. To get an idea of the difference that a perspective can make, look at figure 1.4. Do you see an old woman or a young woman? Similarly, how does your lens affect the way you interpret or react to the latest sport industry news?

For example, do you view a scandal as a repeat of history, a consequence of an overregulating governing body, or a result of ineffective leadership? Any one of these conclusions—and many others—can provide clues to the paradigm that affects your perceptions. It's important to actively analyze how you perceive the world and understand that your view may be very different from that of the person sitting next to you. Your reality is not *the* reality. Effective leaders know this, and they strive to gain a broad perspective by continually stretching themselves to seek greater understanding of differing paradigms and surrounding themselves with individuals who see things differently than they do. The study of history is particularly important in this quest, because many of the issues we face today are eerily similar to issues that plagued the sport industry in past decades and centuries.

Much of the interpersonal conflict that arises within an organization can be attributed to differing paradigms. Just as some see an old woman and others see a young woman in figure 1.4, it is not uncommon for members of a department to see issues, policies, tactics, and decisions very differently. In an effort to understand and appreciate the differences within our organizations, many consultants and leadership teams use the Myers-Briggs Type Indicator (MBTI). The MBTI is a refined questionnaire designed to measure psychological preferences in how people make decisions and perceive the world. The MBTI's four pairs of preferences address the following factors:

1. How you get energy (extrovert versus introvert)
2. How you get information (intuitive versus sensing)
3. How you use information to make decisions (feeling versus thinking)
4. How you take action (judging versus perceiving)

MBTI assessment results may help individuals gain better understanding of what approaches are more natural or more difficult, both for themselves and for their colleagues. Such understanding can help people communicate more effectively, better understand unique perspectives, and defuse tension. The MBTI should

Photo from LC-DIG-ds-00175.

Figure 1.4 **Depending on perspective, a person may see an old woman or a young woman.**

(continued)

LEADERSHIP LESSON *(continued)*

be administered by someone who has been trained and understands MBTI theory. If you are interested in identifying your MBTI preferences, you can do so by visiting www.myersbriggs.org or by exploring a variety of online adaptations of the test.

As we begin our journey of exploring administration in intercollegiate athletics, we do so with a belief that you, the reader, will soon shape the governance of intercollegiate athletics for future generations of students, spectators, and stakeholders. Therefore, it is critical to acknowledge that leadership begins at the individual level and that your paradigm will affect both the decisions you make and, as a result, the future of the industry.

Throughout this text, you will be faced with

The significant problems we face cannot be solved at the same level of thinking we were at when we created them.

Albert Einstein

ethical dilemmas as you strive to balance financial realities, commercial enticements, and educational priorities. As these moments of power arise in your career, it will be critical for you to make decisions based on principles that remain unchanged in the heat of the moment. For now, in *this* particular moment, as you read these words, begin thinking about the principles that you will rely on to guide you through these inevitable challenges. How will your paradigm affect your leadership? What MBTI preferences will help or hinder you in your leadership journey? What is the purpose, in your view, of intercollegiate athletics, and how can you facilitate this purpose in your future leadership roles?

DISCUSSION QUESTIONS

1. Reflect on the chapter's opening scenario and the varying broad sentiments that people express about intercollegiate athletics. Why do you think these differences in perspective exist? Where do you fall in this range? What are your current views about the value of college sport?

2. Explain the notion of a "country club" college. When you were considering which college to attend, did "consumption amenities" influence your choice? How might the "country club" mind-set affect university administrators' views of intercollegiate athletics?

3. If you could go back in time to the period when intercollegiate athletics was just beginning, what might you tell faculty reformers in order to help facilitate greater balance between athletics and academics in the industry for years to come?

4. What are the similarities and differences between "tramp athletes" and current NCAA full-scholarship athletes?

5. Outline the evolution of the concept of amateurism in the NCAA. What has driven this evolution?

6. Explain the role played by college sport in facilitating access to higher education and American society more generally for American Indians, African Americans, and women in the late twentieth century.

7. The 1974 policy statement by the Association for Intercollegiate Athletics for Women (AIAW) advocated "separate but comparable sports for female and male athletes" and argued that the centerpiece of a college sport experience should be "the enrichment of life of the participant. Can you envision the possibility of separate programs for men and women today? Would there be a benefit to having programs separated in this manner today? Why or why not?

8. After researching the AIAW and reading Christine Grant's statement to the NCAA (included in full in the chapter), reflect on the events that transpired in 1981 when the NCAA took over college women's sport.

LEARNING ACTIVITIES

1. In the chapter, you encountered Stanford University president David Starr Jordan, who offered leadership regarding college sport in 1905. Do some research to identify a college president who is providing leadership in college sport today.

2. Columbia student Reed Harris was so passionate in his view that out-of-control commercial interests were distorting "king football" in 1932 that he not only endured being expelled from school but also declined an invitation to return because he preferred to speak out publicly. Are you aware of students who have challenged the status quo in college athletics? If so, what issues they have raised? What do you think of Harris?

3. The chapter's conclusion highlights parallels between past and present-day intercollegiate athletics. Choose one of the issues discussed and research its current status.

©Human Kinetics

CHAPTER 2

Governing Bodies

Erianne A. Weight, University of North Carolina at Chapel Hill

Barbara Osborne, University of North Carolina at Chapel Hill

In this chapter, you will explore

- the variety of intercollegiate athletics governance structures in the United States,
- the principle of institutional control,
- internal and external stakeholders who influence athletics governance,
- conference governance,
- NCAA association-wide and federated governance,
- NCAA Division I governance, and
- NCAA financial structure.

THE CONFERENCE REALIGNMENT DOMINO EFFECT

An announcement of yet another major conference realignment dominated the headlines, continuing the domino effect of football conference hopping. In fact, since the chain reaction began in 2010, all 11 Football Bowl Subdivision (FBS) conferences had gained or lost football members. Changes have also occurred in other divisions. For example, some Football Championship Subdivision (FCS) schools have jumped subdivisions in the hope of capturing a piece of the revenue pie, while others have tapped out and discontinued football. Karl Benson, commissioner of the Sun Belt Conference and former commissioner of the Western Athletic Conference, predicted the situation as follows: "I still think there are other changes that will occur, and it's all linked. . . . If the Big 12 does something, the Big East will react. If the Big East does something, Conference USA will react. If Conference USA does something, we'll react. . . . [T]here's still a lot of movement that will occur" (O'Neil, 2012).

Presidents and athletics directors emphasize the ways in which such moves give their schools opportunities to improve their academic image (Forde, 2010). Other reports assert the primary motives involve conference television revenues. As the ripples spread, headlines are filled with announcements of West Coast football programs joining East Coast conferences, talk about multibillion-dollar television deals, and stories about impoverished athlete-workers. Meanwhile, many stakeholders wonder whether the governance structures of intercollegiate athletics are broken, whether the money filtering through this industry is being handled wisely, and who the key decision makers are in the administrative chain.

The governance of intercollegiate athletics in the United States is based on three levels of control: institutional, conference, and national. An institution holds authority over the level and scope of athletic competition that it wishes to sponsor on its individual campus. Based on its institutional mission and scope of athletic competition, it can choose membership in a national governing body that helps it accomplish its organizational athletics goals.

The institution also decides whether or not conference membership will help it meet its athletics goals. Based on these decisions, athletics at the institution can cover a wide range of purposes, from opportunities for athletes to participate casually in recreational sport to athletics competition on an elite national scale, with the institution hoping to leverage athletics as a vehicle to market and brand their university. Thus institutional goals for athletics vary tremendously, which leads to a variety of related governance structures.

At the base of the intercollegiate athletics hierarchy reside the athletes who compete on the field, track, mat, court, or other setting. The education of these athletes is the reason that the empire exists; as a result, each level of the governance structure is charged with facilitating optimal experiences for this foundational population. Athletes receive the majority of their instruction from—and are governed directly by—their coaches, who are responsible for the competitive direction, athlete development, and overall day-to-day operation of their teams.

The next level of institutional administration is implemented by athletics administrators, who are typically responsible for budget management, facility oversight, fundraising, marketing and promotions, operations, rules compliance, and other management functions. Ultimately, the director of athletics is responsible for all personnel and management decisions, as well as the integration of athletics, university, conference, and NCAA regulatory influences. The highest level of *individual* authority at the campus level resides with the president (or chancellor, depending on the institution's preferred nomenclature). However, even presidents themselves are accountable to a board of trustees (or board of governors). This hierarchy of responsibility at an institution represents the foundational principle of NCAA athletics governance—that of institutional autonomy and control.

Although colleges and universities function independently, sport competition is a cooperative venture. Indeed, intercollegiate athletics could not even exist if schools did not agree on rules. Historically, schools have formed alliances with other schools situated similarly, and this middle layer of regulatory governance takes the form of the athletics conference. Such conferences are voluntary membership associations whose members come together for a specific purpose. Historically, similarities between institutions—such as geographic proximity, type of institution (e.g., public or private; liberal arts, vocational, or technical; large or small), academic standards, and intercollegiate teams sponsored—have motivated schools to band together to develop rules and regulations to facilitate a level playing field and ease burdens such as scheduling and assigning officials.

More recently, however, conference membership appears to be driven by economic incentives, as these organizations pool the inventory of their members to maximize television and marketing revenues. While the members of a traditional athletics conference compete in all conference-sponsored sports (and postseason championships—another revenue opportunity), some conferences administer only one sport. Examples include Hockey East and the East Atlantic Gymnastics League. The largest intercollegiate athletics conference in the country is the Eastern College Athletic Conference, which operates as a regional governing body with postseason championships offered in Divisions I, II, and III.

A college or university may also choose to become a member of a national governing body. The purpose of such bodies is to provide postseason championship opportunities, establish a level playing field through rules and regulations, and promote and supervise intercollegiate competition. The first national athletics organization was the National Collegiate Athletic Association (NCAA), which was founded in 1906 to develop safety rules to protect football players and it subsequently began sponsoring national championships in 1921. It has grown to be the largest national intercollegiate athletics governing body, with more than 1,000 member institutions providing competitive opportunities for more than 400,000 intercollegiate student-athletes participating in 23 sports.

Four other national organizations provide additional options for institutions seeking postseason national championships. Although the NCAA is well known for its March Madness basketball tournament, the National Association of Intercollegiate Athletics (NAIA) sponsors the longest-running national basketball tournament in the United States. Then the NAIA held its first men's basketball tournament in 1937 and was formally established in 1938. The organization was also the first national intercollegiate athletics governing body to invite historically black institutions into membership (in 1953) and to sponsor both men's and women's national championships (in 1980). The NAIA is currently home to almost 300 colleges and universities and some 60,000 student-athletes competing in 13 sports.

Another national organization, the National Junior College Athletic Association, was established in 1938 to promote competition between institutions granting two-year or associate degrees. Today, its nearly 300 members compete in national championships in 17 sports. In 1968, the National Christian College Athletic Association was incorporated. It currently includes about 100 member schools and emphasizes a unique mission of promoting Christian outreach and ministry through sponsorship of national championships in 23 sports. The newest national governing body for intercollegiate athletics is the United States Collegiate Athletic Association, established in 2009 to provide national competitive experiences for small-enrollment schools and nontraditional programs. Member institutions may offer four-year degrees, associates degrees, or trade programs.

With this context in mind, the remainder of this chapter focuses on governance within the framework of the NCAA as it is the largest and most influential of the national governing bodies for intercollegiate athletics in the United States.

INSTITUTIONAL CONTROL

Although the governance and regulation of intercollegiate athletics may appear to be top-down endeavors, the voluntary nature of membership and enforcement necessitates individual compliance from the bottom up. Rules compliance starts with the student-athlete. Individual student-athletes may be recruited, but ultimately the student-athlete chooses to participate and in so choosing also voluntarily agrees to follow the rules of all school, conference, and national governing bodies. The failure of individual athletes to recognize their responsibility to adhere to the rules jeopardizes the success of the team, the coaches, the athletics administrators, and everyone on up through the institution's administrative ranks, all of whom may be subject to sanctions by the conference, the national governing body, or both. Student-athletes can contribute to governance on their own campus through student-athlete advisory committees (SAACs), which are discussed in chapter 5.

Coaches also have a responsibility to follow the rules and to monitor their assistants, staff members, and student-athletes for rules compliance. In fact, recent NCAA rule changes have increased both the head coach's responsibility for monitoring staff members and the penalties enforced against head coaches for recruiting and academic violations in their programs. This role of oversight involves understanding the rules and completing many institutional compliance forms, but it is also critically important that coaches buy into the governance philosophy of intercollegiate athletics. Coaches serve as role models for playing fair and balancing the demands of athletics and academics, and they must lead by example.

Larger athletics programs include various internal units with layers of middle managers who play supervisory (and therefore rules-enforcement) roles. Over the past 20 years, the typical compliance unit in an athletics department has grown in both staff size and importance. The compliance staff's primary responsibility is to educate all members of the athletics program—from student-athletes to alumni—about the rules. This education is generally carried out through informational meetings and the distribution of instructional and reference materials.

In addition to increasing awareness of the rules and identifying areas of risk, the compliance staff work with coaches to provide forms and tools to monitor, assist with monitoring, and supervise rules compliance. When violations or other problems occur, the compliance staff investigates to determine what happened and whether it could or should have been prevented. The staff then reports the violation, self-imposes a penalty (if necessary)

on the institution, and works to prevent recurrence.

The size and sophistication of the compliance staff depends on institutional priorities and resources. The largest compliance unit in an athletics department includes more than a dozen full-time staff, whereas the smallest consists of a single coach or administrator for whom compliance is listed as one of many responsibilities. Regardless of the size or scope of the department, however, compliance is really the responsibility of every individual involved in the athletics department—not just those who work in the compliance unit. This is discussed more thoroughly as we explore compliance as a functional unit in chapter 4.

The athletics director (AD) bears ultimate responsibility for everything that goes on in the athletics program. As the leader of the athletics department, the AD establishes the program's internal compliance culture and also serves as the face of the program for all other institutional and external constituencies. An athletics director's job description can vary widely, depending on the type of institution. At smaller institutions with fewer athletics administrators, the AD is tasked with specific duties as well as general supervisory responsibility, whereas the AD of a larger program assumes a general supervisory role. The AD usually holds approval authority over all athletics department policies and procedures and represents the institution at the conference and national levels.

The president of the academic institution is the final authority in the structure of institutional control. The athletics department is only one part of the educational institution, but intercollegiate athletics may generate more attention than most other university departments combined. Therefore, it is up to the president to retain a holistic view of the institution's mission and determine what role the athletics department plays in achieving that mission. In theory, the president occupies the best position from which to establish the culture and set the rules and limits for the athletics program. On the other hand, because the president is responsible for the entire academic institution, he or she may not be particularly interested in devoting much time to the athletics department or sufficiently educated about relevant issues to make informed athletics policy decisions. Presidential authority is discussed further in the sections addressing internal and external stakeholders and NCAA governance structure.

In general, the philosophy of institutional control provides autonomy for the institution to make its own decisions and control its own destiny in matters such as offering teams, allocating resources, and determining the appropriate balance between academics and athletics. However, because intercollegiate sport cannot exist without rules, institutional autonomy is somewhat problematic in the context of athletics competition. From a governance perspective, sport organizations must balance the need of every institution to chart its own course with the need for all competitors to follow the same rules and achieve a standard of fairness on the playing field. In a narrower view of rules compliance, then, institutional control involves the ability of the college or university to operate the athletics department in a way that abides by the spirit and the letter of the governing rules.

> If you're running a school that has big-time sports, if there's a problem, it can overwhelm you…when you look at all the problems we're having as I see my colleagues around the country struggling, it just makes me wonder whether [presidential control of athletics] was a good idea.
>
> H. Thorpe (qtd. in Stancill, 2013)

INTERNAL AND EXTERNAL STAKEHOLDERS

Authority over the administration of athletics at the institutional level is continually challenged by both internal and external forces. Though faculty members generally possess an important voice in the governance of an academic institution, they have had varying degrees of success in controlling or influencing athletics program policy. Local and national faculty groups calling for reform have proliferated as concerns have risen about the commercial and academic aspects of college sport at the "big-time" level. Examples include the Coalition on Intercollegiate Athletics, the Drake Group, and the American Association of University Professors.

Similarly, varying degrees of influence on athletics administration are wielded by governing boards (e.g., boards of trustees) at the institutional level and by state-level boards (e.g., boards of regents) for public colleges and universities. Powerful influence is also exerted on athletics programs by other external stakeholders, including alumni and other fans, members of the media and entertainment industries (e.g. broadcasters), the sporting goods manufacturing industry, and governmental entities.

Faculty

As one former University of Michigan president recounted, "many members of the faculty believe that the true control of intercollegiate athletics should be their responsibility, either through specific bodies such as faculty athletics boards or through more general faculty governance" (Duderstadt, 2003, pp. 105–106). The rationale for faculty governance hinges on the educational foundation of intercollegiate athletics and on overarching faculty concern for the students for whom the enterprise exists. However, the role and authority of faculty members on their individual campuses vary depending on institutional structures.

This variance was examined in a study of faculty governance across thirty-two institutions in three major athletics conferences (the Big Ten, SEC, and Pac-10), which analyzed formal governing documents detailing the role and authority of faculty governing bodies. The study reported minimal faculty participation and authority; in fact, participatory faculty committees assumed responsibility for the quality of athletics programs and operation at only two schools (Minor & Perry, 2010). However, though few athletics programs appear to operate with mandatory faculty governance in the form of a faculty advisory committee, many athletics departments do voluntarily include faculty members on a variety of athletics department committees to help bridge the gap between athletics and the academy. Examples include student-athlete academic support advisory committees, the NCAA certification committee, Title IX committees, and committees related to student-athlete admissions.

Faculty also play a formal role in athletics governance at all NCAA member institutions through the role of the faculty athletics representative

(FAR). Article 6.1.3 of the NCAA constitution describes the FAR as a faculty member or administrator with faculty rank who does not hold a position in the athletics department. The FAR formally represents the view of the faculty in advising the institution's president on athletics-related issues. The FAR also plays a key communication role on campus by informing the faculty about athletics issues, policies, and procedures. Other duties of the FAR vary, depending on the academic institution, but most FARs are involved in academic oversight of the athletics program and in ensuring the welfare of student-athletes. The role requires substantial knowledge of university, conference, and NCAA rules because the FAR represents the university on various conference and NCAA committees and may serve as the institution's voting delegate if the president is unavailable.

Governing Boards

Internal pressures also arise from university governing boards, which often exert an unusual amount of oversight over the management of intercollegiate athletics. The primary reasoning behind this level of control hinges on the visibility of collegiate athletics programs on many campuses and the political pressures and acclaim that can result from being associated with such programs. Regardless of the motives for intervention, the reality remains that institutional control of intercollegiate athletics is not ultimately held by these internal bodies. Though their concern may be broad and well-intentioned, most faculty or board members have limited knowledge of the system's intricacies and are not in a position to accept or be held accountable for governance in the final analysis (Duderstadt, 2003).

External Stakeholders

External stakeholders range in power and organization, and they are a constant presence among the forces that create intercollegiate athletics governance. These stakeholders include fans and alumni, the media, the entertainment industry (e.g., broadcasters), the sports apparel industry, and the government. Though none of these stakeholders can exert direct authority over an institution, each wields powerful influence.

This power was explored in a study conducted by the Knight Commission on Intercollegiate Athletics (KCIA) related to the costs and financing of intercollegiate athletics within FBS institutions. The research involved nearly 80 percent of NCAA Division I FBS university presidents, and the majority indicated a feeling of possessing only limited power to effect financial change in athletics on *their own* campuses. As one president commented, "The real power doesn't lie with the presidents; presidents have lost their jobs over athletics. Presidents and chancellors are afraid to rock the boat with boards, benefactors, and political supporters who want to win, so they turn their focus elsewhere" (Knight Commission, 2009, p. 16).

Thus, while presidents may reside at the top of the organizational hierarchy, for many of them their power (or belief in their power) has been limited by the strength of external forces. A follow-up study to the KCIA presidential study examined the power felt by conference commissioners in regard to the athletics "arms race." This study found similar results, as the commissioners collectively disagreed with the notion that they held the power to enact change (Weight, Weight, & Schneider, 2013).

CONFERENCE GOVERNANCE

While the concept of a level playing field is attractive in theory, it quickly became apparent to leaders in intercollegiate athletics that not all programs are created equal. To create a more level playing field, schools naturally gravitated toward competing against similar institutions. This self-selection eventually led to the formation of athletics conferences. Initially, intercollegiate athletics conferences were formed by institutions that were similar in the size of their student body, their academic offerings and standards, their status as public or private, their geographic location, and the quality and quantity of competitive opportunities they sponsored. Over time, the conferences became independent organizations with constitutions and bylaws defining their purpose and mission and their members' responsibilities.

The organization of a conference can vary tremendously. Some smaller NCAA Division III conferences operate as voluntary cooperatives in which athletics administrators from member programs carry out leadership and administrative tasks on an assigned or rotating basis. At the other end of the spectrum, most NCAA Division I FBS conferences employ a conference commissioner and a large staff of administrators to provide a wide range of services and generate additional revenue for conference members. The original appeal of conference membership included ease of scheduling and the opportunity to compete in a season-culminating championship. Nowadays, the largest conferences still facilitate scheduling and conference championships but have also expanded to handle officiating bureaus; legislative services; and rules compliance, education, and interpretation.

Conferences also actively promote themselves and their championships through marketing, public relations, media relations, and athletics communication. Conference games and championships are broadcast through a variety of television, radio, and digital communication platforms that are either produced or procured by the conference. Some conferences even own their own television networks. Additional revenues are generated through the sale of conference-licensed merchandise and apparel, through either online stores or physical storefronts—for example, ACC (Atlantic Coast Conference) stores and restaurants in malls and airports.

In addition, conferences provide leadership, governance, and professional development opportunities for athletics administrators and student-athletes of member institutions. Various parties—including presidents, athletics administrators (e.g., ADs and senior woman administrators [SWAs]), faculty athletics representatives, coaches, athletics trainers, sports information and athletics communication directors, and other athletics administrators or personnel—meet regularly to discuss possible or proposed legislation, issues and concerns related to scheduling and conference championships, and various hot topics in intercollegiate athletics. These meetings promote the exchange of ideas and best practices, determine conference policy, and provide networking opportunities.

Conference governance is generally determined through member representation, and the conference commissioner and administrators execute the wishes of the membership on a daily basis. However, as the face of the conference, the commissioner generally also possesses a strong voice in discussions about conference policy and may represent conference members in NCAA governance matters. The voice of athletes is represented at the conference level through the conference-sponsored SAAC, through which athletes share ideas, discuss issues, and vote on whether to support proposed legislation. Conferences may also support students by providing postgraduate scholarships or internship opportunities.

The Big Ten conference has established a reputation as one of the most president- and faculty-driven conferences in the NCAA. The conference's Council of Presidents and Chancellors (COPC) oversees all policy decisions, including approving the annual budget, hiring and determining the duties of the Big Ten commissioner, amending conference bylaws, enforcing conference rules, and admitting new institutions as members. Through this structure, the COPC holds ultimate authority for conference governance (Big Ten Conference, 2013). Under the direction of the COPC, Big Ten commissioner Jim Delany and his staff oversee 60 committees and governance groups in which the Big Ten faculty athletics representatives and campus athletics representatives play a significant role (Big Ten Conference, 2013).

NCAA GOVERNANCE STRUCTURE

The core purpose of the NCAA is "to govern competition in a fair, safe, equitable and sportsmanlike manner and to integrate intercollegiate athletics into higher education so that the educational experience of the student-athlete is paramount" (NCAA Core Purpose, 2014). The operations of the association are managed through the national office, located in Indianapolis, Indiana. The highest-ranking employee of the national office is the president, who is advised by a senior management group that includes a chief policy advisor; a general counsel; a chief operations officer; and vice presidents of communication, membership and student-athlete affairs, championships, and alliances.

The NCAA staff is organized by functional units, providing services in membership and student-athlete affairs, enforcement, communication, finance and operations, championships, and administrative services. Contrary to popular media-driven perception, the national office does not independently dictate an NCAA agenda.

The Conference Realignment Domino Effect

In recent years, conference realignment has often dominated headlines about intercollegiate athletics as long-standing conference partnerships have been severed through realignment. Figure 2.1 provides a snapshot of the nearly 50 schools in 25 conferences that have been affected over a five-year period.

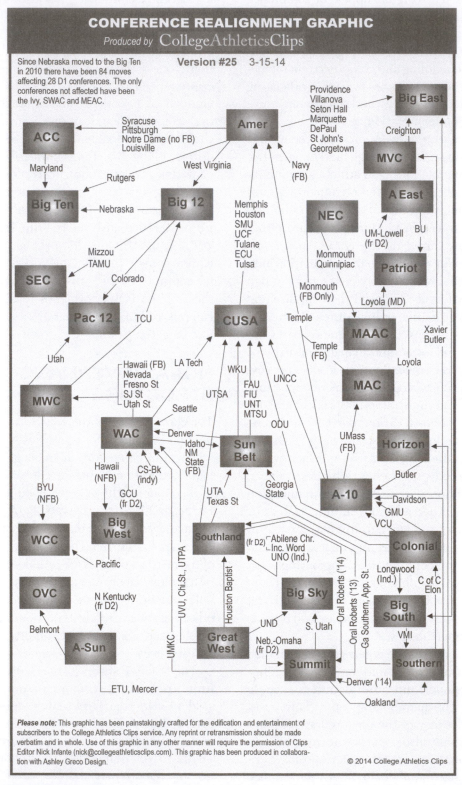

Figure 2.1 Conference realignment.

Industry Profile

Jim Delaney

Commissioner of the Big Ten Conference

Viewed as brilliant, creative, principled, and persuasive by some—and shrewd, arrogant, and smug by others—Jim Delaney has been described as "the most powerful figure in collegiate athletics" (Peter, 2007). Indeed, he has influenced virtually every element of intercollegiate athletics through his leadership of the Big Ten Conference since 1989. From gender equity planning and initiatives addressing good sporting behavior to media negotiations and conference expansion, Delany's innovative leadership is evident in the trailblazing path of the Big Ten. A few of his unique initiatives include the development of the first collegiate version of football instant replay in 2004; the creation of the first conference-owned television network, the Big Ten Network, in 2006;

and the first national TV network commitment to "event equality" for men's and women's events in 2010.

Delany's career path began at the University of North Carolina (UNC) where he studied political science while competing as a guard on the basketball team, with which he made two NCAA Final Four appearances under legendary coach Dean Smith. Following his undergraduate studies, he remained at UNC to study law, after which he practiced law in the state for two years. He then took a job with the NCAA as an enforcement representative for four years before accepting a job as the Ohio Valley Conference Commissioner, where he remained for 10 years before becoming Big Ten commissioner (Peter, 2007).

Rather, the staff handles general promotion of intercollegiate athletics under the NCAA brand, facilitates national championships, and helps interpret NCAA rules and supervises rules enforcement.

Association-Wide Governance

The executive committee is the highest-ranking committee in the NCAA. It hires and evaluates the NCAA president, provides budgetary oversight, engages in strategic planning, identifies important issues, and establishes overall policy for the association. When issues affect the association as a whole, the executive committee holds the authority to convene a joint meeting of the presidential and legislative bodies for all divisions. Similarly, if a constitutional amendment is required, or if a division has enacted legislation that may violate the association's constitution, the executive committee holds the authority to call for a vote of the entire membership. This has been done both at the association's annual January convention and by calling a special convention. Ten committees report directly to the executive committee on topics that concern

the association as a whole (see figure 2.2).

Historically, the executive committee reflected the democratic governance of the association in that all divisions had equal representation and equal voice in the decision-making process. In 1997, association-wide governance was changed to a representative structure that eliminated the one-school-one-vote approach. Instead, Division I, II, and III voting issues were separated, and the composition of the executive committee was altered to heavily favor Division I. The current executive committee includes eight FBS members, two FCS members, two Division I members from the Division I board of directors, two members from the Division II president's council, and two members from the Division III president's council. Ex officio (nonvoting) participants include the NCAA president and the chairs of the Division I leadership council and the Division II and Division III management councils.

As displayed in figure 2.2, the top two layers of NCAA governance put control of intercollegiate athletics policy firmly in the hands of college presidents. This structure is supposed to assure that governance of intercollegiate athletics at the national level remains appropriately integrated into the academic mission of higher education in general. While this philosophy is foundational to the organization of intercollegiate athletics in every division, Division I differs significantly from Division II and Division III in the way in which the divisional governance structure is labeled and organized and in how member representation is appointed.

Federated Governance

The NCAA was divided into three competitive divisions in 1973, and divisional governance (federation) was also established. Each division has a unique operational philosophy and a separate

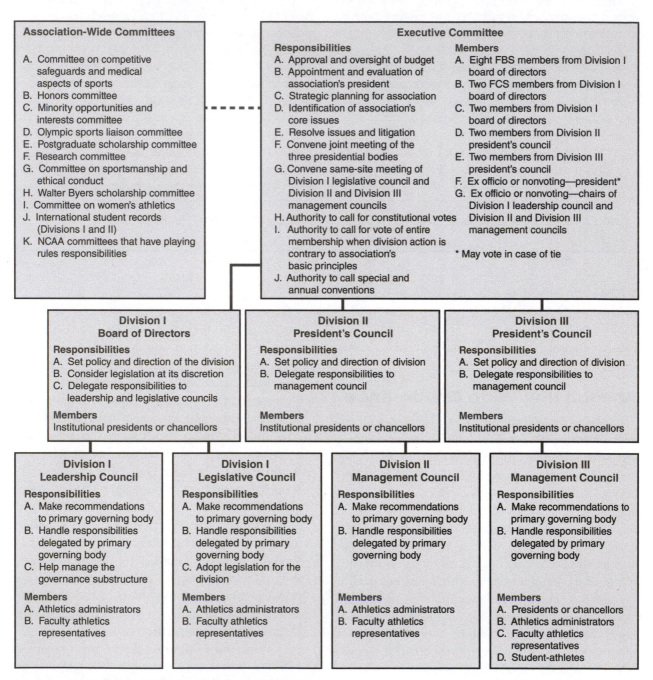

Figure 2.2 NCAA governance structure.

NCAA manual of rules and regulations governing participation in that division. The primary identifying distinction between the three divisions involves the distribution of athletics scholarships. Division I institutions provide the most funding across all sports, Division II provides more limited funding, and Division III athletes receive no athletics-related scholarships. Other differences include the number of required sports, scheduling considerations, and financing sources (see table 2.1).

Division I is the most widely publicized and highly visible of the NCAA divisions. Many Division I schools are athletics powerhouses with elaborate facilities and large budgets. Built on financial inputs such as student fees, conference football television contracts, ticket sales, alumni donations, institutional subsidies, NCAA basketball tournament shares and other NCAA allocations (NCAA Revenues & Expenses Report, 2011), Division I institutions offer the most financial aid

to student-athletes. The amount of aid falls within a range bracketed by a division-specific minimum and maximum.

The importance of football as a revenue sport in Division I was highlighted in 1978, when Division I was further subdivided based on competitive emphasis and funding for football. Originally referred to as I-A, I-AA, and I-AAA, these subdivisions were renamed in 2004. As currently named, Football Bowl Subdivision schools provide a maximum of 85 full football scholarships and strive for postseason bowl bids; Football Championship Subdivision (FCS) schools offer only 63 full scholarship equivalencies, which may be shared among no more than 85 student-athletes; and the remaining Division I members do not sponsor football teams, instead focusing their competitive emphasis and budgets on other sport offerings.

In 2014, the NCAA board voted to allow 64 schools in the richest five leagues (the ACC, Big

Table 2.1 NCAA Divisional Differences

	Membership*	Number of required sports	Average undergraduate enrollment**	Median undergraduate enrollment**	Percentage public	Financial aid
Division 1	345		15,328	12,936	66	Minimum amount of financial aid must be allocated but may not exceed established maximums.
Football bowl subdivision (FBS)	123	16	23,420	22,963		
Football championship subdivision (FCS)	126	14	10,593	8,890		
I-AAA (Division I, no football)	96	14	11,327	7,680		
Division II	295	10	6,015	3,950	52	Few athletes receive a full athletics grant, but most receive some athletics financial aid.
Division III	441	10	3,340	2,202	19	No athletics financial aid.

*These numbers are based on active NCAA membership status in 2013-14 school year.

**The enrollment numbers refer to undergraduate enrollment in fall 2012. Note that schools that did not report to IPEDS are dropped from the enrollment size calculation.

Data from IPEDS enrollment file 2012 from the National Center for Education Statistics (NCES).

12, Big Ten, SEC, and Pac-12) further federation or autonomy to write many of their own rules. Some of the issues which will continue to evolve as this autonomy unfolds include cost-of-attendance stipends, staff sizes, recruiting rules, four-year scholarship guarantees, agency rules, opportunities for athletes to pursue paid career opportunities, provisions and financial support for family members to attend post-season tournaments, and mandatory hours spent on individual sports. Regulations that will not be affected by the autonomy of these schools include rules governing on-field play, postseason tournaments, scholarship limits, transfer policies, and signing day dates. See additional information about the Power 5 Division I conferences in the sidebar titled Autonomy Economics and Division I Implications in the Power 5 Conference.

Division II offers an intermediate-level philosophy, providing limited athletics scholarships and emphasizing an appropriate balance between athletics participation and academics. Community service is also emphasized as an additional educational opportunity to develop productive, socially conscious citizens. Division II athletics programs include few students on full athletics scholarships, but a majority receive some sort of financial assistance for their athletics participation.

Division III is the NCAA's largest and most diverse division in terms of total membership, but 81 percent of the members are private institutions. Division III is philosophically set apart by its financial aid policy, wherein no athletics-based aid is offered. Still, 40 percent of all NCAA athletes compete at the Division III level. The emphasis in Division III is on the participation experience of student-athletes as an extension of their educational experience.

Divisional Membership

A college or university interested in becoming a member of the NCAA must complete a multistep, multiyear process before it is granted full membership privileges. Each division has unique requirements and slightly different processes and timelines for full membership. An institution must first self-evaluate to determine which division's philosophy most closely aligns with its own, then complete a membership application for that divi-

sion. In the following candidacy or exploratory period, applicants are oriented to NCAA rules and regulations, engage in self-study, and determine what changes need to be made in the athletics program in order to be compliant.

If a candidate institution is accepted for provisional or reclassification status, the school must pay a fee and membership dues. Depending on the division, provisional members are expected to engage in more rules education, comply with all NCAA rules, and undergo formal review of their programs for compliance. When the institution has met all requirements for membership, it is granted full membership status, which includes the privilege of qualifying for participation in NCAA postseason championships.

Schools can move their membership from one division to another by completing the membership process for reclassification. More schools have moved to a more competitive division, but some members have reduced the competitive emphasis and financial commitments in their athletics program by moving to a lower division. Similarly, institutions have sometimes chosen to change their affiliation from one national governing body to another. The same membership process applies regardless of whether an applicant was formerly independent or affiliated with another association. Much of the increase in NCAA membership at the Division II level has been from schools that were previously associated with the NAIA.

Division I Governance

The NCAA Division I board of directors is made up of 18 institutional presidents appointed to the board based on conference affiliation. The 11 FBS conferences have permanent representation, while the remaining seven seats rotate among representatives from the FCS and nonfootball Division I conferences. This representative structure ensures that the most competitive football conferences control policy and legislation for Division I. In replacing the one-school-one-vote democratic governance system with this conference-based representative structure, Division I also changed its rule-making process to a top-down system with override authority by the membership in place of the traditional membership-initiated annual legislative process.

In 2008, the Division I management council was

replaced by a leadership council and a legislative council, each of which reports directly to the board of directors and is made up of 31 conference-appointed institutional athletics administrators, conference administrators, and faculty athletics representatives who serve three-year terms. The leadership coun-cil focuses primarily on strategic issues and policy whereas the legislative council considers all legislative proposals and takes action subject to approval by the board of directors.

If members are unhappy with board-approved legislation, institutions can submit override

Autonomy Economics and Division I Implications in the Power 5 Conference

Consider the following 2013-2014 data addressing the financial inequalities between the Power 5 (major conferences plus Notre Dame) and the remaining 81% of Division I institutions:

	Power 5 (65 institutions)	Innervated 1s (286 institutions)
Total enrollment (FTE)	1,785,000	3,515,000
Average enrollment	27,500	12,300
Athletic budgets (combined)	$5,850,000,000	$5,730,000,000
Athletic budgets (average)	$90,000,000	$20,000,000
Athletic subsidies (total)	$380,000,000	$3,700,000,000
Athletic subsidies (average)	$5,850,000	$12,940,000
% athletic subsidies	6.5%	65%
Athletic subsidies (per student)	$210	$1,050

The Power 5 makes up about one-third of the total enrollment in Division I and more than half of the total spending in athletics. The significant measure is the subsidies: Athletic subsidies for the Power 5 are only 6.5% of athletic budgets, compared to 65% (10 times greater) for the Enervated 1s.

An extreme example is Coastal Carolina, which spent more than $22 million on athletics in 2013-2014. Revenues generated by the athletic program were less than 18% of expenditures, resulting in subsidies of over $18 million. All subsidies come from tuition at CCU; therefore, each full-time student has $2,164 (24.5%) of their tuition directed to underwrite the athletic program. Similarly, at Delaware State, athletic spending was $13 million, and the programs generated less than $2 million. For 2013-2014, athletic subsidies equated to $2,856 per full-time student, or 43% of tuition.

Proposed Solution for Enervated 1s: A Five-Year Plan

1. Restructure conferences—by sports and regions, not universities or colleges.
2. Allow institutional choice of sports and competition level.
3. Limit institutional subsidies.

This new model of federation allows room for cost containment at the schools that desperately need to refocus on their academic missions and institutional affordability, allowing the Power 5 to direct their destiny. The implications of their financial models have minimal impact on their students. Their financial issues are centered on lawsuits (e.g., O'Bannon case, players' unions) and payment of players. Possibly they will evolve to a market-driven model of organization through regions, or divisions, and improve the benefits to the student-athletes, students, alumni, and institutions.

Excerpts from *Aligning Athletics within Academic Missions in Division I* by Jeff Smith. Reprinted with permission from the Center for College Affordability and Productivity.

requests. If 30 or more members request an override, the legislative council is required to revisit the legislation; if an override is requested by 100 or more members, the legislation is suspended. The legislative council can then reverse its earlier action, amend the proposal (subject to another override period), or maintain its position, thus requiring an override vote by the membership. The override vote is conducted electronically, and the legislation can be permanently suspended by a supermajority (62.5 percent) of the members voting.

The conference-centered process for leadership delegation has given Division I conferences a strong voice in the association-wide governance of the NCAA. The ultimate role of the president in the governance of intercollegiate athletics is maintained in this structure because institutional presidents and chancellors have ultimate hiring and firing power over conference commissioners; therefore, conference activities are theoretically over-seen by presidents who hold the ultimate authority in the hierarchy. This arrangement resulted from an effort to empower conferences in 1997. While theoretically there is merit to conference empowerment, the variation in conference organizational governance is immense; thus the role of faculty athletics representatives and presidents can differ greatly depending on the conference.

Division II and Division III Governance

Division II and Division III share a very similar governance structure. At the highest level of divisional governance sits the presidents council, which is composed of institutional presidents charged with setting the division's policies and direction. The majority of representatives on the presidents council are chosen by geographic region; the rest are selected at large. All members serve a four-year term. Recommendations are made to the presidents council by the management council, which

---

The Path of NCAA Division I Legislation

1. Schools or conferences propose legislation to the legislative council.

2. The legislative council discusses, revises, accepts, or rejects proposed legislation.

3. The board of directors discusses, revises, accepts, or rejects proposed legislation.

4. Approved legislation is posted for comment.

5. Members who oppose legislation may submit a request to override (see details of override process in text)

6. The working group on rules provides documentation of its discussions and draft proposals and requests feedback from the membership in order to address concerns as new legislation is adopted in the Division I manual.

7. The working group on enforcement provides documentation of its discussions and draft proposals and requests feedback from the membership in order to facilitate the enforcement or infractions process of this new legislation.

8. Legislation is implemented.

The Division I board of directors, leadership council, and legislative council are assisted by a myriad of committees and cabinets with very specific roles. This structure enables experts to evaluate issues, inform decision-making bodies, and carry out organizational tasks. Standards have been established to maintain gender, racial, and positional diversity in virtually all NCAA committees; however, all major leadership positions in Division I are based on conference appointments. Thus the representation of various positions, for instance, is limited to the responsibility that any given conference feels comfortable giving to a faculty athletics representative, athletics director, president, or conference official.

NCAA Board of Directors' Duties and Responsibilities

The Board of Directors shall:

a. Establish and direct general policy;

b. Establish a strategic plan;

c. Adopt or defeat legislative proposals independent of the Legislative Council (e.g., emergency, noncontroversial, or other proposals sponsored by the Board);

d. At its discretion, ratify, amend, or defeat legislation adopted by the Legislative Council;

e. Delegate to the Leadership Council or Legislative Council responsibilities for specific matters it deems appropriate;

f. Appoint members of the NCAA Division I Committee on Infractions and the Division I Infractions Appeals Committee;

g. Review and approve policies and procedures governing the enforcement program;

h. Ratify, amend, or rescind the actions of the Leadership Council or Legislative Council;

i. Assure that there is gender and ethnic diversity among its membership and the membership of each of the other bodies in the administrative structure;

j. Require bodies in the administrative structure to alter (but not expand) their membership to achieve diversity;

k. Approve an annual budget;

l. Approve regulations providing for the expenditure of funds and the distribution of income consistent with the provisions of Constitution 4.01.2.2;

m. Approve regulations providing for the administration of championships;

n. Advise the Executive Committee concerning the employment of the NCAA president and concerning the oversight of his or her employment;

o. Be responsible for the administration, compilation, and disclosure of information concerning the Academic Progress Rate (APR) and Academic Performance Census (APC); and

p. Elect institutions to active Division I membership.

consists in Division II of athletics administrators and faculty athletics representatives and in Division III of presidents, athletics administrators, faculty athletics representatives, and student-athletes. Legislation is proposed by Division II and Division III member institutions on an annual basis, and all members have the opportunity to review proposals, discuss them at the association's annual convention, and then vote. Each member and each qualifying conference may cast one vote.

NCAA FINANCIAL STRUCTURE

It is an expensive undertaking to provide 89 national championships in 23 sports and manage a national office to support services for member institutions. Not surprisingly, much media attention is focused on the millions of dollars generated by and spent on intercollegiate athletics. The association's governance structure is heavily influenced by revenue producers—the Division I programs that command the most media attention. Although the media perpetuates the myth that the NCAA "makes" billions of dollars, the income generated by the association is spent primarily on services for its members and directed back to the affiliated conferences.

This section of the chapter provides an overview of the NCAA's financial structure. This structure is also discussed in the chapter 7.

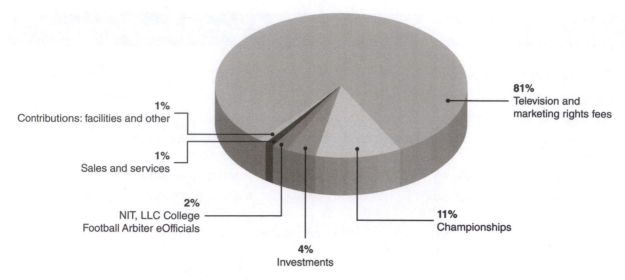

Figure 2.3 Breakdown of NCAA revenue in 2011–2012.

Income

The NCAA is almost wholly financed by the television and rights fees of the Division I men's basketball championship. Representing approximately 81 percent to 87 percent of the roughly US$900 million annual budget, the US$10.8 billion 14-year agreement with CBS Sports and Turner Broadcasting keeps the organization afloat (NCAA Finances, 2014). Most of the remaining revenue (approximately 11 percent) comes from ticket sales at NCAA championship events; other revenue is gained from additional minor contributions from investments and subsidiaries (see figure 2.3).

Expenses

The income generated by the association directly benefits its members, either through services provided or through distribution of revenues. The association's largest expense comes in the form of distributions made to Division I conferences, which account for 63 percent of the budget. The next-largest expense (17 percent) is incurred in providing national championships for all three divisions. The remainder of the budget primarily supports association-wide programs, including postgraduate scholarships and committee support, injury insurance, and educational programs; roughly 4 percent is used to fund NCAA administrative expenses (see figure 2.4).

The distribution of revenue to Division I

members is allocated through five unique funds. More specifically, about 61 percent of the budget is distributed to Division I members through five unique Division I funds (see figure 2.5). The majority of the Division I revenue distribution is based on school and conference performance in the NCAA basketball tournament. Each tournament game that a team plays earns a share (worth about US$250,000 in 2014). Payouts are distributed to each conference based on its member-school appearances in the tournament over a six-year rolling period (Schlabach, 2011; Smith, 2012).

Thus, in 2014, if your team made it to the tournament but lost in the first round, it earned one share for the conference to be paid annually over six years with an approximate 2% increase in share value each year (valued at approximately US$1.58 million total after each of the six payments were made). If the team made it to the Final Four, it earned a share for each game played, thus generating approximately US$9.5 million for its conference over six years (Smith, 2012). Payout amounts per share in 2020, for instance, will be based on the average payouts between 2015 and 2020, and conferences will be paid according to the number of shares that their member schools earned over those six years of tournament play.

For this reason, it is in the best financial interest of each conference to send as many schools as possible to the tournament and keep them in it as long as possible. Thus, though it is tempting for

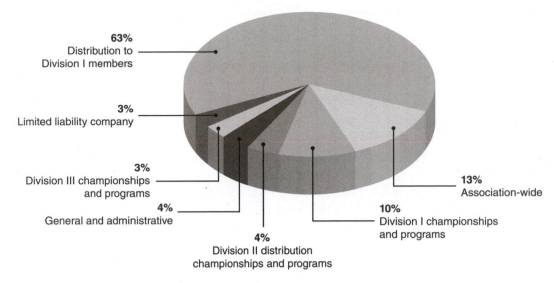

Figure 2.4 Breakdown of NCAA expenses in 2011–2012.

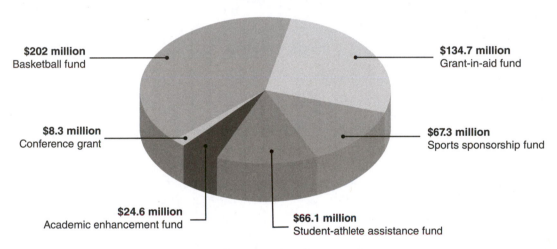

Figure 2.5 Distribution of the US$503 million in Division I revenue in 2011–2012.

fans to celebrate losses by their conference rivals, those losses translate into millions of dollars in lost revenue sharing for their own school. Most wise financial administrators, therefore, cheer fiercely for all conference schools in order to maximize their budgets.

The next-largest funds in the Division I revenue distribution plan are based on the number of scholarships and teams sponsored per institution in certain sports, including those in which the NCAA conducts championship competition, emerging sports for women, and Division I FBS football. The

grant-in-aid fund pays an institution based on the number of full-time scholarship equivalencies it provides to athletes. Institutions sponsoring more scholarships receive more revenue per scholarship (NCAA, 2009). Thus a school offering 80 scholarships might receive an average of approximately US$372 per scholarship, whereas a school offering 160 scholarships might receive an average of approximately US$1,500 per scholarship, and a school offering 250 scholarships might receive an average of nearly US$3,000 per scholarship (Schlabach, 2011).

Leadership Lesson

No Excuses

Intercollegiate athletics is founded on the principle of institutional autonomy—the premise that individual institutions govern athletics. Through their presidents (who are influenced by a myriad of stakeholders), individual schools are responsible for making the decisions that govern the industry. This reality contradicts the popular notion that the NCAA is an all-powerful entity led by a dictatorial czar. Certainly, the NCAA president holds a tremendous amount of power in determining initiatives and areas of emphasis, but in the end, industry-guiding legislation rests in the hands of individual institutions.

Until we acknowledge this reality and take responsibility at the institutional level, the many ills described in chapter 1 will likely continue. In the worst-case scenario, an author writing a similar text 150 years from now might marvel that the same issues remain. The leadership lesson from chapter 1 notes that leadership begins at the individual level and that your paradigm affects both your own decisions and the future of the industry. The leadership lesson presented here emphasizes that such leadership comes with responsibility and accountability.

Sociologists have estimated that even the most introverted people influence 10,000 others in an average lifetime (Elmore, 2010; Maxwell, 2011). Given the public admiration and fandom associated with athletics departments, imagine the lifetime influence you might have as a leader in this industry. As challenges arise, will you be a thermometer or a thermostat? A thermometer reflects the temperature around it—it mirrors the dynamic in the room, and its fate is determined by its environment. A thermostat, on the other hand, sets the temperature. Regardless of the external environment, it remains steady. For

I know of no more encouraging fact than the unquestionable ability of... man to elevate his life by conscious endeavor.

Henry David Thoreau

our part as human beings, we may find it easy to blame our environment, history, colleagues, predecessors, government, or any number of other external influences that affect our circumstances. By doing so, however, we forgo the empowerment that comes from realizing our fundamental freedom to choose.

Victor Frankl was held prisoner in four Nazi concentration camps between 1942 and 1945. His family was killed, and he experienced cruelty, humiliation, misery, and suffering through the daily trials of life in the camps. Surviving this experience, he wrote *Man's Search for Meaning,* in which he said, "everything can be taken from a man but one thing: the last of the human freedoms—to choose one's attitude in any given set of circumstances, to choose one's own way" (1963, p. 66). In every circumstance we arrive in, we can choose to focus our energies on what we can influence. We have the ability to choose how we respond. We have "response-ability" (see figure 2.6).

Contrast this frame of mind with a reactive approach. People who are reactive allow circumstances to determine their frame of mind. They are at the mercy of stimuli because they do not choose their response. Reactive people focus their energies on what they cannot control. They blame others, highlight the weaknesses of their peers, find external excuses and causes for their own circumstances, and ultimately feel trapped as victims of their environment.

Putting into practice the wisdom of Victor Frankl, on the other hand, can foster tremendous personal power. "Until a person can say deeply and honestly, 'I am what I am today because of the choices I made yesterday,' that person cannot say, 'I choose otherwise'"

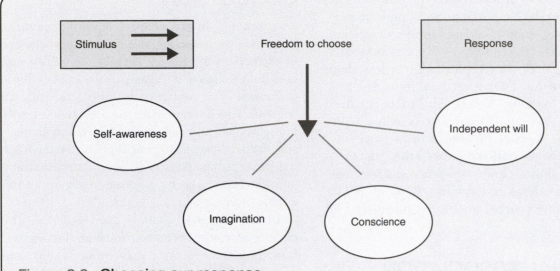

Figure 2.6 **Choosing our response.**

(Covey, 2004, p. 72). Within this proactive paradigm, there are no excuses. We cannot be bullied by external stimuli, and we cannot accept the passivity of a reactive paradigm. Covey urges individuals who find themselves taking an irresponsible position to use their resourcefulness and initiative (their "R and I").

Whatever the stumbling block or confounding issue, accept responsibility and choose how you respond. You may not be able to change the environment—you may not even be able to influence, for example, your president's vote on governance issues—but you will always have the power to choose your response. And as you focus on that which you can influence, your circle of influence will grow.

The sport sponsorship fund also rewards the number of opportunities that Division I schools provide, but, unlike the grant-in-aid fund, it is not weighted. NCAA guidelines for the sport sponsorship plan reward institutions with one unit (approximately US$30,000) per sport offered in a range of 13 sports (Schlabach, 2011).

The student-athlete assistance fund is a combination of two funds, each of which is designed to help athletes in need of special assistance. The first fund, the student-athlete opportunity fund, is designed to provide direct benefits (beyond traditional grants, fees, and other budgeted items) to athletes or their families to meet financial needs that arise in conjunction with participation in intercollegiate athletics or enrollment in an academic curriculum (NCAA, 2009). Many schools base this distribution on student Pell Grant eligibility (which requires a demonstration of low financial support

from the family), but these decisions are made on an institutional basis. The bulk of this funding is allocated for educational purposes, but it can also be used to meet other needs, such as clothing ("NCAA Finances," 2014). The other part of the student-athlete assistance fund—the special assistance fund—is distributed to conferences with the goal of financially assisting athletes who are unable to complete because of medical reasons or have exhausted their eligibility ("NCAA Finances," 2014).

The final portion of Division I revenue distribution is allocated specifically to the enhancement of academic support programs. The fund was created to support efforts to increase team academic progress rates and graduation success rates. Common uses include paying for additional athletics academic support personnel, supplies, academic equipment (e.g., computers), and tutorial services ("NCAA Finances," 2014).

Although these various funds represent financial support from the NCAA in terms of performance incentives (e.g. grant-in-aid and sport sponsorship) and additional athlete support (e.g. academic and special support), they typically cover less than 5 percent of most Division I athletics budgets ("NCAA Finances," 2014). The main sources of revenue for most institutions come from institutional support (in the form of university or student-fee allocations), ticket sales, contributions from alumni, and conference distributions ("NCAA Revenues & Expenses Report," 2011). These revenue sources are discussed further in chapter 7.

NATIONAL ASSOCIATION OF COLLEGIATE WOMEN ATHLETICS ADMINISTRATORS (NACWAA)

NACWAA fosters the empowerment, development, and advancement of women in all aspects of intercollegiate athletics. Through mentoring, networking, and professional development, the organization strives to involve women in positions of influence and power in athletics administration and aspires to help administrators, professional staff, coaches, and student-athletes maximize their opportunities in the field. The group stresses diversity and equity in tackling national issues in college sport. NACWAA also seeks to empower women in their personal lives, pressing women to break through barriers that might restrict their upward mobility or advancement. Growth opportunities are facilitated by a national convention and continuous leadership education. Student memberships are available.

CONCLUSION

As discussed in the chapter-opening scenario, criticism is growing about the governance of intercollegiate athletics. Headlines are filled with multibillion-dollar television deals, multimillion-dollar coaching contracts, lawsuits, and calls for reform. The current governance structures in intercollegiate athletics are under attack, with many stakeholders questioning whether the money filtering through this industry is being handled wisely, and who the key decision makers really are in this administrative chain.

In this chapter, you have learned about the principle of institutional control. You have also learned how conferences serve their member institutions while also facilitating rules compliance and acting as intermediaries with the NCAA. Institutions independently determine what type of athletics program to operate and then choose how they affiliate with others through playing conferences and national governing bodies. In turn, each individual associated with an intercollegiate athletics program—from student-athletes to institution presidents—is responsible for understanding and playing by the rules of the governing bodies. Thus the integrity of intercollegiate athletics is collectively owned.

You now have a greater understanding of how the NCAA functions and how the vast sums of money generated by the NCAA serve its members, and ultimately the student-athletes, both directly and indirectly. The governance of intercollegiate athletics is not a top-down dictatorship but a bottom-up representative governance system that can be only as successful as the individuals who participate in the enterprise enable it to be.

DISCUSSION QUESTIONS

1. What are the limitations of institutional control in intercollegiate athletics?

2. Some argue that the NCAA has grown too big and powerful. Given the purpose of a national governing body as discussed in this chapter, how might you refute or support this argument?

3. The Drake Group, the Coalition on Intercollegiate Athletics, and American Association of University Professors are faculty groups that have called for reform in intercollegiate athletics. Visit the web pages of these groups and explore some of the reforms they suggest. Do you support these suggested reforms? Why or why not?

4. Initially, conferences were organized to help facilitate competition between similarly situated schools with geographic proximity. How have conference missions changed, and what has spurred this change?

5. The top two layers of NCAA governance involve college presidents. What are the strengths and weaknesses of this structure?

6. Explain the differences between NCAA Division I, II, and III institutions. What are some strengths and weaknesses of each division?

7. Given the current NCAA Division I "top-down" legislative process (with override authority residing with the schools), is it possible for individual schools to enact change? How might a president, athletics director, FAR, or athletics administrator pursue a cause that he or she feels is important?

8. Discuss the NCAA's current revenue structure. How might the organization be affected if several power conferences chose to begin their own annual basketball tournament? What are the implications of such heavy reliance on a single revenue source?

9. Why might it be wise to cheer for, rather than against, schools in your NCAA Division I conference during March Madness?

10. What activities are most highly rewarded by the Division I revenue distribution plan? Do you think this is the best rewards structure? What alternatives might facilitate beneficial change?

LEARNING ACTIVITIES

1. Research the rules passed by the Power 5 conferences who were granted autonomy in 2014. What legislation has been adopted and how have these changes affected the industry of intercollegiate athletics?

2. Interview one of the following administrators to gain perspective about his or her role in the NCAA governance process: institutional compliance director, senior woman administrator, athletics director, faculty athletics representative, conference compliance administrator, or conference commissioner.

CHAPTER **3**

Leadership and Management

Erianne A. Weight, University of North Carolina at Chapel Hill

In this chapter, you will explore

- the importance of vision in modern-day intercollegiate athletics administration,

- effective strategies for optimizing resource management,

- tools to help formulate information-driven decisions,

- the importance of effective communication throughout the organization and beyond, and

- strategies for effective personnel leadership.

LEADING WITH VISION

A new athletics director (AD) prepared for her first senior staff meeting. After working in the corporate world for 20 years, she had chosen to apply for the AD position at her alma mater, a Division I Football Bowl Subdivision school with an annual budget of US$60 million. The budgetary demands of the position were familiar—a fact that she had clearly articulated throughout the interview process—but the balance of the budgetary demands and the academic mission of the department was going to be a new challenge.

As she approached her first week in this new position, she hoped to be guided by the vision, mission, and philosophy statements she had presented during the interview process. She had been attracted to this position with a desire to give back to the institution that had given her so much as a fan, student-athlete, and alumna. But as the e-mails, phone calls, and appearance requests piled up on top of the budget cuts and the day-to-day demands of leading 18 teams and a 350-person staff, it became evident that the position would involve a continual battle to maintain vision and perspective through all of the day-to-day operations.

As governmental and institutional financial constraints have led to an expectation for athletics departments to become more self-sufficient, modern-day athletics directors have absorbed many of the responsibilities and challenges typically faced by CEOs, educators, and politicians. As a result, individuals who serve as athletics directors need to be well versed in identifying and building both revenue streams and relationships while maintaining a focus on their role as educators. In fact, they must play a diverse range of roles, as summarized eloquently in the following quotation:

> *Major-college ADs are expected to find ways to keep shoes on hundreds of athletes who will never make the pros while still investing heavily in traditional revenue-generating sports. They have to be fans and dispassionate observers. They must have creativity, imagination and vision, but they better know NCAA rules to the letter. They must lead, follow and get out of the way. They must be contrarians with deft conflict resolution skills. They must make deals and friends (wealthy ones, especially). They must hire and fire. They must understand contracts and contractors, traditions and academicians, Twitter and glitter. (Berkowitz & Upton, 2011)*

An athletics director's responsibilities may include elements of being a lobbyist, designer, or fundraiser for new facilities; a legal expert when making decisions surrounding Title IX, liability, contracts, and other issues; a publicist for promoting the good in an era in which bad news sells; and a strategist with respect to management and financial plans for both the short and the long term. Whether an AD manages the 458-person staff of the Ohio State University athletics department (Easterbrook, 2010) or a staff of 5 at a smaller school, many of the leadership demands of the position are the same. Issues range from competitive coaches vying for scarce departmental resources to often-incessant public commentary about departmental decisions. In this complicated context, the tasks of allocating fiscal, physical, and human resources can be challenging indeed.

LEADERSHIP

The job descriptions of a corporate CEO and a "big-time" athletics director are similar in many respects. They differ considerably, however, in the purpose and structure of their respective organizations. Most corporate CEOs pursue a general organizational purpose of creating value and are charged with maximizing returns for shareholders. In contrast, the purpose of an intercollegiate athletics department should be to facilitate educational opportunities for their athletes. As a result, the athletics director's role is to strengthen the philosophical, financial, and organizational structure necessary to create optimal experiences within the parameters defined through the university's own organization and its national governing body (for information about divisional philosophies, see chapter 2). The AD should clearly define, differentiate, and inspire departmental stakeholders, which requires him or her to delineate a vision, a mission, and core values.

Vision

A vision is a clear, concise, and inspiring statement defining what the athletics department wants to be or should look like in the future. This statement should be easy to remember and should provide a sense of direction and pride for the organization's stakeholders. A powerful vision can motivate and inspire staff members and athletes to accomplish extraordinary feats in an effort to reach for this image of the future. The following list gives a sampling of powerful visions from the corporate sector:

- To solve unsolved problems innovatively (3M)
- To make people happy (Disney)
- Making tools for the minds that advance humankind (Apple)
- Refresh the world, inspire moments of optimism and happiness, create value, and make a difference (Coca-Cola)
- To transform our athletes into world-leaders (possible athletics department vision)

Mission

An organizational mission is a unique statement of purpose describing why an athletics department exists, and what distinctive competences or competitive advantages it uses in striving to achieve its vision. Mission statements can be used to frame SMART (specific, measurable, achievable, realistic, and time-bound) objectives that guide an organization toward achieving its vision. Many organizations have confused their vision and mission statements or melded them into one statement of purpose, and some have used broad terms rather than unique processes and expected performance levels that can set the department apart from others. In doing so, they have often lost the long-term inspiration underlying why the organization does what it does from a broad perspective, as stated in the vision statement. As you peruse the following examples, you will note that many of the mission statements could be used as either a mission statement or vision statement. The differentiation between the two types of statements is far less important than the guiding purpose and inspiration they can bring. Here are some powerful mission statements from the corporate sector and intercollegiate athletics.

- To bring inspiration and innovation to every athlete in the world (Nike)
- Apple is committed to bringing the best personal computing experience to students, educators, creative professionals, and consumers around the world through its innovative hardware, software, and Internet offerings.
- 3M is committed to actively contributing to sustainable development through environmental protection, social responsibility, and economic progress.
- To be the world's best fast-food restaurant that gives excellent service, is clean, provides quality food, and puts a smile on every customer's face (McDonalds)
- To bring students, faculty, and staff together in educational activities that promote healthy lifestyles, enhance a sense of community, foster growth in leadership and teamwork skills, and encourage the pursuit of excellence (Massachusetts Institute of Technology Department of Athletics, Physical Education, and Recreation)
- To provide student-athletes with the opportunity to compete at the highest level while making progress toward completion of a degree of their choice in an environment consistent with high academic standards, a commitment to equity and diversity, sportsmanship, personal growth and development, and ethical conduct (University of Tulsa Athletic Department)
- We educate and inspire through athletics (University of North Carolina at Chapel Hill Athletics).
- To facilitate unmatched educational experiences for student-athletes through holistic training in the classroom, on the field, and throughout their university experience (possible athletics mission)

Core Values

Departmental values are shared beliefs about desired behaviors and outcomes that provide a framework in which decisions are made. Values drive the culture and priorities of an athletics department; therefore, identifying these shared beliefs can allow organizations to create a culture that embraces common goals and outcomes (Abreu, Macedo, & Camarinha-Matos, 2009; Berings, De Fruyt, & Bouwen, 2004). As a result, they should form the underlying current in the development of vision and mission statements.

The core value of candor, for instance, can improve organizational efficiency by encouraging employees to be honest with each other (Welch & Welch, 2005). Alternatively, a core value of excellence can emphasize the importance of process and doing things the right way in every departmental decision or challenge. The stated core values of the NCAA include belief in and commitment to the following ideals:

- The collegiate model of athletics in which students participate as an avocation, balancing their academic, social, and athletics experiences

- The highest levels of integrity and sportsmanship

- The pursuit of excellence in both academics and athletics

- The supporting role that intercollegiate athletics plays in the higher education mission and in enhancing the sense of community and strengthening the identity of member institutions

- An inclusive culture that fosters equitable participation for student-athletes and career opportunities for coaches and administrators from diverse backgrounds

- Respect for institutional autonomy and philosophical differences

- Presidential leadership of intercollegiate athletics at the campus, conference, and national levels

Value Culturization

In 1994, Jim Collins and Jerry Porras released their influential book *Built to Last*, which documented the presence of a core ideology in high-performing organizations. In the wake of this wisdom, corpora-

tions around the globe have adopted organizational statements of vision, mission, and values (Lencioni, 2002). In doing so, corporate leaders have sought to attain the purported benefits derived from a core ideology, including inspiration, motivation, empowerment, organizational effectiveness, and fulfillment of personal aspirations (Berry, 1999; Collins & Porras, 1994; Harmon, 1996; Pattakos, 2004; Van Rekom, Van Riel, & Wierenga, 2006). A well-defined mission also brings external benefits, including the ability to attract well-qualified personnel (Brown & Yoshioka, 2003), define a niche in the industry (Bolon, 2005) that can facilitate brand equity, and, for institutions of higher learning, "attract the best recruits, garner the most donations, earn the most revenue, and reflect best upon their universities" (Meyer, 2008, p. 72).

Scholars have cautioned, however, that value, mission, and vision statements that are insincere or lack organizational buy-in and infusion can be detrimental and ultimately undermine leadership action. In particular, dissonance between stated and practiced values can lead to mistrust, cynicism, and skepticism because the effort is interpreted as an insincere approach used simply to maximize productivity. The result can be more detrimental to the culture of an organization than not having defined values at all (Ferguson & Milliman, 2008; Ind, 2007; Milliman & Clair, 1995; Sull & Spinosa, 2007).

The challenge of creating buy-in through an organizational ideology may be more complex for modern-day athletics directors because the sanctity of college sport in its current form at the big-time level is continually questioned by scholars and the media (Branch, 2011; Deford, 2011; Splitt, 2011; Vedder, 2011). Indeed, the schizophrenic combination of commercial and educational values that often seem at odds with each other can leave stakeholders searching for direction. However, this tumultuous climate can also create an opportunity for leadership as stakeholders search for guidance (Kotter, 1996). Because the NCAA is a member-driven organization, these issues fall within the sphere of influence of directors of athletics through their college presidents, and a powerful vision can facilitate tremendous buy-in, hope, and inspiration for members of an athletics department.

As directors of athletics strive to overcome negative media reports and inspire their employees to fulfill departmental purposes, they must realize that creating and communicating values constitutes only one step in the process of maximizing organizational efficiency. Research has demonstrated that the most successful results come from defining values and achieving organizational infusion through value creation, consistent communication, and synergistic rewards systems (Van Rekom et al., 2006). "From the first interview to the last day of work, employees should be constantly reminded that core values form the basis for every decision the company makes" (Lencioni, 2002, p. 117). This process starts with the example set by upper-level administrators and continues through the integration of these values in all of the organization's processes—a process known as "culturalization." This type of leadership empowers employees to make effective situational decisions through engrained organizational principles (Ouchi, 1979; Sull, 2010).

Most intercollegiate athletics departments have defined vision, mission, or value statements, but they vary in the extent to which they are unique (Meyer, 2008; Ward & Hux, 2011) or effectively used and engrained in the organization (Cooper & Weight, 2012; Cooper, Weight, and Pierce, 2014). In a study examining Division I athletics directors' perceptions of core values, Cooper, Weight, & Pierce (2014) explored the presence of a leader–value continuum in intercollegiate athletics departments. On one end of the continuum, they uncovered efficient administrators who fully embrace departmental core values and proactively root day-to-day decisions in values. On the other end of the spectrum, however, they found evidence of administrators who embrace a hypocritical approach in which they may believe (or proclaim) values to be important yet do not act in accordance with these stated standards.

Undoubtedly, the majority of administrators fall somewhere in the middle of the continuum. They aspire to create efficient organizations driven by culturized values yet have not fully built buy-in or culturization and therefore leave untapped potential in their sphere of influence (Cooper et al., 2014). Ultimately, effective leaders must "create a vision, articulate the vision, passionately own the vision, and relentlessly drive it to completion" (Jack Welch as qtd. in Tichy & Charan, 1989, p. 173).

Situational Vision and Decision Making

In *Developing the Leader Within You* (2005), John C. Maxwell explained that one of the most common questions from people in leadership is how to develop a vision for their organization. This question is crucial because until it is answered a person will be a leader in name only. Maxwell explains how easy it can be for managers to get bogged down in minutia. In order to lead effectively, they must make a conscious effort to see the big picture and look to the future.

Throughout the day-to-day demands of an athletics director, decisions and situations arise in which simply pushing a piece of paper is not sufficient as they may carry long-term or far-reaching implications. In these situations, a leader feeling that he or she is viewing the problem from the weeds rather than from a more objective or vision-centered "30,000-foot" vantage point should take time to proactively step back, reflect, and compose a vision specific to the situation. In some instances, a situational vision may naturally surface, but more often than not, an effective leader needs to consciously invent a process to guide the department through each unique circumstance. Whether facing a contract renegotiation, a personnel problem, an outsourcing decision, or a new initiative, leaders can use certain strategies to create a guide for handling a given complex circumstance. These strategies include beginning with the end in mind (Covey, 1989), pondering the hoped-for result of the decision two or ten years down the road, examining the most significant stakeholders affected, and using a formalized decision-making process.

When confronted with a challenging decision, it is crucial to gather high-quality information. Yet in the increasingly fast-paced communication environment that we live in, administrators often feel pressure to make decisions quickly. In reality, this is a reckless approach perpetuated by the notion that a powerful organizational "quarterback" will be able to assess the field and make snap judgments in order to lead the team to victory. Acting in this matter, intercollegiate athletics administrators have been questioned about irresponsible decisions that clearly contradicted federal law and legal precedent (Ridpath, Yiamouyiannis, Lawrence, & Galles, 2008; Yiamouyiannis & Lawrence, 2009).

Instead, scholars have urged administrators to use rationality in their decision making (see figure 3.1) and to strive to optimize decisions rather than simply "satisficing" (i.e., compromising between satisfying and sufficing) (Simon, 1977). The practice of satisficing reflects the limits of human decision making based on available information, time, and information-processing ability, which is often referred to as "bounded rationality" (Simon). Certainly, there are limits, and in some situations it is acceptable to satisfice and make a "good enough" decision rather than devoting precious resources to a process of maximizing the decision. Too often, however, people jump to the good-enough approach too early and make grave mistakes that could have been easily avoided through a more systematic decision-making process.

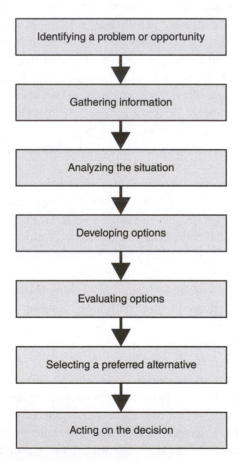

Figure 3.1 The rational decision-making model.

Reprinted from "Rational decision making," *Happy Manager* (Chester, United Kingdom: Apex Leadership). Available: www.the-happy-manager.com/rational-decision-making-model.html.

Another approach, the Delphi method, can be used to capitalize on the skill of experts in forecasting or decision making. In this process, eight to ten experts who remain anonymous are presented with an issue or question. They respond in writing, and a summary of their opinions is prepared and sent back to each expert, who can then modify his or her position based on the feedback of the others. Respondents whose opinions deviate from the median are asked to defend their positions. After multiple rounds, a final summary report is sent to management.

Whether one uses a formal decision-making model such as the Delphi method or another approach, gathering high-quality information increases the likelihood of optimizing a decision rather than merely satisficing. These methods also provide data to justify decisions. This data can be particularly useful if a decision turns out to be less than ideal.

In moments of turmoil, when you receive troubling information, ask yourself, "What is the other side of the story?" Empower those around you to have patience in the face of criticism, to slow down, and to take the time to gather the information needed in order to make an informed decision. After all, you simply don't know what you don't know. The situational vision that led the University of North Carolina at Chapel Hill through the challenge of a major infractions case in 2010 and 2011 (see the case study sidebar) provides a glimpse of the structure that this approach can bring to difficult organizational circumstances.

One of the most significant challenges faced in intercollegiate athletics administration is compliance. No amount of policing or departmental staffing seems to be enough. Instead, compliance needs to be built on a culture of accountability emphasized by each departmental stakeholder. In order for an organization to feel congruence in this and other facets of its mission, it helps to have a leader at the helm who champions the cause. Many intercollegiate athletics stakeholders feel that the industry is on the brink of a renaissance, and athletics directors must embrace the responsibility of challenging the status quo within their organizations and governance structures in order to inspire positive change.

Considerable research has been conducted to examine how a single individual can accomplish

Case Study

Situational Vision in an Infractions Investigation at UNC-Chapel Hill

Richard A. Baddour, former AD at UNC–Chapel Hill

The department of athletics received notification that the NCAA was coming to conduct an on-campus investigation. We knew they wanted to talk to a lot of students and some coaches. We didn't know if this would be big or inconsequential, but one thing I knew was that we needed a set of core values to guide us through the process—that this was a moment that required vision. So, after contemplating the reality of the situation for a few days, I sat at my kitchen table and came up with what I thought would be the best way to guide us through this process. This situational vision took the form of four guiding principles:

1. Every decision we make will be in the best interest of the University of North Carolina.

2. We will be as fair as possible to all the individuals involved.

3. We will go where the information takes us and maintain total cooperation with the NCAA.

4. We will start today to make ourselves better as a result of the experience.

Deciding to be guided by what was best for the university helped us know how to proceed. If, for instance, something might have been in the best interest of football, or of a particular individual, we knew that our stated values for this process meant that we would do our best to be fair—and we wanted the coaches and athletes to know we cared about them and would fight for them—but at the end of the day, our decisions would be guided by what was best for the university. What was best for Carolina would take priority.

The idea of going where the information took us seemed simple and logical, but when the information was piling on, it was not always easy. I sometimes wondered if we really wanted to open a door, but we committed to conduct the investigation in a first-class way, and so we followed each piece of information. This open statement of full investigational compliance was empowering for stakeholders in the department. They heard their athletics director say that we were going where the information took us, and as a result they all knew that it was their responsibility to bring forward any information they had.

It was difficult for us to face this investigation when we prided ourselves on integrity. So, as we began this process, I felt that we needed the hope and the knowledge that the journey to rebuilding our image on the inside and the outside would begin today. It would start by how we conducted the investigation.

extraordinary feats by inspiring dedication, loyalty, and admiration in subordinates. Throughout the 1970s and 1980s, several theories arose founded upon the importance of a leader's ability to express a compelling vision, display charismatic behavior, and lead through personal example (Bass, 1985; Bennis, 1984; Burns, 1978; Graeff, 1983; House, 1971; Vroom & Yetton, 1973). One philosophy that emerged during this era of theoretical advancement was the theory of transformational or visionary leadership (Bass, 1985; Bennis, 1984; Burns, 1987). This theory describes the ability of a leader to transform an organization by expressing a determined vision that infuses and inspires the organization, thus leading to an organizational change or rebirth as employees are motivated and empowered (Bass; Conger & Kanungo, 1987). Theorists have described the effects that can be achieved by a transformational leader, including the metamorphosis of followers into leaders and the intrinsic desire of subordinates to surpass the leader's expectations (Yukl, 1989). Specific dimensions of a transformational leadership approach are listed in table 3.1.

Many documented accounts of transformational leaders exist within intercollegiate athletics. Jeremy Foley, for example, is known as a man with great vision who has led a top-to-bottom team approach in his 20-year tenure as director of athletics at the University of Florida. The mission of the department under his leadership is to produce good citizens, to graduate the athletes who come through the program, and to win with class and integrity (Mondello, 1997). Throughout his tenure, he has led the department to a perfect record of top-10 finishes in the National Association of Collegiate Directors of Athletics all-sport standings, and he is respected for his support of all programs in the department—not just the most visible sports (SECSports.com, 2006). Indeed, in an era in which the vast majority of Division I athletics departments engage in deficit spending, Foley added three women's sports and oversaw a budget responsible for contributing more than US$55 million to help fund University of Florida academic endeavors (Gatorzone.com, 2011).

Responding to Foley's gutsy decision to hire 39-year-old Texas defensive coordinator Will Muschamp as the football head coach successor to the very successful Urban Meyer, Gene Frenette (2010) commented, "He's not afraid to think outside the box or risk being bombarded down the road by an orange-and-blue legion of second-guessers" (p. 94). This hire fit the criteria that Foley values in his coaches: coaches with integrity and commitment to NCAA rules, who respect the other sports in the department, possess a strong work ethic and a high level of passion and energy (Newell, 2008). Foley stated, "In the competitive world, you have to outwork people. I like people who will work very hard and who will focus on the positives rather than the negatives" (qtd. in Mondello, 1997, para. 14). In keeping with this approach, Foley encourages athletics administrators to talk about the positives in intercollegiate athletics that are never as broadly reported as the negatives (Mondello).

Other examples of transformational athletics directors include Ron Wellman and Peter Roby. Wellman, athletics director of one of the smallest schools to compete at the NCAA Division I FBS level, has led Wake Forest to tremendous achievement. Atlantic Coast Conference Commissioner John Swofford has commented on Wellman's success and respect in the industry: "I think he has earned it by the consistency he has had over the years, by the standards he sets for himself and those around him, by his capabilities administratively, which are enormous, by the manner in which he treats people, and the manner in which he conducts himself" (qtd. in Collins, 2009).

Roby is athletics director at Northeastern University and a vocal leader for social change through sport education and values-driven leadership. He freely shares his vision of being in the business of "people development." Roby has modeled his emphasis on education in his athletics department

Table 3.1 Transformational Leadership Dimensions

Dimension	Description
Vision	"The expression of an idealized picture of the future based around organizational values" (p. 332)
Inspirational communication	"The expression of positive and encouraging messages about the organization, and statements that build motivation and confidence" (p. 332)
Supportive leadership	"Expressing concern for followers and taking account of their individual needs" (p. 333)
Intellectual stimulation	"Enhancing employees' interest in and awareness of problems, and increasing their ability to think about problems in new ways" (p.333)
Personal recognition	"The provision of rewards such as praise and acknowledgement of effort for achievement of specified goals" (p. 334)

Reprinted from *The Leadership Quarterly* 15(3), A.E. Rafferty and M.A. Griffin, "Dimensions of transformational leadership: Conceptual and empirical extensions," pgs. 329-354, copyright 2004, with permission of Elsevier.

Culture Is the Shadow of the Leader: Embedding Culture Within an Organization

Primary Embedding Mechanisms

- What leaders pay attention to, measure, and control on a regular basis
- How leaders react to critical incidents and organizational crises
- How leaders allocate resources
- Deliberate role modeling, teaching, and coaching
- How leaders allocate rewards and status
- How leaders recruit, select, promote, and communicate

Secondary Articulation and Reinforcement Mechanisms

- Organizational design and structure
- Organizational systems and procedures
- Rites and rituals of the organization
- Design of physical space, facades, and buildings
- Stories about important events and people
- Formal statements of organizational philosophy, creeds, and charters

by instituting various programs to help athletes stay on top of their studies. One such program is "lecture-capture," wherein the athletics department supports the recording and uploading of lectures for students who miss class due to athletics competition (Roby, 2012). Roby encourages athletics administrators to be led by values of conviction rather than values of convenience and urges leaders to hold themselves accountable to the students they serve.

Regardless of the strategy used in leading an organization, the message must be communicated powerfully and frequently in order for a new vision, mission, culture, initiative, or set of values to take root and flourish. The message can be disseminated both through formalized channels (e.g., meetings, memos, and official departmental lines of communication) and through informal methods (e.g., discussions during casual lunches, modeling through

Meet your teammates. Assess their strengths. Set mutually agreed upon goals. And plan a strategy for achieving success.

Michigan AD David Brandon
(qtd. in McCoy, 2010)

example, and distribution of unique reminders featuring highlighted keywords). For more on this topic, see the sidebar titled Culture Is the Shadow of the Leader.

In most situations where organizational change is needed, buy-in is difficult to achieve without a sense of urgency or need for the change, as well as support for the change from powerful leaders in the organization. John Kotter has outlined an eight-step change management model that details how to implement organizational change (see table 3.2). When pursuing a cultural initiative, it is important to remember that an athletics director's time is one of the most valuable resources in the department. Therefore, how the AD chooses to spend his or her time sends the clearest message of departmental priorities and sets the tone in the department about what is important.

MANAGEMENT

Although a visionary leader can take a good organization to a level of greatness by inspiring stakeholders, a solid management structure is also necessary to facilitate optimal organizational effectiveness. Management functions include leading, planning, staffing, organizing, and evaluating an organization in an effort to accomplish a goal. Thus far in this chapter, we have discussed leading and planning; this section focuses on staffing, organizing, and evaluating.

For an employee, few things are more frustrating than running into bureaucratic roadblocks that don't make sense. Whether it is the structural organization of a department within a larger unit, or a policy that seems to hinder progress, the "way things are done" often impedes forward momentum. Athletics directors can be constrained by the overall university structure in which they function, but there is often a fair amount of latitude in what can be done in the department itself. Specifically, the athletics director can exert considerable control over the *who* (staffing) and the *how* (organization, evaluation, and communication) of athletics department management.

Staffing

The importance of staffing is easily understood by anyone who has fielded an athletic team. You may be the best coach in the world with a highly trained and prepared team, but if your athletes average a 6-inch (15-centimeter) or 50-pound (23-kilogram) deficit compared to the competition, it will be difficult to compete. Successful Cornell University lacrosse coach Jeff Tambroni explained how he attracts great players and builds winning a team year after year: "We know who our type of player is. We have identified what we are looking for in a Cornell lacrosse player. We tell them that we will work and train harder than any other team in the country . . . so if they don't have a strong work ethic they are not our type of player" (qtd. in Gordon, 2009).

In the revolutionary book *Good to Great,* Jim Collins explained that a critical element of successful organizations is the competence to get the right people on the bus and put them in the right seats (2001). In other words, it is critical for administrators to build a team that shares the organization's guiding philosophy. It is also a wise practice for leaders to focus on key responsibilities rather than

Table 3.2 Kotter's Eight-Step Change Management Model

1. Create urgency.	In order for stakeholders to buy in to the change and the strategy, they need to believe that change is needed.
2. Form a powerful coalition.	Change will be facilitated if you create a team of influential people who believe in the strategy. Their power may come from longevity, status, expertise, or political clout.
3. Create a vision for change.	Simplify the strategy into a form that encapsulates its potential and is easily understood by all stakeholders.
4. Communicate the vision.	Communicate the strategy frequently and powerfully. Demonstrate the type of behavior that is integral to the plan and openly address ideas and potential concerns.
5. Remove obstacles.	Alter any structures or processes that can impede the implementation of the plan. Eliminate any barriers to progress.
6. Create short-term wins.	Success breeds success and can be a strong motivator. Set short-term targets that can be celebrated along the journey toward complete implementation of the marketing plan.
7. Build on the change.	Be careful not to declare success too soon. After each victory, analyze what was done right and what could be better. Strive for continuous improvement.
8. Anchor the changes in corporate culture.	In order for the strategy to stick and remain grounded in the organization over time, communicate progress often and emphasize ideals of the strategy in hiring and training new staff members.

Reprinted, by permission, from E.A. Weight and M. Walker, 2012, Ensuring strategic sport marketing success. In *Sport marketing: winning strategies for sport business success,* edited by B. Turner et al. (Dubuque, IA: Kendall Hunt).

job titles. Collins recommends that leaders list key positions, roles, and duties and then determine what percentage of them are currently handled by the right people. Increasing this figure to 100 percent is one of the most difficult tasks that leaders need to be willing to address. Some longtime traveling companions may need to be asked to get off the bus before the newly charted route can be traveled, and some duties may be best fulfilled through outsourcing.

In a different approach toward the same staffing goals, Jon Gordon (2009), consultant for numerous professional and college coaches and teams, recommends an exercise of identifying several people in the organization that you wish you could clone. Write down their characteristics and create benchmarks for identifying the right person for each position. Gordon reminds leaders to hire the right kind of people—those who fit the organizational culture. If you want a creative culture, hire creative people; if you want a positive culture, hire positive people. "Remember," he emphasizes, "the people you surround yourself with will often determine the kind of ride it's going to be" (p. 6).

One pitfall of this approach that should be consciously avoided is hiring staff who all think alike, have similar cultural backgrounds, and similar world views. While Gordon uses "cloning" to illustrate attributes to replicate, administrators should seek to facilitate as much diversity as possible. Research has demonstrated the more perspectives, experiences, empathy, and education garnered, the greater ability an organization will have to harness the considerable benefits of diversity, including increased creativity, productivity, and quality (e.g., Earley & Masakowski, 2000; Ely & Thomas, 2001; Swann, Kwan, Polzer, & Milton, 2003).

Use of Search Firms in Athletics Staffing

At the Division I level, the use of search firms has become an increasingly common practice in high-profile searches for athletics directors and for coaches of football and men's basketball. Each year, Division I schools conduct roughly 35 to 45 searches through the use of an outside agency (Smith, 2011). Dave Brandon, Michigan athletics director and former CEO of Dominos Pizza, generally disliked using search firms in the corporate world but sees tremendous advantages in using them in intercollegiate athletics because of the highly specialized nature of the position.

> *You're dealing with a compressed period of time, and you need to be as efficient as possible. To be productive, you've got to know the agents, the coaches. You've got to set up meetings and move around the country, all while maintaining confidentiality. . . . [O]ur football search was done in six days, and if I had done it on my own, it would have taken two to three weeks, and there would have been a lot of frustrating moments in the process. (qtd. in Smith, 2011)*

Search firms offer an array of services that can be tailored to fit a university's needs (see figure 3.2) including meticulously screening résumés, developing a candidate profile, developing a pool of candidates, enticing candidates to the institution, and negotiating and developing contracts (Ammons and Glass, 1988).

Organizing

In order to maximize an organization's potential, a leader must also create a clear and efficient

Minority Opportunities Athletic Association

The National Association of Collegiate Directors of Athletics (NACDA) promotes the development and advancement of minorities in intercollegiate athletics through the Minority Opportunities Athletic Association (MOAA). This group advocates for greater participation rates by minorities in athletics administration while offering programming that supports diversity initiatives. MOAA hosts an annual symposium in conjunction with NACDA's convention and provides research and solutions related to ethnic minority issues in intercollegiate athletics. The group's resource center offers additional services and resources, including mentoring and networking.

Industry Profile

Brian Hutchinson on Hiring and Firing Coaches

Brian Hutchinson became Morehead State University's (MSU's) ninth director of athletics in 2005. Under Hutchinson's leadership, the athletics department has achieved major improvements in facilities, student-athlete performance, and staffing levels. He was instrumental in the facility's renovations, and during his tenure MSU has won conference championships in men's basketball, volleyball, soccer, and football, as well as women's golf.

Scrutiny and second guessing—by the media, by an institution, and now even by researchers—are heaviest at the time of a firing rather than at the time of a hiring. What aspects of the process (such as ticket sales, fundraising, recruiting) does the media not see?

The media rarely knows the entire story regarding hirings and firings. All of the aspects you mentioned are important, but generally one can just observe a program and determine if the players are executing a game plan and if that game plan is well reasoned. Sometimes exit interviews done with departing players can play a role. Those are important because questions are asked and answered about the day-to-day happenings inside a program that no one really sees. A great deal can be gleaned from that information.

Given the dollar amounts involved in firing a coach and then hiring a new coach, what process do you use to examine the new coach's ability to achieve more success than his or her predecessor?

Clearly, we wouldn't make a change unless we felt the need to improve our performance and/or our team discipline, or in the case of rules violations. That doesn't mean that our young people are in trouble, but it does mean that we want them to approach their studies and their athletic effort with a certain level of performance. We identify the issues within that program, determine the profile of a coach that we might be interested in, and go through a process that would allow us to ascertain if that person fits our needs. I'd have to be certain that a change would matter before I made the move.

When determining the length of a contract for a new coach, how do you balance the need for long-term job security (recruiting perception) against a possibly shorter time line to get results on the field?

I think it is fair for any coach to come in and have a reasonable expectation that they will have enough time to do the job. For us, we typically look at an initial four-year term. We also don't pay out megacontracts, so security can offset that and keep us within some semblance of the market.

Reprinted from B. Hutchinson, 2013. By permission of Winthrop Intelligence. Http://winthropintelligence.com.

organizational structure with defined channels of communication and divisions of labor. If effective people are placed in ineffective structures, they experience frustration, demotivation, and confusion. Putting it in terms of athletics, coaches must not only recruit the right athletes but also give them proper coaching and training. A group of phenomenal athletes with minimal direction may be able to compete with a well-trained competitor for a while, but as the competition continues the team with superior conditioning and coaching is likely to win. In a departmental setting, all of the effort spent to get the right people on the bus can quickly unravel in the face of bureaucratic minutia. The best people will then begin to peruse NCAA job listings on a daily basis in search of alternative professional homes. As with most leadership challenges, departmental organization requires both science and art.

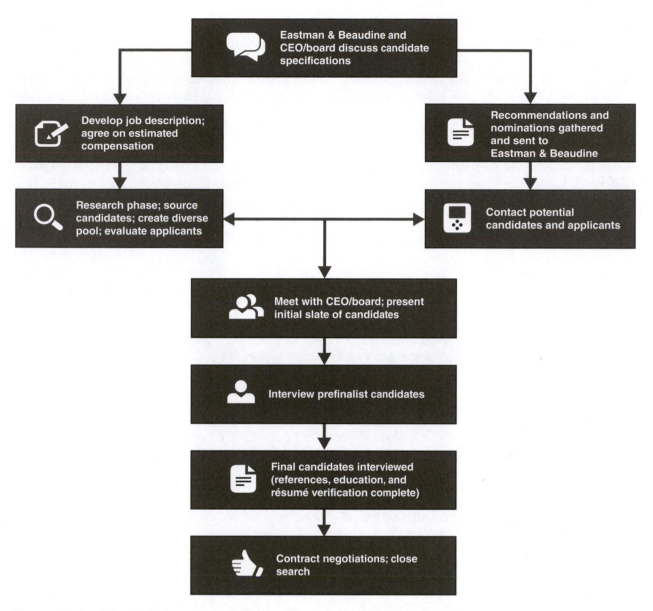

Figure 3.2   The Eastman and Beaudine search firm process.

Reprinted, by permission, from Eastman & Beaudine. Available: http://eastman-beaudine.com/our-approach/our-process-timeline.

An athletics department is typically housed within the larger university organizational structure, and the athletics director usually reports either to the university president or to the vice president of student affairs. The organization of the department itself is generally directed by the AD with help from a senior staff of associate and assistant ADs who are each responsible for unique functional responsibilities (e.g., compliance, marketing, finance, student affairs, operations). A few athletics departments operate as separate men's and women's programs, each with its own director, and many departments are housed with recreation or exercise and sport science departments that administer intramurals, recreational sports, and related educational programs in addition to varsity athletics.

Within the department's senior staff, the NCAA has mandated that one woman hold the designation of senior woman administrator (SWA). In addition, a faculty athletics representative (FAR) represents the institution's faculty in its relationship with the

NCAA and its conference. The FAR is designated by the president or chancellor and does not hold a coaching or administrative position in the athletics department (NCAA Division I Manual, 2013).

Other NCAA regulations related to organizational structure include limits on the number of coaches and graduate assistants per sport. Bylaw 11.7.2 in the Division I manual, for instance, limits the number of football staff within Football Bowl Subdivision institutions to one head coach, nine assistant coaches, and four graduate assistant coaches. Similarly, bylaw 11.7.4 limits the number of coaches and off-campus recruiters for each sport. Division I men's and women's basketball programs, for example, are each limited to four coaches and three off-campus recruiters (NCAA Division I Manual, 2013).

Beyond meeting these requirements, the department should be structured in such a way as to create an efficient chain of command and day-to-day functionality. Learning activity 2 at the end of the chapter encourages you to search online for various athletics organizational charts in order to gain an understanding of the lines of communication and authority, as well as possible career paths. In addition, table 3.3 summarizes the career paths followed by Big Ten athletics directors. Searching organizational charts can also illuminate the multiple levels that are integral to the operation of an athletics department.

One of the best ways to create efficiency in a complex organization is to assign responsibility and delegate authority. With this in mind, effective management has been compared to conducting an orchestra. The conductor is the only person in an orchestra who doesn't make a sound. She is judged by how well she inspires the musicians to perform. Similarly, an athletics director empowers the department's staff to make decisions—to push issue resolution down the organizational chain and eliminate the potential for upper-level bottlenecks.

Because of the highly visible nature of athletics departments, employees who have not been effectively empowered often get nervous about making decisions. They question whether they will receive support and therefore are often slow to make decisions. In contrast, establishing a strong vision—coupled with clear support, evaluation, and communication—allows coaches and other staff members to build a sense of what is important and what authority and responsibility they have to act. Over time, everyone should know what issues to handle themselves, what issues might be best addressed by the senior staff, and when it might be best to involve a task force to investigate an issue at length. Building this strong organizational structure allows the athletics director to focus on the most important leadership functions and maintain a balanced approach to personal and organizational management.

We've all felt the difference between a frazzled leader who carries a high level of stress and one who seems to be composed and always far ahead of deadlines. The difference between these two people likely hinges on the way in which they prioritize and manage their time. Steven Covey created a visual representation of different types of demand faced by individuals in their day-to-day lives and divided the tasks into four quadrants based on importance and urgency (see figure 3.3). Covey urges leaders to strive to live their lives in quadrant II. Certainly, many urgent and important matters will arise, but habitually spending a majority of time in a quadrant-I crisis-management mode leads to stress, burnout, and inefficiency. On the other hand, planning and carving out maximal

> *I may be the AD, but I have no shot at being successful if I don't have a great staff. I have several associate ADs and assistant ADs who, in essence, help run the program. They oversee every sport except for football and men's basketball, which I directly supervise. But it's a team effort. We're all in this thing together. I am very much a delegator. When I first became the AD, I was very much a micromanager because I had done all of those different jobs. So I had to learn to delegate. When you delegate, you show people you trust them. When you delegate, they grow. And when you delegate, you are much more effective as an organization. Our success is due to the fact that we have a lot of quality people working here.*
>
> University of Florida AD Jeremy Foley (qtd. in Newell, 2008, p. 10)

Table 3.3 Career Paths of Big Ten Athletics Directors (ADs)

Name	School	Hire age	Education	Former student-athlete?	Coaching experience?	Previous work experience
Morgan Burke	Purdue University	40	BS in industrial management, MS in industrial relations, JD	Yes, swimming	No	Vice president, Inland Steel Co. (13 positions in 18 years)
Mike Thomas	University of Illinois	50	BS in business administration, MS in athletics administration	No	No	AD at Cincinnati and Akron; associate AD at UVA; assistant AD for internal operations at Denver
Fred Glass	Indiana University	50	BS, JD	No	No	Partner in Indianapolis law firm; president of Indianapolis 2011 Super Bowl bid committee
Gary Barta	University of Iowa	42	BS in mass communication and broadcast journalism	Yes, football	No	AD at Wyoming; director of athletics development and external relations at Northern Iowa; director of development at North Dakota State; senior associate AD at Washington
Dave Brandon	University of Michigan	56	BS in communication	Yes, football	No	Chair and CEO, Domino's Pizza; president, University of Michigan board of regents; CEO, Valassis Communications Inc.
Mark Hollis	Michigan State University	48	BS in communication, MBA	No	No	Assistant commissioner, Western Athletic Conference; assistant and associate athletics director, Pitt; senior associate AD for external relations, Michigan State
Barry Alvarez	University of Wisconsin	65	BS, MS	Yes, football	Yes, college football	Head football coach (Wisconsin), assistant football coach (Iowa, Notre Dame)
Joel Maturi	University of Minnesota	66	BS in government, MS in teaching	No	Yes, high school football	Athletics director, University of Denver, Miami University; assistant AD–facilities and associate AD–compliance, Wisconsin
Tom Osborne	University of Nebraska	70	BS, master's and doctorate in educational psychology	No	Yes, college football	U.S. Congressman (Nebraska); senior lecturer in business administration (Nebraska); head football coach (Nebraska)
Jim Phillips	Northwestern University	42	BS, master's in education, doctorate in educational administration	No	Yes, college basketball	Assistant athletics director of giving, Tennessee; associate director of athletics and senior associate director of athletics for external affairs, Notre Dame
Gene Smith	Ohio State University	56	BS in business administration	Yes, football	Yes, college football	Marketing, IBM; assistant AD, Eastern Michigan; athletics director, Arizona State, Iowa State, Eastern Michigan

time in quadrant II creates a life led by vision, control, balance, and perspective. Therefore, leaders are advised to delegate all matters that are urgent but not important to trusted support staff and to avoid doing activities that are neither important nor urgent, because they result in irresponsible use of time (Covey, 1989).

Evaluating

Returning to the sport analogy of fielding and developing a competitive team, it is difficult to pinpoint the strengths and weaknesses of an offense or of a particular player without some type of evaluative measure, whether it be a game, a time

trial, or a strength test. Just as hundreds of hopeful singers learn for the first time that they might not be cut out for a life of stardom when they receive feedback from the *American Idol* panel of judges, so too are many employees completely unaware of their shortcomings in the workplace until they receive proper feedback.

The best evaluation mechanisms are used on a daily basis, in every interaction. Athletics directors should view employee interactions as a microcosm of the educational mission of the athletics department. Just as opportunities for life lessons can occur on the mat, on the track, or in the training room, they can also be found in meetings, projects, and

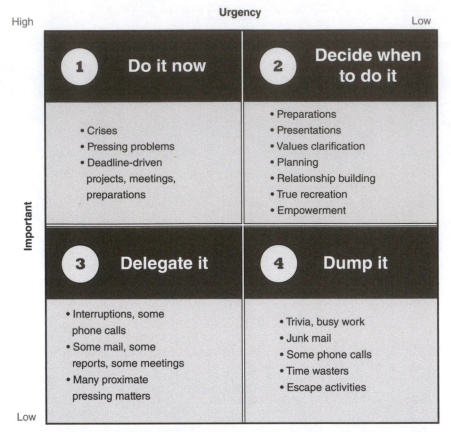

Figure 3.3 Four-quadrant time management paradigm.

Showing Initiative Without Taking Liberties

As a new intern or employee, one of the most difficult challenges is that of taking initiative without overstepping your span of control. The best way to address this challenge is by facing it head on through conversation. One of the first conversations you should have with your supervisor is about how much authority or responsibility he or she hopes for you to wield. Ask your supervisor when he or she wants to see you and when you are being a burden. Explain that you are a person of initiative but you also want to make sure not to overstep the expected boundaries.

If you are the leader in this situation—if you have a subordinate trying to find his or her way—there is generally no simple prescription. Begin the relationship by erring on the side of caution. Have the person see you often, encourage him or her to run ideas by you, and strive to build the person's confidence in the process. If the person is struggling with a challenge, ask what he or she plans to do. If the person is on track, you can say, "You're right—now go do it!" If they are not on track, the oversight necessary to facilitate their success will need to remain until they are able to take the reins In this way, the gap between manager and subordinate responsibility is closed over time. One of the greatest ways to inspire confidence in your subordinates is by clearly articulating the end-goal of a project, and setting check points from the beginning. When the subordinate is able to understand the ultimate purpose of a project and the supervisor's role as the facilitator of success, you can unleash tremendous potential.

Wise individuals also take the time to sit back and debrief after each meeting. Contemplate what the manager or subordinate questioned or learned in this particular instance and how it might be valuable for future interactions. If implemented effectively, situational communication coupled with honest evaluation can help both the manager and the subordinate develop their ability to anticipate each other's thoughts, thus leading to greater self-efficacy, a sense of what is important, and a knowledge of how the other would respond in various situations. If no feedback is sought or given, no learning occurs, and the potential for synchronicity is squandered.

Leadership Lesson

Building a Strong Team and Avoiding Turf Wars

How often have you heard the track-and-field coach compare his or her budget or facilities with those of women's soccer, women's basketball, or even football? Similarly, how often do those in internal marketing look at those in ticketing, external marketing, or sports information with an "us versus them" mentality? "*We* work harder than *they* do, but *they* were able to take their whole team to the convention and *we* only got to send two." "If *they* would read the material *we* sent them about promotions, *we* wouldn't have so many complaints." "*They* get preferential treatment because *they* went on the basketball trip with the AD." And so on . . .

Politics is when people choose their words and actions based on how they want others to react rather than based on what they really think.

Lencioni, 2002, p. 88

Talent wins games, but teamwork and intelligence wins championships.

Michael Jordan

As is the case in most organizations, intercollegiate athletics departments include a number of units that should work together to accomplish a common mission. All too often, however, individual units become myopic in their pursuits and care far more about their own success than about the success of the department as a whole. The result of these divisions is an ongoing political turf war between heavily reinforced "silos," which causes people to compete with each other rather than working together as colleagues on the same team (Lencioni, 2006). Silos develop when leadership teams either do not understand the importance of their interdependence or fail to communicate that importance to the people in their chain of command (Lencioni, 2006).

In order to foster unity from the top down, Lencioni recommends issuing a rallying cry—a single, temporary, qualitative goal that all members of a leadership team (and organization) can share. This "thematic goal" should identify the single *most* important priority of the organization for a time frame of three to twelve months. The objective should capture equal attention from everyone in the organization and rise above the functional specializations (e.g., finance, marketing, operations) that often divide team members. The thematic goal should support the vision and mission of the organization while helping the team focus on current critical priorities. Each thematic goal should also include several supporting objectives that can be measured (e.g., a quantifiable metric or a date by which a supporting activity will be completed). The biggest key, however, is for each department to have a stake in each objective and an understanding of how critical interdependence is to achieving the goal (Lencioni, 2006). The goal should also be distinct from common operating objectives, such as revenue generation, conference finishes, and customer satisfaction; it should capture the most important time-sensitive priority of the organization unique to the current time period.

A great way to establish a thematic goal is to have teams write down an answer to one of the following questions:

- "What is one thing we must achieve during the next 9 months?"
- "We will fail if we do not achieve _____ in the next 9 months" (Lencioni, 2002).

An appropriate rallying cry for an athletics department following a scandal, for instance, might be to "reestablish credibility," whereas an

(continued)

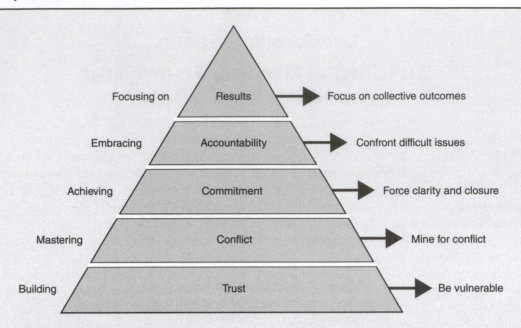

Figure 3.4 Characteristics of High-Performing Teams.
Reprinted, by permission, from The Table Group.

athletics department with limited local support might choose to focus on "building community partnerships" for a time period with each member of the athletics department able to buy in and hold responsibility for specific objectives related to the thematic goal of the period.

Defining the rallying cry and shared objectives are important first steps toward achieving organizational unity, but it is also critical to implement the process through a fully functional team. Members of a truly cohesive team implement the following key practices:

- Trust one another. Team members are willing to be vulnerable within the group and are genuinely open about their mistakes and weaknesses.

- Engage in unfiltered conflict about ideas. They are willing to engage in passionate ideological debate in order to extract the best from each team member.

- Commit to decisions and plans of action. After being able to express their opinions and hear an unguarded discussion of others' perspectives, they are able to fully buy into decisions.

- Hold one another accountable for delivering according to plan. Committed team members challenge and hold one another to clearly defined standards.

- Focus on achieving collective results. Team members put the needs of the team above divisional or individual needs in an effort to achieve predefined, time-bound, measurable results.

Each of these critical team functions is listed in figure 3.4 along with the role of the leader. Again, the leadership team sets the tone for the organization. When egos and turf wars prevail among the senior staff, the stage is set for discord and silos throughout the athletics department. Similarly, when meetings are boring, when consensus comes too easily, when discussions and decisions seem to resurface over and over, when team members focus on individual rather than collective goals, and when deadlines are missed and mediocrity abounds, there is clearly room for improvement. Though many of these issues need to be addressed from the top down, you can also focus on your role as a team member, regardless of whether you are the AD or an intern. There is always someone within your sphere of influence; therefore, you can help your team function effectively.

crises faced in the organization. To ensure a base level of formal appraisal, it is wise to institute at least an annual evaluation system that can be tied to position-specific objectives based on the unique job function of each individual. Beyond the educational and motivational roles that evaluations can play, an additional reason for performing them involves the possibility of legal liability. Consistent and equitable practices in personnel decisions—including salary allocation, promotion, and hiring and firing, to name a few—must be documented in order to provide legal support for those decisions.

As noted earlier, Peter Roby, athletics director at Northeastern University, prides himself on being in the "people development" business. He emphasizes this philosophy not only with his coaches, who are held accountable as educators, but also in his interactions with other staff members. He meets with all new hires and asks them to share their career aspirations. He then commits to support them in their professional pursuits and provides evaluation and feedback as they strive to fulfill their professional objectives.

In the athletics department at the University of North Carolina at Chapel Hill, the annual performance appraisal and review process has traditionally involved a formal evaluation of significant accomplishments and areas of focus over the past year for each employee. In addition, supervisors share their thoughts about each staff member's strongest professional traits and areas that need attention. The review process is concluded by creating a game plan for the future. Employees are encouraged to continually seek evaluation and strive to improve professionally as they accomplish clear, specific, and measurable job assignments with associated time lines and budgets.

COMMUNICATION AND LEADERSHIP

An athletics director spends the vast majority of his or her time hiring, firing, managing, motivating, inspiring, evaluating, solving problems, and building relationships. To succeed in these activities, he or she must practice effective communication both within and beyond the organization on the basis of a strong organizational structure and vision. We have already discussed in this chapter the process of developing and culturizing an inspiring vision. In

this section, we review the relevant communication mechanisms.

One of the primary methods of direct communication within the organization is through meetings. While this method of communication has tremendous potential, most individuals have experienced the frustration that can result from sitting through unnecessary or inefficient meetings. In order to combat this very common practice, administrators can use several rules of thumb to help them run efficient and productive meetings. For additional insight on meetings, see the "Meetings and Movies" Leadership Lesson in chapter 8.

1. Preparing for the meeting:
   a. Determine the meeting purpose.
   b. Determine the desired meeting outcomes.
   c. Ask: Do we need to have a meeting? Is it necessary for people to come together, or are there more efficient alternatives to accomplish the same result?
   d. Who needs to participate in the meeting? If some individuals are not on the agenda or have no input in the work, allow them the option to be informed through the minutes.
   e. Select the meeting place.
   f. Provide a thoughtful agenda and distribute it to all participants in advance so they can prepare for the meeting.
   g. Consider the equipment needed.
   h. Prepare your state of mind to accomplish the desired outcomes in the most efficient manner.
2. Participating in the meeting:
   a. Greet people as they enter the room.
   b. Explain the meeting purpose and allow the agenda to be modified if necessary.
   c. Keep the meeting moving by staying on task and using the agenda as a guide. Use a "parking lot" to respectfully capture ideas that can lead the group off onto tangents.
   d. Close the meeting by reviewing the parking lot, assigning tasks with specific follow-up dates, and providing direction for any open items.
   e. End on time and on a positive note.

3. Following up after the meeting:
   a. Prepare and distribute the minutes within 24 hours in order to allow review while the meeting is still fresh in participants' minds. The minutes also serve as an immediate assignment reminder.
   b. Follow up on any action items that you have been assigned.
   c. Evaluate the success of the meeting through reflection. Ask yourself, and occasionally others, what went well and what could be improved.
   d. Develop an agenda for the next meeting. (Earnest & Cugliari, 2009)

In a study of core values in Division I, II, and III athletics departments, the majority of senior-level administrators cited meetings as the primary mechanism for infusing core values, but a vocal minority voiced concern about dissonance between stated values and leaders' actions (Cooper & Weight, n.d.). As discussed earlier in the chapter, such dissonance can carry damaging organizational consequences (a lack of value culturization). In order to avoid this treacherous organizational pitfall, administrators need to "walk the walk" and examine informal mechanisms of communication.

Edgar Schein, a notable organizational development expert, explained that leaders embed culture through what they "pay attention to, measure, and control on a regular basis" (2010, p. 236). In other words, if a leader purports to value all sports equally within the department but attends only football games, his or her credibility comes into question and the climate of the department morphs into one driven by a football-is-king mentality. Conversely, if an athletics director emphasizes the role of department personnel in fostering educational experiences for athletes and models this mission—for example, by supporting them in leadership development activities, thanking them for their positive representation of the university, and maintaining an open-door policy—the culture in the department becomes one driven by athlete education.

The influence of communicating values through action (or inaction) can be particularly powerful during times of turbulence. In fact, sometimes the most important method of communication is the art of listening. In all situations, the leader should not rush to judgment but rather should assess the situation, seek and hear all sides of the story, and contemplate whether this is a moment that requires vision. A secondary culture-embedding mechanism mentioned by Schein is transmitted through the way in which leaders "react to critical incidents and organizational crises" (2010, p. 236). Though an athletics director does not directly report to shareholders, there are hundreds, thousands, and sometimes hundreds of thousands of stakeholders invested in the output of an athletics department. In this pressured climate, addressing problems directly paves the path for progress.

Often in these times of trial, members of the media are particularly hungry for a story. Therefore, when an athletics leader is approached by the media, he or she is well advised to take a moment to reflect on what message needs to be delivered—and to whom. Most often, the communication should be directed toward the organization's stakeholders. They need to be touched, and they often need a reason to keep believing in the organization.

As conventional media sources seem to focus on news that sells, many intercollegiate athletics leaders have turned to social media as an alternative way to engage the public. Whether driven to this channel of communication out of frustration, in a desire to take charge of communication, or as an alternative marketing vehicle, athletics directors are able to develop a personality and draw allegiance through direct communication with fans. These lines of communication facilitate a more intimate view of the administrator's life than previous modes of public communication, which usually took the form of interviews or media conferences during times of crisis and often left the administrator looking stiff. Social media options, such as blogging and tweeting, can provide effective ways to let people know what the department is all about. Some examples of social media communication from athletics directors are presented in the social media sidebar. Take some time to complete item 6 in the Learning Activities to learn more about how athletics directors are using social media. For information about social media as an element of departmental marketing initiatives, see chapter 6.

Stakeholder Engagement Through Social Media

From University of Michigan AD Dave Brandon's Blog: Preparing Student-Athletes for More Than the NBA

Life on the road recruiting high school basketball players is not easy. Coaches travel many miles, spend a lot of time away from their families and homes, and get only a few hours of sleep as they make coast-to-coast recruiting visits. It is a challenging undertaking to stay one step ahead of other college coaching staffs attempting to recruit a young, star player to their campus.

In the world of big-time college basketball, U-M head coach John Beilein and our Wolverine assistant coaches could be considered renaissance men when you examine the complex phenomenon known as basketball recruiting. They still log the miles and work as hard as anyone in their profession, but the message they deliver is unique, straightforward, and resonates among the type of players who attend the University of Michigan: Come and play for Michigan, do not come and play at Michigan.

It might seem to be in conflict with what has occurred with the NBA Draft this week as three Wolverine underclassmen—Nik Stauskas, Glenn Robinson III and Mitch McGary—were selected to play at the next level. However, when our U-M staff talks to a recruit about playing for the Maize and Blue, professional basketball is not the main talking point.

Most college basketball recruits have dreams and aspirations of going to the pros, and the U-M coaching staff embraces those dreams. They tell prospects if they are going to be a student-athlete, don't plan on attending the University of Michigan if you are in a hurry to leave. Unpack your bags and stay awhile!

Michigan is a destination. It is not to be used as a springboard to jump to the professional ranks. If their athletic career takes off during their time here and it makes sense for them and their families to explore the opportunity to go pro, the staff will counsel and help them every step of the way. The young man may not always heed the advice of our coaches, but they can be assured they will receive an honest and qualified 'assessment of their options and the risks associated with each option (Brandon, 2014).

Reprinted by permission, from D. Brandon.

Tweets From Oklahoma AD Joe Castiglione

Thanks to so many #Sooners who have & will continue to support our student-athletes as they strive for greatness! #Boomer

Very proud of the fight in our @OU_MTennis team. Fell a little short tonight but played like champions. Gr8 yrs ahead #lessons4futuresuccess (Castiglione, 2014)

Reprinted by permission, from J. Castiglione.

Tweets From University of Arizona AD Greg Byrne

And the new Arizona football coach and his family is . . . [Used to announce the hiring of Rich Rodriguez; retweeted by 702, Facebook liked by 584, 71,261 views] (Byrne, 2011).

Flying back to Tucson from Chicago. One hour left…anyone have any @AZATHLETICS questions to ask? Mention @Greg_Byrne (Byrne, 2014).

Reprinted by permission, from G. Bryne.

CONCLUSION

Peter Drucker, the father of modern-day management, eloquently defined the difference between leadership and management: "management is doing things right," whereas "leadership is doing the right things" (qtd. in Covey, 1989, p.101). As leaders in intercollegiate athletics guide the industry through the challenges of the twenty-first century, it is increasingly critical for athletics directors to do the right things—to lead through vision and focus on the mission of their organization. Once this approach is established, leaders can manage through a strong organizational structure and team that is inspired to facilitate educational experiences in the most effective manner.

DISCUSSION QUESTIONS

1. In 2010, the athletics director at the University of California, Berkeley, announced the elimination of five sports in an effort to save an estimated US$4 million per year. Research this decision and its reverberations to decide what type of decision-making framework may have been used. Describe the reasoning behind your conclusions.

2. Select a visible leader with whom you have had contact. How did that leader spend his or her time? Based on this time usage, what values did the leader reflect?

3. Take a moment to review the time management quadrants presented in Stephen Covey's *The 7 Habits of Highly Effective People*. In which quadrant do you focus the majority of your time? What adjustments to your time management could you make to become more effective?

4. Imagine that you are a new AD coming into an institution. In gathering information for strategic planning, you were told by multiple stakeholders that a certain coach is "bad news" and should be fired. What is the best way to handle this situation considering any potential legal, communication, and departmental morale effects?

5. What type of organizational culture will be bred by an athletics director who does the following?
   a. Purports to value all sports equally yet attends only football games
   b. Attends only women's sporting events
   c. Associates with the male head coaches in a weekly workout
   d. Touts the importance of an academic focus but recognizes students and coaches only for athletics-related performance

LEARNING ACTIVITIES

1. Write a unique vision and mission for the athletics department at your school or an athletics department where you hope to work. Utilizing this vision and mission, write down characteristics of people you might wish to hire for a director of marketing or a director of compliance position.

2. Search the web for two athletics organizational charts. What can you learn about the organizations? Do the charts include all levels (coaches, graduate assistants, and support staff)? Why are organizational charts important? How many steps might it take to advance from an intern position to the role of athletics director? Do any of the individuals seem overloaded with responsibility? What jobs look interesting to you?

3. The National Association of Collegiate Directors of Athletics offers a variety of support services and opportunities for professional growth. Explore the group's website (www.nacda.com) to learn about its convention, upcoming events, and affiliated professional organizations. After exploring the site, find two current job postings that you might be interested in pursuing at some point in your career.

4. Ask an athletics department employee if he or she feels that collaboration between functional units (e.g., marketing and ticket sales) is currently optimized. Ask the person to discuss the reasons that this collaboration is currently strong or weak. Drawing on the leadership lesson from this chapter, what areas could be focused on to strengthen the departmental collaboration?

5. Ask two colleagues or former employers to suggest two ways in which you could improve your professionalism as well as two areas of strength.

6. Search Twitter for some athletics administrators who are active on Twitter. Select a month of tweets from one athletics director to analyze. What do their tweets reflect about their priorities?

CHAPTER 4

Compliance and Title IX

Erianne A. Weight, University of North Carolina at Chapel Hill

In this chapter, you will explore

- the logic behind NCAA regulations,

- the primary responsibilities of compliance personnel,

- recruiting and rules education,

- Title IX compliance intricacies, and

- outlets for finding additional compliance information in order to learn more and stay informed as changes arise.

COMPLIANCE AS A CULTURE

While attending a meeting about NCAA compliance issues, an exasperated Football Bowl Subdivision athletics director mentioned he was spending more than US$2 million per year on compliance efforts at his institution. Despite this tremendous investment, a rogue coach who chose to bend some rules had brought the entire department into question. The ensuing discussion revolved around the tremendous pressure placed on ADs to oversee actions taken within their robust departments and the challenge of covering all compliance bases through a single compliance unit (regardless of size).

Indeed, in the face of increasing competitive pressure, media scrutiny, and public skepticism, the importance of compliance oversight in intercollegiate athletics administration has become paramount to long-term success in this volatile industry. In order to avoid facing allegations, sanctions, and a tarnished brand, administrators need to be informed, involved, and heavily invested in federal and NCAA rules compliance. As the discussion among athletics directors concluded, the sentiment shared by most was that in order to maximize departmental functionality, compliance must be everyone's responsibility—and an integral part of the department's culture.

Throughout the last decade, the headlines have been full of scandals involving athletics personnel who chose to push the envelope with respect to the rules and regulations designed to ensure a level playing field. From the days of paid nonstudent ("tramp") athletes in early intercollegiate athletic competition to the academic, agent-related, booster-recruiting, point-shaving, administrative, and pay-for-play issues we have seen in more recent years, the pressure to skirt the rules in order to gain a competitive advantage has been a constant presence in collegiate athletics. For this reason, the NCAA manual has grown thicker year after year as rules have been adopted to maintain the principles to which members commit. These principles include the following:

- Institutional control
- Student-athletes' well-being
- Gender equity
- Good sporting behavior and ethical conduct
- Sound academic standards
- Nondiscrimination
- Diversity in governance structures
- Rules compliance
- Amateurism
- Competitive equity
- Recruiting governance
- Eligibility governance
- Financial aid governance
- Governance of playing and practice seasons
- Governance of postseason competition
- Governance of economic program operation

Each rule has been driven by issues that threaten the sanctity of these governing principles. Rules are also usually driven by unique situations specific to the division for which they are written. For this reason, the NCAA provides a different manual for each of its three divisions. Division I in the NCAA has the most complex regulations of any governing body, so for this reason, we focus primarily on NCAA Division I athletics, although we address other divisions and governing bodies throughout the chapter as well. Conversely, Title IX, the federal law that will also be addressed within this chapter, applies equally to all governing bodies and institutions that receive federal funding. As we explore both types of legislation, be cognizant of how a thorough understanding of current practices and regulatory rationales can facilitate buy-in and cultures of compliance throughout your future athletics departments. Informed administrators can also shape future legislation in an effort to sustain the integrity of intercollegiate athletics. As your understanding deepens, your power to affect change grows.

Acknowledgements: Emily Garr (Debbie Yow profile) and Natalie Lutz (Compliance Resources section).

COMPLIANCE

The principle of rules compliance is established in the NCAA constitution in article 2.8, which outlines the association's responsibility to assist member institutions in their efforts to abide by the regulations. It also provides for "disciplinary and corrective actions as may be determined by the Association" (National Collegiate Athletic Association, 2013a, p. 4) for an institution found in violation of the rules. It describes institutional responsibility for compliance as follows:

> *Each institution shall comply with all applicable rules and regulations of the Association in the conduct of its intercollegiate athletics programs. It shall monitor its programs to assure compliance and to identify and report to the Association instances in which compliance has not been achieved. In any such instance, the institution shall cooperate fully with the Association and shall take appropriate corrective actions. Members of an institution's staff, student-athletes, and other individuals and groups representing the institution's athletics interests shall comply with the applicable Association rules, and the member institution shall be responsible for such compliance. (National Collegiate Athletic Association, 2013a, p. 4)*

The nearly 450-page NCAA Division I Manual outlines the association's constitution and the operating bylaws and administrative bylaws to be followed by each member institution. Athletics administrators are responsible for understanding the manual and other applicable regulatory materials in addition to facilitating compliance by all staff members, student-athletes, boosters, and any others representing the institution's athletics interests. This is no small task, and, as bemoaned by the athletics director in this chapter's opening scenario, even a fully staffed compliance department leaves room for error.

Compliance Office Overview

As with many positions in intercollegiate athletics, there is no real typical day for a compliance staffer. Depending on the time of year, his or her day may consist of entering data and generating reports with Compliance Assistant (CAi) (discussed later in the Compliance Resources section), referencing the NCAA Legislative Services Database (LSDBi) to find case precedents and rules interpretations, reviewing new NCAA legislation, preparing coaches for their annual certification exam, administering the student-athlete opportunity fund, ordering NCAA manuals for staffers, organizing compliance forms, conducting eligibility meetings, monitoring schedules for playing or practice seasons, reviewing coaching designations, compiling athlete book-purchasing forms, reviewing recruiting logs, self-reporting an infraction, conducting rules education, or approving official or unofficial visits. Each of these tasks requires a firm understanding of the rules, appropriate forms and procedures to follow, and the ability to achieve understanding and adherence among departmental stakeholders.

A compliance officer is often an athletics department's most important—and perhaps most resented—employee (Rhoden, 2009). As big-time athletics departments are increasingly scrutinized, a violation can tarnish the reputation of an entire university and affect hundreds of student-athletes and thousands of fans. With these risks in mind, the compliance officer's primary responsibility is to protect the university, and doing so often creates departmental tension as coaches strive to maximize their competitive advantage. This "cordial but often contentious relationship" was explained by compliance director Amy Herman: "There will always be that inherent tension; really it's probably better that way for the protection of the institution. If that tension were to go away, I think you would have trouble" (qtd. in Rhoden, 2009).

Traditionally, compliance has been handled as an internal function in the athletics department with an external reporting obligation. However, in response to the scrutiny associated with major infractions, several new models of compliance structure have emerged. Ohio State moved its compliance office out of the athletics department umbrella with the stated purpose of maximizing objectivity. This adjustment was made in order to centralize all university compliance offices, including those that address research and medical practices (Infante, 2011; Ludlow, 2011). Oregon advertised a position on its compliance staff for an

Organization of the NCAA Manual

The separate manuals for Divisions I, II, and III each contain legislation specific to the relevant division. Since each division's manual does not contain legislation specific to the other divisions, some bylaws may have gaps in their numbering.

Constitution

Articles 1 through 6 form the constitution, which addresses the association's purposes, structure, membership, and legislative processes, as well as the more important principles for the conduct of intercollegiate athletics.

Article 1: Name, Purposes, and Fundamental Policy

Article 2: Principles for Conduct of Intercollegiate Athletics

Article 3: NCAA Membership

Article 4: Organization

Article 5: Legislative Authority and Process

Article 6: Institutional Control

Operating Bylaws

Articles 10 through 23 are the operating bylaws, which consist of legislation adopted by the membership to promote the principles enunciated in the constitution and to achieve the association's purposes.

Article 10: Ethical Conduct

Article 11: Conduct and Employment of Athletics Personnel

Article 12: Amateurism

Article 13: Recruiting

Article 14: Eligibility: Academic and General Requirements

Article 15: Financial Aid

Article 16: Awards, Benefits, and Expenses for Enrolled Student-Athletes

Article 17: Playing and Practice Seasons

Article 18: Championships and Postseason Football

Article 19: Enforcement

Article 20: Division Membership

Article 21: Committees

Article 22: Athletics Certification

Article 23: Academic Performance Program

Administrative Bylaws

Articles 31 through 33 are the administrative bylaws, which set forth policies and procedures for implementing (a) the general legislative actions of the association, (b) the NCAA championships and the business of the association, (c) the association's enforcement program, and (d) the association's athletics certification program. These administrative bylaws may be adopted or modified by the Division I board of directors or the legislative council for the efficient administration of the activities that they govern. These same bylaws also may be amended by the membership through the regular legislative process.

Article 31: Executive Regulations

Article 32: Enforcement Policies and Procedures

Article 33: Athletics Certification Policies and Procedures

To download a free PDF of the comprehensive NCAA manual, visit www.ncaapublications.com.

individual with law enforcement or investigative experience. The position is intended to serve as a liaison between the athletics department and the law enforcement community in addition to assuming responsibilities including student–agent and cyberspace surveillance and student-athlete self-defense training. Finally, West Virginia added an employee with experience working for the NCAA, the U.S. government, and legal entities to help with compliance measures, but rather than working in the compliance office, the employee works specifically for the football team (Infante, 2011). As the stakes continue to escalate in intercollegiate athletics, new approaches will likely emerge.

Rules Education

Because of the depth and detail of NCAA legislation, it is rare to find any coach, athlete, or even compliance officer who claims full understanding of all areas for which universities are held strictly accountable. As a result, education is a fundamental area of emphasis for compliance personnel. Most universities require coaches and student-athletes to participate in workshops reviewing compliance basics, and many distribute weekly newsletters with compliance reminders to help administrators, athletes, and coaches understand the repercussions of their actions, the philosophy behind the rules, and the accountability they each carry. Educational efforts must also extend beyond the walls of the department to include boosters, prospective student-athletes, and any others who promote the interests of the department. The NCAA has mandated education for each of these stakeholder groups.

Pursuant to NCAA bylaw 11.1.2.1, a head coach is responsible for creating an atmosphere of rules compliance and monitoring the activities of his or her staff. Therefore, a coach can be held respon-

sible for the actions of the individuals within the program. Informing coaches of this responsibility should facilitate an understanding between compliance personnel and head coaches in which coaches have an ongoing desire to create efficient monitoring systems, learn more about legislation that affects their processes, and ask questions when in doubt. If red flags do arise, coaches should clearly understand that it is their responsibility to immediately report suspected and actual rule violations. Building strong relationships and facilitating an atmosphere that encourages continuing education are critical to efficiency in a compliance system.

Compliance director Amy Herman addressed the dynamic between coaches and compliance officers: "We don't expect them to know all the rules, because we don't know all the rules, and we deal with it on a daily basis. What we expect of them is that they know enough of the rules to know when to ask. If they have a question about something or if something raises even a tiny red flag, that they know to pick up the phone and make the call to us" (qtd. in Rhoden, 2009, para. 8). Similarly, an assistant athletics director explained the policy at Memphis for coaches to ask before they act: "When in doubt, let us figure it out" (qtd. in Rhoden, 2009, para 10).

Recruiting

Recruiting is a vital—and volatile—step in the pursuit of competitive excellence in intercollegiate athletics. This importance has led coaching staffs to work long hours reviewing junior film and senior recruiting lists in order to narrow a class of 1,000 prospects down to 25 signers (Feldman, 2007). Because of the need to bring in a top class year after year, staffers feel constant pressure to entice student-athletes by demonstrating bigger and better facilities, unique selling points specific to a

Test Your Knowledge: An NCAA Recruiting Quiz

1. On Thursday night, an institution's coach picks up a prospective student-athlete from the nearest major airport on arrival for an official visit. The coach drives the prospective student-athlete directly to an off-campus hotel and instructs the prospective student-athlete to have dinner on his or her own at some point during the evening. The next morning, the coach transports the prospective student-athlete from the hotel to campus. When does the 48-hour period begin for this prospective student-athlete's official visit?

   A. once the coach begins to transport the prospective student-athlete from the nearest airport

   B. once the prospective student-athlete arrives on campus on Friday morning

   C. once the prospective student-athlete arrives at the hotel on Thursday night

   D. once the prospective student-athlete has dinner on his or her own

2. An institution may arrange which of the following for a prospective student-athlete during an OFFICIAL visit?

   A. personalized jersey

   B. game-day simulation activities

   C. personalized scoreboard presentation

   D. none of the above

3. An OPEN EVENT conducted by or held on the campus of an institution is not considered a tryout provided which of the following?

   A. The event is not classified by age group or grade level.

   B. Selection of participants is limited ONLY by number, geographical area, and/or some objective standard of performance.

   C. All participants must be amateurs.

   D. *a* and *b*

4. Which of the following methods of communication with a prospective student-athlete prior to graduation from high school is NOT permissible?

   A. an institutional postcard with an athletics logo on one side and a handwritten message on the other side

   B. a mass electronic mail letter noting the team's accomplishments

   C. a personalized recruiting message to the prospective student-athlete placed on a DVD

   D. an institutional note card with one athletics logo on the outside and no preprinted information on the inside

5. A representative of an institution's athletics interests (i.e., booster) may attend a game in which a prospective student-athlete participates, notify the prospective student-athlete of the institution's interest, and correspond with the prospective student-athlete through e-mail.

   A. true

   B. false

6. An enrolled student-athlete has a friendship with a prospective student-athlete currently attending the student-athlete's former high school. The student-athlete may write the prospective student-athlete provided the correspondence is not at the direction of the institution and the institution does not provide any of the expenses related to the written correspondence (e.g., stationary, postage).

   A. true

   B. false

Answers (with specific bylaws referenced in parentheses):

1. b. once the prospective student-athlete arrives on campus on Friday morning (13.5.2.4, 13.6.4.1)
2. d. none of the above (13.6.7.9)
3. d. *a* and *b* (13.11.3.1)
4. c. a personalized recruiting message to the prospective student-athlete placed on a DVD (13.4.1.1, 13.4.1.2, 13.4.1.2.2, 13.4.2)
5. b. false (13.02.14)
6. a. true (13.1.2.7-[c])

program, and anything else that might convince an up-and-coming superstar to sign a national letter of intent. Successful Michigan State basketball coach Tom Izzo described recruiting as the worst part of his job.

> *It has gotten to the point where there are too many people involved. There are too many people that do not have anyone's best interest in mind, and I struggle with that. I also struggle with being able to go into a kid's home and telling the kid what he wants to hear instead of what he needs to hear. I'm not a very good used car salesman, and I don't want to be a good used car salesman.* (qtd. in Hemminger & Bensch, 2007, p. 59)

Each year, college coaches, graduate assistants, and other staff members involved in the recruiting process are required to pass an exam demonstrating knowledge of NCAA bylaws in order to become certified to recruit off campus. These exams serve as an educational tool to inform coaches of new legislation and to verify their knowledge of the bylaws. Theoretically at least, this process should negate the possibility of violations deriving from lack of knowledge about the bylaws. The exam is 30 questions long, and in order to pass it a test taker must correctly answer 80 percent of the questions and complete the exam within an hour. If a person fails, he or she is allowed to retake the test an unlimited number of times with a minimum of 30 days between attempts.

Each division and each sport has unique contact periods and specific rules; however, a similar vernacular is used in all recruiting bylaws (see the Recruiting Definitions sidebar). Each year, the NCAA releases the recruiting calendars for Division I and Division II sports that have specific recruiting time periods. The calendars designate dates for contact, evaluation, quiet, and dead (no-contact) periods. Division III institutions are allowed to begin recruiting through unlimited telephone calls and recruiting material as early as a prospect's first year in high school. Division I coaches are allowed to begin recruiting prospects following their sophomore year in all sports other than football and women's basketball' Bylaw 13 covers specific regulations for each sport and

Recruiting Definitions

Contact

A contact occurs any time a coach has face-to-face contact with you or your parents off the college's campus and says more than hello. A contact also occurs if a coach has any contact with you or your parents at your high school or any location where you are competing or practicing.

Contact Period

During this time, a college coach may have in-person contact with you and/or your parents on or off the college's campus. The coach may also watch you play or visit your high school. You and your parents may visit a college campus and the coach may write and telephone you during this period.

Dead Period

The college coach may not have any in-person contact with you or your parents at any time in the dead period. The coach may write and telephone you or your parents during this time.

Evaluation

An evaluation is an activity by a coach to evaluate your academic or athletic ability. This would include visiting your high school or watching you practice or compete.

Evaluation Period

The college coach may watch you play or visit your high school but cannot have any in-person conversations with you or your parents off the college's campus. You and your parents can visit a college campus during this period. A coach may write and telephone you or your parents during this time.

Official Visit

Any visit to a college campus by you and your parents paid for by the college. The college may pay the following expenses:

- your transportation to and from the college;
- room and meals (three per day) while you are visiting the college; and
- reasonable entertainment expenses, including three complimentary admissions to a home athletics contest.

Before a college may invite you on an official visit, you will have to provide the college with a copy of your high school transcript (Division I only) and SAT, ACT, or PLAN score and register with the NCAA Eligibility Center.

Prospective Student-Athlete

You become a "prospective student-athlete" when

- you start ninth-grade classes; or
- before your ninth-grade year, a college gives you, your relatives, or your friends any financial aid or other benefits that the college does not provide to students generally.

Quiet Period

The college coach may not have any in-person contact with you or your parents off the college's campus. The coach may not watch you play or visit your high school during this period. You and your parents may visit a college campus during this time. A coach may write or telephone you or your parents during this time.

Unofficial Visit

Any visit by you and your parents to a college campus paid for by you or your parents. The only expense you may receive from the college is three complimentary admissions to a home athletics contest. You may make as many unofficial visits as you like and may take those visits at any time. The only time you cannot talk with a coach during an unofficial visit is during a dead period.

Verbal Commitment

This phrase is used to describe a college-bound student-athlete's commitment to a school before he or she signs (or is able to sign) a national letter of intent. A college-bound student-athlete can announce a verbal commitment at any time. While verbal commitments have become very popular for both college-bound student-athletes and coaches, this "commitment" is NOT binding on either the college-bound student-athlete or the school. Only the signing of the national letter of intent accompanied by a financial aid agreement is binding on both parties.

recruiting method. Additional recruiting rules and processes are covered in this book in chapter 5.

Violations and Infractions

Despite a compliance officer's best efforts, most institutions commit several violations a year. These are generally innocent mistakes, referred to as "secondary violations," and they typically involve an isolated or inadvertent breach that does not or is not intended to provide a significant recruiting or other type of benefit. Rather, they stem from a lack of knowledge about intricate legislation, a miscommunication between personnel, or an oversight. Most secondary violations are self-reported through a standard form and resolved administratively, often through self-imposed minor penalties.

Repeated secondary violations, however, may be elevated to major infraction status, in which case the institution becomes subject to the process and penalties associated with such infractions. Major infractions provide an extensive recruiting or competitive advantage. Institutions accused of major infractions are investigated by the NCAA enforcement staff. An investigation is generally launched because the staff has reason to believe that an institution has intentionally broken rules in a way that yielded a significant competitive advantage (NCAA Rules Enforcement, 2014).

When sufficient information is discovered to warrant an investigation, the enforcement staff provides a letter of inquiry to the university president or chancellor. At this point, the enforcement staff conducts an investigation to determine whether rule violations occurred. Primary methods used in the investigation typically include interviews and information collection through documents such as telephone records, bank records, and academic transcripts. If a major violation is discovered, a notice of allegations is sent to the member school's president or chancellor, copied to the athletics director, the executive officer of the conference, and the institution's faculty athletics representative. At this point in an investigation, the school must respond to the allegations, and a hearing date is set with the relevant NCAA infractions committee.

The enforcement committee compiles a case summary outlining the allegations, the individuals involved, and any other relevant information. All parties receive the information at least two weeks before the hearing date. If all parties accept the allegations in the report, a summary disposition may be conducted in which the school, the individuals involved, and the enforcement staff cooperate to confirm the violations and propose penalties in an effort to bypass an in-person hearing. The committee on infractions then reviews the report to decide whether the terms are acceptable or a hearing is needed. If a hearing is necessary, penalties

Selected Major and Secondary Violations

Major Violations

Violation summary: Violations of NCAA legislation in the men's lacrosse program involving ineligible participation, failure to maintain squad lists, and lack of institutional control. Violations of NCAA legislation in the football program involving impermissible inducements and extra benefits, inconsistent financial aid packages, and lack of institutional control.

Penalty summary: Public reprimand and censure; three-year probation; NCAA regional rules seminar required for the directors of admissions, athletics, compliance, and financial aid, as well as the vice president for institutional advancement and head coach; vacation of lacrosse wins while the ineligible student-athlete competed; lacrosse postseason ban for the following year; limit of five official paid football visits for the following two years; vacation of football wins in which two student-athletes competed while ineligible; financial penalty of US$70,000; and required annual compliance reporting.

Violation summary: Violations of NCAA legislation involving impermissible recruiting of a prospect by a representative of the institution's athletics interests; impermissible phone calls and text messages; impermissible inducements; impermissible entertainment; unethical conduct; failure to promote an atmosphere of compliance; and failure to monitor by the institution.

Penalty summary: Public reprimand and censure; three-year probation (the institution had proposed a two-year period); reduction by 1 (from 13 to 12) of the permissible number of grants-in-aid in men's basketball for the following academic year; reduction by 40 (from 130 to 90) of the permissible number of "recruiting person days" for the following two academic years; limit of no more than five official paid visits in men's basketball for the following two academic years; show-cause order placed on the former operations director for a period of three years; suspension of the head coach from all coaching duties for the first three conference games of the following season; informing of all prospective men's basketball student-athletes about the term of probation for the institution; requirement that the institution permanently disassociate the representative of the institution's athletics interests involved in this case; and required annual compliance reporting.

Violation summary: Academic fraud by four baseball student-athletes and a women's tennis student-athlete.

Penalty summary: Public reprimand and censure; one-year probation; student-athletes ruled ineligible for competition for the remainder of the current baseball season and the entire following season; student-athletes ruled permanently ineligible for and removed from the baseball and women's tennis teams; vacation of records.

Secondary Violations in Football

Violation: During the fall semester, an assistant football coach had telephone contact with two prospective student-athletes on two occasions, each during the same week. The coach misunderstood what constituted a recruiting week.

Institutional action: Letter of admonishment issued to involved assistant coach; rules education for entire coaching staff; preclusion of entire staff from using next permissible calling opportunities with both involved prospective student-athletes.

Enforcement action: Preclude the entire football coaching staff from having telephone contact with prospective student-athletes for the next two calling opportunities.

Violation: An institution paid for additional hotel charges incurred by the parents and siblings of prospective student-athlete (PSA) 1 and PSA 2 while accompanying the prospective student-athletes on their official visits. Specifically, PSA 1 and PSA 2 had their parents and siblings accompany them on their official visit, which resulted in a $40 hotel charge for a rollaway bed for two nights on each PSA's bill. The violation was discovered when the director of compliance reviewed all travel reimbursement documents related to the football program. PSA 1 promptly repaid the $40, and when reported, the institution was waiting on PSA 2's payment.

Institutional action: Prior to the next official visits, compliance will meet with hotel staff to educate them about rules regarding what the institution can pay for and the fact that any room charges for a PSA other than those for parents are the responsibility of the PSA's parents. Football coaches have been informed that they must educate PSAs' parents regarding additional charges incurred by bringing other family members and siblings.

Enforcement action: No further action. However, please note that PSA 2 is ineligible for intercollegiate competition at the institution until restitution is made to a charity of his choice or until his eligibility is restored by the NCAA student-athlete reinstatement staff.

Violation: During the spring semester, an assistant coach (AC) sent one text message to a PSA. Specifically, the PSA was preparing for his official visit to the institution and sent a text message to the AC to inform him of his SAT score. The AC responded to the text message without realizing his mistake. The AC subsequently reported the violation to the compliance office.

Institutional action: Entire football coaching staff prohibited from initiating phone calls or correspondence with involved PSA for a two-week period; rules education provided to all coaches at next rules education meeting.

Enforcement action: No further action.

Violation: Two football student-athletes participated in one countable athletics-related activity prior to completing the compliance paperwork.

Institutional action: A letter of admonishment was issued to the head football coach. The institution is required to conduct a rules education session about the applicable NCAA legislation with the involved staff member(s). The SAs are ineligible for further practice and competition at the institution until completion of the forms.

Enforcement action: No further action.

---

are announced six to eight weeks after the hearing.

Each NCAA division has a committee on infractions. The number of members on the committee ranges from five (Division III) to ten (Division I), and the membership includes lawyers, member-school law professors, and individuals from the general public. The committees serve as independent groups responsible for assessing penalties against institutions and individuals who break NCAA rules (NCAA Rules Enforcement, 2014).

Penalties for major violations vary depending on the severity of the case but generally involve termination of the guilty staff member's employment, preclusion of postseason competition, forfeiture of wins throughout the time frame of the noncompli-

ance, fines, and limits on scholarships or recruiting visits. The most significant penalty, often referred to as "the death penalty," can include eliminating a sport for at least one year, eliminating athletic scholarships for two years, and eliminating NCAA voting privileges for four years. This penalty is applicable only to repeat offenders, and to date it has been implemented only once—at Southern Methodist University in 1987 after a series of major violations.

The NCAA has been criticized by some for punitive and seemingly unfair methods of rules enforcement. The effort to govern is complicated by the fact that the association's investigative and enforcement power is limited. An institution or individual that commits a major infraction has not committed a crime addressable by the legal system but a violation for which the response is limited to NCAA sanctions on member institutions, staff members, and student-athletes. The penalties, therefore, for past violations are often shouldered by future administrators and athletes.

The burdens associated with the investigation process—and the negative publicity and financial implications that can come with a postseason ban or other penalty—have caused many institutions to employ outside legal counsel to regularly self-investigate. This action can head off an NCAA investigation and the associated strife.

Institutional Response to Major Infractions

For an administrator involved in an investigation, it is wise to seek outside legal counsel and create a guiding vision for the investigation. Several firms that specialize in addressing infractions employ highly experienced lawyers, some of whom have served on infractions committees. Seeking advice, experience, and insight from outside counsel in a major infractions case can help tremendously, and it has become a common practice in major NCAA infractions cases.

As discussed in chapter 3, the University of North Carolina developed a situational vision as a guide for handling a major NCAA infractions case. At difficult times during the process, the philosophical approach adopted at the beginning of the investigation helped administrators make effective decisions and keep the process in perspective. Such a vision also helps employees muster the courage to bring forward information that is potentially damaging. Indeed, if a director of athletics does not lay out a clear philosophical approach in such a situation, it might be wise for an employee to suggest doing so. Administrators are often so inundated with intense day-to-day operational demands that they fail to step back and devise an approach that looks at the big picture in order to help them best navigate a difficult situation.

Compliance Resources

Compliance administrators can find a wealth of information in two NCAA resources: the Legislative Services Database (LSDBi) and the Compli-

ance Assistant (CAi). The LSDBi fulfills two main functions: to provide a comprehensive collection of information about NCAA bylaws and processes and to serve as a resource regarding prospective student-athletes' eligibility. One of the main purposes of the LSDBi is to allow compliance administrators to search for any and all NCAA bylaws, interpretations, and legislative proposals. This capacity is especially valuable when administrators are asked rules questions by coaches and staff members, because it allows the compliance administrator to look up any relevant bylaws or interpretations. The LSDBi also allows administrators to search for all major and secondary infractions committed by NCAA institutions, which can provide points of comparison if a similar situation arises at a particular institution.

In addition, the LSDBi is one of the sources for administrators to access educational materials and compliance forms and check the status of various submitted waivers—for example, initial eligibility, progress-toward-degree, legislative relief, and student-athlete reinstatement. The LSDBi is also the home of the NCAA Eligibility Center. This resource focuses on information relevant to prospective and current student-athletes. Compliance administrators use this site for a variety of purposes, including adding a prospective student-athlete to their institutional request list (IRL) once a coach has decided to pursue the athlete. The site also contains guidelines, checklists, and instructions for completing a national letter of intent (NLI). These documents may be sent to prospects in order to increase their awareness of the NLI process.

Administrators can also view an NLI report that contains a list of all signees in a certain sport in a particular year and check the status of an NLI. Finally, the Eligibility Center gives administrators the opportunity to view information regarding its current student-athletes. A detailed report is kept for each prospect and includes demographic information, academic qualifier status, amateurism status, IRL and NLI information, transcripts and test scores, and a list of items needed by the NCAA in order to complete the prospect's initial eligibility evaluation.

The Compliance Assistant (CAi) website is another resource that allows compliance administrators to keep detailed records regarding their institution's current student-athletes and athletic teams. Administrators can upload or input each team's playing and practice season, which includes items such as start and end dates of practice, competition days, and required days off. The institution's academic calendar can also be added in order to provide a comprehensive view of a team's schedule for a specific year. The site provides a recruiting calendar for each sport by specifying what type of period (i.e., contact, evaluation, quiet, or dead) is in effect for the sport on any given day of the year. Administrators can also input information regarding each prospective student-athlete being recruited by the institution and therefore house all data in one location.

CAi can be used to run a multitude of reports on topics such as eligibility and financial aid, and the reports can be customized for each institution. Each student's profile contains information about enrollment, recruitment status, seasons of competition used in the applicable sport(s), financial aid received, eligibility status, degree progress, waivers applied for and received, forms completed, and transfer information (if applicable). Administrators are not required to fill out every possible piece of information on CAi, and some institutions input data for certain sections but leave others blank. The site simply provides a one-stop shop that administrators can choose to use for managing information about their student-athletes and teams. Though CAi is used primarily by compliance administrators, some coaches have purchased their own software to prevent violations and manage information. Leading software options in this category include JumpForward and FieldLevel.

GENDER EQUITY

Title IX of the Education Amendments of 1972 is a federal law that prohibits sex discrimination in any educational program or activity at any institution that receives federal funds. The 37 words that form this law—along with supplementary statutes, regulations, policy interpretations, case law, and secondary sources—form the basis of which the law is interpreted and applied. The following discussion provides an overview of the law with particular focus on current interpretation and application.

Title IX Time Line

- 1963—Hourly women workers are included in the Equal Pay Act.
- 1964—Title VII of the Civil Rights Act prohibits discrimination in employment based on race, color, sex, national origin, or religion.
- 1969—Bernice Sandler files complaints of discrimination against more than 200 universities.
- 1970—U.S. Congresswoman Edith Green, chair of the Subcommittee on Higher Education, holds the first Congressional hearings on women in education and hires Bernice Sandler to compile the findings of the hearings.
- 1971—Senator Birch Bayh introduces a proposal to ban sex discrimination in schools. The legislation is not approved because it would open The Citadel to women.
- 1971—The U.S. House of Representatives approves an amendment authored by Congresswomen Patsy Mink that includes Title IX.
- 1972—The U.S. Senate approves Title IX, which is enacted into law.
- 1974—The Tower Amendment to exempt revenue-producing sports from Title IX is rejected.
- 1975—Bills to alter Title IX athletics coverage die in committee.
- 1975—The U.S. Department of Health, Education, and Welfare issues final regulations banning sex discrimination and establishing a three-year time frame for institutions to become compliant with Title IX.
- 1975 and 1977—The U.S. Senate rejects bills to curtail Title IX enforcement.
- 1978—The mandatory Title IX compliance date arrives.
- 1980—Title IX enforcement is assigned to U.S. Department of Education's Office for Civil Rights.
- 1984—Title IX is suspended after *Grove City College v. Bell* establishes Title IX's applicability only to programs receiving specifically targeted federal funding.
- 1988—The Civil Rights Restoration Act of 1987 is approved by Congress (over the veto of the president). The act reverses Grove City, restoring Title IX's institution-wide coverage in any program or activity in an educational institution receiving federal funding.
- 1992—The private right of action is established in *Franklin v. Gwinnett*. Title IX plaintiffs can

Leadership Lesson

The Importance of a Vision Framework

Responding to tremendous criticism related to overregulation, complexity, and legislation unfriendly to athletes, the NCAA Division I board of directors adopted a set of 25 proposals in 2013 aimed at creating "a more flexible manual based on common sense" (Hosick, 2013, p. 1). This move was the first step toward deregulation in several areas, which, as NCAA president Mark Emmert noted, "refocuses our attention on things that really matter, the core values of intercollegiate athletics" (Hosick, p. 4). Indeed, things that matter can sometimes be lost in the seemingly never-ending onslaught of paperwork to complete, recruiting materials to prepare, fires to put out, and legislative changes to absorb.

It can also be easy to lose sight of the *spirit* of the law (in the case of Title IX, to prohibit sex discrimination in education) and get bogged down in the *letter* of the law (e.g., limiting male opportunities, inflating female rosters, and cutting sports). This type of focus, one might argue, could be the reason for a 450-page Division I rulebook. Rule "patches" were stitched together to help control problems in a system that had lost sight of what was truly important.

In the *Adventures of Alice in Wonderland*, Alice came to a fork in the road and politely asked the Cheshire Cat which road she should take. "Where do you want to go?' responded the Cheshire cat. 'I don't know,' Alice answered. 'Then,' said the Cat, 'it doesn't matter'" (Carroll, 1865). As we pursue the tasks that fill our days, it is very easy to become busy—very, very busy. We might work from sun up to sun down, trudging along a path only to realize when we reach the end that we took the wrong one. If we don't know where we hope to go, it is extremely difficult to get there. In chapter 3

> *If you want to build a ship, don't drum up people to collect wood and don't assign them tasks and work, but rather teach them to long for the endless immensity of the sea.*
>
> Antoine de Saint-Exupéry

(Leadership and Management), we discussed the importance of vision in an organization. In this leadership lesson, we explore the concept a bit more on an organizational *and individual* level.

While differing somewhat in composition and scope, virtually all leadership experts emphasize the importance of this long-term, big-picture approach to organizational leadership. Kotter (1996) calls it "setting a direction," Covey (2004) refers to it as "beginning with the end in mind," and Drucker (1967) asks "what needs to be done." Collins and Porras (1994) define what they call a vision framework as one that preserves the core ideology, purpose, and values of an organization while stimulating progress and envisioning a future through a 10- to 30-year "big hairy audacious goal (BHAG)."

Collins and Porras (1994) also refer to the yin-yang symbol from Chinese philosophy, which is used to describe how seemingly contradictory or opposing forces are often complementary and interconnected (figure 4.1). With this in mind, they urge leaders to "embrace the 'genius' of the *And"* by simultaneously preserving the core while stimulating progress; holding a long-term focus while also effectively focusing on the short-term; and, possibly for our purposes here, pursuing excellence both in athletics *and* in academics. In this way, the core of a business or department can remain constant with a clear vision and core values amid continual change in the NCAA rule book as the organization maneuvers in the competitive marketplace to drive toward progress and the future vision (Collins & Porras, 1994).

With this concept of the yin-yang vision framework in mind, let's transition now from an organizational paradigm to a personal one. As

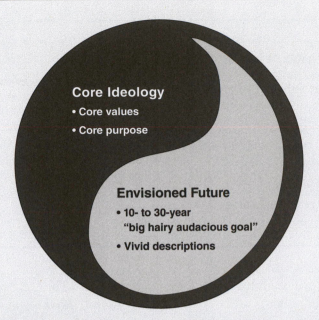

Figure 4.1 **The yin-yang symbol can represent a vision framework, which focuses on core values *and* future progress.**

Copyright © 2002. Reprinted by permission of Curtis Brown, Ltd.

explored in chapter 1, all leadership begins with the individual. But how does vision play out on the individual level? The importance of a vision framework in organizational health is apparent. Indeed, you should soon be able to recite the vision or mission statement of the organization where you intern, work, or hope to work. Perhaps there is even a big hairy audacious goal that the department is working toward. But what is *your* mission? What is your envisioned future? Do *you* have a firm grasp on a core ideology that will stay constant through your journey toward your envisioned future? If not, we urge you to forge one now. Just as vision is important in the direction of an organization, it is also important in your path as a leader.

Covey has argued that all things are created twice—first mentally, then physically. As a result, he urges individuals to begin with the end in mind, to have a clear idea of their destination and the steps necessary to get there. Toward this end, it is helpful to write personal mission statements to serve as a guide through life's journeys. In order to envision our "end," we must start by understanding our core.

> *Management is doing things right; leadership is doing the right things.*
>
> Peter Drucker

Echoing the yin-yang philosophy, Covey notes that "people can't live with change if there's not a changeless core inside them. The key to the ability to change is a changeless sense of who you are, what you are about and what you value" (2004, p. 108).

Change, as the saying goes, is the only constant in life. Understanding our desired destination makes it possible to maintain a proactive approach—to act rather than to be merely acted upon—through all of the changes and curveballs that we may encounter (Covey, 2004). Taking the time to write a personal mission statement allows you to reap the rewards on an individual level that have been well documented on an organizational level. If you are struggling with what you might write in a mission statement, or what your core is made of, try the following exercises to help solidify the values and principles that are of *most* importance to you.

- Visualize your own funeral, the people who might attend, and the things that you hope might be said. How do you hope to be remembered? What will you wish you spent more—or less—time doing?

(continued)

LEADERSHIP LESSON *(continued)*

- Imagine that you have only one semester to live and that during this semester you must remain in this course as a standout student. What might you do differently? What would you do the same?
- List the differing roles you currently hold and the goals you hope to achieve in each role. (Covey, 2004)

When you walk into a visionary company—a company with a strong core and an envisioned future—you should be able to feel the culture and sense the vision as it emanates from everyone and from everything that is done. Can your coworkers sense your core and your vision? Take some time to ponder, write a personal mission statement, and then review it often. Take time first to create mentally what you will then accomplish physically. Stay true to your core while continually stimulating personal progress, and begin with the end in mind…for if you know where you're going, it's a whole lot easier to get there!

recover monetary damages and attorney fees for intentional discrimination.

- 1993—*Favia v. Indiana University of Pennsylvania* established that budgetary difficulties are not an excuse for noncompliance with Title IX.
- 1994—The Equity in Athletics Disclosure Act is passed, requiring disclosure of compliance data.
- 1996—The Office for Civil Rights issues Clarification of Intercollegiate Athletics Policy Guidance explaining how schools can comply with each prong of the three-part test of the participation requirements of Title IX.
- 1996—The three-part test is sustained in *Cohen v. Brown University.*
- 2000—The Office for Civil Rights issues Revised Sexual Harassment Guidance reaffirming standards described in 1997 guidance.
- 2001—The U.S. Department of Justice issues the Title IX Legal Manual.
- 2002—The Commission on Opportunity in Athletics is established by the U.S. Secretary of Education to evaluate the law.
- 2003—The Office for Civil Rights (OCR) issues further clarification: Title IX does not encourage limiting men's opportunities.
- 2005—Additional clarification issued by the Office for Civil Rights introduces controversial survey method approach to prong-three test of participation compliance. It is rejected by the NCAA and later rescinded by OCR in 2010.

- 2005—The U.S. Supreme Court rules in *Jackson v. Birmingham Board of Education* that schools are prohibited from retaliating against those who protest against sex discrimination.
- 2010—The Office of Civil Rights rescinded the 2005 "Additional Clarification."
- 2011—The Department of Education issued a policy guidance which made clear that Title IX's protections against sexual harassment and sexual violence apply to all students, including athletes. It requires schools to use the same procedures that apply to all students to resolve sexual violence complaints involving student-athletes.

From Carpenter & Acosta 2014; DeJulio et al. 2008; National Coalition for Women and Girls in Education 2008; Women's Sports Foundation 2014.

The landscape of educational equality prior to the passage of Title IX is clearly illustrated by the following scenario. Throughout a three-year period in the 1960s, more than 20,000 female applicants were denied admission to colleges and universities in the state of Virginia. During that same time frame, no men were denied admission. Until the championship of Title IX, there was no legal precedent for preventing sex-based discrimination in educational institutions. Title VII of the Civil Rights Act prohibited discrimination in employment on the basis of race, color, religion, national origin, or sex, but this law was not applicable to employment in educational institutions. Title VI prohibited discrimination in federally assisted programs, but only on the basis of race, color, and national origin—not

Industry Profile

Debbie Yow and Title IX Compliance at Maryland

Debbie Yow has been applauded for her contributions as director of athletics at the University of Maryland between 1994 and 2010. Maryland won 20 national championships under her leadership even as she reduced the department's debt (from US$51 million to US$5.5 million) and expanded opportunities for women. Her efforts to comply with Title IX are also notable; she added two varsity sports for women and improved facilities without cutting any men's varsity teams (Peeler, n.d.).

As athletics directors strive to achieve proportionality in the percentage of female and male undergraduates and student-athletes, many choose to eliminate sports rather than add opportunities for women. Athletics directors have claimed budget shortages as a factor that makes it difficult to expand opportunities. Yow joined Maryland shortly after the school was investigated for Title IX violations (Brown, 2010). Rather than cut men's track, which was not fully funded at the time, Yow chose to add two women's sports—competitive cheer and water polo—for which significant interest and ability already existed. The cheerleaders had applied for varsity status for numerous years, and the university had a successful water polo club (McKee, 2004). Yow's attitude of meeting the law's requirements without sacrificing teams or student-athletes' funding is an excellent example for others to follow.

From Brown 2010; McKee 2004; Peeler (n.d.).

sex. The Equal Pay Act prohibited salary discrimination on the basis of sex but did not cover professional and administrative employees, such as professors. Finally, the Fourteenth Amendment to the U.S. Constitution assured all persons "equal protection of the laws," but before Title IX no case concerning discrimination against women in education had ever been decided in favor of women by the U.S. Supreme Court.

After years of determined effort by early pioneers, Title IX of the 1972 Educational Amendments to the 1964 Civil Rights Act was adopted, and the following 37 words became part of the Constitution of the United States: "No person in the United States shall, on the basis of sex, be excluded from participation in, be denied the benefits of, or be subjected to discrimination under any education program or activity receiving Federal financial assistance" (Title IX of the Education Amendments of 1972, 44 Fed. Reg. at 71413). Over the years, Title IX has received the most attention in relation to gender equity in athletics, but the law was passed primarily to address discrimination in access to education, with no focus on athletics.

Broadly, Title IX offers legal protection from any form of sex discrimination in public or private educational programs receiving federal funding. As a result, most private institutions are covered under Title IX because of federal financial aid packages for students. The law addresses discrimination in admissions and counseling, discrimination against pregnant or married students, sexual harassment, and inequities in extracurricular activities.

From its inception, the law's application to intercollegiate athletics has been attacked. Critics have labeled Title IX an unfair quota system that limits men's opportunities. A growing body of scholarly research and legislative interpretation, however, support the conclusion that many administrators are using Title IX as a scapegoat for lavish expenditures in football and men's basketball that deplete resources and opportunities for both men and women in athletics departments. Though many administrators choose to limit opportunities for men rather than expand opportunities for women, the spirit of the law reflects a hope for equality and increased opportunity for both sexes.

TITLE IX COMPLIANCE

In 1979, the U.S. Department of Health, Education, and Welfare issued a policy interpretation that still stands as the gold standard of compliance measurement in athletics. This document outlined three areas of compliance: (1) participation, (2) scholarships, and (3) other benefits. For a visual representation of this policy interpretation, see figure 4.2. For each area of compliance, the document defined in detail key factors to be measured. Since then, the foundation set by this policy interpretation has been supplemented by clarifications and judicial decisions. These intricacies—and the ways in which they are viewed by the current regulatory body charged with enforcing Title IX, the U.S. Office for Civil Rights (OCR)—are discussed in the following sections.

In order to most effectively comply with the requirements of Title IX, an athletics department should rely on an institutional Title IX policy or a plan led by an institutional Title IX coordinator. In addition to following university guidance, most athletics departments engage a Title IX committee that is consulted regularly. This committee is often responsible for preparing an extensive gender equity plan every five years in accordance with NCAA requirements for gender equity self-studies.

Participation

The 1979 policy interpretation outlines the method through which institutions can demonstrate effective accommodation of students' interests and abilities. This method has become known as the three-part or three-prong test. Though highly contested, this method of demonstrating participation compliance has been supported time and again in legal cases because it provides flexibility for an institution in how it chooses to demonstrate effective accommodation. Despite a pervading belief that prong 1 is the only method for achieving participation compliance, institutions have successfully demonstrated compliance in OCR reviews by using *any* of the three prongs:

- Prong 1—Providing athletics participation

Title IX of the Education Amendments of 1972

"No person in the United States shall, on the basis of sex, be excluded from participation in, be denied the benefits of, or be subjected to discrimination under any education program or activity receiving federal financial assistance."

Participation	Scholarships	Other Benefits
Three-prong test Prong one: Provide athletic participation opportunities that are substantially proportionate to the undergraduate student enrollment; **or** Prong two: Demonstrate a history and continuing practice of expanding opportunities for the underrepresented sex; **or** Prong three: Full and effective accommodation of the interest and ability of the underrepresented sex.	The actual percentage of athletics-based aid must be proportionate to the respective percentage of male-to-female student-athletes within 1%.	Equality between sexes in the following areas: 1. Provision and maintenance of equipment and supplies 2. Scheduling of games and practice times 3. Travel and per diem allowances 4. Opportunity to receive coaching and academic tutoring 5. Assignment and compensation of coaches and tutors 6. Provision of locker rooms and practice and competitive facilities 7. Provision of medical and training services and facilities 8. Provision of housing and dining services and facilities 9. Publicity 10. Recruiting 11. Support services

Figure 4.2   **1979 policy interpretation of compliance measures.**

opportunities that are substantially proportionate to the undergraduate student enrollment

- Prong 2—Demonstrating a history and continuing practice of expanding opportunities for the underrepresented sex
- Prong 3—Full and effective accommodation of the interest and ability of the underrepresented sex

In 1996, the OCR issued a clarification of the three-part test, and the document's introductory letter referred to prong 1 as a "safe harbor." Despite this indication, the 1996 clarification, and each of the following transmissions, have maintained the viability of each of the prongs as a method for participation compliance. Let us now take a closer look at each of these compliance methods.

Prong 1—Proportionality

An institution can establish compliance with prong 1, "the proportionality prong," by providing athletics participation opportunities to a substantially proportionate percentage of the underrepresented sex as compared with its percentage of the school's full-time undergraduates. Thus, if women make up 60 percent of the undergraduate population, approximately 60 percent of the athletics participation spots in the athletics program should be filled by women. The Office for Civil Rights defined "substantial proportionality" in its 1996 clarification as one of the following: (1) exact proportionality; (2) a disparity of 1 percent caused by an increase in the current year's enrollment after a year of exact proportionality; or (3) an institution's pursuit of proportionality over a five-year period and in the final year—when proportionality would otherwise have been reached—enrollment of the underrepresented sex increased so that there was up to a 2 percent disparity.

The OCR and courts have allowed schools to comply with this prong in the way that they see fit. In practice, this freedom has allowed many schools to use practices that are detrimental, and even fundamentally opposed, to the spirit of the law. One such practice is roster management, in which the number of participants in men's sports is artificially capped by limiting the number of walk-ons and eligible athletes while coaches of women's sports are pressured into padding their participant numbers,

thus leading to a less-than-[...] all athletes on the team. Th[...] sion I level has altered the [...] of the other divisions, as me[...] have been able to compete [...] now seek opportunities in t[...] the same time, women who [...] able to compete in Division [...] sometimes without being equ[...] handle that level of competition (Staurowsky & Weight, 2011). Although this practice is legal, it is not encouraged, and if an institution chooses to use it, the institution will not be able to demonstrate compliance in the history or interest tests.

The first prong preserves women's right to equal opportunity and avoids freezing discrimination into place. The first prong recognizes that women are entitled to equal opportunity, and adopts the common-sense principle that schools can comply with Title IX when they provide their female students with the same number of athletics opportunities they provide their male students. (Samuels, n.d.)

Prong 2—Program Expansion

An institution can establish compliance with prong 2 by demonstrating a history and continuing practice of expanding opportunities that are responsive to developing interests and abilities of the underrepresented sex. Administrators determining whether this method of compliance is sufficient should gather detailed records demonstrating institutional decisions to add programs. These records should indicate the time line of program expansion, how the expansion affected the male-to-female ratio of participants, and how these additions were responsive to interests and abilities of the underrepresented sex.

Adding programs based on factors other than interest (e.g., financial factors) may create skepticism about the spirit of compliance and could jeopardize an institution's case. Specific time-frame parameters have not been stated for adding programs or increasing participation, but expansion should be undertaken as part of a long-term plan in order to demonstrate a history *and* continuing

of program expansion. In assessing an
tution's participation compliance through the
ns of history and a continuing practice of program
expansion, the OCR examines the following factors:

- Record of adding intercollegiate teams by sex
- Record of upgrading teams to intercollegiate status by sex
- Record of increasing the number of participants of the underrepresented sex
- Affirmative responses to requests by students or others to add or elevate sports
- Current implementation of a policy or procedure for requesting the addition of sports that includes the elevation of club or intramural teams
- Effective communication of that policy or procedure to students
- Current implementation of a plan or program expansion that is responsive to developing interests and abilities of the underrepresented sex
- Demonstrated efforts to monitor developing interests and abilities (and timely reaction to the results of those efforts)

Opportunity expansion requires a definitive increase in the participation opportunities for the underrepresented sex in the athletics department's offerings. Therefore, expansion of opportunity for the underrepresented sex cannot be demonstrated by a narrowing of the male-to-female ratio based on a diminished men's program or by upgrades to female facilities.

> Under the second prong, schools that do not provide equal opportunity can show instead that they have made, and are still making, progress toward equality. This prong offers a flexibility that is unprecedented in the history of civil rights law. We would never, for example, allow an employer to continue paying women less than men on the basis that it was moving toward equality. (Samuels, n.d.)

Prong 3—Accommodation of Interests and Abilities

An institution can establish compliance with prong 3 by demonstrating full and effective accommodation of the interests and abilities of the underrepresented sex. This prong is often overlooked as

a legitimate method of participation compliance because it has been left somewhat fuzzy in terms of how a school can demonstrate compliance. Administrators should be aware that this is a completely legitimate method of participation compliance for institutions that cannot demonstrate either proportionality or a history and continuing practice of program expansion. In fact, an institution can add participation opportunities for the overrepresented sex as long as it can also prove a good-faith effort to conclusively demonstrate that there is no interest, demonstrated ability, or reasonable expectation of competition by the underrepresented sex in the institution's competitive environment.

On March 17, 2005, the Office for Civil Rights issued an additional clarification specifically aimed at aiding institutions in their participation compliance using prong 3. This clarification had many flaws which were inconsistent with the 1996 clarification, including a survey methodology as a primary method of gauging student interest that shifted the burden of proof to female students and provided an opportunity to evade the law. Though flawed in methodology, the 2005 additional clarification did shed light on the pervasive concern that it is no easy task to demonstrate effective accommodation and that clarification is needed regarding how it might be demonstrated. In response, the NCAA issued guidelines for institutions searching for unmet need and potential compliance with the third prong. Following this guidance release, the U.S. education department's assistant secretary for civil rights, issued a follow-up letter rescinding the controversial elements of the 2005 "additional clarification" and detailing the methods by which OCR determines whether schools can justify compliance with prong 3 utilizing the following measurement criteria (2010):

- Whether an institution uses nondiscriminatory methods of assessment when determining the athletics interests and abilities of its students
- Whether a viable team for the underrepresented sex was recently eliminated
- Multiple indicators of interest
- Multiple indicators of ability
- Frequency of conducting assessments
- Competitive opportunities offered by other schools against which the institution competes
- Competitive opportunities offered by other

schools in the institution's geographic area, including those offered by schools against which the institution does not now compete

The document outlines recommendations for effective assessment procedures and technical assistance. A primary indicator of interest is the ongoing assessment of club and intramural participation. If substantial participation and competitive experience in an interscholastic sport has the potential to sustain it as a varsity sport—and if participants have an interest in competing at the varsity level—the OCR would likely determine that the interests and abilities are not being accommodated. Proactive methods of ascertaining interest levels are necessary for this method to suffice in participation compliance.

Under the third prong, schools can show that they are fully meeting the actual interests and abilities of women on their campuses, even if they are not giving women the same opportunities to play as their male students. This prong enables schools to adjust the requirements of equal opportunity where their female students are shown to be, in fact, less interested than men in participating in sports. (Samuels, n.d.)

Sport Defined

The Office for Civil Rights has provided guidance about what constitutes an athletic team by listing the primary factors as areas of consideration to determine whether an athletics program "counts" for Title IX purposes in an intercollegiate athletics department. Some of the questions to consider include the following:

- Does the team prepare for and engage in competition in the same way as other teams in the program in terms of coaching, recruiting, budget, tryouts, eligibility, length and number of practice sessions, and competitive opportunities?
- Is the activity administered by the athletics department?
- Is the primary purpose of the activity athletic competition or support and/or promotion of other athletes or athletic teams?
- Do organizations knowledgeable about the activity agree that it should be recognized as an athletic sport?
- Is the activity recognized as part of the intercollegiate athletics program by the athletics conference to which the institution belongs and by national intercollegiate athletics associations?

While these criteria are easily applicable to some sports traditionally operated as competitive team sports, their application to other activities (e.g., cheerleading, dance squads, and rodeo) are not as clear-cut. The NCAA has tried to simplify this process for many women's sports by designating emerging sports recognized by the NCAA and OCR. Traditionally, the OCR has held the position that cheerleading is not to be considered a varsity sport because of its supportive rather than competitive nature; however, this view is changing

Title IX Literacy

A series of studies conducted by Staurowsky and Weight (2011, 2013, & 2014) found that a majority of NCAA coaches were lacking in basic Title IX knowledge. In addition, nearly 30 percent of coaches indicated hesitancy in raising Title IX issues, and more than 10 percent feared losing their job if they were to bring up concerns related to Title IX. Administrators were slightly better off but still demonstrated limited knowledge and moderate fear in some areas. The study findings demonstrate that training and education related to Title IX can empower coaches and administrators to be fiscally responsible and creative in order to make decisions that are in the best interest of the broad-based athletics program. Ongoing educational efforts will facilitate the greatest buy-in as we strive to provide educational opportunities for student-athletes of both sexes.

From Cook 2010; Staurosky and Weight 2011.

as competitive opportunities have increased and schools have begun to offer support services similar to those provided to their traditional offerings. Despite this trend, neither the NCAA nor the OCR has officially recognized cheer as a sport, but they are evaluating programs on an individual basis.

Participant Defined

A common misunderstanding in compliance determination involves the definition of a participant. A primary reason for this confusion lies in the unfortunate reality that a participant is defined in three ways in three gender-equity analyses—Title IX participation, financial aid, and the Equity in Athletics Disclosure Act (EADA). For purposes of Title IX participation analysis, a participant is defined in the 1996 OCR clarification as someone

1. who receives the institutionally sponsored support normally provided to athletes competing at the institution involved (e.g., coaching, equipment, medical and training room services on a regular basis during a sport's season); and

2. who participates in organized practice sessions and other team meetings and activities on a regular basis during a sport's season; and

3. who is listed on the eligibility or squad lists maintained for each sport; or

4. who, because of injury, cannot meet 1, 2, or 3 above but continues to receive financial aid on the basis of athletics ability. (U.S. Department of Education, 1996)

The 1996 clarification specifies that participant

Case Study
The NCAA Emerging Sport List

In 1994, the NCAA Gender Equity Task Force recommended the creation of a list of emerging sports for women to help athletics departments increase athletics opportunities. The list was soon established, and it included nine emerging sports: archery, badminton, bowling, ice hockey, rowing, squash, synchronized swimming, team handball, and water polo. As of 2012, only four of these sports have emerged as championship sports, and the other five have been taken off of the list due to insufficient interest to fulfill the requirements to become championship sports.

In order for a sport to rise to "emerging sport" status, it must meet the NCAA definition of a sport; cite 20 or more existing varsity or competitive club teams on college campuses; and demonstrate governing body support at the high school, professional, coach association, conference, or Olympic level. Finally, a minimum of 10 letters of commitment must be submitted by the athletics director and president of institutions intending to sponsor the sport. Once on the list, an emerging sport has 10 years to demonstrate steady progress toward championship status or meet the championship status requirement of being sponsored by 40 programs.

If a sport is removed from the list, it may be reinstated after at least 12 months through the same process; however, 15 letters of support are needed, and they must address how conditions have changed since the initial trial period. Sports added to the list since the initial nine include equestrian, rugby, and sand volleyball. Triathlon and competitive cheer may be added soon.

Case Study Questions

1. Which sport currently on the emerging sport list do you think has the best chance of being elevated to championship status? Why?

2. If you were an athletics administrator who needed to increase participation numbers for women in your athletics department by adding a new sport, how might you determine which sport to add?

count should be based on the number of athletes listed on the NCAA roster on the first day of competition. Despite this specificity, OCR routinely checks for significant changes in roster count after the initial competition, and in at least one court case a broader definition has been used that views a participant as one who participated for the majority of a season. In participation analysis (not to be confused with Title IX financial aid or EADA accounting), a multisport athlete counts as a participant for each sport in which he or she participates. For instance, an athlete who runs cross country and indoor and outdoor track could count as three participants (see figure 4.3).

Scholarships

Thus far in our Title IX discussion we have focused on the participation requirements of the legislation. The 1979 policy interpretation also addresses equivalence in athletics financial assistance as a necessary area in which to demonstrate compliance. The OCR's assessment of compliance in this area is very clear. Institutions that provide financial assistance to student-athletes must demonstrate that the percentage of athletics-based aid given (not just budgeted) is proportionate, within 1 percent, to the respective percentage of male and female student-athletes. Therefore, if an institution has 60 percent male participants, the men should receive between 59 percent and 61 percent of the scholarship dollars awarded, including the real-dollar

amount of tuition, room, board, fees, supplies, summer tuition, and post-eligibility aid.

Participants are calculated here based on the number of student-athletes in the athletics department. This means that—unlike the participation formula, in which a student-athlete competing in two sports can count as two participant opportunities—the scholarship calculation under Title IX allows an athlete competing in multiple sports to count only once in financial participation figures. Where a discrepancy greater than 1 percent exists, a school must demonstrate a nondiscriminatory rationale for financial disbursement based on gender-neutral policies or unforeseen events; such factors are evaluated on a case-by-case basis. Examples of potentially legitimate nondiscriminatory factors include the following:

- Differences between in-state and out-of-state tuition at public colleges
- Actions taken to promote athletics program development
- Legitimate efforts undertaken to comply with Title IX requirements (e.g., participation requirements)
- Unexpected fluctuation in participation rates
- Phasing in of athletics scholarships pursuant to a plan to increase participation
- Unexpected last-minute decisions by scholarship athletes not to enroll (U.S. Department of Education, 1996)

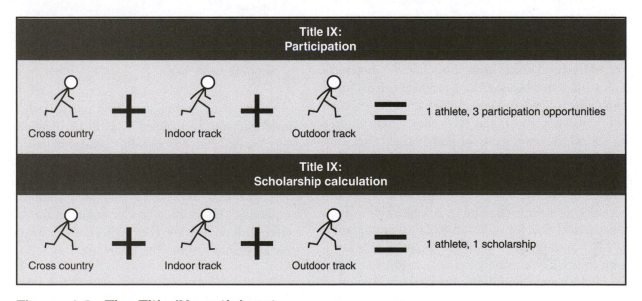

Figure 4.3 **The Title IX participant.**

Though not directly related to Title IX requirements for compliance in scholarship allocation, tiering is a common practice for dividing an institution's athletics offerings into differing levels of equal treatment. The top tier—which might include, for instance, football, men's basketball, women's basketball, soccer, volleyball, and gymnastics—would likely have the largest budgets, the nicest facilities, and the most comprehensive scholarship offerings. This practice enables an institution to treat different sports equitably within a tier, while recognizing that not all sports will be fully funded or treated equally.

This practice has been used for years, but budget cuts have spurred an increase in formalized practices over the past decade. When tiering is practiced, it is important for officials to be open about the process with departmental stakeholders so that they are aware of the reasons for differences between sports. Any tiering should also be done with equity in mind. For Title IX purposes, and in particular for the financial aid and "other benefits" components of the law, each tier should include a proportionate percentage of male and female student-athletes. In addition, if proportionality has not been reached within the department, an additional percentage of the underrepresented sex should perhaps reside in a top tier of financial aid distribution.

Institutional decisions about which sports to place in the top tier are often influenced by the NCAA Division I financial aid designation of a given sport as a "head-count" sport or an "equivalency" sport. In head-count sports, each athlete who receives athletics aid of any amount is counted toward the head-count limit. Thus, it is common for each athlete in a head-count sport to receive a full scholarship in order to maximize competitiveness. In equivalency sports, on the other hand, limits are set on the total value of financial aid that an institution may provide in any academic year. For example, under bylaw 15.5.3.1.1, the maximum equivalency for men's tennis teams is 4.5. Thus, if the value of a full scholarship is US$25,000, the men's tennis coach is allotted $25,000 multiplied by 4.5—or $112,500—to distribute to all of his or her recruits. The coach may choose to give two full scholarships and a multitude of partial scholarships, or all partial scholarships, but in any case the total

amount spent must not be greater than the equivalency of 4.5 full scholarships. An institution can use either actual or average cost for determining equivalency calculations regarding room, board, tuition, and fees as long as the same method is used for both the numerator and the denominator in individual calculations. Table 4.1 provides Division I head-count and equivalency limits.

Other Benefits

The third area of compliance outlined by the 1979 policy interpretation is equivalence in "other" athletics benefits and opportunities. This category is commonly referred to as "the laundry list" because it addresses equality in a multitude of treatment issues, including the following:

- Provision and maintenance of equipment and supplies
- Scheduling of games and practice times
- Travel and per diem allowances
- Opportunity to receive coaching and academic tutoring
- Assignment and compensation of coaches and tutors
- Provision of locker rooms and practice and competitive facilities
- Provision of medical and training services and facilities
- Provision of housing and dining services and facilities
- Publicity
- Recruiting
- Support services

In addressing compliance, and particularly in considering the intricacies of Title IX, it is easy to get bogged down in details because individual components of the legislation's interpretation can appear complicated. At the root of every test and every court case, however, is a simple question: Is it equitable? Describing gender equity in the collegiate athletics setting, the NCAA Gender Equity Task Force has written the following:

An athletics program can be considered gender equitable when the participants in

Table 4.1 Division I Equivalency and Head-Count Limits

HEAD COUNT LIMITS	
FBS football	85 (with an additional limit of 25 initial counters* per year)
Men's basketball	13
Women's basketball	15
Women's gymnastics	12
Women's tennis	8
Women's volleyball	12
EQUIVALENCY LIMITS	
Men's sports	
Cross country and track and field	12.6
FCS football	63 (with an additional limit of 30 initial and 85 total counters*)
Fencing	4.5
Golf	4.5
Gymnastics	6.3
Lacrosse	12.6
Rifle	3.6
Skiing	6.3
Soccer	9.9
Swimming and diving	9.9
Tennis	4.5
Volleyball	4.5
Water polo	4.5
Wrestling	9.9
Women's sports	
Bowling	5
Cross country and track and field	18
Equestrian	15
Fencing	5
Field hockey	12
Golf	6
Lacrosse	12
Rowing	20
Rugby	12
Skiing	7
Soccer	14
Softball	12
Swimming and diving	14
Water polo	8

*Counters are individuals who receive financial aid and are countable against the aid limitations in the sport. FCS schools are allowed 63 scholarships among no more than 85 individual players, whereas FBS schools are allowed 85 players, all of whom may receive full scholarships.

From 2011-2012 Division I manual 2011.

both the men's and women's sports programs would accept as fair and equitable the overall program of the other gender. That is to say, an athletics program is gender equitable when the men's sports program would be pleased to accept for its own the overall participation, opportunities, and resources currently allocated to the women's program and vice versa. (DeJulio, et al., 2008, slide 3)

This sentiment lies at the heart of each laundry list element. The men's and women's programs do not need to look exactly the same, but the treatment of the entire men's and women's programs needs to be equitable. If disparities exist, they are assessed individually. If disparities in one area for the underrepresented sex can be offset by disparities in another, then the department may still be viewed as being in compliance. If, however, clear disparities exist that cannot be offset, the OCR will likely view the school as noncompliant in that area. We will now explore two of these "other benefit" categories in depth to demonstrate how compliance of each of the laundry list issues might be demonstrated.

Provision and Maintenance of Equipment and Supplies

Equitable provision and maintenance of equipment and supplies require institutions to provide equitable uniforms, other apparel, sport-specific equipment and supplies, instructional devices, and conditioning and weight-training equipment. In monitoring these factors, a review should consider equipment quality, amount, suitability, maintenance and replacement, and availability. While every team would like the latest practice and game equipment, maintenance and replacement schedules are often dictated by economic reality. Ideally, an institution should adopt a consistent and uniform policy to eliminate grey areas that might be considered inequitable practices. The policy needs to take into account sport-to-sport variation and specific unique needs.

In this area of compliance, financial expenditures are not measured; rather, the criterion is overall equity. For instance, outfitting a men's hockey or football player is likely to be considerably more expensive than outfitting a female cross country or soccer athlete. The cost of these uniforms,

however, is not the primary concern, as long as the teams are treated in an equitable manner in regard to the quantity and quality of their equipment and clothing. Another area where interpretation can be difficult involves access to weight-training equipment and coaches, because some sports rely more heavily on weight training than others do. If the differences can be justified with an equitable rationale, they may be permitted.

A relevant caveat may arise here and in related areas regarding the potential presence of funds raised. A common misconception about external funding is that it supersedes Title IX equity requirements and therefore that any inequities resulting from contributions are acceptable. This is inaccurate. All funds—regardless of a coach's popularity or ability to attract fundraising dollars to a unique project, endowment, or supply fund— are viewed as institutional funds. As a result, they need to be used in an equitable manner. If several coaches are outstanding fundraisers and are able to provide benefits that create an imbalance between the sexes in the department, the department may need to allocate budgetary funds to balance the discrepancy created by the fundraising effort.

Travel and Per Diem Allowances

The 1979 policy interpretation outlines five areas to be examined in assessing travel and per diem allowances. Specifically, an institution should be able to demonstrate equivalence for men and women in (1) modes of transportation, (2) housing furnished during travel, (3) length of stay before and after competitive events, (4) per diem allowances, and (5) dining arrangements. As with each of the laundry list components, formal nondiscriminatory policies can help administrators make good decisions and demonstrate equitable treatment. Specifically, it is helpful to outline departmental travel policies based on team size, class schedules, and cost.

Differences may exist for larger teams related to access to appropriate transportation and nourishing meals. Traveling with a group of 80 involves different logistical needs than traveling with a group of 20. The larger group may need a catered meal and a larger hotel with meeting rooms, whereas the smaller group may not need such arrangements. Justifications in quality differences, however, need to be very clear. Overall, policies and practices

Title IX Simplified

- Is it fair?
- Are the benefits provided to students equally available?
- Is a benefit being provided to one sex but not the other? If so, why?
- Is the underrepresented sex denied or limited any benefit provided to the other sex? If so, why?

should be formulated in an equitable manner for the men's program and the women's program.

The OCR views equity both from the perspective of the student-athlete and from a broader look at the women's program as compared with the men's program. Therefore, sport-to-sport comparisons, and even overall budget comparisons, may not highlight overall equity. One common misconception in athletics departments is that expenditures on the women's basketball team need to mirror expenditures on the men's basketball team because they are equivalent sports. This is not necessarily the case. For example, a school might choose to highlight its men's basketball team and its women's soccer team, which could mean that both of those teams have equipment far superior to that of the women's basketball team. As long as the overall men's and women's programs are equivalent, a school can decide to elevate certain sports to top-tier status or to treat all sports equally. When tiering is practiced, the philosophy should be expressed to coaches and student-athletes so that they understand the department's overall gender-equity strategy and fair practices.

Permissible Differences

Because not all sports are created equal, it often makes sense and is not discriminatory to treat some sports differently than others. In particular, because of the large roster sizes of football teams, they often have unique needs that can create sex-neutral discrepancies in treatment. The OCR investigation manual outlines the following nondiscriminatory differences that may be deemed appropriate in an investigation.

- Differences inherent in the operation of specific sports because of rules of play, the nature or replacement of equipment, rates of injury resulting from participation, the nature of facilities required for competition, and the maintenance or upkeep requirements of those facilities

- Differences caused by sex-neutral factors arising out of special circumstances of a temporary nature, such as fluctuations in recruiting activities based on a team's annual needs and desires

- Differences directly associated with the operation of a competitive event in a single-sex sport that creates unique demands or imbalances that may be associated with large event-management issues

- Differences resulting from an institution's voluntary affirmative actions to overcome effects of historical differing treatment

As long as these factors are addressed in an equivalent manner for both sexes and do not reduce the opportunity for equality, the differences can be acceptable.

INSTITUTIONAL PERFORMANCE PROGRAM

It is easy to get caught up in the details of compliance, but it is important for athletics stakeholders to remember the purpose of the educational endeavor of intercollegiate athletics. Toward that end, an annual initiative is now required of all Division I institutions—the Institutional Performance Program (IPP). The IPP is a tiered data-collection process that annually assesses performance in academics, student-athlete experience, inclusion, and fiscal management. It was rolled out in 2012 to replace a burdensome and costly certification process that had been instituted in 1993 at the Division I level. The ultimate purpose of the IPP is to help institutions meet NCAA commitments

The Senior Woman Administrator

The designation of senior woman administrator (SWA) has evolved since 1981, when the NCAA first established the position (then referred to as primary woman administrator) to help with the transitional merger of the NCAA and the Association for Intercollegiate Athletics for Women (Tiell & Dixon, 2008; NCAA Education Services, 2003). The SWA has evolved into a position held by the highest-ranking female in each athletics department or conference.

The designation of SWA is intended to encourage and promote the involvement of female administrators in meaningful ways in the decision-making process in intercollegiate athletics. The designation is intended to enhance the representation of female experience and perspective at the institutional, conference, and national levels and to support women's interests. The SWA's daily responsibilities can include any departmental tasks and must include senior management responsibilities. When an institution has a female director of athletics, the AD may designate a different female to assume the designation of SWA (NCAA, 2013a).

From NCAA 2008; Tiell and Dixon 2008; NCAA Education Services 2003.

to integrity in order to provide appropriate experiences for student-athletes.

NATIONAL ASSOCIATION FOR ATHLETICS COMPLIANCE

The National Association for Athletics Compliance (NAAC) is dedicated to maintaining high standards and ethics in athletics compliance. NAAC members enjoy access to educational forums and training to help them tackle the constantly evolving compliance rules and other issues related to preserving integrity in intercollegiate athletics. The organization also supports the professional development and advancement of its members through a symposium held at the annual convention of the National Association of Collegiate Directors of Athletics, as well as educational webinars conducted throughout the year. Members can be nominated and recognized for excellence in compliance integrity as the mem-

bership strives to protect the highest standards of the profession. Student memberships are available.

CONCLUSION

The collegiate model of athletics participation is founded on an ideal of education through participation in athletics. The proliferation of rules speaks to the ever-present temptation for commercial and competitive interests to outweigh the pure purpose of athletics within the academy. For this reason, administrators should remember the student-focused foundation of all rules as they lead the association and their departments into the future. Although NCAA compliance procedures and Title IX interpretation can be intimidating at first glance, the common themes of fair play and opportunity enhancement should serve as the foundation for each bylaw and each Title IX interpretation.

DISCUSSION QUESTIONS

1. Why are the relationships between coaches and compliance staff so important? If you were a director of compliance, how might you suggest strengthening these relationships?

2. What does a "culture of compliance" mean? How might you help instill a culture of compliance as an athletics director, a coach, or an intern?

3. Why has Title IX received the most attention related to gender equity in athletics even though it is applicable to any educational program that receives federal funding?

4. Do you agree with the definition of a sport for Title IX purposes? Why or why not? How might the equation of proportionality change on your campus if current "non-sports" were accepted as sports under the umbrella of Title IX? What would be the implications of this change?

5. Discuss potentially legitimate nondiscriminatory factors that might explain a discrepancy in financial aid allocations between male and female athletes.

6. Without getting bogged down in the specifics of Title IX legislation and interpretation related to athletics, what is a simple way to test whether an athletics program is in compliance with Title IX?

LEARNING ACTIVITIES

1. The NCAA has been criticized for seemingly punitive and unfair methods of rules enforcement. Search the web for a specific example of such criticism. In your chosen situation, why do you think the NCAA acted as it did? Was there an alternative approach that might have been better for the individual(s) and institution(s) involved? How might this alternative action have affected other individuals and institutions?

2. Using the NCAA Legislative Services Database (LSDBi), find an example of a secondary violation. If you had been an administrator at the involved school, how might you have prevented this violation? What would you have done immediately upon finding out about it? How might you have addressed your stakeholders once the sanction or self-imposed penalty had been decided?

3. Create your own graphic overview of Title IX that demonstrates the intricacies of the legislation as it relates to intercollegiate athletics.

4. If possible, evaluate an element of the "other" or "laundry list" athletics benefits and opportunities that should be provided equitably to male and female student-athletes at your high school, college, or other athletics program. Based on your analysis, how is the program doing in this area of Title IX compliance?

CHAPTER **5**

Academics, Eligibility, and Life Skills

Erianne A. Weight, University of North Carolina at Chapel Hill

Sally R. Ross, Grand Valley State University

In this chapter, you will explore

- initial academic eligibility standards for incoming first-year students and recruits,
- regulations related to NCAA visits and letter-of-intent process,
- academic standards for continuing student-athlete eligibility,
- resources and practices for athletics academic advisors, and
- examples of student development programming.

NAVIGATING THE WORLD OF STUDENT-ATHLETE SERVICES

A young former Division I athlete is hired as the student-athlete career development coordinator at a large Big Ten institution. During a typical week, she handles day-to-day advising and eligibility demands for student-athletes as they navigate the intercollegiate athletics experience. She also provides leadership for student-athletes in 26 sports as they work toward professional careers in life after sport. Charged with improving the experiences of 800 student-athletes, she must keep up with trends in the challenging twenty-first century job market, understand the demands of each individual sport, and establish rapport with a departmental staff of more than 300 people, including 10 senior staff members and 70 coaches.

As this young professional navigates the leadership demands of her new role, her success will depend in large part on programming aimed at helping student-athletes balance their student role with their athlete role. However, efforts to promote holistic programming for this higher education population are not always appreciated by campus administrators who are skeptical of athlete-specific programs. As a result, this young professional often feels that she is working under a microscope, especially in light of media upheavals about commercialization, academic scandal, and exploitation of student-athletes. Her athletes have a difficult time focusing on life after athletics, skeptics continually question the legitimacy of her job, and NCAA eligibility standards loom as hurdles for athletes who come to the department academically underprepared. With all this in mind, as she begins her work, she wonders how best to press forward in developing, sustaining, and justifying the work she does with this unique population.

Parham (1993) identified six challenges with which student-athletes are often confronted: (1) balancing athletic and academic endeavors, (2) balancing social activities with the isolation of athletic pursuits, (3) balancing athletic success or lack of success with maintenance of mental equilibrium, (4) balancing physical health with the need to keep playing, (5) balancing the demands of various relationships, and (6) dealing with the termination of a collegiate athletic career. For administrators in intercollegiate athletics, it is critical to understand these and other experiences and challenges faced by student-athletes. Toward this purpose, this chapter focuses on regulations, standards, and programs designed to facilitate optimal educational experiences for students who pursue intercollegiate athletics. Although rules and regulations exist within each of the national governing bodies, the NCAA is by far the most regulated. As such, the majority of our attention throughout this chapter will be specific to regulations adopted by NCAA member schools.

STANDARDS FOR INITIAL ACADEMIC ELIGIBILITY

In an effort to protect high school students, create competitive parity, and limit the time and effort spent on recruiting, the NCAA has developed numerous stipulations on permissible recruitment behavior for campus personnel and boosters. Bylaw article 13 in the NCAA manual outlines these guidelines and rules for Division I, II, and III institutions, and some of the stipulations are outlined in chapter 4 of this book. Building on the concepts introduced in the previous chapter, this section focuses on the academic considerations and processes the NCAA has established to help ensure that student-athletes are prepared for the rigors of college.

Incoming First-Year Recruits

The NCAA Eligibility Center, formerly called the NCAA Clearinghouse, was created to evaluate and certify the initial eligibility of prospective first-year student-athletes. Registration with the eligibility center is required for students from U.S. high schools, those who are home schooled, and international student-athletes wanting to play sports in NCAA Division I or Division II programs.

Minimum academic requirements must be met in order to compete in either Division I or Division II athletics. The requirements have changed over time and were most recently amended for the 2016-2017 academic year. In general, student-athletes wishing to play Division I or Division II college sports must complete a required number of core academic courses in high school with a minimum grade point average (GPA) of 2.0 (on a 4.0 scale) to qualify for aid and practice. Division I athletes must have a GPA of at least 2.3 to be eligible for competition. A sliding scale is used in Division I to determine initial eligibility—as a student's GPA increases, the required standardized test score decreases (see table 5.1). Therefore, a student with a lower GPA would need a higher test score than one with a higher GPA. For Division II, eligibility requires at least a 2.0 GPA, and there is no sliding scale; there is, however, a required minimum test score. Eligibility requirements for Division III athletes are determined and certified by the school for which they choose to compete.

Meeting NCAA eligibility standards does not guarantee admission to any university. Therefore, prospective students should also be aware of university admission standards.

Special Admits

The NCAA sliding scale allows students with low test scores to gain eligibility to compete for a Division I or Division II institution if their high school GPA is sufficiently high, or vice versa. Based on data from three special-admit categories, Winters and Gurney (2013) criticized the sliding scale as inherently flawed. Their study concluded that standardized test scores below the threshold were more indicative of readiness in this population than a combination of GPA and test scores, because GPAs appeared to be inflated as compared with baseline measures. If the combination of test scores and GPA falls below traditionally accepted university standards but above NCAA minimum standards indicated by the sliding scale, a "special admit" may be approved at the university level.

Administrators' philosophies vary in regard to special admits. Dick Baddour, former athletics director at the University of North Carolina (UNC) at Chapel Hill, studied special admits in his master's thesis. He believes that if an institution commits to bringing in an underprepared student, it has an obligation to support that athlete. At the same time, because of the resources necessary to facilitate supplementary education (through learning specialists, counselors, and tutors), special admits must be limited unless the institution has unlimited resources to support them. In general, then, a special admit should be a "difference maker"—an athlete of unique talent worthy of the tremendous time, energy, and money that will be spent in order to help him or her succeed in the classroom. Baddour encouraged administrators to ask coaches to prove that an athlete can succeed academically before considering a special admittance request (R. Baddour, personal communication, 2012).

Table 5.1 NCAA Division I Sliding Scale

SLIDING SCALE B (USE FOR DIVISION I BEGINNING AUGUST 1, 2016.)		
Core GPA	SAT (verbal and math only)	ACT sum
3.500	420	39
3.400	460	42
3.300	500	44
3.200	540	47
3.100	580	49
3.000	620	52
2.900	660	54
2.800	700	57
2.700	740	61
2.600	780	64
2.500	820	68
2.400	860	71
2.300	900	75
2.200	940	79
2.100	980	83
2.000	1,020	86

Regardless of the coach or AD's recommendations for admittance, the ultimate decision about what standards are utilized to determine student admittance is held by the university admissions office. The University of North Carolina utilizes a Committee on Special Talent to carefully support the University Admission's commitment to "comprehensive and individual evaluations" of all candidates for undergraduate admissions in order to "draw together students who will enrich each other's education, strengthen the campus community, contribute to the betterment of society, and help the University achieve its broader mission" (The University of North Carolina at Chapel Hill Office of Faculty Governance, 2014, para 1). This committee evaluates "prospective students presented by university programs requiring special talent—currently defined as programs administered by the departments of athletics, dramatic art, and music—who

a. have predicted first-year grade-point averages lower than 2.3;

b. require review for possible breaches of community standards for academic or personal behavior; or

c. may only be admitted as exceptions to UNC-system policies and regulations because they do not meet minimum course or admissions requirements established by the Board of Governors" (The University of North Carolina at Chapel Hill Office of Faculty Governance, 2014, para 5).

The UNC Department of Athletics strategic plan outlines an initiative to reduce the number of students recommended for admissions with predicted first-year GPAs below 2.3.

International Student-Athletes

With an increase in global recruiting, more international students are participating in U.S. college athletics than ever before. In order to participate in NCAA competition, students who have completed all or part of their education outside of the United States are required to register with the NCAA Eligibility Center and meet academic and amateurism standards outlined by the association. International student-athletes must arrange to have standardized test scores and a number of academic documents sent to the Eligibility Center and, if necessary, translated into English. To help with this process, the Eligibility Center publishes an online (and downloadable) document called the Guide to International Academic Standards for Athletics Eligibility.

Transfer Student-Athletes

The NCAA also publishes a transfer guide that is available for download through the Eligibility Center website. This guide assists student-athletes who wish to transfer from one four-year school to another, as well as those looking to attend a four-year college or university after attending a two-year school. The guide outlines the "basic transfer rule" for Division I and Division II schools, which states that any transfer student must spend one academic year in residence at the new school before becoming eligible to compete. A transfer student must also meet all NCAA, conference, and school rules. The student's athletics eligibility is also affected by his or her initial eligibility status as certified by the NCAA Eligibility Center and the Division (I or II) of the school to which he or she is interested in transferring.

STANDARDS FOR RECRUITMENT

The NCAA defines a prospective student-athlete as a student who has started classes for the ninth grade (NCAA Division I Manual, 2013). Although an institution is not allowed to provide recruiting materials to a prospect until the beginning of the student's junior year in high school, the recruiting process for many athletes and coaches begins much earlier in an unofficial manner. Bylaw 13 in the NCAA manual details NCAA recruiting regulations and should be reviewed if recruiting becomes a major part of your oversight responsibilities. Two elements of this process that include many individuals throughout the department of athletics include the campus visit and the national letter of intent, which we will now explore.

Campus Visits

The campus visit is an integral part of the process through which high school students choose an institution. Students can explore their options in one of three general ways: through camps, unofficial visits, and official visits. Camps are a good way to get to know the coaching staff, facilities, and team members early in the recruiting process—even as a youth. Students can attend as many individual camps as permitted by high school regulations (limits often apply to team camps); the camps are, however, generally costly. Unofficial visits offer another way for students to explore as many programs as they like on their own time with their own agenda. Again, these visits must be paid for by the student, though the university can provide up to three complimentary admissions to campus athletic events.

Official visits are initiated and paid for by the recruiting school and indicate that the school is very interested in attracting the recruited student. The recruiting institution is allowed to provide transportation, meals, lodging, and entertainment to a prospect in his or her senior year of high school, as well as transportation, meals, and lodging for the student's parent(s) or legal guardian(s). Official visits are limited to 48 hours but still offer an excellent way to learn about an institution's priorities based on how time is allocated during the visit. Only five official visits are allowed per athlete to Division I and II schools (with no more than one visit per school regardless of the number of sports in which the athlete is involved); there is no limit for Division III schools. Division I institutions are also limited in the number of official visits that can be provided—for example, 56 for football, 12 for basketball, and 25 for baseball (NCAA Division I Manual, 2013).

In Division I and Division II, a prospect cannot be offered an official visit without receiving initial clearance from the NCAA Eligibility Center. For students with many recruiters, it can be difficult to choose which five schools to visit. As a five-star football recruit said, "I have about 45 offers, and all of them want me to come visit. You have to make some of them, just to see what you like and don't like. If you don't go at all, you'll probably pick the wrong school" (qtd. in Olson, 2012). In order to narrow the decision, he and his family took a cross-country trip to see 10 schools in 11 days, and he committed to the University of Florida in July—before his senior year of high school and prior

to making any official visits (Olson).

Because of the strict time line for official visits during one's senior year, as well as the trend toward early commitments, unofficial visits have become increasingly important. As a result, concerns have arisen that coaches (particularly in football and basketball) are having third parties finance unofficial visits, giving coaches plausible deniability regarding how the prospect arrived on campus. Such behavior is tantamount to a major NCAA violation (Thamel, 2011). Given the tremendous expense of unofficial visits (see figure 5.1) and the resulting disadvantage faced by high school prospects with limited resources, many coaches, administrators, and reformers are calling for a ban on unofficial visits and a rewriting of recruiting rules to facilitate more official visits earlier in a prospect's career (Infante, 2012).

National Letter of Intent

Once a student-athlete recruited in Division I or Division II decides which school to attend and is offered an athletics-based scholarship, he or she is sent a national letter of intent (NLI) and an accompanying athletics aid agreement from the recruiting university or coach. Once signed by the athlete and his or her parent or legal guardian, the letter of intent serves as a legal document of commitment to the university that signifies the end of the recruiting process. The NLI process was first created in 1964 by seven conferences and eight independent institutions in an effort to curb the recruiting insanity that had characterized football throughout the late 1940s and the 1950s. During that time, coaches had engaged in endless efforts to outdo each other in attracting top recruits to their programs, which were increasing in notoriety due to television exposure. Signifying the fervor of the process, accounts surfaced of coaches who attempted to lure recruits to their programs even after the students were enrolled at other institutions (Hosick, 2011).

Although the NLI program is completely voluntary for both recruits and universities, it provides certainty and finality to the recruiting process. Recruits (who are offered athletics-based financial aid) are assured of their financial package by the recruiting university for one academic year, and coaches (who offer the athletics aid) are assured that the recruit will in fact participate in their program for one academic year.

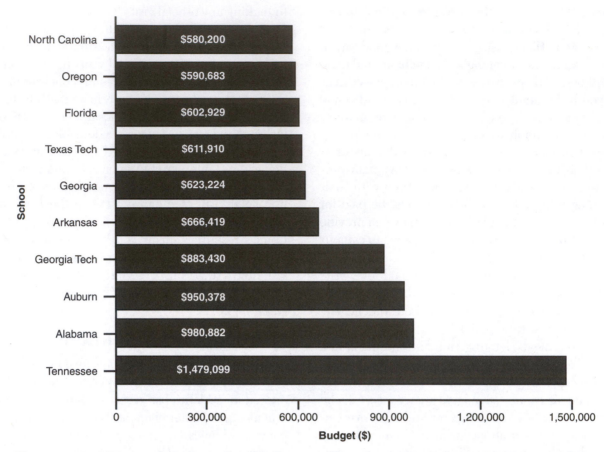

Figure 5.1 **Money spent on football recruiting (average of the 2010 and 2011 fiscal years).**

Therefore, competing coaches can continue recruit a "verbally committed" player, but the NLI legally concludes the recruitment process. Despite this general finality, however, even a national letter of intent can be declared null and void if any of the following conditions occur:

- A recruit is denied admission to the university
- A recruit does not meet NCAA, institutional, or conference eligibility requirements
- A recruit does not enroll for at least one academic year and the scholarship (in its original amount) is no longer available
- A recruit serves in the military or on a church mission for one year
- The institution discontinues the sport
- The institution violates recruiting rules

Based on NCAA, *National letter of intent,* 2013. Available: national-letter.org.

Though originally intended for football, the letter of intent is now used across all Division I and Division II sports, and each sport has specific signing periods. In addition, coaches cannot talk about recruits before having a valid NLI on file; as a result, national signing days have become akin to national holidays as the media and fans eagerly await announcements from universities about newly signed players. NLIs bind the recruit with the institution, not the coach, which means that the agreement remains in effect if a coaching change occurs. For annual signing dates and additional NLI information, see www.nationalletter.org.

CONTINUING ELIGIBILITY STANDARDS

Once initial eligibility has been secured and an athlete begins the collegiate experience, he or she must continue to meet amateurism and academic benchmarks in order to remain eligible. NCAA academic benchmarks are often referred to as "progress toward degree" or "continuing eligibility" rules. They were set up to encourage athletes to stay on track toward graduation, ensure that schools in the same division apply equal academic requirements, and fulfill part of the NCAA's mission to "integrate athletics into the fabric of higher education" (NCAA, 2014a).

Collegiate administrators must understand the eligibility standards specific to their division of competition in order to facilitate optimal experiences for the athletes in their programs. Institutions are responsible for determining and certifying the academic eligibility of athletes and for withholding academically ineligible students from competition. This responsibility, paired with pressure from often-overzealous coaches for their athletes to be "kept eligible," has led to heightened NCAA regulation, criticism, and preventive measures. We will now address minimum academic standards and progress-toward-degree requirements, then turn our attention to amateurism rules and other concerns related to all of these continuing eligibility regulations.

Academic Standards and Progress Toward Degree

Minimum academic standards are established to encourage students to commit to pursuing a degree rather than focusing solely on athletic endeavors. Division I athletes experience the highest level of regulation, which includes minimum GPA requirements, a "40-60-80 rule" that sets milestones for moving along in their academic work, and the academic progress rate (APR). Minimum GPA requirements are based on the institution's minimum overall GPA required for graduation. Athletes must earn a GPA that is at least 90 percent of the institution's minimum required for graduation at the beginning of their second year, 95 percent at year three, and 100 percent at year four. If, for instance, the minimum GPA required for graduation is 2.0, as it is at Florida State University, an athlete must have at least a 1.8 at the beginning of his or her sophomore year, a 1.9 at the beginning of the junior year, and a 2.0 at the beginning of the senior year in order to be eligible for competition. Schools in some conferences may collectively agree to increase the minimum GPA standard and

require that additional hours be completed for an athlete to remain eligible. Such conference-wide eligibility requirements may not fall below the NCAA requirements.

The 40-60-80 rule provides an eligibility standard for Division I athletes based on their progress toward earning a degree. Student-athletes are required to earn a minimum of six credit hours per term in order to remain eligible for the following term, and they must also complete 40 percent of the coursework required for a degree by the end of their second year, 60 percent by the end of their third year, and 80 percent by the end of their fourth year. Thus, if an athlete's degree requires completion of 120 credits, 48 credits must be completed by the end of the second year. Because of this flexibility, many Division I athletes choose to take a "lighter load" during the competitive season, and those who can also take summer classes to remain on track for graduation. In 2011, however, the NCAA imposed a rule mandating that football players pass at least nine (increased from six) credits in the fall semester or face a four-game suspension.

The APR was instituted in 2004 in response to low Division I graduation rates in football (51 percent) and basketball (41 percent) based on a six-year graduation time line. The APR is used to gauge and enforce student-athletes' academic progress (Beland, 2004). It serves as an early indicator of eventual graduation rates based on term-by-term measures of Division I scholarship athletes. The measure is calculated by giving each scholarship athlete per team one point for remaining in school and one point for remaining eligible. The point total earned by the team is divided by the total number of possible points and then multiplied by 1,000. An APR of 1,000, therefore, would be a perfect score.

Provisions exist by which athletes who choose to transfer or play professionally before exhausting their eligibility do not count against the team's APR as long as the athlete leaves in good academic standing. If, for example, the men's basketball team fulfills the maximum scholarship allotment of 13, 26 points are possible. If two players remain in school but are academically ineligible (–2 points), one player drops out due to being academically ineligible (–2), and one player joins the NBA but is in good academic standing at the time of his departure (0), the team's score would be 26 – 2

– 2 = 22. The APR, then, would be 846 (see the following calculation).

Sample 1-semester Team APR Calculation APR = (22 ÷ 26) × 1000 = 846

Fortunately, the team's APR is based on a four-year rolling average, and the team in our example has had perfect APR scores (1,000) over the other seven semesters over a four-year period, thus their overall APR would be 980.75. Teams with a four-year-average APR below 930 are banned from postseason play. An APR of 925 is equivalent to a 50 percent graduation rate. Teams that score below 925 can lose scholarships, and teams with APRs below 900 face additional sanctions with increased severity for each consecutive year the team fails to meet the standard.

Academic requirements for Division II athletes are quite similar to those for Division I athletes. To remain eligible for competition, Division II athletes are required to earn a 1.8 GPA after 24 semester hours (or 36 quarter hours), a 1.9 GPA after 48 semester hours, and a 2.0 GPA after 72 and 96 semester hours. In addition, Division II athletes must complete at least 24 hours of degree credit per year, at least 18 of which are taken during the traditional fall-to-spring academic year, and 6 credit hours per full-time term.

Maintenance of eligibility for Division III and NAIA athletes is determined based on individual institutional standards of academic good standing and satisfactory progress toward degree completion. Division III athletes are required, though, to enroll in at least 12 credit hours per term regardless of an institution's definition of "full-time." Overall, however, it is clear that the level of academic (and other) regulations are significantly decreased in Division III, NAIA, and institutions under other governing bodies. This difference is a factor to consider as one chooses which type of athletics department to work in.

Academic metrics can be helpful for student-athletes as they research institutions. The NCAA maintains a searchable database that reports academic progress rates for Division I and Division II schools, along with graduation success rates (GSRs), federal graduation rates (FGRs), and other indicators of academic performance. Whereas the APR is a term-by-term measure, the FGR and GSR are based on a percentage of first-time, full-time students who graduate in a six-year time frame. The FGR is compiled by the U.S. Department of Education, and the GSR is compiled by the NCAA.

The GSR was developed in response to criticism that the FGR understates graduation rates because transfers students are not taken into account. The GSR reflects the unique nature of student-athletes by considering transfer students who come to a university from a two-year school or another four-year school, as well as students in good academic standing who leave an institution to pursue additional playing time, a different major, or a professional career. The GSR and FGR are simply informational tools, whereas the APR can be used as a basis for punitive measures. Examples of GSRs and FGRs are listed in tables 5.2 and 5.3.

Amateurism

Another aspect of initial and continuing eligibility is the highly contested "bedrock principle" of amateurism in college athletics (National Collegiate Athletic Association, 2014b, para. 1). The NCAA cites the importance of amateurism in maintaining a "student first, athlete second" mentality and establishing national uniformity and fairness. All prospective Division I and Division II athletes, therefore, must complete amateur certification through the NCAA Eligibility Center. In order to be deemed "amateur" and eligible, an athlete must abstain from all of the following:

- Contracts with professional teams
- Salary for participating in athletics
- Prize money above actual and necessary expenses
- Play with professionals
- Tryouts, practices, and competition with a professional team
- Benefits from an agent or prospective agent
- Agreement to be represented by an agent
- Delayed initial full-time collegiate enrollment to participate in organized sport competition

These guidelines clearly leave much room for interpretation. As a result, any case flagged by the NCAA eligibility monitoring system is reviewed individually. Typically, 90 percent of prospective student-athletes are automatically preliminarily

Table 5.2 2011–2012 Graduation Success Rates at the University of North Carolina at Chapel Hill

MEN'S SPORTS			WOMEN'S SPORTS		
Sport	GSR (%)	FGR (%)	Sport	GSR (%)	FGR (%)
Baseball	94	44	Basketball	79	79
Basketball	91	71	Cross country and track	95	81
Cross country and track	71	56	Fencing	100	100
Fencing	100	100	Field Hockey	100	92
Football	75	57	Golf	100	88
Golf	89	80	Gymnastics	100	89
Lacrosse	89	84	Lacrosse	100	100
Soccer	78	64	Rowing	100	83
Swimming	91	91	Soccer	67	64
Tennis	100	100	Softball	89	85
Wrestling	76	75	Swimming	100	96
			Tennis	100	86
			Volleyball	100	90

GSR denotes graduation success rate; FGR denotes federal graduation rate. .

Created from NCAA Education and research database, 2013.

Table 5.3 2011–2012 Graduation Success Rates for Atlantic Coast Conference Men's Basketball

Institution	GSR (%)	FGR (%)
Boston College	88	43
Clemson University	75	46
Duke University	100	54
Florida State University	57	33
Georgia Institute of Technology	18	15
University of Maryland, College Park	50	36
University of Miami	87	53
University of North Carolina at Chapel Hill	91	71
North Carolina State University	73	46
Virginia Polytechnic Institute and State University	90	64
University of Virginia	64	50
Wake Forest University	100	64

GSR denotes graduation success rate; FGR denotes federal graduation rate.

Created from NCAA Education and research database, 2013.

certified (National Collegiate Athletic Association, 2010). If violations of NCAA amateur conditions are suspected, case managers analyze reports about prospective athletes and communicate with the athletes and with leagues who may have contributed to the violation. If violations are substantiated, it may still be possible for the athlete to receive eligibility with conditions attached. If the conditions specified by the NCAA are met (e.g., repaying an award or sitting out a specified number of competitions), eligibility can be granted. If an athlete is initially deemed either ineligible or eligible with conditions, the recruiting school can facilitate a request for interpretation, reinstatement, or appeal.

Concerns About Continuing Eligibility Measures

NCAA measures to enhance the academic focus and graduation rates of its members' athletics programs have led some to believe athletes "major in eligibility" (Steeg, Upton, Bohn, & Berkowitz, 2008). Though academic reform measures may be well intended, they have produced several unfortunate by-products. For instance, NCAA officials have pronounced the rules regulating an athlete's course load, GPA, and progress toward a degree have led to higher graduation rates. However, critics contend that higher graduation rates do not necessarily indicate higher levels of academic focus or enhanced educational experiences (Grasgreen, 2012).

Steven Cline, a defensive lineman for Kansas State University, expressed regrets about his academic experience. He had always dreamed of becoming a veterinarian, but after he performed poorly in first-year biology an academic advisor encouraged him to take an easier path toward a social sciences degree—one that about a third of his teammates were pursuing. He completed the degree but later told USA Today reporters that after finishing his eligibility he would work in construction to save money in order to return to school as a pre-veterinary student (Steeg et al., 2008).

This practice of "academic clustering"—in which a number of athletes choose or are advised to choose a course of study representing the path of least resistance toward eligibility—is one consequences of academic standards and pressure for athletes to remain eligible. When the NCAA announced higher standards in 2012, academic advisors voiced concern that additional clustering would result. As one academic advisor said, "I will have no choice but to allow our at-risk players to only pursue certain degrees" (Grasgreen, 2012, para. 15; Castle & Myers, 2012).

Because of the penalties associated with academic ineligibility, many coaches are now given incentives related to their team's academic performance. Ideally, strict academic standards coupled with financial incentives for coaches might alter the type of player that a coach chooses to recruit. This mind-set might even filter down to emphasize the importance of academics in youth sport. Unfortunately, some evidence suggests "the reforms designed to open access to higher education to more athletes came at the expense of the integrity of the academy" (Gurney & Southall, 2013, p. 1).

In addition to academic clustering and pressures from academic advisors and coaches to "just stay eligible," a growing number of fraudulent behaviors are littering the landscape of NCAA institutions, including admissions scandals, academic fraud, and "gaming of the system" in order to fudge APR numbers. In these circumstances, the values on which intercollegiate athletics is supposed to be founded can get washed away in a torrent of unethical pressure. Often caught in the middle of this torrent are the athletics academic advisors who are commissioned to facilitate optimal educational experiences for the athletes. This can be a challenging role that often requires them to juggle messages from demanding coaches, academically underprepared athletes, rigorous university professors, and powerful university officials.

Among the plethora of criticisms levied at the NCAA over a variety of practices, none has gained more momentum and traction than the movement against amateurism. Sack and Staurowsky (1998) led the modern attack on the NCAA's version of amateurism in their powerful book *College Athletes for Hire: The Evolution and Legacy of the NCAA's Amateur Myth*, wherein they outlined the evolution of rules that transformed college athletes into college employees devoid of workers' rights (see also Zimbalist, 1999). Shortly thereafter, a class action lawsuit was initiated by former UCLA basketball star Ed O'Bannon challenging the NCAA's right to profit in perpetuity from the names, images, and likenesses of college athletes without ever compensating them. As the lawsuit progressed, Pulitzer Prize winner Taylor Branch (2011) released an article in *The Atlantic* titled "The Shame of College Sports," wherein he compared participation in intercollegiate athletics to indentured servitude.

The salient arguments levied by Branch and Sack and Staurowsky have been supported by columnists in the *Wall Street Journal,* the *New York Times,* and the *Chronicle of Higher Education* under titles such as "Players Should Be Compensated" (Bilas, 2012), "Admit Amateurism Is a Sham" (Whitlock, 2012), and "The NCAA's Ethics Problem" (Nocera, 2013). Taken together, such critiques have created an atmosphere in which the notion of compensating athletes seems to be emerging as a real possibility (Zola, 2013). Though the NCAA relentlessly argues that the value of a college education provides fair compensation for athletic performance, the services performed by some athletes are estimated to be worth more than a million (U.S.) dollars per year—far above the cost of an athletics scholarship (Huma & Staurowsky, 2011). This mounting criticism of the amateur notion within big-time intercollegiate athletics may catalyze some changes in the coming years, but most likely, as long as intercollegiate athletics remains within the academy, it will be founded on the educational experience of the athletes. We will now turn our attention to the athletics structures that support athlete education: athletics academic advising.

ATHLETICS ACADEMIC ADVISING

The field of athletics academic advising, sometimes called athletics academic counseling, student-athlete support, or student-athlete development, has greatly expanded in the last three decades. These units are now characterized by a great deal of diversity both in the services provided and in the number of staff members involved. The size and scope of services depends largely on the size, institutional philosophy, and budget of the athletics program.

Just a few decades ago, even the largest Division I universities had small academic counseling staffs of two or three people. Until recently, athletics academic advising was largely handled by sport coaches with varying degrees of assistance from academic advisors working in university academic programs or the athletics department. Athletics academic support staffs have grown for several reasons, including the expansion of NCAA rules, comprehensive eligibility certification procedures, and the perception that placing coaches in charge of academics creates a potential conflict of interest. In the largest programs, it is now common for an academic support unit to employ eight to ten academic counselors who each work closely with a few teams, as well as two or three learning specialists dedicated to helping students who are at risk, have a learning disability, or have come to college otherwise underprepared. The staff may also include individuals who specialize in life-skills development.

Athletics academic advisors typically work with academic advisors and faculty in a variety of departments on campus to ensure that student-athletes are taking the correct classes. Because academic curricula are commonly updated, it is critical that athletics academic counselors develop collaborative relationships with others across campus to gain assistance in giving student-athletes proper advice. In addition to athletics academic advisors, student-athletes often have access to university academic advisors who work with all students in a given major or specialization.

Academic advisors must possess a breadth of knowledge about classes and requirements. They also need knowledge of student development theory in order to help students with current challenges and planning for the future. Collaboration between athletics academic advisors, faculty, and other advisors on campus can help inform student-athletes of all advising resources available to them.

Learning Specialist Position

Prior to the 1990s, few athletics departments employed learning specialists. In more recent years, however, the position has often become a necessary part of athletics academic support units due to increasing recognition and admission of athletes who are academically at risk. Individuals who work in this position possess specialized training in student development and are hired to work independently with students who need extra help and support because they are underprepared for the challenges of college and in some cases have been diagnosed with learning disabilities. Learning specialists typically develop individualized learning strategies and connect athletes with relevant resources on and off campus to help them succeed academically and achieve good life balance amid the rigorous demands of being a student-athlete.

Organizational Structure and Related Challenges

A University of Washington (2009) study found three reporting structures used in academic support units for student-athletes: some units reported solely to the athletics department; others reported to someone outside of athletics (e.g., the university provost or dean of student affairs); and still others had dual reporting structures, reporting to individuals both inside and outside of the athletics department. When the unit is situated in the athletics department, the athletics director is ultimately responsible for directing staff and allocating resources to aid in the academic performance of student-athletes. Because athletics participation depends on academic eligibility, it is not difficult to surmise that this configuration—in which the athletics director controls academic support—constitutes a conflict of interest. As a result, some believe it necessary to use an administrative structure that requires athletics academic support units to exist under the control of administrators who are not part of the athletics department.

Donna Lopiano (2008), former athletics director and current president of the college sport consulting firm Sports Management Resources, discusses best practices in the development of athletics academic support services. According to Lopiano, academic support units have commonly developed and expanded in response to major changes and crises rather than in more strategic, intentional ways that match up with university missions and values. Lopiano believes that it is not only practical, but also essential, for academic support units to be monitored by the institution—not by the athletics department.

Clearly, when an academic support unit for student-athletes is housed outside of athletics, it is easier to establish faculty oversight and operational transparency. Strategic design of academic support programs that focus on the educational mission of the university may result in less pressure on athletics academic support employees, coaches, and other athletics department employees.

PROFESSIONAL ORGANIZATIONS AND SUPPORT

The National Association of Academic Advisors for Athletics (N4A), created in 1975, provides professional development opportunities to people who advise in the unique area of college athletics. Over the years, the organization has evolved considerably due to growth in the field. Most recently, it became affiliated with the National Association of Collegiate Directors of Athletics (NACDA). Other organizations under the NACDA umbrella support individuals who work in collegiate marketing, development, licensing, compliance, and two-year college administration. Affiliation with NACDA provides members with economic support, opportunities for networking, research, and access to potential corporate sponsorship. N4A holds an annual national convention where members work together to enhance the field through professional development.

Most athletics academic advisors join N4A as their primary professional organization, but some also join the National Academic Advising Association (NACADA), which supports general academic advising outside of athletics. This organization facilitates professional academic advising conversations and initiatives throughout the college or university as athletics and departmental advisors from across campus work together in the best interest of students.

STUDENT DEVELOPMENT PROGRAMMING

In 1991, the NCAA Foundation and the Division I-A Athletic Directors' Association initiated an effort to create a total development program for student-athletes. This effort was unveiled in 1994 in the form of the CHAMPS/Life Skills program (Challenging Athletes' Minds for Personal Success). This program has evolved over the years as individual programs and NCAA support staff have developed, implemented, and shared resources (National Collegiate Athletic Association, 2008).

Currently, nearly every school has a life skills program of some kind, but the way in which it is run (and what it is called) can vary dramatically from one institution to another. Some programs are mandatory, whereas others are optional; some are for credit, whereas others are noncredit; some are for first-year students, whereas others for seniors; and some involve coaches, whereas others do not. Most deliver programming through speakers, workshops, classes, socials, and orientations. Instructional guidance varies from school to school and can include a wide range of activities, including mentoring and career networking with alumni, stress management guidance, study skill development, nutrition education, media relations education, leadership training, and just about everything in between.

Case Study

Student-Athlete Career Construction: A Phenomenological Study

Kristina M. Navarro, PhD

During the twenty-first century, the American labor force has experienced considerable challenges. As the economy declined and the job market became increasingly unstable, the ways in which people constructed career identities also changed. Throughout career development literature, the higher education experience is viewed as a crucial time period for forming a sense of career identity and for choosing and preparing for a career. Although this period of time poses developmental challenges for all students, researchers highlight the fact that student-athletes, a specific subset of individuals nested within the general student body, face additional challenges in constructing meaningful career plans.

The qualitative study we focus on here used the method of multiple semi-structured interviews to look at the life experiences of 25 junior and senior student-athletes at a large midwestern university representing 19 sports. The purposes of this study were (a) to further understand the career aspirations of student-athletes who are approaching the transition to life after intercollegiate athletics and (b) to learn what life experiences have helped these individuals construct career identities as they explore, choose, and prepare for career fields.

Data analysis confirmed two previous findings in the literature about student-athlete development. First, participants confirmed that they faced an internal psychosocial struggle to balance the dual roles of *student* and *athlete* during their higher education experience. This role conflict was most prevalent in individuals who participated in the revenue-generating sports of men's hockey, men's basketball, and football. In addition, 20 of the 25 individuals expressed a desire to pursue a career in a sport-related role. Such findings confirm previous literature suggesting that student-athletes may fail to fully explore career opportunities outside of their predominant skill sets and activities (Adler & Adler, 1987; Baille & Danish, 1992; Chartrand & Lent, 1987; Danish, Petitpas, & Hale, 1993).

Second, student-athletes in this study shared that they were subjected to academic clustering, a practice that funnels student-athletes to specific majors in order to maintain their eligibility (Case, Greer, & Brown, 1987). Moreover, 17 of the 25 student-athletes interviewed noted that they changed their major direction after realizing the time commitment required by their sport. For example, student-athletes noted their inability to pursue time-intensive majors, such as education, or majors with high entrance requirements, such as business and kinesiology. They also said that their realization of the time commitment required by Division I athletics following their first year was a primary reason for pursuing a less laborious major. These findings confirm previous studies suggesting that the time commitment required by athletics participation influences student-athletes' drive to pursue meaningful degree paths (Case et al., 1987; Fountain & Finley, 2009, 2011; Renick, 1974).

Continuing Education and Graduate Work

Many individuals who work with student-athletes in academic support services have earned an advanced degree. Some of the degrees pursued by those working in student-athlete support include higher education leadership or student affairs; clinical and educational counseling; social work; and sport management. Some unique programs, such as one at Kansas State University, emphasize developing specific knowledge about advising the student-athlete population, but other programs focus more on overall student development.

Leadership Programming

The Richard A. Baddour Carolina Leadership Academy at the University of North Carolina at Chapel Hill has been recognized as the nation's premier leadership development program in collegiate athletics. The program "challenges and supports student-athletes, coaches and staff in their continual quest to become world-class leaders in athletics, academics, and life" (GoHeels.com, 2013). Like many such programs across the nation, the Carolina Leadership Academy was born out of unique needs identified at its particular institution (see the sidebar titled Dick Baddour Reflects on the Establishment of the Carolina Leadership Academy).

In addition to monthly professional development workshops for coaches and athletics department administrators, the Carolina Leadership Academy provides a four-year program of leadership training for student-athletes that begins with a focus on personal leadership during every student-athlete's first year. Upper-class student-athletes serve as peer mentors and discussion leaders for first-year participants in an effort to facilitate social connections and ease the transition into college as they discuss responsibility, accountability, ethics, and character building. Selected sophomores and juniors are invited to continue their leadership development through discussion of leadership strategies and skills as they strive to support and learn from team captains and leaders.

The top tier of the program, designated "veteran leader," is designed for team captains and veteran student-athletes. At this level, athletes engage in advanced leadership training and support one another in their roles as vocal leaders. Each level of leadership training "provides comprehensive and cutting-edge leadership development programming through interactive workshops, 360-degree feedback, one-on-one coaching, peer mentoring, and educational resources" (GoHeels.com, 2013).

According to athlete exit interviews and surveys, the Carolina Leadership Academy is consistently ranked as one of the highlights of the student-athlete experience at UNC. It has directly influenced athletes' success both on and off the field and serves as a unifying agent for individuals throughout the department. Because of the academy's tremendous success, many other universities have begun to implement similar programming.

On a national scale, the NCAA student-athlete affairs advisory group pursues the mission of developing leaders for life. Toward that end, the NCAA provides resources to help member institutions in their leadership programming efforts. The NCAA also sponsors an annual student-athlete leadership forum to foster student-athlete development and empower participants to bring leadership lessons home to their campuses. Typically, students selected to attend the leadership forum are members of their campus, conference, or national student-athlete advisory committee.

Student-Athlete Advisory Committees

One of the best ways to facilitate leadership growth is to provide opportunities for people to lead. Student-athlete advisory committees (SAACs) provide this opportunity to selected student-athletes who contribute to the governance of intercollegiate athletics at the campus, conference, and national levels. Specifically, SAAC members provide insight into student-athlete experiences and offer input on rules, regulations, and policies that affect student-athletes'

Student-Athletes in Academic Counseling Careers

The staff directories of intercollegiate athletics programs are filled with academic support staff members who were once college sport participants themselves. Former athletes possess in-depth understanding of the demands faced by student-athletes, and they can serve as effective advisors because they themselves have graduated and in many cases obtained an advanced degree. As a result, both student-athletes and coaches view them as credible sources of information. They can also be inspiring and share messages of balance, persistence, and the value of higher education.

Former varsity athletes working in student-athlete support services may also face some challenges. Young professionals who are not far removed in age from the student-athletes with whom they work must take care to develop professional relationships rather than friendships. In addition, former student-athletes have often developed into "team players" who are willing to sacrifice for the team and are eager to please coaches. People working in student-athlete support services, however, need to practice a high level of integrity in order to respect and understand the pressures faced by coaches and athletes without sacrificing their own professionalism.

Though many former athletes pursue careers in student-athlete support and development, it is not necessary to have a background as a college athlete in order to successfully provide support services to athletes. Persons interested in working with student-athletes should review job descriptions for positions they might like to pursue in order to identify the knowledge and experience required for the job.

lives ("About SAAC," 2014). The functions of campus SAACs are summarized in the following list as published on the NCAA website:

- Promote communication between athletics administration and student-athletes
- Disseminate information
- Provide feedback and insight into athletics department issues
- Generate a student-athlete voice within the campus athletics department formulation of policies
- Build a sense of community in the athletics program involving all athletic teams
- Solicit student-athletes' responses to proposed conference and NCAA legislation
- Organize community service efforts
- Create a vehicle for student-athlete representation on campuswide committees
- Promote a positive image of student-athletes on campus.

The NCAA recommends that campus SAACs be organized into executive committees with elected positions including a chairperson, a secretary, a treasurer, and chairs of standing subcommittees. Outstanding campus SAAC members are often selected to serve on the conference or national SAAC. National SAAC members are selected by the Division I, II, or III management council from a pool of conference nominees. National SAACs provide a student voice within the NCAA legislative process as national SAAC members recommend, review, and respond to proposed legislation. National SAAC members also serve as liaisons between their own campuses and conferences and the national governing body of the NCAA.

The organization and support of SAACs can differ from campus to campus; whatever their specific form, however, their potential effect is immense. It would be a wise practice for institutional SAACs to create an annual report covering initiatives, concerns, and other relevant topics to distribute to campus stakeholders. Through such efforts, leaders in training can help effect change on a broad scale.

Leadership Lesson

Interdependence and the Win-Win Paradigm

Student-athlete services have been referred to as the heart of an athletics department. Whether for study table, student-athlete advisory committee meetings, scheduling, tutoring, counseling, or leadership training, athletes from different sports come together through student services to learn and grow in their nonathletic pursuits. With this in mind, it is fitting that we now return to the beginning of our leadership lessons by revisiting the heart of any leadership quest—the paradigm. In the leadership lesson in chapter 1, we put forward the notion that leadership begins at the individual level. In the leadership lesson presented here, we add an understanding that leadership efforts are also inherently interdependent and can often be enhanced through a win-win paradigm.

Before we explore this paradigm, let's focus for a moment on the point that leadership is inherently interdependent. There is no way to lead in a vacuum; therefore, interpersonal communication and understanding are essential. Daniel Goleman (1995) has theorized that the differentiator between good and great leaders is what he calls emotional intelligence (EI), which consists of five components that can be strengthened through practice: self-awareness, self-regulation, motivation, empathy, and social skill. Through research, Goleman has found that when a leader possesses a critical mass of EI capabilities, his or her units outperform others in yearly earnings by 20 percent.

These capabilities allow a person to contribute to what Covey (1989) calls an emotional bank account—a balance of trust accumulated in a relationship. Deposits in the account are made through acts of courtesy, honesty, follow-through, and kindness. When a significant

Maturity is the ability to express one's own feelings and convictions balanced with consideration for the thoughts and feelings of others.

Hrand Saxenian, researcher and Harvard business school professor

balance of trust has been built up, communication is most effective. The parties give each other the benefit of the doubt and accept communication at face value. However, the trust account can also get drawn down or overdrawn as a result of withdrawals in the form of disrespect, deception, lack of follow-through, or malice. In this case, communication is difficult, words are minced, flexibility is scarce, and deeper meanings are often attributed to even the simplest exchanges.

Covey outlines six methods of making deposits to build a strong balance of trust in the emotional bank account.

1. Understand the individual. Some deposits mean more than others, depending on the unique attributes and capabilities of each person. What one person considers a large deposit (e.g., spending time going to lunch) might be considered a withdrawal by someone else!

2. Attend to the little things. Small efforts at courtesy or attentiveness can translate into large deposits. Similarly, small discourtesies or acts of disrespect can translate into large withdrawals.

3. Keep commitments. Keeping promises and delivering on expectations are ways to make deposits. Failing to keep a commitment, on the other hand, makes a large withdrawal.

4. Clarify expectations. It can pay dividends to invest the time up front to make sure that each person partakes of a shared vision. Lack of clarity, however, leads to unfulfilled or differing expectations and reduces the account balance.

5. Show personal integrity. "One of the most important ways to manifest integrity is to *be loyal to those who are not present.* In doing so, we build the trust of those who are present. . . . Integrity in an interdependent reality is simply this: you treat everyone by the same set of principles. As you do, people will come to trust you. They may not at first appreciate the honest confrontational experiences such integrity might generate. Confrontation takes considerable courage, and many people would prefer to take the course of least resistance, belittling and criticizing, betraying confidences, or participating in gossip about others behind their backs. But in the long run, people will trust and respect you if you are honest and open and kind with them" (Covey, 2004, pp. 196–197).

6. Apologize sincerely when you make a withdrawal. We will make mistakes—that is inevitable. When we do, if we can sincerely apologize, we may be able to mitigate the withdrawal. However, repeated apologies with no change in behavior make large withdrawals.

In effect, emotional bank account deposits boil down to being respectful and truly valuing those with whom you work. This sentiment is expressed in Thaler and Koval's *The Power of Nice—How to Conquer the Business World with Kindness* (2001), in which they demonstrate that nice people live longer, are healthier, and make more money—and that "nice" companies have lower turnover, lower recruitment costs, and higher productivity. We urge you to utilize this strategy by seeking to create strong emotional bank accounts in order to cultivate a win-win paradigm. "Win/Win is a frame of mind and heart that constantly seeks mutual benefit in all human interactions. . . . [It is] based on the paradigm that there is plenty for everybody, that one person's success is not achieved at the expense or exclusion of the success of others" (Covey, 2004, p. 207).

We can use this paradigm as we bring high school students to our university for recruiting visits, as we facilitate the contract negotiation for a new hire, and as we cultivate a corporate partnership. We should approach each situation with an abundance mentality—with the idea that we need to either find a solution that benefits both parties, or "agree to disagree agreeably" (Covey, 2004, p. 213). When this approach becomes our standard operating procedure, we will find our emotional bank accounts overflowing, and we will be able to expand the benefits of each exchange.

Community Service

College and university athletics departments possess a great deal of social capital, which in its most simplistic form means college sport has the ability to use its "people power" to do admirable work—if people are inspired to do so. Even so, intercollegiate athletics is commonly critiqued as a single-minded money-making venture that operates in a silo, isolated from the rest of campus. This does not have to be the case, nor should it be.

Everything rises and falls on leadership, and if we're going to have success, our student-athletes need to have an understanding of leadership and the roles that they play.

Doug Peters, athletics director, Minnesota State University Moorhead (qtd. in Richards, 2011)

Many college athletics programs participate in some type of community service initiative. These efforts may be coordinated by any number of athletics employees and are sometimes programmed through the campus student-athlete advisory committee (as in the Special Olympics partnership mentioned earlier). For example, the University of Illinois athletics department coordinates Hometown Heroes, an outreach program that encourages student-athletes to interact with local youth

Dick Baddour Reflects on the Establishment of the Carolina Leadership Academy

In a meeting with head coaches at the University of North Carolina (UNC) at Chapel Hill, athletics director Dick Baddour asked the coaches what he could do to help their teams succeed. The coaches responded that they needed the members of their teams to be leaders. Baddour recalls 22-time national championship soccer coach Anson Dorrance saying, "I can have the most talented team in the country, but without leaders on the field, I will not win." This meeting, Baddour later recalled, was the seed from which the Carolina Leadership Academy grew.

A few years after this meeting, Baddour attended a dinner at the head football coach's house where the seniors were establishing goals for the upcoming year. The coach said to Baddour, "I think we're in trouble. . . . I don't sense strong leadership in this group." As Baddour drove home, he marveled at the fact that millions of dollars were being poured into the football team yet the lack of leadership meant that no amount of training would lead to success on the field. Indeed, the next season was one of the worst in school history.

Soon after, a student-athlete advisory committee discussed recent events involving alcohol-related issues that had surfaced among some athletes. Baddour asked the students what could be done to prevent these incidents. The athletes initially answered that more education was needed, but the exasperated athletics director countered with a different thought: "You've had education about substance abuse since elementary school. Isn't this about decision making and team standards?"

He then posed a question to the athletes: "You're in a bar, and your teammate is about to do something really stupid. How many of you would grab him or her and say, 'You're done'?" Only a few of the athletes raised their hands. Upon questioning them, he got mixed messages as to why they wouldn't take action. Some didn't want to risk being a leader, others didn't want to "get in their teammate's face," and still others said they didn't think their teammates would respect their intervention.

Baddour remembers feeling disappointed. As he rode the elevator after the meeting, he reflected on what he had been taught in U.S. Army officer school: leaders are made, not born. The coaches' meeting early in his tenure, the conversation with the football coach prior to the weak season, and the meeting he had just attended with the student-athletes all ran through his mind. By the time he got off the elevator, he was inspired to help his institution become the school known for developing student-athletes as leaders. It seemed that through training leaders, the department could address many of the issues it faced.

Shortly thereafter, the associate athletics director for student-athlete affairs began researching what was being done around the country. Several limited leadership initiatives were discovered, and many programs brought in speakers, but none had a developmental program. Baddour knew that he wanted to build a solid program, and he reflected again on his time in the U.S. Army, where classes built on what was discussed in the previous class. Initially the athletics department looked into offering leadership training as a class, but after running into obstacles the leadership team decided to make the class so enjoyable and such a high-quality experience that student-athletes would want to be a part of it. Jeff Janssen, a local leadership expert, was brought on as a consultant, and soon thereafter the program was up and running. The comprehensive leadership development program will continue to evolve, and it stands as an integral and desirable part of the athletics experience for UNC's student-athletes.

and community members to promote positive messages. Syracuse University athletics coordinates 'Cuse Cares, which encourages athletes to participate in community service activities, such as childhood literacy events, delivery of holiday meals to underprivileged families, and charitable walks for cancer research. In mounting such efforts, administrators must keep in mind that if an organization seeks to have an athlete appear at or be involved in an event, permission must be granted by the athletics department according to NCAA legislation governing the use of student-athletes' names, pictures, and appearances.

CONCLUSION

The intercollegiate athlete population faces unique pressure to represent their schools athletically, perform academically, balance demanding time-constraints, adjust to living on their own, and, for a few students, complete all of these tasks while academically unprepared for the rigors of a university education. Therefore, it is critical to provide the necessary resources to allow all within this population to succeed. Departments that deliver academic and developmental support to student-athletes seek to help them succeed both in the classroom and as individuals. These support programs have expanded in the last two decades and are now often responsible for advising resources, tutoring, developmental programming, and monitoring of academic performance. Student-athlete support units are configured in a variety of ways. They collaborate widely with other individuals and departments on campus, as well as with NCAA representatives, to evaluate eligibility, academic performance, and overall experience.

DISCUSSION QUESTIONS

1. What is the purpose of regulating the initial eligibility standards for NCAA athletes? Are the regulations accomplishing their purposes? What are the implications of higher or lower academic standards for athletes hoping to pursue NCAA intercollegiate athletics?

2. The term "special admit" refers to a student who falls below average university admissions standards but is admitted because of his or her athletic ability. What issues are involved in allowing special admits? Why is it important for athletics administrators to be aware of these issues?

3. Do you agree with reformers who call for a ban on unofficial visits? How could recruiting rules be rewritten to decrease the tremendous expense of unofficial visits in light of the trend toward early commitments (prior to the senior year of high school) by recruiting prospects?

4. Regulation is significantly decreased in every area for NCAA Division III and NAIA institutions as compared with NCAA Division I and II institutions. Why do you think this is the case? Do you believe that NCAA Division I and Division II institutions are overregulated? Why or why not?

5. Some unintended consequences of "academic reform" in the NCAA are discussed in this chapter. Search the web and outline an example of one of these issues that has emerged in the last several years. What could the NCAA or the involved member institution have done to prevent the issue?

LEARNING ACTIVITIES

1. Take a moment to research the APR, GSR, and FGR of schools in your conference by using the NCAA Education and Research Database (fs.ncaa.org/Docs/newmedia/public/rates/index.html). What trends do you discover?

2. Explore the resources provided on the NCAA Eligibility Center's website. Describe one of the areas about which you learn the most.

3. Search the web for athletics department service initiatives. What purpose is fulfilled by the initiatives you find?

4. Visit athletics department websites for a variety of institutions and search for the academic support unit. How many athletics academic advisors or counselors does the athletics department employ, and what are each person's duties? Do some of the academic advisors work with a number of sports? Does the university have a football team? If so, how many academic advisors are employed to work with football players? Does the unit have learning specialists who work with at-risk or underprepared students? Does the unit offer assistantship, study-hall monitor, and tutoring opportunities for current students?

Photo courtesy of Robert H. Zullo

CHAPTER 6

Media Relations

Robert Zullo, Seton Hill University

In this chapter, you will explore

- why publicity is important,
- how to produce media,
- how to work with media outlets,
- the evolution of media,
- media training,
- the difference between forecasting and speculation,
- crisis management strategies,
- social media concerns, and
- privacy issues related to students' academic and medical records.

THE FISHBOWL: ALL EYES ARE ON YOU

With their most recent win, the student-athletes had earned the opportunity to compete in the postseason and were excited to celebrate their hard work with a night out. Unfortunately, they were baited into a full-scale brawl after defending a female restaurant patron who was being picked on by locals. Team members were attacked with a glass bottle and flying chairs, but the videos that captured the scene happened to show only the taller, bulkier team members defending themselves in the ensuing fistfight. Police were called to the scene, and both locals and student-athletes were arrested. The head coach was notified, as well as the athletics director (AD), and the videos found their way onto social media before sunrise.

Local media outlets, scanning social media in search of breaking news, quickly posted reports of the fight on their websites. In response to those reports and to still pictures extracted from video footage—and before the facts were presented to the public by the police or the AD—public opinion began to settle on the idea that the student-athletes had been looking for trouble. As a result, the team's reputation was sullied, and anonymous fans and critics poured onto news websites, commenting about who should be suspended and calling for the head coach to be fired. The institution's board of trustees was embarrassed and demanded answers from the president.

How does a sports information director proactively control crisis scenarios such as this one in a day and age when technology allows inaccurate stories to be distributed to thousands of people at a moment's notice?

In intercollegiate athletics, media relations and public relations are generally blended together in the function known as (depending on the school) sports information, sport communication, or athletics media relations. This branch of intercollegiate athletics administration is typically handled by a sports information director (SID), who may be supplemented by associate and assistant directors, as well as graduate assistants, interns, and student workers, when the school can afford such resources (Stoldt, 2000).

The sports information department is vital to the athletics department because it deals with the mass media, which possess the greatest reach to the general public (Stoldt, Dittmore, & Branvold, 2006). Through this reach, media outlets shape opinions about the athletics department by affecting what people see, hear, and read. The role of the sports information department is to help

> *Our primary area of responsibility is with the media, and good public relations can't be beat. We also work a lot with coaches, and a willingness to work with them is critical.*
>
> Rod Commons, former assistant athletics director and sports information director, Washington State University (qtd. in Schultz, 2005, p.210).

shape the information distributed in this manner (Andrews, 2005). It does so in part by proactively disseminating information, which requires it to maintain statistics and create media releases, media guides, game notes, programs, and other documents (Stoldt et al., 2000; Panella, 2012). The department also holds media conferences, facilitates media training, and educates members of the athletics department about how media outlets function and what "sells."

Another critical function of the sports information department is to oversee the athletics department's website so that fans and other stakeholders can access information about their favorite team 24 hours a day, 7 days a week, 365 days a year. Proper control of the website also fosters greater coverage of women's athletics and Olympic sport programs that traditional, for-profit media outlets do not tend to cover (Cooper & Cooper, 2009;

Industry Profile
Claude Felton

Senior associate athletics director for sport communication, University of Georgia

Educational Background

University of Georgia, ABJ in journalism (major in public relations) and MA in journalism

Current Position

Responsible for overall supervision of sport communication department programs, establishing and maintaining the direction of the overall media relations programs for sport, and developing all annual publications of the communication office, including media guides, game event programs, and recruiting publications

How did you get into your current field of work?

I was pressed into duty as a high school senior to serve as sport editor of the school newspaper and concurrently took a required journalism class. I enjoyed the experience and decided to major in journalism at UGA. After serving a dual role in university public relations and sports information at Georgia Southern, I made the transition to full-time sports information and media relations and had the opportunity to return to UGA in that role.

What are the most enjoyable aspects of your position?

Working in sport on a college campus with student-athletes and coaches. It's a terrific atmosphere to spend a career in.

My busiest time of the year is . . .

Football season

To unwind and relax, I . . .

Go fishing or hunting, but I don't get to do it often enough.

Advice for students and others seeking to work in this field?

Start early. Volunteer to help out with your high school sport teams—keeping stats, helping publicize the teams in local media. Also, working on the high school paper is great experience. Find the sports information office in college and tell them you want to help out. Jobs in this field are plentiful, but there is a lot of competition. Two, three, or four years of sports information and media relations experience in college will be essential to getting into the job market.

Reprinted, by permission, from Campus Game. Available: http://thecampusgame.wordpress.com/2011/06/20/careers-in-sport-profile-claude-felton.

Cunningham, Sagas, Sartore, Amsden, & Schellhase, 2004; Cooper, Eagleman, & Laucella, 2009). The sports information office also helps other branches of the athletics department develop their online reach. For example, the website can be used to publicize upcoming promotions (for the marketing department), educate fans about NCAA rules (for the compliance office), provide directions and behavior policies for events (for facilities and event management), sell tickets (for the ticket office), procure donations (for the development office), and provide fans with their favorite merchandise (Salas, 2012; Menaker & Connaughton, 2010).

In addition, sports information directors must be able to handle the inevitable highs and lows of the athletics department with calmness and integrity while leveraging the department's publicity through various human interest stories, awards, honors, and other unique angles (Anderson, 2012). They must also strike a balance between understanding what the media expects and trying to put their department in the best light, whether in terms of a national championship or a reading program implemented through a local community service project. For most athletics departments, this obligation requires a heavy time commitment from the SID, who must be on call while at home for the night or away on vacation.

IMPORTANCE OF PUBLICITY AND GOOD PUBLIC RELATIONS

Publicity is a no-cost alternative to advertising (Stoldt et al., 2006); in order to get it, however, as former Ohio State SID Heather Hirschman notes, "there needs to be a personal element to the relationship" (qtd. in Schultz, 2005, p. 210). The key is to present information to the mass media—including print, television, radio, and web outlets—in a manner that is informative and will not be construed as a manipulated version of advertising. Ries and Ries (2002) stress that, through the continuous release of such information, high-quality public relations can be used to build stakeholders' trust in an organization. Consider the broad range of stakeholders for an intercollegiate athletics department as summarized in the following list.

Stakeholders in an Athletics Department

- Students in general
- Student-athletes
- Parents
- Alumni
- Coaches
- Athletics department staff
- Athletics department administrators
- School staff
- School faculty
- School administrators
- Fans
- Donors to the school
- Donors to the athletics department
- Sponsors of the athletics department
- School's athletics conference
- School's peers in the athletics conference
- School's athletics governing body
- School's accrediting body
- Local community
- State community

Communicating effectively with each of these constituent groups must be a high priority for the department. The preferred methods and content for such communications continue to evolve in order to best address the diverse issues that arise (Jackowski, 2007).

PRODUCTION OF MEDIA

As noted by Bill Lamberty, assistant athletics director of media relations at Montana State University, "Sports information is at its essence a service industry. The first and foremost function is to disseminate information, but at the same time to maintain relationships with media members and provide them with the information they need in a manner that fits their needs" (qtd. in Schultz, 2005, p. 210). Sports information departments produce media releases, create media guides, oversee the athletics department website, maintain historical records (including statistics), and produce other publications (e.g., programs and annual reports). They also host media conferences and handle other game-day duties at sporting events.

Amid these various duties, Battenfield and Kent (2007) suggest that the overwhelming primary duty of sports information staffers is to serve as "producers of information." With an ample staff size, the department's production of media can even grow to include a magazine generated in-house, as well as oversight of sport photography (Salas, 2012). As a result, students aspiring to work in sports information are well advised to pursue courses in communication or journalism. In addition, duties such as creating media guides and other publications require sports information staff to be knowledgeable of desktop publishing tools, such as Photoshop, InDesign, and Adobe's Creative Suite and Acrobat Professional (Panella, 2012). Additional relevant courses can be found in public relations, graphic design, and other media production departments.

WEBSITE INTERACTIVITY AND INNOVATION

Greg Byrne, director of athletics at the University of Arizona, uses the athletics website to speak to Wildcat fans en masse. In this setting, he answers questions directly and has complete control of the message he is trying to convey. Athletics directors use this type of outreach both in stressful times and in times of celebration because, unlike the mass media, the athletics website allows the sports information department to control the message without fear of editing or omission (Stoldt et al., 2006). Examples include sharing community relations or academic success stories that might not be deemed sufficiently dramatic by the mass media.

Websites also provide interactive options where fans can engage with the athletics program by, for example, voting for their favorite teams and registering to win contests (Schultz, 2005). Sports information staffers can be heavily involved in creating both the appearance and the content of material designed for fans' consumption (Reichart-Smith, 2011). Some schools develop their websites in-house for greater control, whereas others use such firms as XOS Digital, PrestoSports, NeuLion, CBS Technologies, and Sidearm Sports, because of their online expertise and familiarity with newer features (Salas, 2012). Such features help athletics departments' websites develop "stickiness"—the quality of keeping visitors on the site for extended periods of time.

For example, fans of Mississippi State athletics can see who won a basketball game by visiting the school's website, the ESPN site, the Fox Sports site, or any number of other sport sites. To stand out in this crowd, Mississippi State University's sports information department enhances its website's stickiness by including live statistics from games and posting sound bites and video clips that competing websites may not include (Andrews, 2005). The school also created an appealing website domain—www.hailstate.com—to appeal to Bulldog fans through their recognized rallying cry used at sporting events. The shortness and simplicity of the domain's address make it easy to remember (Bruno & Whitlock, 2000).

These efforts are intended to maximize unique visitors to the website. Unique visitors are people who visit a website; regardless of if, or how many times they return to the website, each visitor only counts once. Another measurement tool for web traffic is the "hit," which is defined as a single request from a browser to a server (Stoldt et al., 2006). One valuable tool for assessing such metrics is Google Analytics.

In addition to providing information to departmental stakeholders, athletics websites can also serve as revenue generators (Schultz, 2005). Possible ways to generate revenue through the website include pursuing sponsorships, selling tickets or merchandise, offering a secondary ticket exchange, hosting online auctions, giving donors the opportunity to log in and make a contribution, and providing specific subscription content. Thus the website is not merely a publicity tool but has gained importance to the athletics department in many ways (Blaine, 2012; Cooper & Pierce, 2011; Menaker & Connaughton, 2010).

GENERATING PUBLICITY

Producing media is important, but the information itself is relatively useless unless properly disseminated. Therefore, in order to generate effective publicity, sports information professionals must understand media channels. The mass media, taken together, constitute a highly competitive business that helps keep people informed and entertained (Schultz, 2005). Economic theory indicates that media look to increase their market share of consumers, and this focus affects what is carried in the news, in what order, and in what quantity (Cooper et al., 2009). Thus the media have evolved to interpret the news, thus shaping society's views and influencing ideology for the masses (Stoldt et al., 2006).

Media outlets often share experiences with readers, listeners, and viewers as if they were attending the event themselves (Andrews, 2005). Therefore, the information presented may include the specifics and details of the event, as well as the associated histrionics. Andrews observes that media information also traditionally blends in opinions, analysis, and criticism. The result can prove entertaining for many viewers, as evidenced by such sport-themed television shows as *Pardon the Interruption* and *The Jim Rome Show*.

The sports information department must work with various types of media and recognize that the media are part of a business. Consequently, the director is charged with being a forward thinker who identifies prospective stories that will sell (Andrews, 2005). The director must also formulate strategies about which stories should be directed to which media outlets, each of which has its own rhythm and deadlines (Howard & Mathews, 2000).

It is a wise practice for athletics department personnel to walk in the shoes of the media, viewing available content through the lens of how it might increase newspaper readership or website visitors for a media company seeking to generate revenue. What will raise ratings on a television or radio show looking to add sponsors through commercials? As relationships are built with media outlets by providing them with marketable content, the outlets may be more willing to highlight the program in a positive light or fact-check with the department before running misleading stories such as the one in the chapter-opening scenario.

At many Division I schools, the sports information department works with a "beat writer" who is assigned to cover athletics (Schultz, 2005) and focuses on the daily happenings of the athletics department. The department must also contend with columnists, who write to foster discussion and debate over their opinionated views in print or online articles (Andrews, 2005). The beat writer is traditionally hesitant to critique the athletics department harshly, since his or her access might be restricted, but the columnist is not subject to such restriction and strives simply to create the greatest impact.

To understand what it takes to "sell" a story, consider the acronym TIPCUP, which refers to news that is timely, important, prominent, conflict oriented, unusual, and proximate (close) to those in the readership (Thompson, 1996). In terms of timeliness, sport news from two years ago seems outdated as compared with something that happened last weekend, yesterday, or perhaps an hour ago. In terms of importance, a team winning a national championship is obviously far more important than a team winning a scrimmage. Prominence comes into play, for example, when a head coach gets arrested and makes the headlines, whereas a graduate assistant in the same situation might go unnoticed. Conflict can take many forms, such as a decision about who will start in the conference championship game—something that fans will want to weigh in on even though the decision rests, of course, with the head coach. The unusual can also take many forms, such as a football player on special teams who served in the military prior to enrolling in college. And proximity dictates, for example, that the athletics department at the state's major public institution will get more media coverage than the conference rival from four states away.

Coaches and student-athletes sometimes assert that negativity is all that "sells" in the media; however, the TIPCUP acronym provides a more informative look at what the media tend to find worthy of coverage. Journalists write about what passionate fans want (Wigley & Meirick, 2008). Regardless, some coaches and staff continue to decry sportswriters and the media as wielding the "poisonous pen"—thus the importance of educating athletics department members about media relations.

Despite the need to cultivate good media relations, Howard and Mathews (2000) observe that media requests are sometimes rejected. Here are some reasons that sports information directors can use strategically.

- The issue in question simply cannot be discussed (e.g. a personnel matter, legalities, or privacy including injuries or academic situations).
- The time required to gather the information is unavailable due to the broad nature of the request.
- The reporter does not know what he or she wants.
- The host has a record of asking loaded questions.
- The request asks someone in athletics to appear on a scandal-driven program.
- The request cannot be confirmed as coming from a reporter on assignment.
- The request comes from someone with a clear bias or a careless approach to journalism.

In similar fashion, strategy can be implemented in the way in which a story is released. Many SIDs do not hesitate to acknowledge that releasing a story on Monday generates more attention, whereas Tuesday is traditionally a slow media day (Johnston, 2012). Along the same lines, releasing a story on a Friday afternoon helps bury it, because many media outlets have already established the storylines for their weekend sport coverage (Howard & Mathews, 2000; Anderson, 2012).

SENSATIONALISM

Today's journalism has broadened from local newspaper, radio, and television outlets to Internet coverage by tabloids and investigative journalists (Andrews, 2005; Howard & Mathews, 2000). Howard and Mathews note that this trend is not going to change. Yahoo Sports, for example, has established a strong niche in its ability to research and uncover hidden stories through investigative methods (Fisher, 2011). TMZ Sports, following TMZ's general paparazzi model of providing details about celebrities, now spotlights the activities of athletics figures. DrunkAthlete.com works in similar fashion but also asks viewers to upload their own pictures and videos captured in public.

In this context, newspapers and radio and television stations also operate websites that enable breaking news coverage, and fan sites have been dedicated to specific teams (Butler & Sagas, 2008). Butler and Sagas observe that while such sites focus on providing information to viewers about their favorite teams, they are not traditional media in the sense that fans use them to create forums and communities where they offer their unfiltered views, opinions, and feedback on message boards. Though fans flock to such websites, the parent companies running them may not adhere to industry ethics because they are newer forms of media operated independently of traditional sites (Yanity & Edmondson, 2011). The accuracy of the fan-generated content can also be questionable (Butler & Sagas).

At the same time, comments posted on fan-generated sites and online columns can make it easier for athletics administrators to gauge the mood of the fans (Andrews, 2005). Many newspapers now also permit fans to comment on articles (Butler & Sagas, 2008). These practices further build the "soap opera" that sport provides to fans; they also help journalists shape future stories (Andrews; Wigley & Meirick, 2008). Sensationalism will likely continue to grow with the development of more online media that allow for increased fan participation. As a result, sports information professionals must develop the needed skill set to shape and learn from these activities.

MEDIA POLICY

Though one core principle of sports information is to facilitate information transfer to the media, the department also needs to identify "guiding principles and behaviors to ensure consistent, fair,

and ethical communication with all constituents" (Mathews, 2004, p. 46). To this end, it is essential to develop and implement a media policy for the following reasons:

- The media policy designates who will serve as the calm and credible spokesperson to the media in times of crisis (Ruihley & Fall, 2009; Satter, 2012; Braun, 2012).
- It helps the athletics department staff be aware that members of the media should work with sports information to obtain official quotes, interviews, and comments.
- It establishes the stringent philosophy to the media that student-athletes are students first and are not to be disrupted during classes or while studying (Hubbard, 2012).

For example, Yanity & Edmondson (2011) found that many high school recruits were contacted in high volume by recruiting websites at all times of the day. A media policy establishes that this is not acceptable practice in intercollegiate athletics by informing the media of the proper procedures for setting up an interview with a student-athlete.

The media policy should also specify when and how to contact head coaches, who may be occupied with recruiting, watching film, or preparing for a game (Bratton, 2012). The policy informs members of the media that student-athletes and coaches could be unavailable for interviews at certain times (Schultz, 2005). Possible reasons for limiting media access range from keeping the team focused on academics during exams to a coach's desire to better monitor a team that has spoken too freely with the media, perhaps making inflammatory comments about opponents (Bratton; Lovings, 2012; Thompson, 2012). In addition, the policy should advise the media against conducting ambush interviews, such as questioning coaches or student-athletes during community service appearances outside of prearranged interview times (Andrews, 2005).

The media policy should also specify cool-down periods after practices and especially after competition to enable coaches and student-athletes to calm down, control their emotions, and get their thoughts together before speaking with the media (Johnston, 2012). A coach or student-athlete caught up in passionate feelings may speak without thinking rationally, thus making it harder to control the message delivered to the media. For example, Nolan Richardson, former head coach of the 1993 national championship Arkansas Razorbacks men's basketball team, once noted in postgame comments that the school could have his job if they exercised the contractual buyout provision (Associated Press, 2006). The comments were made in haste, but the media firestorm that ensued led the school to terminate the head coach in the following days even though the season was not yet over.

In addition, the media policy may provide for using teleconference calls to expedite the media process and avoid redundancy in questions (Masteralexis, Barr, & Hums, 2008). The policy should also establish priorities for postgame interviews; for example, the television or radio broadcast partner should have priority in interviewing the star player or head coach on the playing surface before the individuals depart to the locker room. This partnership is arranged through the media rights deal in place with the school, conference, or governing body (Gale, 2012).

MEDIA TRAINING

Sports information departments use media training to help coaches, administrators, and student-athletes avoid debacles (Stoldt et al., 2006). Media training can promote a stronger, more conducive environment for interacting with the media and help eliminate the fallout that comes with negative interviews (Johnston, 2012). The media are capable of fueling stereotypes, for example, through illustrations of the big-business nature of college sport, the supposed "dumb jock" mind-set of college athletes, and other stereotypes (Harrison, Lawrence, Plecha, Bukstein, & Janson, 2009). Media training assists in combating such stereotypes and promoting a more positive image.

Members of the media may build mutual trust and respect with coaches and student-athletes, but it remains a wise move to avoid friendships due to the business nature of the mass media industry (Schultz, 2005). Media training helps coaches and student-athletes anticipate questions and best formulate in advance the messages that they would like to get across. Media training also informs coaches and student-athletes about how their behavior and reactions on the playing field, court, or other surface may be subjected to interpretation

by the media, even if such interpretations are inaccurate (Earnheardt, 2010). Regardless of all these wrinkles, the media's views play a significant role in shaping fans' opinions of coaches, student-athletes, and programs.

Media training helps educate those in the athletics department not only about what can go wrong when interacting with the media but also how it might be fixed (Johnston, 2012). Certain members of the media have a particular story angle in mind before they start talking with a coach or student-athlete, but proper training helps interviewees redirect the conversation or eliminate the angle completely if it portrays the team or athletics department in a negative light (Andrews, 2005). Here are two examples of such angled questions and cautionary responses by a coach or student-athlete.

> Question: Did your teammates' poor shooting cause you great frustration?
>
> Answer: It is a team game, and collectively we did not play well enough to win.
>
> Question: Did the cautious play calling from the coaches hinder your ability to win the game?
>
> Answer: Our coaches put us in position to be here tonight, but the other team just played better.

Howard and Mathews (2000) highlight the fact that some reporters, in their effort to grow their audience, resort to trickery during interviews. Examples include needling, false "facts," reinterpretation of responses, and putting words into someone's mouth. Coaches and student-athletes can defuse such situations by calmly sticking to the key message, kindly correcting the interviewer, avoiding loaded responses, and steering clear of arguments (Howard & Mathews).

Members of the media are also trained to notice if a responder's body language gives any messages that could be used in a negative fashion (Andrews, 2005). For example, a roll of the eyes, an unwillingness to look someone in the eye, or increasing sweat on the forehead can be portrayed negatively in the media, even though each of these mannerisms could simply be a function of being interviewed in a hot locker room after a lengthy game or being tired from studying the previous evening. Therefore, proper training should provide examples of the

Industry Profile

Brian Morrison

Associate commissioner, media relations, Atlantic Coast Conference

Straight Shooter: Brian Morrison Fields Media Calls, Conducts Weekly Teleconference

Bill Cole, Posted Friday, May 2, 2008

GREENSBORO—The phone rang late on the night of January 23 in Brian Morrison's home—an unexpected but important call about ACC business.

On the line was Steve Kirschner, North Carolina's sports information director, in need of immediate help at 11:15 after a basketball game at Miami. Kirschner was leading the UNC beat writers to the team locker room for interviews when Miami's athletics director, Paul Dee, standing in a corridor, told him that the UNC locker room was closed to media and prevented anyone from entering.

Kirschner explained the situation to Morrison and handed his cell phone to Margaret Belch, a Miami assistant sports information director. Morrison told her that ACC regulations called for open locker rooms and that the media had to be granted access, although by then Dee had found an ACC manual and read the regulations and was relenting on his stance.

Such a late-hour interruption is not unusual for Morrison, an ACC associate commissioner and the conference's director of media relations. Urgent requests can come at almost any time on any day from the ACC media and reporters from all over the country, as well as ACC school officials in need of clarification on issues.

"When you have 12 schools, there's a lot going on," Morrison said. "I appreciate those calls from the media because most of the time they're calls for background or for edification when they're trying to make sure that they get their facts straight. Those are the calls I'd rather have—making sure that they get their facts straight. I have no problems with those calls. I'd rather get it done right."

Morrison started working for the ACC in 1981 as an intern to the late Marvin "Skeeter" Francis, the conference's longtime media relations director. He returned on a full-time basis in 1985 as Francis' assistant and took over five years later when Francis retired.

Morrison has worked for the past three ACC commissioners: John Swofford, the current commissioner; Gene Corrigan, who preceded Swofford; and Bob James. Francis taught Morrison to know his media and to attend personally to everyone's needs. Communication was one of the most important aspects of the job, Francis said, and it is to Morrison.

The ACC has expanded three times in 17 years, adding Florida State in 1991, Miami and Virginia Tech in 2004, and Boston College in 2005. The conference has become an important member of the football Bowl Championship Series (BCS)—the football playoff post-season—and has long been a national power in basketball.

Such reporters as Tony Barnhart of the *Atlanta Journal-Constitution* have relied upon Morrison to help them in covering conference business. Barnhart, a veteran ACC reporter, will call Morrison to talk about college athletics issues because Morrison knows what's going on and why.

"Brian's going to level with you about what's going on, either in his conference or what's going on in college athletics," Barnhart said. "The thing I've always liked about him is if you ask him a question, he won't try to weave and dodge. He'll either give you the answer or tell you, 'I don't know,' or he'll tell you, 'I can't talk about it.' He never tries to talk his way around it."

Now Morrison handles only basketball for the ACC. He used to handle football, too, but that role was taken by Mike Finn, another associate commissioner, to ease Morrison's load after the conference grew to 12 members.

(continued)

INDUSTRY PROFILE *(continued)*

Morrison used to direct the now-defunct ACC football writers' tour, in which he and a busload of media members visited the conference's campuses for preseason stories each August over about a two-week period. Now he conducts the weekly ACC teleconference for the 12 basketball coaches with media across the nation. He also moderated the football conference call until Finn took his place.

Morrison is the person who decides which media are credentialed for the ACC's showcase event, the conference basketball tournament. Limited working space means that not everyone is granted access. He has had his share of strange requests.

One year, Morrison received a request for credentials from the sports editor of the school newspaper at McGill University in Montreal. Morrison turned down the request after figuring out that the student was heading to Florida for spring break and wanted to watch the tournament on the way.

Three days before the tournament, Morrison received a call about 10 p.m. at the ACC office. It was the McGill student who, speaking in a French-Canadian accent, pleaded his case for almost 20 minutes.

"At the very end in exasperation he goes, 'Mr. Morrison, in the name of bettering Canadian-American relations, would you consider it?'" Morrison recalled with a laugh. Morrison left international relations to the diplomats. The student didn't get his press pass.

And there was the tournament when, a few minutes before the championship game, Morrison spotted a rather large fellow wearing only a T-shirt and gym shorts sitting on the stanchion of one of the baskets. Morrison asked the man if he had a pass to sit there, and received no answer.

Morrison asked again and told the man that if he didn't have a media pass, he would have to sit in the stands if he had a spectator's ticket or leave the building. The man looked at him and pointed toward the ceiling. The man then told Morrison, "God wants me here."

Divine intervention was of no help with the title game ready to begin. "I said, 'Did God give you a pass?'" Morrison said, laughing again. "He shook his head. I had to get a state trooper to get him out of the building."

Expansion was tough on almost everyone involved, from ACC officials to school officials to the reporters who cover Virginia Tech, Boston College, and Miami. Bill Dyer, Virginia Tech's basketball sports information director, found that Morrison's expertise eased everyone's adjustment.

"For me as a basketball guy, it's been really good," Dyer said. "We get things when we need them. We seldom, if ever, go into a basketball game without an updated (ACC) release. We don't want for a whole lot because of Brian."

Reprinted, by permission, from B. Cole, 2008, "Straight shooter: Brian Morrison fields media calls, conducts weekly teleconference," Winston-Salem Journal May 2.

media taking liberties based on body language in order to emphasize the importance of the responder's smile, attire, and posture at all times.

Media training also helps remind responders that they do not possess a crystal ball that enables them to see what is going to happen in the future (Adkison, 2012). The media are capable of asking the same question in many different ways; therefore, media training prepares responders to answer consistently even in times of crisis. Though such responses have been called clichés, responders have to be comfortable acknowledging that they lack information, are looking into something, or cannot answer a certain question due to such reasons as laws about privacy or personnel matters (Adkison). Media training also helps athletics administrators effectively share sympathy if someone is injured at a sporting event without expanding on their answer to the point that their response is used against them in a court of law (Braun, 2012).

Media training should also emphasize the fact that "off-the-record" answers simply do not exist (Howard & Mathews, 2000; Schmidt, 2012). The media operate as a business, and businesses and their employees typically operate in their own perceived best interest. Therefore, if a supposedly off-the-record comment can help create better business for the media outlet, chances are that it will be used even if the interviewee indicated that the conversation was not for official release.

Regardless of whether he or she implements formal media training, the SID is obliged to guide student-athletes and coaches, especially those who are in the media spotlight or are subject to regular public scrutiny (Johnston, 2012). Using the analogy of a fishbowl, the sports information staff can advise a star student-athlete or coach that members of the media are watching their every move, both on and off the playing surface. For example, Larry Eustachy, former head basketball coach at Iowa State University, left his team after a road game at the University of Missouri, choosing to stay in the opposing team's town to take part in a fraternity party (Associated Press, 2003). Members of the media were alerted to the behavior through pictures of the coach taken at the party, resulting in national embarrassment for the basketball program, the athletics department, and the university—and leading to Eustachy's termination.

SPECULATING VERSUS FORECASTING

Forecasting is another element of media training that can help administrators control the messages relayed to the public. In this approach, the SID uses his or her familiarity with the media's strategies for finding an appealing story angle to forecast questions that will be asked. From time to time, for example, media personnel ask speculative questions related to events that *could* happen in the future. For instance, a reporter might ask a head coach about a player's eligibility for an upcoming season when grades have not yet been submitted. Similarly, an athletics director might be asked about forthcoming sanctions immediately after the announcement that violations have been submitted to the NCAA. In these scenarios, neither the coach nor the athletics director possesses enough information to make an informed response.

Forecasting allows administrators, coaches, and student-athletes to examine forthcoming issues behind closed doors in an effort to identify potential scenarios and prepare desired responses in advance (Howard & Mathews, 2000; Record, 2012; Smith, 2012). In the case of the student-athlete's eligibility, for example, if an individual's forthcom-

ing grades determine whether he or she can play during the next semester, the SID can help athletics department members forecast what types of question will be asked by the media regardless of whether or not the student-athlete ends up eligible to compete. Here are some specific examples.

If eligible, the student-athlete could be asked the following questions:

- How were you able to improve your grades?
- Were you motivated to get better grades in order to maintain your eligibility?
- What role did your teammates play in supporting you?
- What will keep the academic problems from reoccurring in the future?
- What role did your family play in this process?

If ineligible, the student-athlete could be asked the following questions:

- Have academics been a continuous issue for you?
- Do you feel that you were offered enough academic support by your coach, team, or athletics department?
- Now that you are ineligible, what is your next step?
- Will you consider transferring?
- How disappointed are you?

Although forecasting helps SIDs prepare for many potential scenarios, it is an imprecise science. Despite attending conferences and keeping up with the news, no SID is immune to crisis, and all will face an unanticipated issue at some point. In times of duress, the head of sports information is the face that many administrators, coaches, and student-athletes look to for calmness and direction (Schmidt, 2012). In being mindful of what sells in the media, a good SID can take some solace in the limited shelf life of today's negative news (Anderson, 2012); however, the best preparation is to avoid such issues in the first place through regular education (Montoro, 2012).

CRISIS MANAGEMENT

By definition, a crisis is disruptive; it may also be unexpected, and it is frequently characterized by

Examples of Recent Crises in College Sport

- Academics—A Florida State University cheating scandal involves numerous student-athletes.
- Agents—The University of Southern California is criticized for failing to monitor football star Reggie Bush's involvement with an agent while Bush was still competing.
- Alcohol—The University of Wisconsin and the University of Minnesota require student fans ejected for drunken behavior to take a breathalyzer test upon return to future games at their football stadiums.
- Allegations—Allegations of sexual assault are made by an exotic dancer against members of the Duke University men's lacrosse team.
- Alumni—Former NFL All-Pro Dexter Manley asserts that he graduated from Oklahoma State University despite being unable to read.
- Arrests—The Fulmer Cup website monitors which athletics departments annually have the most arrests of student-athletes.
- Band—A hazing scandal at Florida A&M University implicates band leaders.
- Band equipment—A cart holding band equipment at the field level of the Marshall–Houston football game causes injury to a University of Houston student-athlete who runs out of the back of the end zone while attempting to catch a pass.
- Benefits—Terrelle Pryor and other Ohio State University football players receive fringe benefits, thus affecting their eligibility.
- Brawl—Players from the University of South Carolina and Clemson University brawl during their 2004 rivalry game.
- Cell phones—Former University of Arkansas football head coach Houston Nutt's cell phone records are requested by a football fan through the Freedom of Information Act.
- Cheerleaders—A member of the Mississippi State University cheerleading squad poses naked in Playboy.
- Cheerleading coach—The University of Georgia terminates a cheerleading coach for imposing Christian views and requests on the squad in violation of the separation of church and state.
- Coaches and affairs—Former University of Arkansas head football coach Bobby Petrino's affair with a fellow athletics department staffer is revealed in his attempted cover-up after a motorcycle accident involving the two individuals.
- Coaches and coaches—Former West Virginia University football head coach Bill Stewart asks members of the media to find dirt on head-coach-in-waiting Dana Holgorsen.
- Conference—Conference hopping results in litigation between departing schools and the conferences they are leaving.
- Death—A fan is killed while tailgating at a Yale–Harvard football game when a truck transporting beer strikes three women.
- Donors—University of Miami football players are implicated in receiving benefits directly from a prominent university supporter.
- Drugs—University of Kansas basketball players are implicated in a drug ring after the arrest of an alleged supplier.
- DUI—The University of Missouri head football coach is arrested on suspicion of drunk driving.
- Flags—Confederate flags depicted on state flags affect South Carolina's and Mississippi's ability to host NCAA postseason events.

- Fundraising—The University of Missouri Paige Sports Arena, named in honor of a donor's daughter after a US$25 million naming-right gift, is renamed after revelations that the daughter committed academic fraud at another university.
- Health—Former University of Notre Dame head coach Charlie Weis' postsurgery complication results in inquiries about his availability to coach from the sidelines.
- Heat—The *International Journal of Biometeorology* reports in a 2012 article that heat-related deaths among college and high school football players tripled since 1994, increasing to three per year in between 1994 and 2009.
- Honor code violations—A Brigham Young University men's basketball student-athlete is suspended due to violation of the school policy requiring a chaste and virtuous life.
- Injury—A Rutgers University football student-athlete is paralyzed while making a tackle on special teams.
- Interim—Former Ohio State University interim head coach Luke Fickell assumes the leadership role with the football team in the aftermath of the head coach's resignation.
- International—The University of Georgetown men's basketball team is involved in an in-game brawl on a goodwill and educational trip to China.
- Jersey sale—University of Georgia wide receiver A.J. Green is suspended for four games after selling a jersey he wore during a game.
- Mascot death—A University of North Carolina student who served as the school's mascot dies on a men's basketball postseason trip after being struck by a car while walking to a local store.
- Mascot fight—The Oregon Ducks mascot is suspended for a game after an in-game fight with the Houston Cougars mascot.
- Murder of a teammate—A Baylor University basketball student-athlete is convicted of murdering a teammate, as well as a head coach's attempt to cover up significant NCAA violations.
- Parking—UCLA football players are charged with illegally acquiring parking permits intended for persons with a disability.
- Past coaches—Former Penn State University football defensive coordinator Jerry Sandusky is convicted on charges of child abuse.
- Postseason—The University of Connecticut men's basketball team is banned from postseason play due to continuous poor graduation rates.
- Racial slurs—Two Texas A&M football student-athletes are required to attend a multiculturalism course after yelling racial slurs at patrons at a fast food restaurant.
- Recruiting—Allegations surface that Cam Newton's father solicited bids from Mississippi State University for his son's football services.
- Snowballs—Members of the student section at the University of Notre Dame pelt their football team and staff with snowballs to express their displeasure at the team's performance.
- Social media—Louisiana State University swimming and diving student-athletes are kicked off the team after posting negative comments about their coaches on Facebook.
- Stadium stampede—Seventy-three students are injured, six critically, in the aftermath of an on-field celebration following a Wisconsin–Minnesota football game.
- Strip club—University of New Mexico football student-athletes and recruits are shot at during an unauthorized trip to a strip club.
- Tailgating—Restrictions are put in place at the University of Georgia after littering and poor social behavior damage the campus after football games.

(continued)

EXAMPLES OF RECENT CRISES IN COLLEGE SPORT *(continued)*

- Ticketing—University of Kansas ticket office officials are charged with stealing and reselling tickets for personal profit.
- Travel—A member of the Kenyon College swimming and diving team dies when the team's van flips in icy conditions while traveling home from a competition.
- Trustee—Auburn University trustee Bobby Lowder flies during midseason with athletics director and school president to secretly visit Louisville head football coach Bobby Petrino for the purpose of luring him away.
- University-wide—A Binghamton men's basketball scandal results in job loss for the president, the provost, two athletics officials, and the head coach in the aftermath of arrests and academic fraud.
- Videographer—A Notre Dame videographer dies at football practice when the tower from which he is filming topples due to high winds.
- Weather—Rampant thunderstorms delay, postpone, and eventually cancel the 2000 season-opening Black Coaches Association football game between Virginia Tech and Georgia Tech, resulting in ticket-refund woes.

allegations that are not completely founded or proven, which can lead to erroneous assumptions (Connaughton, Spengler, & Bennett, 2001). Crises can happen due to injury, improper recruiting, arrests, fights, academic improprieties, and other reputation-damaging issues. They can occur on campus, at off-site events, or even overseas during international goodwill trips. They can involve any number of departmental stakeholders—fans, donors, alumni, parents, coaches, student-athletes, cheerleaders, cheerleading coaches, and even mascots. Crises can take place in season, out of season, during the academic year, and throughout the summer. As a result, sports information departments are never immune to the concerns of crisis management (Barrow, 2012).

Seitel (2010) suggests that when a crisis occurs, administrators should adhere to the following guidelines.

- Speak early and often.
- Don't speculate.
- Go off the record at your own peril.
- Stay with the facts.
- Be open and concerned, not defensive.
- Make your own point and repeat it.
- Don't war with the media.
- Establish yourself as the most authoritative source.

- Stay calm, and be truthful and cooperative.
- Never lie.

Dealing with a crisis has become more difficult with the growth of the Internet and, as mentioned earlier, the emergence of online tabloid journalism outlets such as TMZ Sports, DrunkAthlete.com, BadJocks.com, and independent fan sites' chat rooms (Andrews, 2005; Butler & Sagas, 2008). In past generations, journalists traditionally verified their sources to ensure the accuracy of their reporting. Power has now shifted, however, from the mainstream media to uncontrolled information intermediaries who often possess sensationalist agendas or ulterior motives (Howard & Mathews, 2000). The race to break stories, and thereby enhance an organization's ratings or readership, has reduced the importance of credibility (Howard & Mathews; Stoldt et al., 2006). Unnamed sources may be less credible, but they are still sources that help shape a story (Andrews, 2005). Thus it is important to develop an ample crisis management team and a plan that alerts all involved to possible tripping points.

As cited in Stoldt et al. (2006), a crisis can grow if the athletics department is not prepared to avoid the following pitfalls: stalling (Helitzer, 2000), telling lies (Stoldt, Miller, Ayres, & Comfort, 2000), withholding negative news (Helitzer), ignoring tough questions (Stoldt et al., 2000), stating "no comment" (Stoldt et al., 2000), downplaying a crisis (Cutlip, Center, & Broom, 2000), going off the record (Cutlip et al., 2000), estimating monetary damages or medical diagnoses (PRSA, 2000), shifting blame (PRSA), and adding inappropriate humor (Schmidt, 2012). All are valuable points about which to educate one's athletics department members well in advance.

The last tripping point (humor) felled Ohio State chancellor Gordon Gee during the crisis that encompassed the university's football program in 2011. When asked if he would fire head football coach Jim Tressel in the aftermath of a scandal in which players received extra benefits, Gee joked that he hoped the coach, given his tremendous success on the field, would not fire *him* (Thamel, 2011). Further investigation uncovered the fact that Tressel had known more than he had initially revealed, after which he resigned, leaving the media to mock Gee's leadership during the time of crisis. As Earnheardt (2010) observed, even overzealous fans will judge antisocial behavior in a negative light; thus it is critical to take all crises seriously.

Despite our best efforts to educate and forecast, crises will inevitably occur. When they do, issues management is essential. Issues management is "the process of prioritizing and proactively addressing public policy and reputation issues that affect an organization's success (Pinkham, as qtd. in Stoldt, Dittmore, & Branvold, 2006). With this need in mind, administrators should be aware of and familiar with the following four-step process for optimally managing any issues that arise:

1. Anticipate and analyze the issue(s).
2. Develop the organization's position.
3. Identify key publics.
4. Specify the desired behavior of these groups.

During such times, an SID who is viewed with trust and credibility by local media outlets is generally the person they turn to for answers (Masteralexis et al., 2008). "The ideal relationship is based on trust," according to Maxey Parrish, former SID at Baylor University. "The media have to trust the SID to be fully factual, whether the news is good or bad. The SID has to trust the media to treat his (her) school fairly" (qtd. in Schultz, 2005, p. 210). As a result, it is the SID who traditionally advises

senior administrators about what to do when a crisis reduces the available reaction time from hours to minutes (Adkison, 2012).

CRISIS MANAGEMENT PLAN

Because of the tendency to rush to reaction by key publics—including fans, alumni, sponsors, ticket holders, students, and others—athletics departments stress a proactive approach to controlling the media and their story angles. The idea is to maximize reaction time and minimize clean-up (Stoldt et al., 2006), which requires careful creation of a detailed crisis management plan. Such a plan is analogous to a fire evacuation route in one's home. You hope you never need it, but in case you do, you want it be as efficient as possible and to include a proactive step for every circumstance.

A crisis management team, frequently led by an SID in conjunction with other senior administrators, is established to explore potential worst-case crisis scenarios (Record, 2012; Smith, 2012). The sports information director can be instrumental as a "problem-solving process facilitator" and catalyst in the communication effort (Ruihley & Fall, 2009). For each scenario, the crisis management team identifies response outcomes and needed support. Does the president or chancellor need to be informed? Is legal counsel necessary? If the crisis does in fact arise, the plan is then implemented to keep all involved parties consistent in working with the media.

Afterward, the plan's implementation is assessed to see what worked and what didn't. Crises can arise unexpectedly, but the crisis management team can prevent them or prepare to manage them effectively through practices such as observation, discussion, and analysis of organizational crisis management tactics (Braun, 2012). In addition, in a crisis that could damage an entire university's reputation, the institution's overall department of media and public relations may step in to assist or oversee media relations because the central administration wants greater control over the response in order to prevent further damage (Adkison, 2012).

REPUTATION

Reputation has been defined as the "ability of an organization to meet the expectations of its publics and the strengths of the relationships [that] various stakeholders have with the organization" (Stoldt et al., 2006, p. 35). Depending on the scale of a crisis and the institution's reputation, the institution may be able to withstand a damaging blow to its reputation quotient (Fombrun, Gardberg, & Sever, 2000). The reputation quotient accounts for various factors that may be affected by a scandal: emotional appeal, products and services, vision and leadership, workplace environment, social responsibility, and financial performance.

In one dramatic example, Penn State's reputation has been tarnished by a football scandal in which the president, vice president, athletics director, and head football coach have been accused of failing to act effectively on allegations of child abuse against former assistant coach Jerry Sandusky. Located in a community known as Happy Valley, Penn State has seen its emotional appeal damaged among students, alumni, and fans alike as trust in and admiration of Penn State football have suffered. The athletics department offers many other products and services, including sporting events and camps, that have suffered decreased attendance. In addition, in such situations, sponsors may consider withdrawing their services and their support of Penn State athletics.

Prior to the disclosure of the scandal, former head coach Joe Paterno's legacy was characterized by a vision of high-quality academics, leadership, and integrity. That legacy took decades to build but has now been severely diminished. In addition, the workplace environment for Penn State faculty and staff is stained by the allegations that football was prioritized above child welfare on campus. The scandal has even hindered the school's efforts to exercise social responsibility because of the perception that it undertakes such activities merely as a form of damage control. The school also faces potential harm to its financial performance in terms of lost donors, decreased alumni support, departing sponsors, mounting legal costs, and costly settlements. Despite the tremendous impact of the crisis, Jamie Singer, a specialist in crisis communication and reputation management with Cone Communications, notes that Penn State University can emerge from the crisis through a three-step process: distancing itself from those involved in the scandal, focusing on team leadership as the school moves forward, and restoring values by example

(not rhetoric) across the campus (Cone, 2011).

SOCIAL MEDIA AND CONTINUOUS SURVEILLANCE

The evolution of online technology has forced sports information directors to assume a new role as social media police. Because the media can now pull information from a student-athlete's Facebook page or a coach's Twitter account, the athletics department's message has become more difficult to monitor (Gregory, 2009; Sanderson 2011). Continuous education should advise all members of the department about how the media can use details from any social media outlet at any time (Sanderson, 2011). Because of the rapidity of the social media evolution, many athletics departments lack applicable policies, management plans for social media crises, and oversight procedures (Syme, 2012).

Similarly, many departments are unsure how to use their own department's social media outlets in a time of crisis. Syme (2012) recommends that schools embrace the following five strategies during this period of social media evolution:

1. Implement a social media monitoring system.
2. Develop a social media policy.
3. Implement a social media management policy.
4. Establish registration of department social media accounts.
5. Establish a community manager for department social media.

Sports information staff must also strongly emphasize to coaches and student-athletes that the audiovisual recording functions of mobile phones mean that their actions, both good and bad, can be captured by anyone at any time (Sanderson, 2009)—and that the media can use the results in their reporting. Video footage, for example, can lead to a coach's or student-athlete's unwanted appearance on tabloid websites while engaging in drunken behavior, drug use, physical violence, competition in an unauthorized sporting activity while rehabilitating an injury, or other dangerous or otherwise undesirable activities. In such cases, the sports information staff must address issues in a reactive fashion as sport talk radio shows or websites quickly frame the story line for their own economic gain (Sanderson, 2009).

Student-athletes and coaches may express concern about invasions of their privacy, but sports information directors need to remind them of their heightened visibility due to the economic realities of the media (Sanderson, 2011). Therefore, whereas profane postings, provocative pictures, and evidence of alcohol consumption may be considered acceptable by some traditional college students or staff members (Miller, Parson, & Lifer, 2010), the behavior of a student-athlete or coach is more visible and is held to a higher standard.

These cautions also apply to student-athletes who use social media (e.g., Twitter) to lash out at a coach or teammate (Ballouli & Hutchinson, 2010). Athletes who use Twitter as a medium for sharing their personal life should be warned of the potential pitfalls (Pegoraro, 2010). Fans of rival schools have disguised their identities to lure or entice student-athletes and then taunt them at a sporting event. In addition, stalkers, agents, and persons affiliated with gambling interests may also use social media to reach student-athletes (Sanderson, 2011). As Mandel (2010) notes, social media postings can even result in NCAA investigations, as evidenced by the investigation into former University of North Carolina football player Marvin Austin who tweeted about "bottles comin' like it's a giveaway" while in attendance at a Miami nightclub.

Some coaches, including John Calipari of the University of Kentucky men's basketball team, have revoked student-athletes' social media privileges after their postings led to undesirable media coverage (Staples, 2011). The sports information director should emphasize that the time spent in strategically repairing a program's brand could be better used in pushing proactive positive messages, thus heightening the importance of media education in the athletics department (Sanderson, 2011). Preventive monitoring by coaches and sports information staff can include such measures as having student-athletes send social media "friend" requests to coaches and sports information staff members.

Social Media as a Marketing Tool

Pitfalls notwithstanding, when social media are used strategically they can serve as critical elements of an athletics department's marketing toolkit (Williams & Chinn, 2010; Pegoraro, 2010). A captivating link or picture, for example, can stimulate fan avidity and draw traffic to the department's website (Pegoraro). Similarly, tweets by student-athletes and coaches can be used to highlight charity work, off-season training, travel, and reflection on large-scale events, such as postseason competition. Tweets and images can be used to enhance relationship marketing efforts that boost ticket sales, merchandise retailing, donations, and other means of support (Williams & Chinn). In addition, Phua (2010) has found that fan identification is stronger among online media users than among fans who connect through print and broadcast media.

Dos and Don'ts of Social Media

To avoid "making news" in a negative manner, tweets should not comment on issues involving politics, religion, or military actions (Pegoraro, 2010). Departments should also be careful to properly balance their own tweets. Reichart-Smith (2011) found that athletics departments have produced tweets that publicize men's programs more than women's programs. This concern needs to be addressed throughout the sports information or sport marketing department given Title IX's application to intercollegiate athletics, as well as the potential for missed opportunities to promote Olympic sport programs (Cooper, 2008). In addition, tweets from student-athletes should not endorse such things as movies, restaurants, or other products for fear of violating the amateur status of NCAA participants (Sanderson, 2011).

Despite all these caveats, social media provide a valuable way to highlight rivalries, give updates about facility construction, thank fans, share about community goodwill efforts, and offer a look at past or current success stories—all of which can enhance the department's brand (Wallace, Wilson, & Miloch, 2011). If communication is a two-way platform between the athletic departments and its supporters, athletics department staff can type in the answers to tweeted questions directed towards coaches or student-athletes. This practice increases efficiency and eases the time constraints faced by student-athletes. Syme (2012) observes that athletics departments also use other social media, including YouTube, blogs, and Foursquare.

STUDENT-ATHLETE PRIVACY: FERPA AND MEDICAL ISSUES

The Family Educational Rights and Privacy Act (FERPA) requires that students' records be protected from release. The law is not limited to student-athletes, but, given the heightened scrutiny applied to this population, sport administrators must understand the law thoroughly because the media often inquire about related issues, such as academic eligibility and graduation rates (Hubbard, 2012). The law also protects student-athletes from searches of their medical records and drug tests (Lewis, 2012). As a result, if a student fails a drug test, sports information staff traditionally note merely that a violation of team rules has warranted a suspension. Even if anonymous sources attribute the suspension to the use of illicit drugs, the sports information department should stand by its response that the student-athlete was disciplined due to a violation of team rules, while neither confirming nor denying the allegation (Lewis).

Medical records are also protected when a student-athlete is injured. Minor injuries may be disclosed as the reason that a student-athlete did not play or practice. In the case of severe injury, however, athletics departments traditionally have a media policy requiring that the sports medicine staff first notify family members, then ask their permission before sharing a diagnosis publicly (Anderson, 2012; Schmidt, 2012). However, it is not unusual for members of the media to ask medical practitioners for a diagnosis and a description of the recovery faced by a student-athlete, especially if he or she is a star figure.

FREEDOM OF INFORMATION ACT

The sports information department must educate coaches and other athletics staff members (including administrators and central administrators) about the fact that documents, including e-mail correspondence, are subject to request by the media (Montoro, 2012). This is particularly important at public institutions, although employees at private schools should act under the premise that their words could be read by others, as well. The media can file requests through the Freedom of Information Act, otherwise referred to as the Open Records Act or an Open Records Request, thereby compelling the release of such documents in a timely manner.

Though the request may not be as narrow as securing all e-mails related to the firing of a head coach, the media can request all e-mail correspondence between two designated times, and reporters will then read through the e-mails and convey their findings. As a result, coaches and other members of the athletics department are advised to treat their correspondence as if the general public will read it. Phone records are also commonly requested by the media in order to find patterns of calls or text messages, as well as any communication that is out of the ordinary. For example, the media used the Freedom of Information Act to discover that a former Arkansas head football coach had texted a female reporter 1,000 times during a six-week period (Associated Press, 2007).

PUBLIC RELATIONS CAMPAIGNS

Although the sports information department focuses primarily on media production and relationships with media outlets, it must occasionally mount a public relations campaign (Stoldt, Miller, & Comfort, 2001). Such campaigns are designed to change behavior, affect attitudes, build knowledge, or generate awareness (Mullin, Hardy, & Sutton, 2007). They typically pursue specific short-term goals and are targeted at selected publics (Smith, 2002). For example, Virginia Tech has worked to generate good sporting behavior at events through the Hokies Respect program. Other examples include efforts urging patrons to keep an athletics facility "green" or clean during events or promoting a student-athlete for an award (e.g., the Heisman Trophy or the John Wooden award).

Despite the importance of such campaigns, Stoldt and Narasimhan (2005) have found that sports information directors lack proficiency in adequately measuring or assessing the effectiveness of their publicity efforts. Ballouli and Hutchinson (2010) conclude that many sports information directors view themselves more in the role of providing technical expertise than of providing the managerial expertise necessary for public relations campaigns.

More generally, assessment is a difficult task for many who work in public and media relations, regardless of whether sport is involved (Howard & Mathews, 2000). Website success can be measured in terms of quantifiable metrics, but traditional media may not offer comparable patterns of analytics (Ballouli & Hutchinson, 2010). Consequently, public relations campaigns seek assessments that measure the target audience's changes in attitude or behavior (Howard & Mathews). However, these goals are difficult to gauge and analyze accurately with the limited staffing typically found in sports information departments.

CAREER CONCERNS

Those who work in sports information enjoy the benefits of close involvement with sporting events, coaches, and participants, but there are also downsides. Sports information directors work extensive hours and are always on call for any crisis or emergency. In addition, job promotions can be very difficult to obtain, especially for females, who can be restricted to working with sports other than football and men's basketball. The following sections address these issues in more detail.

Time Obligations

Working in sports information requires a large time commitment. As noted by Maxey Parrish, former SID at Baylor University, SIDS typically "put in stretches of about 100 to 120 days twice a year in which they work seven days a week without a break. That's 60 to 70 hours a week. And time and circumstances make it impossible to please everybody" (qtd. in Schultz, 2005, p. 210). Intercollegiate athletics seasons are traditionally scheduled in conjunction with the academic school year, but the sports information department never has an off-season. As the staff moves from sport to sport, they find little downtime amid the ongoing creation of media guides for upcoming seasons. This is true even during the summer, which is condensed by sporting events that run as late as June (for postseason play) or start in mid-August.

In addition, while in season, teams compete on nights, weekends, and holidays, thus keeping sports information staff members in the office, at events, or traveling with their teams for an extended period of time to produce statistics, media releases, and

video or audio content (Panella, 2012). The need for crisis management responses also ensures that sports information departments are on call 24 hours a day. "No one other than SIDs realizes the amount of time required for the job today. I'm in the office or on the road with the team every day, including Saturdays and Sundays, from August to April," noted Southern Illinois University SID Fred Huff (qtd. in Schultz, 2005, p. 210).

Because of these demands, the College Sports Information Directors of America (CoSIDA) was formed to bring sports information colleagues together to tackle what was a growing morale issue in the industry (Stoldt, 2008). The group's initial strategic plan focused on advances in the profession, including image building, visibility, and of course morale (Stoldt, 2008). John Humenik, executive director of CoSIDA from 2008 to 2013, pushed for the evolution of the sports information department's role from that of "information director" to that of "strategic communication director." This shift promoted the value of sports information in public relations in terms of a broader range of skills, including strategic vision, rather than simply overseeing statistics and producing media releases and media guides (Stoldt, 2008).

Gender

Though many females working in sports information are reluctant to speak about a "glass ceiling," Whiteside and Hardin (2011, 2012b) found that women in this field face career fears related to balancing a family with the large time commitment required by the job. A glass ceiling is an artificial barrier restricting the upward mobility of qualified individuals. For women, the glass ceiling can be maintained by a lack of mentoring, a lack of access to informal networks, an unwelcoming work environment, or misleading stereotypes about ability. In addition, the lack of female senior administrators can be perpetuated by "homologous reproduction," in which male interviewers hire male candidates (Whisenant & Mullane, 2007).

Whiteside and Hardin (2012b) observed that women in sports information internalize the lack of opportunity for advancement in sports information due to the perception that oversight of the traditional revenue sports of men's basketball and football is reserved for men. In fact, Whiteside and

Hardin (2011, 2012b) found that women leave the profession sooner than their male counterparts due to a lack of upward mobility, concerns about family, and the true existence of a glass ceiling. The same pair of researchers (2012a) also indicated the existence of a "friendliness trap," which emphasizes certain skills (e.g., listening, empathy, and teamwork) as helping women begin their careers in sports information, even though such traits are later perceived as unrelated to the desired traits of leadership or power when it comes time for promotion.

In response, Whiteside and Hardin (2011, 2012a,b) stress the importance for younger female sports information staffers of networking with and seeking mentoring from women of greater experience and responsibility. This kind of professional development can help create strong female leaders in sports information, whereas at present only 12 percent of the sports information directors are women (Carpenter & Acosta, 2010).

CURRENT ISSUES

Sports information staffs continue to grow in their responsibilities. As the media evolve, SIDs must account for new media outlets, including websites, bloggers, and social media. Whereas the sports information department once produced and distributed mass quantities of media releases, media guides, and other informative pieces, directors now use online distribution options to keep costs down. They also play a greater role in revenue generation.

Evolution of the Media

There was an era when the news was reported primarily through the morning newspaper and the evening newscast. Today's news is brought to the consumer at a much faster pace. Joe Hernandez, associate athletics director for media and alumni relations at Ball State University, observes that "media demands have changed dramatically. With the advent of the fax machine, e-mail, and the Internet, the world wants news faster and faster. The technology has caused more and more media outlets to arise and require information" (qtd. in Schultz, 2005, p. 210).

Indeed, in the 24-7 news cycle, media outlets demand immediate attention and assistance (Stoldt, 2000). This new reality includes the use of Twitter by the media to promote breaking news before a complete story is written (Schultz & Sheffer, 2010). In addition, websites overseen by traditional outlets must compete with team-specific fan sites, thus affecting the revenue streams gained through advertising and subscriptions (Butler & Sagas, 2008). Even the profiles of message board users are broken down by demographics for the benefit of online advertisers interested in details about factors such as gender, race, age, and income (Clavio, 2008).

The commercial nature of the media also affects the framing of information. According to Bobby Parker, associate athletics director for communication at Bradley University, "the growth of sports talk radio and the Internet have created a more negative approach to coverage. The Internet has provided another avenue for the media to get information, but it's not always reliable" (qtd. in Schultz, 2005, p. 210). This environment leads to increasing concern about credibility and accuracy and makes it difficult to police the information available to the general public (Andrews, 2005). When errors do occur, Howard and Mathews (2000) suggest the following steps for rectifying the situation.

1. Acknowledge the difference between what is incorrect and what you don't *like* about the story.

2. In most cases, be charitable and do nothing.

3. In some cases, contact the reporter to request that the item be corrected for the record.

4. In a few cases, write a letter to the editor.

5. In rare cases, ask the publication to print a correction.

6. In no case contact a competing media outlet to tell them of the incident and ask them to set the record straight.

7. If the error is critical, post the correction on your website.

Many sports information departments have embraced proactive approaches to solving the problem of inaccurate reporting (Ruihley & Fall, 2009). In this area of sports information, the athletics department's website is an even more important tool than usual for the athletics department to convey its message to the public. One great example of this proactive approach occurred at

Leadership Lesson

Negotiation

Revenue generated from media contracts serves as the lifeblood of many intercollegiate athletics departments. As a result, the negotiation of these contracts has become vitally important. The need for negotiation skills also extends into nearly every facet of an administrator's duties—from day one as a prospective employee, to the annual budgeting cycle, to the allocation of facility space and practice time between antagonistic coaches, to multi-million-dollar facility naming and sponsorship opportunities. In each of these situations, a savvy administrator can break out his or her negotiation toolkit and approach the communication with confidence and excitement.

Excitement? Absolutely. Each of these situations requires give and take, the understanding of moving parts, the ability to put together pieces of a puzzle, and the skill of uncovering value that can invigorate each person at the table. These moments can get your adrenaline pumping and simulate in your own work the game-day experience that you are trying to facilitate for your athletes. There is, however, one tremendous difference. Generally, the negotiation process should not be viewed as a competitive sport. Rather, it is helpful to view both parties as being on the same team and working toward a "win-win" result.

In the chapter 5 leadership lesson, "Interdependence and the Win-Win Paradigm," we discussed the win-win frame of mind, which is "based on the paradigm that there is plenty for everybody, that one person's success is not achieved at the expense or exclusion of the success of others" (Covey, 2004, p. 207). In other words, rather than dividing a fixed pie, both parties expand the pie through integrative synergy. This win-win mentality is very different from the common image of hard-nosed bargaining sessions in which parties threaten to walk away, try to take advantage of each other, exaggerate concessions, and attempt to squeeze every ounce of value for themselves out of the negotiation. This "distributive

approach," in which each party battles for the largest possible piece of a fixed pie, can be appropriate in situations where you will never work with the other party, but it is generally not appropriate in most ongoing working relationships.

This is not to say that you don't try to maximize satisfaction of your interests. You certainly do; but you do so with an awareness of the context and the interests of both parties. Before beginning a negotiation, then, there is a tremendous amount of work to be done. As you prepare for and begin each phase of a negotiation, strive to do so with the vision framework discussed in chapter 4. Begin with the end in mind. The following steps will help you enter any negotiation full of confidence.

1. Recognize the type of issue involved. There are three types, and each calls for its own strategies.

   a. Distributive—This is the typical "divide the fixed pie" situation. A fixed amount of resources is equally valued by both parties, and a gain for one party is viewed as a loss for the other. The best strategy in this situation is to get as much information as possible from the other party while limiting what you share. Be willing to make concessions for a realistic outcome.

   b. Integrative—There is a fixed amount of resources, but the issue is differently valued by the parties. Something might be very important to one party but minimally important to the other. Seek to maximize integrative issues for both parties. The only way to understand these preferences is through honest information sharing in an effort to "expand the pie."

   c. Compatible—Both parties want the same outcome. Emphasize this mutual commonality.

(continued)

LEADERSHIP LESSON *(continued)*

2. Research the issue itself. When you arm yourself with data, you bring additional power to the negotiation. If, for example, you have done a competitive analysis, know the standard industry rates, possess relevant testimonials, and are equipped with pro-forma budgets for a set of possible scenarios, the person who is negotiating with you is also negotiating with the data (and associated experts) that you bring to the table.

3. Define *your* interests. Prioritize your interests related to the issues that will be discussed. Define your negotiating zone and set points where accepting an impasse will be the best outcome for both parties (win-win or no deal). One way to do so is by understanding your BATNA—an acronym for "best alternative to a negotiated agreement" (Fisher & Ury, 2011). The BATNA is a predetermined alternative action that will be taken if your interests are not met in the negotiation. A strong BATNA (e.g., an alternative partner, offer, product, or employer) can empower you as a negotiator.

4. Research *their* interests. The more you understand the driving factors behind the other party's interests, the more creative you can be in approaching the issues. Ask questions, seek alternatives, and research past negotiations and possible options that the other party could bring to the table in order to recommend trade-offs.

5. Focus on interests rather than positions. Asking "why" can reveal the underlying interests behind positions. Finding out the motives behind stated positions can bring information to the table that facilitates integrative win-win outcomes.

Completing a tough, multiround negotiation can be tremendously rewarding. When two parties come together armed with preparation and an understanding that compromise is not the *desired* outcome, it is possible to create tremendous synergistic value. This type of negotiation involves both parties seeking to maximize integrative interests, identify and highlight compatible issues, compromise on distributive issues, and dig deep to find alternative solutions.

Unfortunately, this often does not happen. As you may have noticed, the tactics for maximizing value on distributive issues are contrary to the tactics for maximizing value on integrative issues. This contradiction can foster negotiation approaches with minimal information sharing, minimal understanding of interests, and maximal likelihood of an impasse. If one party shares information with a "value creator" mind-set, and the other approaches the discussion with a "value claimer" mind-set, the claimer will likely crush the creator, as the claimer can use the information shared by the creator to their advantage while concealing their own interests. The long-term consequences of the "claimer" approach, however, include a lack of trust and merely average future outcomes as both parties withhold information.

Other Resources

Cialdini, R.B. (2006). *Influence: The psychology of persuasion.* New York: HarperBusiness.

Fisher, R., & Ury, W. (1983). *Getting to yes: Negotiating agreement without giving in.* New York: Penguin Books.

Louisiana State University, where fans could use a feature called Cyberchat with Skip to interact with Skip Berman, who served as the school's athletic director from 2001 to 2008 before stepping into an emeritus role. Similarly, Old Dominion University's director of athletics promotes upcoming events and posts illustrations and explanations of facility construction plans preemptively in order to address potentially contentious issues. Such approaches illustrate the evolution of sports information's role from information provider to strategic adviser, and duties will continue to change as new issues and media emerge (Ruihley & Fall).

Cost Containment and Green Effect

Technological advances such as websites and e-mail can also be used to contain costs. Whereas media guides, releases, and game notes used to be produced in mass quantities and then faxed or mailed to the media, they can be distributed today in non-print form, thereby reducing cost and supporting an eco-friendly approach (Benko, 2012).

Revenue Generation

In addition to publicizing the athletics department, the sports information department plays a vital role in revenue generation for athletics. Specifically, sports information staff can enhance vital revenue streams in the following ways:

- Producing game-day programs sold at sporting events
- Providing subscription-based services on the athletics department website
- Displaying backdrops at interviews and media conferences that exhibit athletics department sponsors' names and logos (Andrews, 2005)
- Working with the media at sporting events to determine awards affiliated with sponsor recognition (Andrews, 2005)—for example, the Dairy Queen MVP of the game, the Chili's student-athlete of the week, or any other similar award voted on by members of the media

Game-Day Blogging

With the advent of sizable financial radio and television deals, sports information directors must balance what is contractually obligated to their media partners with requests from other media outlets looking to provide information rapidly to their consumers. Whether it is the Big Ten Network, a national ESPN contract, or a regional radio contract, television and radio outlets pay a rights fee for the opportunity to broadcast an event and deliver related information first to their viewers and listeners (Andrews, 2005). At the same time, their media rivals, including websites from traditional media and team-specific sites, seek to provide comparable details about the event via Twitter, blogging, live stats, or video and audio content, thus ambushing the priority rights afforded through the media deal (Butler & Sagas, 2008; Schultz & Sheffer, 2010).

COLLEGE SPORTS INFORMATION DIRECTORS OF AMERICA (COSIDA)

As previously mentioned, CoSIDA is the preeminent organization for people working in sports information. Originally part of the American College Public Relations Association, the organization provides its members with a strategic focus on the sports information niche. The association holds an annual conference that allows members to network and engage in professional development. Attendees can learn about cutting-edge issues in intercollegiate athletics through educational sessions about current events in the industry, such as the monitoring of social media or the media's growth and evolution. The organization also advocates for advancement in such areas as efficiency, effective organization, and proactive approaches to the field (Stoldt, 2008).

CoSIDA links colleagues regardless of school or conference affiliation, ranging from schools in the National Association of Intercollegiate Athletics to NCAA Football Bowl Subdivision schools. It facilitates education and connection of peers through committees and councils that work on solutions, proposals, and recommendations about key issues (Stoldt, 2008). The group's signature program is the annual awarding of Academic All-American honors. CoSIDA offers student memberships for those interested in starting their professional affiliation early.

Students in communication, journalism, public relations, and comparable majors can also join the Public Relations Student Society of America (PRSSA). Doing so is a way to engage in further professional development that is advantageous to persons interested in a career in sports information. Membership provides access to networking opportunities, strategic career plans, internship and job boards, competitions, and a national convention. You can visit the organization's website at www.prssa.org.

CONCLUSION

Sports information is a time-intensive field that requires a committed effort to help the athletics department communicate concertedly and informatively through the commercial mass media and other avenues, including social media and the department's own website. The flow of information stems from interviews with administrators, coaches, and student-athletes, as well as the production and distribution of various pieces such as media releases, media guides, and game notes. Sports information directors must balance the needs and deadlines of the media with fostering publicity for women's athletics and Olympic sports that frequently lack media coverage. Media training and crisis management planning can greatly help athletics departments striving to maintain a strong reputation and credibility with various stakeholders. Those who work in sports information must continue to adapt to the evolution of media, including social media and the web.

DISCUSSION QUESTIONS

1. As the sports information director for a small athletics administrative staff, you are charged by the new athletics director with generating publicity for your small Division I school, which is not competitive on the playing field. What strategies would you implement? How would your strategies differ at a Division II or Division III school?

2. After a competitive sporting event that ended in a controversial loss, you as the sports information director find that the mandatory cool-down period has not helped the team or the head coach. Would you let the student-athletes and the coach visit with the media? Defend your decision.

3. A star player is arrested in his or her hometown during the off-season. Local media in that area try to contact the student-athlete and family members for quotes. The media are not privy to or cognizant of the school's media policy, and time is of the essence. As sports information director, what would you do?

4. A controversial website continues to report inaccurate stories and headlines that create negative publicity about your institution. Though you know the stories to be false, the website producers are excited about the growing popularity of their online content, especially with your fan base. How would you address this issue?

5. A student-athlete decides to transfer and takes to social media to bash the school, the athletics department, the coaches, and teammates. What steps do you take to control the damage?

LEARNING ACTIVITIES

1. Create a "hot-seat" class exercise. Identify one student to be the athletic director and one to be the sports information director. The rest of the class acts as members of the media in a press conference. The instructor should explore national media outlets, pick a current event in intercollegiate athletics, and share it with the class. With the students playing their roles, see if the athletics director is properly prepared by the sports information director to navigate the questions that stem from the mock press conference. Repeat the exercise with new students assuming the roles of the SID and AD.

2. Imagine that you approach your athletics director with the recommendation that he or she make a monthly post on the website to educate fans. The athletics director, however, is not a big proponent of technology. You want to share examples of this practice becoming more common. Students should examine Division I athletics websites to see which institutions use their website to enable the athletic director to personally communicate with fans. Students can also identify common themes in their online postings. Using their findings, students can discuss how best to educate an athletic director who is reluctant to embrace technology.

3. At a senior staff meeting, the director of athletics asks for a discussion regarding making certain portions of the athletics website subscription based. Students should examine Division I athletics websites to see which institutions offer subscription-based content to their followers. The students can also identify what type of content requires a subscription and the rates charged for such content.

CHAPTER 7

Financial Operations

Stephen L. Shapiro, Old Dominion University

Brendan Dwyer, Virginia Commonwealth University

In this chapter, you will explore

- the current financial environment in college athletics, including trends in media rights revenue, conference realignment, and the growing financial disparity between athletics programs;

- the unique nature of financial operations in college sport, including its operating structure within higher education, the nonprofit status of college sport, and the tiered financial structure of the NCAA, conferences, and individual athletics departments; and

- general financial knowledge and skills in the context of college athletics, including financial operations, financial statements, planning, and budgeting.

THE CHALLENGE OF BALANCING AN ATHLETICS BUDGET

The athletics program at a Football Bowl Subdivision (FBS) school has just completed its annual budget review. Meanwhile, with a new fiscal year approaching, word is spreading across campus that the state legislature, which has a budgetary shortfall, has pulled back a considerable portion of university funding. In an effort to make up for the expected cut in state funding, the university president has chosen to take back US$750,000 allocated to athletics through student fees—amounting to 5 percent of the total athletics budget—in order to redistribute it across the university. The cut comes at a time when the athletics department is already operating at a slight deficit. In response, the athletics director (AD) faces the challenge of balancing the budget by properly managing financial operations and making decisions that could lead either to additional revenue generation or to budget cuts.

From humble beginnings as an extracurricular activity for college students in the mid to late nineteenth century, college athletics has grown into a tiered business operation with an industry value estimated at well above US$40 billion. More than a thousand member institutions compete in the National Collegiate Athletic Association (NCAA) alone ("About the NCAA," 2012), and hundreds of additional programs compete in other associations, such as the National Association of Intercollegiate Athletics (NAIA) and the National Junior College Athletic Association (NJCAA). The large numbers of participants, coaches, administrators, officials, and spectators mean that substantial economic activity is developed through the operation of college athletics. This chapter provides an overview of financial operations in college athletics departments, as well as an overview of issues associated with the current financial landscape in this environment.

A glimpse into the revenues and expenses of the most visible athletics departments in the NCAA's Football Bowl Subdivision provides insight into the finances at play in this industry. This financial information is available from such sources as the NCAA Division I Revenues and Expenses Report (Fulks, 2012), the Equity in Athletics Disclosure Act annual report, and the USA Today college athletics finances database ("USA Today Sports," 2012). Median revenue for Football Bowl Subdivision institutions in 2012 totaled US$52.7 million, which constituted a 9.1 percent increase from 2010 and an 86.8 percent increase from 2004 (Fulks).

In terms of individual athletics departments, the University of Texas tops the revenue chart, generating nearly US$150.3 million in 2010–2011, and eight other programs also generated more than US$100 million ("Texas' $150 million," 2012). At some institutions, the revenue growth has been staggering. For example, between 2006 and 2011, the University of Oregon and the University of Louisville have seen revenue growth of 89.9 percent and 69.7 percent, respectively. Growth in college sport appears to be an ongoing trend.

However, the substantial growth at the highest level of competition presents a very slanted view of the industry as a whole. In fact, the vast majority of athletics programs struggle financially. Only 23 FBS institutions reported a surplus in 2012, which represents only 19.2 percent of FBS programs and 9.5 percent of all programs competing in Division I football (Fulks, 2012). Most Division I programs operate at a deficit, with a median loss of approximately US$12.1 million in FBS competition and US$5.9 million in Football Championship Subdivision (FCS) competition.

In addition, the disparity continues to grow between the haves and the have-nots, and the gap currently stands at about US$21 million between financially successful programs and others (Fulks, 2012). For example, while the University of Texas, generated over US$150 million in 2011, the University of North Texas (another public institution competing at the FBS level) generated just US$11.2 million ("USA Today Sports," 2012). Table 7.1 lists the highest- and lowest-revenue-generating programs at the FBS level.

In the scenario described at the start of the chapter, then, the athletics director faces funding cuts that are not uncommon in today's college athletics environment. Many athletics departments operate at a deficit while attempting to compete with the small percentage of programs that enjoy significantly more resources.

FINANCIAL DISTINCTIVENESS OF INTERCOLLEGIATE ATHLETICS

The disparity in athletics department budgets results from a number of factors, including revenue generation opportunities, conference realignment, the need for resources to remain competitive, and the current economic climate in higher education. These factors create a complex financial environment in college athletics, in which athletics programs have to maneuver through financial challenges to remain competitive on the field and fiscally sound off the field. These factors are addressed in some detail in the following sections.

Television Broadcasting Deals

Although disparity in financial resources has existed in college athletics for decades, the gap between the haves and the have-nots has escalated in recent years, largely due to television broadcasting deals. Broadcasting contracts for the five major FBS conferences—the Southeastern Conference, the Atlantic Coast Conference, the Big Ten, the Pac 12, the Big 12, and the Big East—range from US$200 million to US$3.6 billion. Contract lengths range from 6 to 25 years, and annual per-school payouts run from US$15 million to US$28 million (Dosh, 2012a).

Trends indicate that these numbers will continue to increase in the foreseeable future, because negotiating windows exist within all of these contracts, and schools continue to change conferences to position themselves for greater financial reward. In fact, the considerable conference realignment in recent years has been attributed largely to the desire to maximize revenue from broadcasting rights. Major conferences can command more revenue in these contracts by increasing their number of member

Table 7.1 Athletics Department Revenue at NCAA Division I Public Institutions (2011)

Institution	Conference	Total revenue in US$	Allocated %	Profit (loss) in US$
HIGHEST REVENUE				
1. University of Texas	Big 12	150,295,926	0	16,609,111
2. Ohio State University	Big Ten	131,815,821	0	9,528,952
3. University of Alabama	SEC	124,498,616	4.2	19,430,464
4. University of Florida	SEC	123,514,257	3.5	16,356,426
5. University of Michigan	Big Ten	122,739,052	0.2	10,894,499
LOWEST REVENUE				
1. Chicago State University	Great West	5,033,060	84.5	(163,486)
2. Alcorn State University	SWAC	5,995,743	69.4	418,812
3. Alabama A&M University	SWAC	6,003,172	75.2	(997,411)
4. Grambling State University	SWAC	6,212,914	46.5	0
5. Indiana University-Purdue University Indianapolis	Summit	6,495,982	88.5	23,757

Notes: Allocated % indicates percentage of revenue generated through institutional allocations in the form of student fees. SEC indicates Southeastern Conference. SWAC indicates Southwestern Athletic Conference.

From "USA Today sports' college athletics finances," 2012, USA Today. Available: http://usatoday30.usatoday.com/sports/college/story/2012-05-14/ncaa-college-athletics-finances-database/54955804/1.

institutions, and individual schools are willing to change conferences in order to stake their claim to guaranteed annual payouts from television deals (Thamel, 2011).

Conference realignment has also added a new financial layer for conferences and member institutions in the form of the exit fee. In response to the movement by programs, conferences have increased their exit fees to deter schools from leaving. The Big 12 levies an exit fee equal to one year's worth of conference revenue. The Atlantic Coast Conference (ACC) recently voted to change its exit fee from US$20 million to US$50 million in an effort to deter members from leaving (Smith, 2012). Perhaps in the future, these fees will be too high for athletics departments to afford, and realignment will come to a halt. In the meantime, the athletics director in the chapter-opening scenario could consider a conference move if other, more lucrative conferences have an interest. The additional revenue could go a long way toward making up the department's 5 percent budget cut.

> *Our TV revenue overnight is going to jump from $2.8 million to about $20 million. That's enabled us to invest in facilities and hire a coach like Mike Leach and his staff. Once the Pac-12 networks are going strong, institutions are going to see another $10 million-plus per year.*
>
> Bill Moos, athletics director, Washington State University (Smith, 2012).

Arms Race

The race to compete for conference and national championships has never been more competitive. Even though Texas and North Texas have vastly different resources, they compete in the same NCAA category, illustrating the fact that many institutions in smaller conferences feel pressure to compete with financially larger programs. Areas of competition include building and renovating facilities, expanding recruiting budgets, acquiring top-of-the-line equipment, and hiring the best coaches. All of these strategies lead to significant debt service, and smaller institutions do not have the capacity to take on such debt.

In 2010, Hofstra University dropped its football program, citing a lack of funding. Cutting the program saved the institution an annual total of US$4.5 million (Armstrong, 2009). However, program cuts are not limited to smaller Division I programs.

Recently, the University of Maryland eliminated eight sports to account for a US$4 million deficit that was growing annually (Gerstner, 2012). The race to compete creates a spending frenzy, further separating the haves from the have-nots in college sport. Table 7.2 lists sample program spending for both large and small institutions.

Current Economic Climate in Higher Education

The U.S. recession of 2008 has had a major effect on higher education, including cuts in state funding for public colleges and universities. According to Mincer (2012), state funding was approximately US$6,200 per student on average in 2012 compared with US$8,000 in 1986. For larger athletics programs, these cuts may not have a direct impact, because many of these athletics departments receive limited state funding. However, the majority of Division I and lower-division institutions rely heavily on allocated revenues from the university. These programs are affected greatly by funding cuts to higher education, which increases the gap between large programs and their smaller competitors.

ORGANIZATIONAL STRUCTURE WITHIN INTERCOLLEGIATE ATHLETICS

The organizational structure of intercollegiate athletics is unique as compared with those of its counterparts in professional and amateur sport. The primary point of distinction is that college athletics departments operate within the bureaucratic structure of higher education. For the most part, this setup is unique to U.S. sport, because higher education and sport are not connected directly in most of the world. This approach means that the mission of college sport in the United States should be driven by the overall academic mission of

Table 7.2 Athletics Department Expenses at NCAA Division I Public Institutions (2011)

Institution	Conference	Total expenses in US$	Allocated %	Profit (loss) in US$
HIGHEST EXPENSES (BCS INSTITUTIONS)				
1. University of Texas	Big 12	133,686,815	0	16,609,111
2. Ohio State University	Big Ten	122,286,869	0	9,528,952
3. University of Michigan	Big Ten	111,844,553	0.2	10,894,499
4. University of Florida	SEC	107,157,831	3.5	16,356,426
5. University of Alabama	SEC	105,068,152	4.2	19,430,464
HIGHEST EXPENSES (NON-BCS INSTITUTIONS)				
1. University of Nevada, Las Vegas	MW	60,555,156	54.2	(1,010,287)
2. University of Central Florida	C-USA	42,806,123	50.9	(43,498)
3. University of New Mexico	MW	40,428,116	41.2	(141,008)
4. University of Memphis	AAU	40,307,245	37.6	77,020
4. U.S. Air Force Academy	MW	39,430,241	64.6	393,541

Note: Allocated % indicates percentage of revenue generated through institutional allocations in the form of student fees. C-USA indicates Conference USA. MW indicates Mountain West Conference. SEC indicates Southeastern Conference.

From "USA Today sports' college athletics finances," 2012, *USA Today*. Available: http://usatoday30.usatoday.com/sports/college/story/2012-05-14/ncaa-college-athletics-finances-database/54955804/1.

colleges and universities. This purported focus has been an overarching issue throughout the history of U.S. college sport, and it affects financial operations through public funding, student fees, and the ability of athletics departments to raise capital.

The NCAA is a governing body controlled by a portion of member institution presidents. Therefore, the president of the NCAA has no direct control over decisions about regulations, conference alignments, the media rights of conferences or individual programs, or other organizational components that affect athletics department finances. In addition, the NCAA, its member conferences, and individual institutions all operate as nonprofit organizations. Nonprofit status affords these organizations tax exemption and the ability to generate revenue through charitable contributions. The nonprofit status of college sport is discussed in more detail later in the chapter.

Revenue Theory of Cost

The organizational and legal structure of college sport as a nonprofit endeavor under the umbrella

of higher education has considerable effects on the financial operation of the industry. The continuing trend of expenditures increasing at a similar rate to revenues is not uncommon in a nonprofit setting. By their very nature, nonprofit organizations must spend all the revenue they generate. This phenomenon is the foundation of Bowen's (1980) revenue theory of cost, which states that in a nonprofit setting, expenditure increases are a direct result of increased revenue that must be spent by the organization in order to avoid a significant surplus. Martin (2009) refers to this spending environment as the revenue-to-cost spiral.

Bowen (1970, 1980) articulated five laws to explain cost in higher education (see figure 7.1). The primary goals of institutions are educational excellence, prestige, and influence. In the quest to achieve these goals, there is no limit on what an institution will spend. There are never "enough" resources. Since current resources are never acceptable, institutions always attempt to increase revenue and subsequently spend all that they raise. Following these laws leads to a consistent

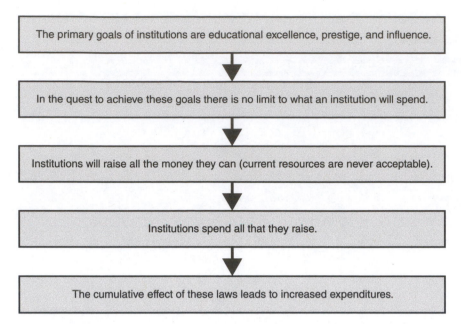

Figure 7.1 Bowen's revenue theory of cost cost—five "cost laws."

Reprinted from H.R. Bowen, 1980, *The costs of higher education* (San Francisco: Jossey-Bass).

increase in expenditures. Limits are not set in this environment because there is no determination of the minimal amount needed to run a high-quality college or university. Therefore, a cycle is created wherein revenue increases are the source of increases in expenditures.

College athletics departments are unique segments of higher education, yet they operate in a similar environment. Due to their nonprofit nature, they must spend all of their revenue in a given year. Although the revenue theory of cost and the revenue-to-cost spiral concepts were not developed for college athletics, they provide a framework for understanding financial decisions made by athletics departments (Suggs, 2009). The primary goals for college athletics programs are success, prestige, influence, and, ultimately, a positive reputation. In pursuit of these goals, athletics departments will exhaust all resources, which is evident in the vast number of programs losing money (Fulks, 2012). In addition, there is no limit on the amount of revenue that athletics departments will attempt to generate, and any revenue generated by the departments is spent. Finally, this behavior is cyclical in college sport, which provides a continued motivation to win and garner a positive national reputation.

Thus Bowen's (1970, 1980) revenue theory of cost should be considered throughout this chapter as we dissect financial operations and decision making in intercollegiate athletics. This theory plays out in a considerable number of athletics departments. In the chapter-opening scenario, the athletics director is already operating at a deficit due to the cyclical nature of spending in college sport. This situation becomes a challenge as generating additional revenue almost certainly leads to additional expenses, thus leaving the athletics department again with a similar deficit.

Sport Sponsorship

Another distinctive factor in college athletics is the operation of multiple sport programs under one umbrella, most of which generate limited or no revenue. For the vast majority of athletics departments, no programs are profitable, and in a select few departments one or two programs are profitable. These profitable sports are generally football and men's basketball. The revenue generated from these two sports often subsidizes the other sports in the department. Division I institutions must offer at least 14 sports (and Division II and Division III institutions must offer at least 10 and 5 sports, respectively), which adds to the department's overall operational costs ("Differences Among," 2012).

From an economic perspective, it is not logical to continue to fund programs that are not self-sufficient, let alone to use revenue from profitable programs to subsidize programs that lose money. However, this is the unique nature of present-day college sport, and athletics departments must work successfully in this environment.

Title IX

The groundbreaking federal legislation known as Title IX of the Education Amendments of 1972 has had a tremendous effect in providing opportunities for women in sport by mandating equal opportunity based on sex in all federally funded educational settings. Since its inception in 1972, participation rates for women in college sport have increased by 545 percent (Gregoire & Kohl-Welles, 2012). Some would argue that this legislation has also created financial challenges for athletics departments. This argument is based on the financial reality that programs face if they have not demonstrated equality in opportunity and treatment. As discussed in chapter 4, if one sex is provided with greater facilities or opportunities, this federal law stipulates equality. As a result, many departments face financial challenges associated with equalizing their overall treatment of male and female athletes when discrepancies are evident.

Many facets of present-day college sport make it a unique and challenging environment from a financial operations perspective. The following section provides detail about financial structure and operations and how these components of finance in college sport can be used to navigate this distinct environment.

FINANCIAL CONFIGURATION

For-profit and nonprofit organizations are structured differently, and this difference affects both revenue generation and costs. When dealing with financial components of college athletics, therefore, we must understand the structure of nonprofit organizations and how it affects financial decisions.

Nonprofit Status

Every sport organization has a business structure that influences operations from both a legal and a financial standpoint. Business structure dictates taxes, sources of funding, and personal and organizational liability. The NCAA, NAIA, NJCAA, and their respective member conferences and institutions all operate as nonprofit entities. Nonprofit organizations are established for charitable or educational purposes (Reider, 2001). In the case of college sport, organizations are a function of higher education, which affords them nonprofit status.

Nonprofits are driven by a civic cause to provide services to the community. Therefore, their organizational structure differs from that of a profit-seeking organization. Due to this social mission of providing for the community, the legal structure of nonprofits provides these organizations with specific benefits, including tax exemption, the ability to receive charitable contributions, lower prices and fees, and indemnification in certain situations for management (Bryce, 2000). These benefits make nonprofits distinct from for-profit organizations that have to deal with issues such as taxes and liability, which can play a significant role in the financial success of a business.

Tax Exemption and Legal Status

One of the main advantages enjoyed by nonprofit organizations is the ability to maintain a tax-exempt status, because taxes constitute one of the largest expenses for commercial organizations (Besley & Brigham, 2006). Colleges and universities (and affiliated departments and associations) operate under section 501(c)(3) of the U.S. Internal Revenue Code, which provides exemption for educational organizations. According to the Internal Revenue Service (IRS), organizations that meet the requirements of 501(c)(3) are exempt from federal income taxes, and donors who make charitable contributions to these organizations can receive a tax deduction (Internal Revenue Service, 2011). In order to receive exemption under 501(c)(3), an organization must meet two criteria. First, it must be established as a state-law nonprofit organization with a mission and goals that are charity focused (Columbo, 2010). Second, it must operate as a charitable entity, with the majority of its activities serving a charitable cause, while limiting resources spent on noncharitable purposes (e.g., lobbying or excessive employee compensation) (Columbo).

This second requirement has been a point of contention in college athletics due to some areas of substantial cash flow in major college athletics departments related to sports such as football and men's basketball. According to Columbo (2010), the NCAA should fall into a category of its own, with certain components of operations having tax-exempt status and other operations being taxed under the unrelated business income tax (UBIT). This has been a point of debate because the NCAA and member institutions are provided with significant financial incentives through tax exemption. For example, if the University of Texas' change in net assets for 2011 (US$16.6 million) were subject to UBIT rates, which is the corporate tax rate of 35 percent, its tax expense would be approximately US$5.8 million.

Charitable Contributions

Not only does 501(c)(3) allow for tax exemption, which is one of the main organizational expenses. It also provides for a tax deduction for charitable contributions to the organization, which attracts many individuals and corporations looking to make donations. Fundraising is a key revenue source for nonprofits, so 501(c)(3) status is extremely valuable.

In 2012 college athletics programs, charitable contributions accounted for 25 percent of generated revenues at NCAA Division I FBS institutions and 28 percent at Division I FCS programs (Fulks, 2012). These substantial revenues highlight the significance of fundraising—and the importance of 501(c)(3) status—in college sport. In 2011, the University of Florida generated more than US$41 million in charitable contributions, which amounted to 34 percent of its total athletics department revenue. This benefit is not exclusive to major athletics programs; for example, Wichita State University's athletics program raised more than US$6.2 million, which represented 29.8 percent of its revenue ("USA Today Sports'," 2012).

From a financial perspective, then, fundraising is an athletics department priority, particularly in times of slow economic growth (Steinbach, 2012). In this environment, donations can increase or decrease based on the performance of major programs. For example, Arizona State University estimated a seven-figure loss in charitable contributions due to the poor performance of the football team during the 2011 season (Steinbach).

When an athletics department relies heavily on fundraising, as most do, such shifts can have drastic effects on financial operations. Unlike ticket sales, where seating capacity limits sales, there is, at least in theory, no limit on the amount of revenue that can be generated through fundraising. There is also, however, no guarantee of consistent annual contributions. Development and the intricacies of athletics department fundraising are discussed in more detail in chapter 11.

In situations where additional revenue needs to be generated rather quickly, such as in the chapter-opening scenario we have discussed here, raising funds through additional contributions is a common strategy. In fact, many institutions use charitable contributions to directly fund the hiring of coaches or the building or renovation of facilities. In the scenario, this strategy could be used to overcome the substantial deficit created by the cut in allocated revenue.

Tiered Structure

College athletics operates according to a tiered structure in which an overarching association governs member institutions housed in conferences. The largest college sport association is the NCAA, which includes 1,066 active member schools, 340 of which are in Division I, 290 in Division II, and 436 in Division III ("About the NCAA," 2012). Other associations include the National Association of Intercollegiate Athletics (NAIA) and the National Junior College Athletic Association (NJCAA); however, this section will only discuss the NCAA. In terms of financial operations, the relationships between the NCAA, the conferences, and individual athletics programs can be complex. Some revenues and expenses are distributed from the association, through the conferences, to the programs. However, other revenues and expenses start at the level of conference or individual program and are not associated with the NCAA. The following sections provide an overview of each tier.

NCAA

The NCAA is a large nonprofit entity whose 2011 assets totaled more than US$607 million. Total revenues during the 2011–2012 fiscal year was $871.6 million. As shown in the NCAA revenue breakdown in chapter 2, 81 percent of association revenue is generated through television and marketing rights—specifically, through the agreement with Turner/CBS Sports to broadcast the men's Division I basketball tournament. This broadcasting deal is worth US$10.8 billion over 14 years. Projected NCAA revenue for 2012–2013 was US$797 million, with US$702 million coming from the broadcasting deal ("Revenues," 2014).

The majority of NCAA revenue is distributed back to member institutions. As shown, again, in the breakdown of NCAA expenses presented in chapter 2, more than 60 percent of revenue is distributed to Division I members, and 17 percent is used to run programs and championships at all levels. These distributions accounted for more than US$137 million in 2012 ("Expenses," 2013).

As shown in the breakdown of Division I revenue distribution in the Governing Bodies chapter, in 2012 US$202 million was distributed through the basketball fund, which rewards long-term performance in the men's basketball tournament. Another US$134.7 million was distributed through the grant-in-aid fund, which provides more funding to schools with the most scholarship funding to student-athletes ("Distributions," 2013). The NCAA also distributes revenue based on the number of sports sponsored and the academic performance of student-athletes. Additional funding is provided for student-athletes with special financial needs.

Conferences

The majority of revenue generated by the NCAA is funneled down to conferences to be distributed to member institutions. Conferences have the authority to decide how this revenue will be distributed, and the approach varies from conference to conference. For example, the Pac-12 uses a multilevel financial distribution strategy (Pac 12 2012–2013 Handbook, 2012). All media rights and football conference championship revenue is distributed equally among the 12 member institutions. However, for football bowl games and preseason classic basketball games, participating teams receive an additional portion of revenue to cover team transportation and unsold bowl tickets. For all other sports, championship revenue is distributed based on NCAA guidelines or detailed conference bylaws limiting expenses and in some cases requiring reimbursement applications (Pac 12 2012–2013 Handbook). A share of revenue is also kept by the conference office for general operations, marketing and advertising, and conference championship operations.

The Pac 12 Conference also follows a distribution plan related to licensing royalties involving the use of the conference logo or individual institution logos. Royalties generally amount to 14 percent of sales (12 percent for the institution and 2 percent for the conference office). Finally, the Pac 12 maintains a reserve fund of US$500,000 for situations resulting in lost conference revenue (Pac 12 2012–2013 Handbook, 2012). In general, the goal of conference distributions is to provide revenue to each member school in order to strengthen competitiveness at all schools. This system promotes success throughout the conference. Therefore, a conference that occupies a strong financial position allows member schools to have the resources to pursue championships, which increases conference revenue for future years.

Financial distributions vary significantly in smaller conferences. All conferences receive similar distributions from the NCAA (varying based on sports sponsored and post-season appearances), but compared with major conferences, mid-major and small conferences do not receive significant media rights revenue to share. Most of the revenue they do receive through smaller media rights deals is split equally among member institutions, and some additional revenue is given to institutions with programs that compete in postseason play.

Athletics Departments

Although athletics departments rely on revenue distributions from the NCAA and conferences, these funds are not the most significant sources of revenue. Most athletics department revenue is generated through the athletics department or institution itself (as discussed in detail later in this chapter). For FBS programs, the median revenue distribution to athletics departments in 2011 was US$8,386,000, or 15.9 percent of total revenue. At the FCS level, these distributions are considerably smaller. In 2011, the median distribution for FCS programs was US$661,000, or 4.9 percent of total revenue (Fulks, 2012).

Table 7.3 provides a summary budget for the University of Michigan athletics department. In fiscal year 2011–2012, Michigan received just

Table 7.3 University of Michigan Athletics Department Summary Budget (2011–2012) and Projections (2012–2013)

REVENUE SUMMARY		
	2011–2012 budget in US$	2012–2013 projection in US$
Spectator admissions	45,588,000	44,051,000
Conference distributions	21,948,000	23,283,000
Preferred seating and other contributions	26,153,000	27,416,000
Corporate sponsorship	14,328,000	15,050,000
Facility revenues	1,825,000	6,847,000
Licensing royalties	4,774,000	5,650,000
Other revenue	6,602,000	8,025,000
Total revenue	121,218,000	130,322,000
EXPENSE SUMMARY		
	2011–2012 budget in US$	2012–2013 projection in US$
Salaries, wages, and benefits	39,205,000	44,235,000
Financial aid to students	17,293,000	18,348,000
Team and game expenses	18,109,000	19,053,000
Facility expenses	9,834,000	10,620,000
Deferred maintenance fund transfer	4,500,000	4,500,000
Other operational and administrative expenses	7,674,000	13,073,000
Debt service transfer to plant fund	13,220,000	14,688,000
Total expenses	109,835,000	124,517,000

Data from "UM regents briefed on athletic budget," *Ann Arbor Chronicle* June 21, 2012.

under US$22 million in conference distributions, which amounted to 18.1 percent of its total athletics revenue. The majority of overall athletics revenue (including allocated revenue) was generated from spectator admissions. However, this percentage is likely to go up as conference broadcast deals for football and men's basketball continues to escalate.

This pattern is generally consistent across the majority of athletics departments. However, athletics department revenue from conference distributions continues to grow at the highest level of competition. Major bowl games currently generate US$155 million per year through bowl games alone, and this revenue is not distributed evenly. Revenue for major conference schools will most likely increase considerably with the new media rights package for the FBS college football playoff system,

which is projected to generate US$7.3 billion over the course of 12 years. This amounts to roughly US$500 million in revenue annually from media rights alone (Ourand & Smith, 2012). Distribution of this revenue is weighted heavily, however, toward the power conferences (Kerkoff, 2012).

Meanwhile, the vast majority of athletics departments are operating at a deficit and will receive a limited amount of revenue from the new football playoff system. At the same time, expenses continue to increase at a faster rate than revenue. As a result, many schools face a challenging financial landscape as they move forward. Ways of dealing with the complex financial environment of college athletics are discussed in greater detail in the following sections.

FINANCIAL OPERATIONS

Due to the considerable revenue associated with college athletics, and the complexities of the tiered distribution system, financial operations form an essential component of organizational management. The NCAA, the conferences, and the individual athletics departments generally maintain a department of business and finance that is managed by a person at the associate director level who operates as the chief financial officer (CFO) and reports directly to the chief executive (e.g., the athletics director, president, or commissioner). In the NCAA, the CFO oversees financial resources, risk management, insurance, investments, travel management, physical plant operations, the NCAA Hall of Champions, purchasing and procurement, publications and printing, and information technology. For an example at the athletics department level, consider Ohio State, which employs a senior associate athletics director who oversees planning and implementation of all aspects of the department's operating budget, the athletics business office, facility operations, event management, human resources, and information technology. Each organization has a business office that employs a team of people who oversee daily business transactions, accounting, investments, insurance, debt service, and travel.

This section introduces and defines an athletics department's most common streams of revenue and expenditures; it also provides examples of dollar figures and growing trends. From ticket sales and licensed merchandise to grant-in-aid funding and team travel, some of today's largest athletics departments manage tens of thousands of transactions per week in an attempt to become financially self-sustaining.

Revenues

For the purposes of this chapter, *revenues* are incoming monies or assets of an athletics department through a commercial transaction, charitable contribution, contractual agreement, transfer, or gift. This category includes income from capital assets, investment vehicles, and in-kind products and services. Two major categories of revenue are generated revenue and allocated revenue, which differ fundamentally in where they come from. *Allocated revenue* is defined as all support from noncommercial activity (e.g., student fees) directly allocated to athletics, as well as institutional support and government support. *Generated revenue* is broadly defined as income derived from commercial activities of the athletics department. These activities often involve actions in which a good or service is provided in exchange for a fee.

In an era of dwindling state appropriations, generated revenue sources have become the strategic focus of most athletics departments, since they are most often variable. In other words, the pressure to become self-sustainable as a department has shifted greater attention to revenue-generating strategies such as sponsorship, donor relations, ticket sales, and media coverage. As compared with other functional departments on campus, athletics departments at the highest level have been estimated to generate seven or eight times more revenue from commercial sources (Congressional Budget Office, 2009).

As a result, in the chapter-opening scenario, the athletics director could increase emphasis on activities related to revenue generation. For instance, the shortfall might be remedied at least in part by either a slight increase in the price of single-game tickets or an uptick in donations. Another possible way to bring in more revenue would be to creatively develop new sponsorship inventory. The challenge for the athletics director is to avoid upsetting fans, donors, or potential sponsors by gouging them too dramatically.

A considerable amount of revenue sources exist for athletic departments. The following list includes the common sources of revenue in college athletics:

• Ticket sales—Advanced ticket sales are a vital source of revenue for an athletics department because they not only provide guaranteed income but also ensure an audience for the department's most important product—intercollegiate athletic competition. Stadiums and arenas filled to capacity create an exciting atmosphere, improve efficiency, and often provide the home team with an advantage. From an accounting perspective, ticket sales should include all tickets sold or provided to the general public, students, faculty, staff, and visiting teams. Ticket sales to conference and national tournaments are typically excluded, as these revenues go to directly to conferences or the NCAA (Congressional Budget Office, 2009).

Season tickets are particularly important because they provide a steady, up-front revenue stream from the organization's most passionate fans. For many institutions—particularly those with demand equaling or exceeding supply—it has become customary for season ticket holders to provide a donation to the athletics department just to gain the right to purchase their yearly tickets. As with personal seat licenses at the professional level, a person who seeks a higher-quality seat is expected to make a larger donation. More information about priority seating and annual giving is provided in chapter 11.

• NCAA and conference distributions—Conference distributions include any revenue received from the conference's participation in tournaments, bowl games, and any other form of NCAA distributions (as discussed in the Tiered Structure section of the chapter). In addition, revenue from conference agreements with television and radio broadcasts are often received via distributions as well (e.g., the Big Ten Network).

• Guarantees—*Guarantees* are contractual agreements between teams in which the home team pays the away team to participate. At some levels of football and basketball, guarantees represent a substantial revenue source for an athletics department. Although most guarantees are also intended to facilitate a guaranteed victory for the home team, visiting teams occasionally take both the money and the victory. Recent examples include Arkansas State (US$550,000 and a win over Texas A&M), James Madison (US$400,000 and a win over 13th-ranked Virginia Tech), and Appalachian State (US$400,000 and a win over 5th-ranked Michigan).

• Donations—Another growth area for athletics departments can be found in fundraising or donor relations. From major gifts such as bequests to small club membership fees, contributions are central to an athletics department's financial vitality. Donations are defined as revenue received directly from individuals, corporations, clubs, associations, foundations, or other organizations that are designated specifically for the operation of the athletics department. Examples of donations include cash, securities, and in-kind products and services. More information about annual donations is given in chapter 11.

• Third-party support—This category refers to all agreed-upon income from a third party that is not included on the institution's W-2 form. Examples of this kind of support include golf club memberships, vehicle allowances, clothing, entertainment, housing, money from speaking engagements, shoe and apparel contracts, and television appearances. As an example of the potential magnitude of third-party support, the University of Michigan was paid US$7 million annually by Adidas starting in 2008 for the opportunity to completely outfit the athletics department's 25 teams (Vosgerchian, 2007). As a reference point, that sum is greater than the average annual nonsubsidized revenue of 127 other Division I athletics programs between 2006 and 2011 (Schnaars, Upton, Mosemak, & DeRamus, 2012).

• Game-day inventory—*Game-day inventory* includes ancillary sales such as parking, program sales, merchandise, and concessions. For well-attended events, this category can represent a viable source of revenue for athletics departments. For smaller events, it provides an opportunity to offset costs. In 2010, for example, the University of Louisville grossed more than US$2.6 million in concession revenue at seven home football games. After accounting for the approximate 30 percent revenue share with concessionaire Centerplate, the athletics department took home US$785,000 (Jessop, 2011).

• Media rights—Another category involves all the forms of media rights that athletics departments count on: contracted revenue received from television and radio broadcasts, television packages, program networks (e.g., Big Ten Network) Internet subscriptions, and e-commerce. For some programs, media rights have become a massive stream of revenue. For example, in addition to the yearly conference payouts discussed earlier, the University of Texas athletics department garners an estimated US$11 million from its Longhorn Network contract with ESPN (Fornelli, 2011).

• Royalties, advertising, and sponsorship—This category includes all revenue from licensing, advertising sales, trademarks, corporate sponsorships, and royalties (Fulks, 2012). Corporate sponsorship is becoming another essential source of revenue for athletics departments. Revenue from corporate partners can come in several forms, such as advertising sales, promotions, trademark usage, licensing, in-kind products and services, royalties, and naming rights. This remains a growth area of revenue for most programs as the inventory associated with sponsorship continues to grow. For instance, Allstate made a major splash in 2005 with its "Good Hands" field goal net sponsorship. Though it began with just a few schools and championship games, it is now being used at 75 Division I football stadiums (Allstate, 2012).

• Sport camps—Sport camps and clinics hosted by the university and conducted by team coaches and staff members provide an important source of revenue, especially for assistant coaches. These weeklong camps typically occur over the summer months and operate as an annual income generator and a low-level recruiting function.

• Investments—Some of the contributions listed earlier are rolled into investments or endowments for the athletics department, from which the organization generates revenue in the form of interest gained. In the world of higher education, an endowment refers either to an organization's total investment from which it earns interest or to a large investment earmarked to fund a specific purpose (e.g., a scholarship, a coach's salary, or a building maintenance fund) in perpetuity through interest earned from the investment. Table 7.4 lists the largest sport endowments, as well as comparisons with the general institutional endowment.

• Miscellaneous—This category accounts for other forms of departmental revenue, such as facility rentals. In the event that a stadium or arena is not being used by the athletics department, the opportunity exists to rent it to other sport organizations, live entertainment companies, or convention organizers. In fact, not only does the rent provide a source of revenue, but also the event inventory itself is often up for negotiation (e.g., a percentage of ticket sales revenue). This category also includes anything and everything not specifically listed otherwise.

• Allocated—As mentioned earlier, allocated revenue represents all support from noncommercial activity, including but not limited to student fees, government funding, and institutional support.

Table 7.4 Athletics and Institutional Endowments

Institution	Sport endow-ment in US$	Athletes	Endowment per athlete in US$	Overall endowment in US$	Undergrads	Endowment per student in US$
UNC at Chapel Hill	212,000,000	437	485,126	2,164,444,000	17,628	122,784
Duke University	150,717,426	339	444,594	5,910,280,000	6,394	924,348
Boston College	100,000,000	262	381,679	1,670,092,000	9,860	169,380
Georgia Tech	80,058,950	292	274,174	1,608,682,000	12,565	128,028
University of Virginia	61,873,981	477	129,715	4,370,209,000	15,078	289,840
University of Washington	56,000,000	380	147,368	2,184,374,000	28,570	76,457
University of Georgia	51,000,000	403	126,551	705,316,000	25,335	27,840
Penn State	49,390,069	450	109,756	1,590,000,000	36,815	43,189
University of Connecticut	48,051,366	340	141,328	337,945,000	16,348	20,672
Ohio State	46,139,682	660	69,909	2,338,103,000	39,209	59,632

• Direct institutional support—Most universities understand the importance of their intercollegiate athletics program in attracting and retaining students, media attention, and public attention. As a result, institutions are willing to invest funds to keep the athletics department competitive—and in some cases soluble. Direct support from the institution can come in many forms, including money transfers, tuition waivers, and state appropriations.

• Indirect institutional support—This support also comes in many forms, and it is offset by an equal expense item. The most prominent sources include the value of facilities and services provided by the institution yet not charged. This indirect support may include an allocation for institutional administrative cost, facilities and maintenance, grounds and field maintenance, security, risk management, utilities, depreciation, and debt service (Fulks, 2012).

• Student fees—In addition to tuition, enrolled students pay a set of fees each semester that cover a litany of administrative and overhead costs of the institution. For some NCAA institutions, a portion of these fees is allocated to intercollegiate athletics. For departments receiving this support, it can be a substantial source of revenue. For instance, Norfolk State University students pay more than US$1,300 in athletics fees each year, and these fees account for nearly 83 percent of the athletics department's revenue (Lorenzen, 2012). Some large schools also use student activity fees to support their sport programs. For instance, Dosh (2011) reported that the University of South Florida used more than US$13 million in student fees, and the University of Virginia athletics program was allocated just over US$12 million. These amounts represented 33.2 percent of South Florida's athletics revenues in 2011 and 14.9 percent of Virginia's (Dosh).

• Direct government funding—Government support can come from the municipal, state, or federal level. Funding from these entities is often earmarked explicitly for the operation of intercollegiate athletics. The notion of subsidizing major college sports has been a hot-button topic for decades, as critics believe this money should be used solely for academically focused ventures. Despite the controversy, nearly 72 percent of the 227 schools in the *USA Today* NCAA financial database ("USA Today Sports," 2012) reported receiving at least 40 percent of their revenue as a subsidy.

Expenses

Expenses are outgoing monies or assets that most often take the form of costs incurred in order to operate. As with revenues, costs in intercollegiate athletics can vary greatly from institution to institution. For the most part, the largest departmental expenses include salaries, capital projects, scholarships, and travel. In recent years, the cost of doing business in college athletics has garnered a great deal of attention. In 2012, the NCAA reported that median spending related to athletics operations increased 94.1 percent between 2004 and 2012, whereas median revenue generated grew only 77.5 percent (Fulks).

The following is a list of the more common expenses athletics departments deal with on a regular basis. There are a multitude of direct and indirect costs associated with athletics department operations. These costs must be considered heavily when assessing the financial well-being of the athletics department.

• Grants-in-aid—This expense includes the total amount of athletics-related student scholarship funding awarded for a given year, including the summer. It should account for tuition remission and waivers provided by the school. It should also include tuition expenses paid to nonathlete students such as graduate assistant coaches, managers, and training staff.

• Guarantees—For home teams looking to secure visiting opponents, guarantees can be an expense for an athletics department. In 2011, for example, the University of Minnesota paid US$645,000 for its nonconference men's basketball guarantees (Krammer, 2012).

• Salaries and benefits—Salaries represent the largest expense for an athletics department. They include not only the wages paid to coaches, administrators, and support staff members but also bonuses and benefits. Benefits vary greatly between institutions and within departments. The more extravagant benefits include exclusive golf memberships, entertainment and clothing allowances, and private jet use. Coaches' salaries have skyrocketed over the past two decades, and some of these benefits have gotten out of control. According to Brady, Upton, and Berkowitz (2012), the average head football coach salary at NCAA Division I FBS institutions (US$1.64 million) is up nearly 12 percent from 2011 and 70 percent since 2006. For some high-profile coaches and administrators, salary costs have been partly subsidized by third-party entities such as shoe and apparel companies, broadcast companies, and local businesses.

• Team travel—Travel costs include air and ground travel, lodging, and meals for teams, coaches, administrators, and other travelers related to preseason, regular season, and postseason competition. They also include lodging for home teams staying in hotels before games. In addition, with the landscape of college athletics changing due to geographically illogical conference realignments, this expense will surely grow as conference members get farther apart. One example of the potential magnitude of these expenditures can be seen in the tab incurred in 2011 by the Louisiana State University football team, which spent US$754,118 on meals and lodging while attending the BCS championship game held in nearby New Orleans (Wetzel, 2012).

• Recruiting—Recruiting expenses include transportation, travel, meals, and lodging incurred throughout the recruiting process. Specific costs include travel and meal costs during recruiting trips, as well as costs incurred while hosting prospective student-athletes and their family members for official and unofficial visits. This expense category also includes other institutional personnel, telecommunication costs, and postage.

• Equipment—This expense includes team-related equipment, uniforms, and supplies that are not considered capital expenditures. It also includes materials for administrators and support staff that meet the same standard.

• Marketing and fundraising—Marketing and fundraising expenses include the costs associated with promoting athletic events and maintaining donor relations and corporate partnerships. Examples include the costs of hosting a golf outing, designing game-day programs, and evaluating the effectiveness of a sponsorship. The category also typically includes funding associated with spirit groups, such as bands, cheerleaders, and mascots.

• Game operations—This category includes all expenses required to run an intercollegiate athletics competition. Examples include security, event staff, ambulance services, officials, food and beverages, and catering services.

• Medical—This category includes both medical expenses and medical insurance premiums for student-athletes. Like general medical costs, this category has ballooned in recent years. For instance, the University of Iowa, which provides very comprehensive medical coverage for its student-athletes, paid US$776,454 in 2008 for more than 4,200 medical bills, according to an Iowa Public Records Law request (Peterson, 2009). This is definitely an area of concern for the NCAA and its member institutions.

• Membership dues—This category includes all memberships and conference and association dues paid by an athletics department.

• Sport camps—This category includes all expenses paid by an athletics department related to the operation of an on-campus sport camp or clinic.

• Facilities and maintenance—These expenses include operating leases, utilities, rental fees, equipment repair, and building and grounds maintenance. In the athletics arms race mentioned earlier, first-rate athletics facilities form a key battleground. From stadium expansions to plush student-athlete living spaces, the costs of renovating and building on campus are excruciatingly high. For instance, the price tag for renovating the football stadium at the University of California, Berkeley, was US$321 million, and, though the funding was originally supposed to come primarily from private sources, shortfalls shifted a larger-than-expected burden onto California taxpayers (Bachman, 2012). At the same time, facility maintenance is an area that an athletics director could cut for a budget cycle or two when pressed to reduce expenses. In the chapter-opening scenario, for example, the AD might find a logical solution in postponing noncritical updates or stadium renovations until state funding returns to previous levels.

• Debt service—*Debt service* is the amount of money required to cover the interest and principal of a debt for a given period of time. These financial obligations for athletics department are typically calculated annually and are most often related to major capital projects, maintenance, or renovations. Even in an economic downturn, new facility construction and upgrades continue to grow; for more on this topic, see Bennett (2012). With new projects, however, comes debt. For instance, according to Dosh (2012b), the University of Michigan, the University of Florida, and the University of Georgia had debt service amounts for fiscal year 2012 of US$13.2 million, US$83.9 million, and US$8.5 million, respectively.

- Other—Other expenses include miscellaneous operating costs, such as printing, subscriptions, business insurance, utilities, postage, equipment leases, severance pay, and travel not related to competition.

With the profitability of the major programs at an all-time high, one interesting trend is for institutional support to flow in the opposite direction. For example, Louisiana State University administrators recently agreed to transfer US$7.2 million per year from the athletics department to the school's academic programs (Bachman & Futterman, 2012).

FINANCIAL STATEMENTS

College athletics departments, like any other nonprofit entity, must account for all of their financial operations. In addition, financial managers must have a clear format for analyzing current and previous financial data and projecting revenue and expenses for budgeting purposes. These data help guide financial decisions regarding revenue opportunities, investments, and cost-cutting measures. The primary source of data for financial planning and forecasting comes from financial statements. These statements provide a record of all financial actions in an organization for the purposes of reporting and financial strategy.

Financial statements serve as the basis for planning and budgeting in both for-profit and nonprofit organizations. These statements are similar in the two types of organization but do include subtle differences in the data and reporting. Financial statements also serve as the basis for annual reporting to the government and other agencies in charge of monitoring nonprofit financial activity. In addition, from a nonprofit perspective, donors and certain stakeholders may have access to this information as part of efforts to evaluate the direction of the organization.

In terms of college athletics, financial statements provide a standard on all tiers of operation, including the NCAA, the conferences, and individual athletics departments. It is not mandatory for all college athletics data from financial statements to be made public. However, the U.S. Department of Education requires public institutions to provide financial data through the Equity in Athletics Disclosure Act (EADA). This act requires all postsecondary educational institutions that receive federal student financial assistance and have intercollegiate athletics programs to report specific information annually about their athletics programs, including some financial data (U.S. Department of Education, 2012). Various aspects of athletics department financial data are available through the EADA Report.

Three financial statements are commonly used in nonprofit operations: the statement of financial position, the statement of activities, and the statement of cash flows. The NCAA provides a public annual report that includes nonprofit financial statements ("NCAA Consolidated," 2013). Therefore, the NCAA report is used in the following sections to further explain the three kinds of financial statement.

Statement of Financial Position

The *statement of financial position* displays the financial condition of a nonprofit organization at a certain point in time. It includes three parts: *assets* (tangible or intangible resources owned or controlled that produce value for a business), *liabilities* (obligations of a business entity arising from past transactions or events), and *fund balances* or *net assets* (assets minus liabilities). Total assets must always equal total liabilities plus net assets. This structure is similar to that of a commercial balance sheet. However, in for-profit companies, which have shareholders and owners who hold an equity stake in the business, shareholder equity is used instead of fund balances or net assets. Since nonprofits do not have such stakeholders, net assets are used to detail the difference between a nonprofit's assets and liabilities.

Assets are listed from the most liquid to the least liquid. *Liquidity* refers to time it takes for an asset to be converted into cash. Assets that can be converted to cash within a year are considered *cur-*

rent assets, whereas assets that would take longer than a year to convert to cash are considered *fixed assets.* Liabilities for the organization are listed in the same manner, from short-term (must be paid in less than a year) to long-term (will take more than a year to pay off). Fund balance (net assets) indicates the remaining assets above liabilities that can be used for reserves. However, if an organization is in a poor financial position, liabilities could outpace assets, leaving a negative fund balance.

Table 7.5 provides the NCAA's statement of financial position for 2011. Assets include cash, investments, prepaid expenses, and accounts and contributions receivable (bills expected to be paid in the short term). Commercial balance sheets include only accounts receivable, whereas nonprofits can also include contributions that have yet to be collected. The NCAA did not separate current from long-term assets in the statement, but assets are listed in order of liquidity. Total assets for 2011 were approximately US$607.2 million. Liabilities include accounts payable (outstanding short-term debt to be paid), distributions payable (payments to conferences), deferred revenue (revenue received but spread over a period of time), and deferred deposits (deposits made but not immediately reported on an income statement). Total liabilities were approximately US$111.4 million.

The difference between assets and liabilities is reported as net assets, totaling approximately US$495.5 million. Net assets are broken down by restriction, because assets can be either unrestricted, temporarily restricted, or permanently restricted. The NCAA appears to be financially sound at the period for which the statement of financial position was created. However, this statement tells you only part of the organization's financial status.

Statement of Activities

The statement of activities shows a nonprofit organization's revenue and expenses over a period of time, usually one year. This statement is similar to the income statement for a commercial business. The difference between revenues and expenses over a period of time is reported as a change in net assets. This change can be broken down as a total fluctuation in net assets or as a change at the beginning and/or end of a given period, thus providing more detailed information about financial position throughout that period. Statements of activities generally provide information about the current and previous period of interest in order to offer detail about changes from one period to another. One component missing from the statement of activities is taxes. This is a distinguishing factor between for-profit and nonprofit sport, and it is a considerable advantage for nonprofits since taxes are a primary expense for commercial firms.

Table 7.6 provides the NCAA's statement of activities from 2011. The majority of revenue is generated through television and marketing rights (US$690 million)—specifically, for the Division I men's basketball tournament. Additional revenues are generated through other postseason tournaments, investments, and charitable contributions at the individual and corporate level. In terms of expenses, the primary cost is distribution, totaling approximately US$608 million. Additional expenses include association programs provided to institutions and the general operations of the association.

In 2011, the NCAA experienced a net assets increase of almost US$66 million, which includes US$5.6 million generated through reclassification fees. These assets (minus approximately US$16 million from a change in accounting, stemming from either a previous accounting error or a change in standard procedures for reporting income) are part of total net assets, which were reported as approximately US$460 million after fiscal year 2011.

Not all revenues are free flowing in nonprofit organizations. Some revenues are permanently or temporarily restricted, either by donors or by grant-funding agencies. For example, a donor can

> *Maintenance of facilities is the primary thing that we'll do away with this year. That entails upkeep on Washington-Grizzly Stadium and other facilities that we have, like Dornblaser Field and the soccer fields.*
>
> Kent Haslam, athletics director,
> University of Montana
> (qtd. in Green, 2013)

Table 7.5 NCAA Statement of Financial Position

	2011 in US$	2010 in US$
ASSETS		
Cash and cash equivalents	6,183,004	12,250,965
Investments	470,180,042	451,202,188
Prepaid expenses	9,134,174	9,217,528
Receivables 　Accounts receivable 　Contributions receivable 　Total receivables	 29,298,004 35,514,450 64,812,454	 11,726,854 31,506,703 43,233,557
Goodwill	8,630,568	23,784,589
Intangible assets	2,844,499	4,078,835
Investment in Youth Basketball, LLC	1,316,975	871,945
Properties	42,798,313	24,937,310
Other assets	1,318,003	1,376,583
Total assets	607,218,032	570,953,500
LIABILITIES		
Accounts payable and accrued liabilities	29,850,630	24,626,771
Distributions payable	7,816,598	11,357,632
Deferred revenue and deposits	24,855,290	22,444,460
Bonds payable—net	45,199,726	47,939,712
NIT payable—net	-	19,262,432
Accrued lease expense	3,683,720	1,412,752
Total liabilities	111,405,964	127,043,759
NET ASSETS		
Unrestricted—attributed to NCAA	460,759,475	407,795,576
Temporarily restricted	34,607,305	32,667,250
Permanently restricted	148,034	148,034
Total NCAA net assets	495,514,814	440,610,860
Noncontrolling interests net assets—unrestricted	297,254	3,298,881
Total net assets	495,812,068	443,909,741
Total	607,218,032	570,953,500

Data from NCAA. Available: www.ncaastudent.org/wps/wcm/connect/public/ncaa/finances/ncaa+consolidated+financial+statements.

designate that his or her contribution be used for a specific sport. All nonrestricted revenues are available for use by the organization as it sees fit (Bryce, 2000).

It appears from the NCAA statement of activities that the organization is in a good financial position, since revenue considerably outpaces expenses. However, this difference can be an issue when assessing a nonprofit organization, in which all revenues should be covering costs.

Statement of Cash Flows

The *statement of cash flows* provides sources and uses of cash during a specified period of time. The statement is usually broken down into three categories: operating activities, investing activities, and

Table 7.6 NCAA Statement of Activities

	Unrestricted	Temporarily restricted	Permanently restricted	Total	2010 Summarized total
				2011	**2010**
REVENUE IN US$					
Television and marketing rights fees	690,314,434	-	-	690,314,434	645,691,980
Championships and NIT tournaments	93,412,324	-	-	93,412,324	71,922,650
Investment income—net	32,883,900	569,844	-	33,453,744	24,404,962
Sales and services	21,756,945	-	-	21,756,945	18,031,455
Contributions—other	-	190,382	-	190,382	239,276
Contributions—facilities—net	-	6,823,352	-	6,823,352	(10,468,065)
Total revenues	838,367,603	7,583,578	-	845,951,181	749,822,258
RECLASSIFICATIONS IN US$					
Temporarily restricted resources used for occupancy costs	4,885,482	(4,885,482)	-	-	-
Temporarily restricted resources used for program services	758,041	(758,041)	-	-	-
Total reclassifications	5,643,523	(5,643,523)	-	-	-
EXPENSES IN US$					
Distribution to D-I members	480,012,096	-	-	480,012,096	434,648,083
D-I championships, programs, and NIT tournaments	74,375,700	-	-	74,375,700	67,662,850
D-II championships, distributions, and programs	31,696,364	-	-	31,696,364	28,510,292
D-III championships and programs	22,019,890	-	-	22,019,890	19,897,645
Associationwide programs	134,253,166	-	-	134,253,166	124,135,246
Management and general	35,706,613	-	-	35,706,613	32,370,217
Total expenses	778,063,829	-	-	778,063,829	707,224,333
Net increase in net assets before other changes in net assets	65,947,297	1,940,055	-	67,887,352	42,597,925
Other changes in net assets—change in accounting principle	(15,985,025)	-	-	(15,985,025)	-
Total change in net assets	49,962,272	1,940,055	-	51,902,327	42,597,925
Change in net assets attributed to noncontrolling interest	3,001,627	-	-	3,001,627	588,597
Change in NCAA net assets	52,963,899	1,940,055	-	54,903,954	43,186,522
NCAA net assets—beginning of year	407,795,576	32,667,250	148,034	440,610,860	397,424,338
NCAA net assets—end of year	460,759,475	34,607,305	148,034	495,514,814	440,610,860

Data from NCAA. Available: www.ncaastudent.org/wps/wcm/connect/public/ncaa/finances/ncaa+consolidated+financial+statements.

financing activities. Operating activities include net assets, changes in assets and liabilities, and gains or losses from investments. Investing activities include acquisition of property, land, and equipment, as well as changes in overall investments.

Examples of investing activities for the NCAA include the costs associated with purchasing the National Invitation Tournament for men's and women's basketball and the revenue generated from this investment. Financing activities include payments on bonds and revenue accumulated through dividends. Examples of financing activities for the NCAA include distributions to conferences and principle payments on bonds.

Cash flow from these activities is compared at the beginning and end of a specified period, thus providing a net change in overall cash flow. In the NCAA statement of cash flows (table 7.7), you can see a breakdown of cash flow from fiscal years 2010 and 2011, including components from both the statement of financial position and the statement of activities. The NCAA has significant cash flows from operations but is limited in investing and financing, because these are not core components of the association's business model.

In practice, financial statements highlight areas of potential growth and areas where cost cutting would be financially beneficial. Although these are financial statements for the NCAA, an athletics director (such as the one in the chapter-opening case) also uses financial statements to forecast revenue and establish the need for resources in the upcoming fiscal year. In the case study, financial statements could be used to highlight areas that could be adjusted to account for the budget shortfall. Possibilities might include delaying planned facility renovations, increasing resources to help raise charitable contributions, and adjusting scheduling to limit travel expenses.

BUDGETING

At its core, a budget is nothing more than a planning document. Whether creating a yearlong, multimillion-dollar operating budget or managing a monthly household budget, the process of budgeting is merely planning that requires organization, forethought, and, most important, communication. A *budget* is a financial document that involves the strategic allocation of organizational funds to operations, activities, projects, or capital resources. The document itself and the budgeting process should provide a department, program, or unit with guidance, clarity, and direction. However, without good communication and a shared vision, budgets often create confusion and frustration.

Budgets come in all shapes and sizes. Regardless, the potential benefits of proper budgeting in intercollegiate athletics are numerous. A well-organized and well-communicated budget offers the following benefits:

- Allows decision makers to better control and monitor spending
- Offers a clearer picture of organizational priorities
- Alerts management to revenue shortfalls
- Prevents rash financial decisions
- Provides a working document for strategic planning
- Proffers a precise measurement source for financial performance
- Motivates constituents to meet important goals and objectives

Another reason that budgets are essential in departmental operations is that, like consumers, athletics departments are constrained by time and money. As a result, managers are required to make strategic decisions about how much to allocate and for how long. For example, a given team's travel budget is often set at a specific amount (e.g., US$150,000) at the beginning of the fiscal year (July 1) and is available to finance the team's travel for only one year. A good budget should also provide an accurate projection of revenue and expenses detailing the projected costs of each planned trip. Thus, it can provide a source of stability in unpredictable times.

Planning, Forecasting, and the Budgeting Process

The budgeting process typically consists of three stages: data collection, planning, and budget development. *Data collection* for budgeting is the process of gathering internal and external financial information that may affect the planning, forecasting, and ultimate development of an organization's budget. Internal sources typically involve private

Table 7.7   NCAA Statement of Cash Flows

	2011	2010
CASH FLOWS FROM OPERATING ACTIVITIES IN US$		
Change in NCAA net assets	54,903,954	43,186,522
ADJUSTMENTS TO RECONCILE CHANGE IN NET ASSETS TO NET CASH PROVIDED BY OPERATING ACTIVITIES IN US$		
Depreciation and amortization	3,513,194	10,757,129
Amortization of bond premium	(179,986)	-
Change in unrealized gain on investments	(21,326,296)	(17,276,248)
Impairment	15,985,025	-
Loss in equity of joint venture	428,152	1,181,648
Realized loss (gain) on investments	(4,326,336)	739,480
Loss on disposal of properties	5,555	-
Changes in noncontrolling interest	(3,001,627)	(588,597)
CHANGES IN CERTAIN ASSETS AND LIABILITIES IN US$		
Receivables	(21,578,897)	18,096,260
Prepaid expenses	83,354	1,260,218
Other assets	58,580	(157,846)
Accounts payable and accrued liabilities	3,464,667	(6,284,821)
Deferred revenue and deposits	2,410,830	13,734,131
NIT payable	(7,842,309)	(1,472,222)
Accrued lease expense	2,270,968	(4,507,823)
Net cash provided by operating activities	24,868,828	58,667,831
CASH FLOWS FROM INVESTING ACTIVITIES IN US$		
Capital expenditures	(19,796,255)	(9,359,590)
Increase in accounts payable and accrued liabilities related to capital expenditures	579,026	1,268,230
Purchases of investments	(38,581,463)	(133,329,367)
Proceeds from sales of investments	45,256,242	71,255,262
NIT payable	(11,420,123)	(3,777,778)
Investment in Youth Basketball, LLC	(873,182)	(1,839,584)
Net cash used in investing activities	(24,835,755)	(75,782,827)
CASH FLOWS FROM FINANCING ACTIVITY IN US$		
Distributions payable	(3,541,034)	3,060,009
Proceeds from issuance of bonds payable	-	20,141,773
Principal payments on bonds payable	(2,560,000)	(1,630,000)
Net cash provided by (used in) financing activities	(6,101,034)	21,571,782
Net increase (decrease) in cash and cash equivalents	(6,067,961)	4,456,786
CASH AND CASH EQUIVALENTS IN US$		
Beginning of year	12,250,965	7,794,179
End of year	6,183,004	12,250,965
Supplemental cash flow information—cash paid for interest	1,631,411	1,347,055
Noncash transactions —purchases of property, plant, and equipment	1,847,256	1,268,230

Data from NCAA. Available: www.ncaastudent.org/wps/wcm/connect/public/ncaa/finances/ncaa+consolidated+financial+statements.

data from previous operations within the organization. Another common data source for an athletics department is primary research in the form of fan or consumer surveys. External sources might come in the form of industry trends, local or regional economic data, or competitor analyses. Data collection must be a systematic and comprehensive process; most important, the sources must be valid and reliable.

Planning is a vital financial activity for any organization, particularly in conjunction with budgeting. In finance, *planning* is the process of creating strategies, based on recent history and on forecasts, to guide the development and implementation of the budget. Given that a budget is nothing more than a component of the overall financial plan, it makes sense that the plan must be implemented first (Bergeron, 2002). Most often, the planning process is broken down into short-term planning and long-term planning. However, forecasting revenues and expenses is the primary aspect of planning that is used in the budgeting process.

Forecasting is the process of using financial data to predict and quantify future events. In particular, forecasting involves using statistical methods of prediction based on the relationships of various factors in an economic environment. In intercollegiate athletics, some of these factors, including most forms of revenue, lie outside of the organization's control (Brown, Rascher, Nagel, & McEvoy, 2010). For instance, an athletics department may use forecasting techniques to predict the number of single-game tickets that will be bought or the major gifts that will be donated. Forecasting can be a powerful tool for an organization if, once again, the data analyzed are correct and the organization's financial plan has been clearly communicated. Forecasting should go hand-in-hand with strategic planning, yet often does not as those tasked with developing the forecast are not often tuned into the broader strategic vision (Hagel, 2014).

Finally, it is vital to develop a progressive yet realistic budget. The budget should be developed for conservative growth based on sound planning and data-driven forecasting. In particular, revenue estimations should be crafted with the idea of pushing the organization forward as a means of goal-oriented action. Likewise, expense forecasting should be carefully devised to include general inflation as well as the increased cost of developing new revenue.

Budget Types

This section highlights two budget types commonly used in intercollegiate athletics. Operational budgets which impact the day-to-day functions of an organization, and a capital budgets which reflect one-time, financed expenses. Several types of operational budgets exist and will be discussed below. In addition, formats, strategies, and implications associated with each type will be provided.

Operational Budgets

An operational budget is a statement that anticipates revenues and expenses required for the day-to-day functions of a unit over a given period of time. The time period for an operational budget is typically one year, but the budget may also be segmented by quarter or month to provide measurable benchmarks. At the beginning of a budget cycle, the figures in the budget are estimates; as the time period elapses, these estimates are compared with the actual amounts. The difference or variance between the two figures provides vital information about potential revenue shortfalls or overspending. This process is called *variance analysis*, and it provides a mechanism for monitoring and controlling revenue collections and spending. Table 7.8 provides an example of variance analysis for an athletics department over four quarters.

Returning to the chapter-opening scenario, the athletics director would certainly benefit from conducting a variance analysis in order to find expenses to cut for the upcoming fiscal year. Identifying quarterly shortfalls, for example, would help the department identify sources of wasteful spending or inefficient programming; meanwhile, a surplus could identify a potential area to revise in the budget.

Line-Item Budget A *line-item budget,* or object-of-expenditure budget, is a document in which individual financial items (revenues and expenses) are grouped by department and itemized by function. For instance, revenue generated from website subscriptions would be itemized as such and grouped under digital media. Line-item budgeting is often considered to be traditional

Leadership Lesson

Feed the Opportunities

As we pursue the tasks that fill our days, it is very easy to become busy—very, very busy. You may recall the anecdote from *Alice's Adventures in Wonderland* in the chapter 4 leadership lesson. The main idea was that if you don't know where you want to go, it doesn't matter which path you take. We might work from sun up to sun down, trudging along a path only to realize when we reach the end that we took the wrong one. If we don't know where we hope to go, it is extremely difficult to get there.

It may seem like a pretty straightforward idea that we should manage our time based on importance. But how do you determine *importance?* We hope that by this point in the text, (building on previous leadership lessons) you have crafted your personal mission statement. If you have, simply ask yourself whether a given task helps you get closer to your vision or to high-priority goals associated with your various roles. If it does, then it is important (Covey, 2004). As discussed in chapter 3 (Leadership and Management), Covey describes a four-quadrant grid (recall figure 3.3) for categorizing the various tasks we encounter, and he urges leaders to strive to live their lives primarily in quadrant II (addressing matters that are important but not urgent). Certainly, many matters arise that are both urgent and important (quadrant I), but habitually spending a majority of time in crisis management mode leads to stress, burnout, and ultimate inefficiency. Planning and carving out maximal time in quadrant II, on the other hand, creates a life led by vision, control, balance, and perspective. Therefore, effective leaders are advised to delegate all matters that are urgent but not important to trusted support staff and to avoid doing activities that are neither important nor urgent, since they result in irresponsible use of time (Covey, 2004).

This vantage point differs from viewing your time in terms of efficiency. Crossing tasks off of a list may provide a temporary sense of accomplishment, but if the achievements are quadrant III or IV tasks—not driven by importance—then you're just spinning your wheels. In fact, "efficient scheduling and control of time are often counterproductive. The efficiency focus creates expectations that clash with the opportunities to develop rich relationships, to meet human needs, and to enjoy spontaneous moments on a daily basis" (Covey, 2004, p. 150). In order to balance the need for efficiency and focus on importance, Covey recommends scheduling your week based on one or two important goals in each role you play. When you allocate time to these goals throughout the week, you enhance your flexibility, allow time for the quadrant I activities that are bound to pop up, and enable yourself to proactively balance the roles you play.

Such clarity is equally important in organizational priorities. The following questions are included in an exercise consultant Patrick Lencioni (2000) has recommended for executive teams to do as they strive to embark on an element of strategic planning. Employees in a healthy organization should be able to unambiguously answer the following questions:

- Why does the organization exist, and what difference does it make in the world?

> *Even when the urgent is good, the good can keep you from your best, keep you from your unique contribution, if you let it. . . . It's almost impossible to say "no" to the popularity of Quadrant III or to the pleasure of escape to Quadrant IV if you don't have a bigger "yes" burning inside. . . . [O]nly then will you have sufficient independent willpower to say "no," with a genuine smile, to the unimportant.*
>
> Covey, 2004, pp. 157–158

(continued)

LEADERSHIP LESSON *(continued)*

- What behavioral values are irreplaceable and fundamental?

- What business are we in, and against whom do we compete?

- How does our approach differ from that of our competition?

- What are our goals for this month, this quarter, this year, next year, and the next five years?

- Who has to do what in order for us to achieve our goals for this month, this quarter, this year, next year, and the next five years? (Lencioni, 2000, p.154-155).

*In every area of effectiveness within an organization, **one feeds the opportunities and starves the problem.***

Drucker, 1967, p. 98, emphasis original

As you strive to become more effective on the individual and organizational levels, ask yourself what quadrant you're spending the majority of your time in. Do your individual weekly planning sessions or organizational meetings emphasize tasks focused on what is most *important?* Does the department allocate finances based on a clear organizational vision, or is there tremendous imbalance between the stated values and the priorities that are funded? It is very easy to forget about the big picture and get sucked into a quadrant I mentality, both in departmental budget management and in life.

budgeting, and it is implemented for a number of reasons, including simplicity, flexibility, and the ability to measure over time.

As shown in table 7.9, a line-item budget allows a manager to quickly populate a budget by looking at the previous year's line. It can be used by a wide range of programs and organizations, and it can also be as detailed as necessary because it is relatively easy to add or subtract a line during the planning process. Finally, line-item budgeting optimizes the control feature of budgeting, because it is easy to monitor from one period to the next but difficult to transfer money from one line to another.

However, this type of budget also has its drawbacks. Although simplicity is a strength of line-item budgeting, it is also a weakness, because it does not require much managerial analysis. In other words, the process of incrementally adjusting the previous year's budget puts focus on the cost of a function but does not oblige the manager to analyze the need for it. This drawback can produce a disconnect between strategic planning, efficiency, and line-item budgeting.

Program Budget A *program budget* is a document in which funds are allocated directly to a program. The unit then has the freedom to spend the money as it chooses so long as it does not exceed the allocated amount for the program. This is a top-down approach as compared with line-item budgeting. It allows an organization to evaluate the efficiency of a given activity without the control afforded through other budgeting formats.

For example, in line with an athletics department's goals and objectives, it may have several ongoing yet clearly delineated programs, such as a campaign to sell more season tickets or a promotion to attract more youth to home games. The use of a program budget system with these programs would entail creating and maintaining a separate budget document for each program. In the end, then, a program budget assesses the effectiveness of the department's pursuits by assessing each program separately, whereas the next type, the performance budget, evaluates the efficiency of management.

Performance Budget *Performance budgeting* links allocated funds to measurable results; therefore, it is the most result-oriented budgeting process. A performance budget typically consists of three sections: the result, the strategy, and the activity (Segal & Summers, 2002). The information gained from these elements is intended to aid in the decision-making process for allocating

Table 7.8 Example of Variance Analysis at XYZ Athletics Department

	Q1—September 30			Q2—December 31			Q3—March 31			Q4—June 30			Total variance
	Budget	Actual	Variance	Budget	Actual	Variance	Budget	Actual	Variance	Budget	Actual	Variance	
REVENUE IN US$ (THOUSANDS)													
Ticket sales	117	118	1	215	211	(4)	195	207	12	47	48	1	10
Conference distributions	900	900	0	900	900	0	900	900	0	900	940	40	40
Donations	220	206	(14)	400	418	18	300	288	(12)	220	215	(5)	(13)
Sponsorships	650	656	6	13	18	5	13	13	0	650	623	(27)	(16)
Institutional support	1,200	1,200	0	0	0	0	0	0	0	10	25	15	15
Other	50	51	1	25	27	2	25	24	(1)	50	54	4	6
Total	**3,137**	**3,131**	**(6)**	**1,553**	**1,574**	**21**	**1,433**	**1,432**	**(1)**	**1,877**	**1,905**	**28**	**42**
Total revenue	**8,000**	**8,042**	**42**										
EXPENSES IN US$													
Grants-in-aid	325	329	(4)	0	0	0	325	311	14	195	201	(6)	4
Guarantees	125	125	0	75	75	0	0	0	0	0	0	0	0
Salaries and benefits	1,200	1,210	(10)	1,200	1,215	(15)	1,200	1,205	(5)	1,200	1,216	(16)	(46)
Team travel	185	196	(11)	400	421	(21)	250	279	(29)	150	166	(16)	(77)
Recruiting	45	46	(1)	65	64	1	59	68	(9)	45	49	(4)	(13)
Medical	110	116	(6)	190	188	2	85	88	(3)	40	41	(1)	(8)
Maintenance	88	96	(8)	88	85	3	88	85	3	88	98	(10)	(12)
Other	37	34	3	41	43	(2)	41	40	1	60	62	(2)	0
Total	**2,115**	**2,152**	**(37)**	**2,059**	**2,091**	**(32)**	**2,048**	**2,076**	**(28)**	**1,778**	**1,833**	**(55)**	**(152)**
Total expenses	**8,000**	**8,152**	**(152)**										
Total variance	**(110)**												

budgetary funds. Within specific programs of an athletics department (e.g., marketing or the men's golf team), this type of budgeting allows for a more comprehensive evaluation of actions.

For example, if a golf coach invests US$800 in access to an online recruiting database that leads to four additional offers and one additional recruit, the detail of a performance budget provides an opportunity for the coach to weigh the benefits and costs of the action. In general, then, this approach should result in budgeting that is more in line with the program's mission and strategies. At the highest level of the department, however, this budgeting process may not work, because eliminating programs due to performance may not be possible (due to Title IX and NCAA rules on minimum number of sponsored sports). This type of budgeting is also more time consuming and requires more detail than other forms.

Table 7.9 XYZ Athletic Department, Line-Item Budget

	Last year	Q1	Q2	Q3	Q4	Total
REVENUE IN US$ (THOUSANDS)						
Ticket sales	600	188	220	225	46	679
Conference distributions	3,500	900	900	900	910	3,610
Donations	1,250	250	450	350	220	1,270
Sponsorships	1,360	650	13	13	650	1,326
Institutional support	1,200	1,200	0	0	10	1,210
Other	90	25	25	25	25	100
Total	**8,000**	**3,143**	**1,608**	**1,513**	**1,861**	**8,125**
EXPENSES IN US$						
Grants-in-aid	830	325	0	325	180	830
Guarantees	225	150	75	0	0	225
Salaries and benefits	4,750	1,200	1,250	1,200	1,200	4,850
Team travel	1,064	190	450	283	166	1,089
Recruiting	205	45	65	50	45	205
Medical	425	110	190	85	40	425
Maintenance	352	88	88	88	88	352
Other	149	37	41	41	30	149
Total	**8,000**	**2,145**	**2,159**	**2,072**	**1,749**	**8,125**

Capital Budgets

Capital budgeting is a much different process than operational budgeting and requires separate documentation due to the unique nature of the items being financed. Depending on the subject, capital can be defined in many ways. For the purposes of this chapter, *capital* refers to money or assets put to use for productive gain. In most instances, forms of capital are costly one-time investments that are not fully consumed within a year yet provide some sort of financial return or public benefit. Typical examples in college athletics include an air-conditioning unit for the football locker room, a scoreboard for the hockey rink, and a cargo van for the golf team.

Given the high cost of most capital projects, it is logical to separate capital from the operational budget so as not to burden a recurring budget with a high-cost nonrecurring item. In addition, most capital projects are financed; as a result, capital purchasing decisions must consider the factors of time, interest rate, and rate of return. Several methods are available for deciding between capital projects, including the payback rule, net present value, internal rate of return, and discounted cash flow methods.

Financial Reporting for Institutions

The NCAA requires institutions to report athletics revenue and expenses in order to facilitate monitoring of the financial health of intercollegiate athletics departments (see the NCAA Bylaw sidebar). The dashboard indicators provided by this standardized reporting also provide university decision makers with a potentially powerful set of metrics for benchmarking and strategic planning. The U.S. Department of Education also requires institutions to file annual financial and participation reports in order to comply with the EADA.

Both of these reporting functions are a step in the right direction for an industry that went without regulation for nearly a century. However, a good deal of the NCAA data are not available to the general public—for example, departmental financial statements from individual institutions. In addition, no standardized accounting principles are required (e.g., generally accepted accounting principles, or GAAP), and the data required for reporting are allowed to be broadly categorized.

For instance, common incomparable financial aspects include the reporting of coaches' salaries subsidized by shoe and apparel companies and the reporting of tuition waivers for grant-in-aid athletes. Each university may have a different approach to classifying these substantial expenses, which leads to significant inconsistencies between institutions. For example, institutional support in the form of new facility construction or rent is a significant expense for an athletics department, but given similar pursuits and shared property it is easy to see how expenses between a university and an athletics department can be interchanged. To illustrate the level of interpretation available to

general accountants, the 2011 Federal Accounting Standards Advisory Board's handbook, which serves as the clearinghouse for GAAP, is more than 2,000 pages long.

COLLEGIATE ATHLETIC BUSINESS MANAGEMENT ASSOCIATION (CABMA)

CABMA is devoted to people who serve specifically to oversee business or fiscal matters in intercollegiate athletics. The group holds an annual symposium at the convention of the National Association of Collegiate Directors of Athletics to bring its members together to share ideas, policies, and procedures related to efficient fiscal management in college sport. The group also facilitates problem solving through continuous dialogue between members aimed at achieving greater cost efficiency

NCAA Bylaw 3.2.4.16—Operating and Capital Financial Data Report

An institution shall submit financial data detailing operating revenues, expenses, and capital related to its intercollegiate athletics program to the NCAA on an annual basis in accordance with the financial reporting policies and procedures. The required data shall include, but is not limited to, the following: (Adopted: 1/17/09 effective 8/1/09)

a. All expenses and revenues for or on behalf of an institution's intercollegiate athletics program, including those by any affiliated or outside organization, agency, or group of individuals;

b. Capital expenditures (to be reported in aggregate for athletics facilities), including capitalized additions and deletions to facilities during the reporting period, total estimated book value of athletically related plant and equipment net of depreciation, total annual debt service on athletics and university facilities, and total debt outstanding on athletics and university facilities;

c. Value of endowments at fiscal year-end that are dedicated to the sole support of athletics;

d. Value of all pledges at fiscal year-end that support athletics; and

e. The athletics department fiscal year-end fund balance.

3.2.4.16.1 Verification and Certification. The report shall be subject to annual agreed-on verification procedures approved by the membership (in addition to any regular financial reporting policies and procedures of the institution) and conducted by a qualified independent accountant who is not a staff member of the institution and who is selected by the institution's chancellor or president or by an institutional administrator from outside the athletics department designated by the chancellor or president. The independent accountant shall verify the accuracy and completeness of the data prior to submission to the institution's chancellor or president and the NCAA. The institution's chancellor or president shall certify the financial report prior to submission to the NCAA. (Adopted: 1/17/09 effective 8/1/09) in daily operations, strategic planning, and other areas of business management.

CONCLUSION

The current growth in college athletics emphasizes the need, now more than ever, for financial responsibility and accountability in athletics departments. The unique nature of this industry provides challenges and opportunities for sport managers to grapple with as athletics departments operate both under the umbrella of higher education and under intense commercial pressures. As a result, today's college athletics administrators must have the ability to generate revenue, raise capital, and budget effectively in order to help provide an opti-

mal educational experience for the student-athletes for whom the organizations exist.

This chapter provides an overview of the financial landscape of college sport and some challenges for the future. It also discusses in detail the nonprofit status of college athletics in order to provide an understanding of the unique nature of the industry. Finally, it covers financial concepts (e.g., business structure, financial statements, planning, and budgeting) in the context of this unique environment. It is critical to understand and implement these concepts as college athletics departments continue to increase costs and are forced to find creative methods for operating in a fiscally prudent manner.

DISCUSSION QUESTIONS

1. Scheduling guaranteed games is a hot-button topic for both teams involved. Why would an organization guarantee revenue to an opponent? What issues should be considered by an athletics department before offering a game guarantee?

2. What are the potential benefits and drawbacks of each of the following budget types: line-item, program, and performance? As a senior associate athletics director, which budget type would you choose, and why? As a head coach in charge of your team's budget, which budget type would you prefer, and why?

3. Bowen's revenue theory of costs is discussed in the chapter as a framework for spending in college athletics. Explain how the additional revenue generated through new television broadcasting deals might affect athletics department spending based on the cycle proposed in Bowen's theory.

4. In situations where athletics departments are out of compliance with Title IX, cutting nonrevenue male sports has been a common but unfavorable strategy used to comply with the legislation. From a financial perspective, how might athletics departments comply with Title IX without necessarily cutting sports? What financial strategies could be used in an effort to limit the damage to student-athletes' participation opportunities?

5. Currently, coaches' salaries for revenue-generating sports such as football and basketball are whatever the market will bear. As a result, these salaries have become a primary expense for Division I athletics departments looking to remain competitive. Do you believe that the current salary structure for coaches in revenue-generating sports is sustainable? Why or why not? What strategies could be used to reduce the expenses associated with coaches' salaries in football and basketball?

LEARNING ACTIVITIES

1. Suppose that you work in an athletics department in which a few teams outperformed expectations this year for tournament results and home-game attendance. As a result, your department is heading toward your first year of posting a profit (revenues = US$48 million, and expenses = US$39 million). There are only a few weeks until the end of the fiscal year, and you cannot roll forward the difference; thus you must spend it. Work in a small group to determine the best expense categories to which the US$9 million surplus could be allocated. Be ready to defend your decisions.

2. Interview an administrator who oversees financial operations in a Division I athletics department. What is the overall budget for the department? How much of the budget involves generated revenue versus allocated revenue? What are the main points of emphasis for generating revenue and controlling costs? Where does the athletics department budget rank in the conference? What is the general expectation for revenue growth each year?

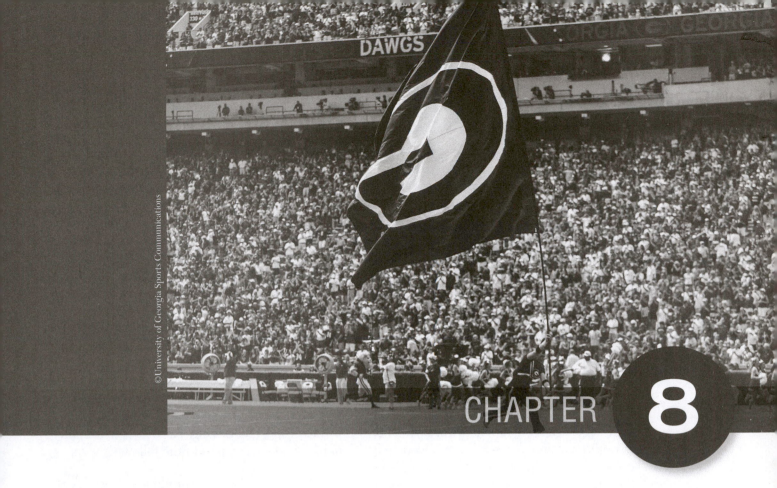

CHAPTER 8

Marketing
Tickets and Promotions

David J. Shonk, James Madison University

Alyssa T. Bosley, James Madison University

In this chapter, you will explore

- the 5 Ps of sport marketing,
- differences between online and traditional advertising,
- licensing and why colleges and universities use licensees,
- how atmospherics affect a consumer at an intercollegiate sporting event,
- community relations and corporate social responsibility,
- community relations initiatives at various institutions,
- the National Association of Collegiate Marketing Administrators,
- the secondary ticket market,
- the effect of dynamic ticketing in intercollegiate athletics, and
- various types of promotion in intercollegiate athletics.

THE CHANGING NATURE OF MARKETING INTERCOLLEGIATE ATHLETICS

Teresa Martin is hired as the new director of athletics marketing at a large public institution in Virginia. She is excited about returning to her alma mater after graduating 12 years earlier. However, she notices that the process of delivering the product to fans has changed considerably since she interned with the athletics department at the end of her senior year. The most noticeable difference involves the use of social media to communicate with the fan base. She did not have a Twitter account 12 years earlier, nor did she use Facebook or LinkedIn. Now, however, it is expected that she use social media platforms to announce promotional information. Her duties also include placing advertisements about various events on the athletics department's Facebook and Twitter pages. In addition, the department has recently implemented dynamic ticket pricing, and she must note how ticket prices change based on date, opponent, and sometimes a specific promotion.

Marketing, ticketing, and promotion are vitally important functions for intercollegiate athletics programs. The marketing of athletics programs is big business, and athletics departments use both traditional and online forms of advertising to sell tickets and multiple forms of social media to reach their target audiences. Intercollegiate sport marketers also use various licensees to create products bearing the name of the university. In addition, in an effort to market the appeal of the physical setting and sensory elements, colleges and universities are constantly building and renovating sport facilities. Athletics programs also use the celebrity status of their athletes and coaches to reach out to and connect with their local communities through various community relations initiatives.

In this complex environment, athletics programs and consumers alike are increasingly affected by dynamic ticket pricing and the secondary ticket market. Various types of promotion are used by athletics programs in an effort to persuade consumers to buy tickets and to communicate with fans. Athletics programs use both in-game promotional activities and sales promotion.

MARKETING INTERCOLLEGIATE ATHLETICS

Marketers of intercollegiate athletics use a variety of methods to appeal to their audience. This section discusses how advertising, social media, licensing, atmospherics, and community relations are used to promote intercollegiate athletics. First, however, it examines how marketers appeal to fans through five primary factors—product, price, promotion, place, and public relations—commonly referred to as the five Ps of sport marketing. The 5 Ps can be applied to highly identified fans in the following ways.

1. Product—The core product in sport is the sporting contest itself. Some fans are highly identified with a particular sport (e.g., basketball) or a particular team (e.g., the University of Louisville Cardinals).

2. Price—A fan may be willing to pay more to attend a marquee game, such as Duke versus North Carolina in basketball or Alabama versus Auburn in football.

3. Promotion—Fans at Penn State University may be motivated to attend a game against a rival team when the athletics program promotes a whiteout (in which spectators wear white shirts to the game) or offers a bobblehead giveaway featuring a popular player.

4. Place—Appealing venues can attract visitors to attend simply because of the atmosphere. Examples include the Palestra basketball arena in Philadelphia and classic football stadiums, such as the Horseshoe at Ohio State University.

5. Public relations—The media attention given to certain celebrity student-athletes (e.g., quarterback Johnny Manziel) or teams (e.g., Notre Dame football) can be a primary motivator for some individuals to attend a sporting event.

ADVERTISING

Advertising has been defined as "any paid form of non-personal presentation of ideas, goods, or services by an identified sponsor" (Irwin, Sutton, & McCarthy, 2008, p. 4). However, advances in technology, including the rise of social media, have created opportunities to advertise at little or no cost. Most collegiate sport marketers use a combination of both traditional and online advertising to effectively reach their entire fan base.

Traditional advertising in intercollegiate athletics usually consists of print, outdoor, and broadcast media. Although these types of media are thought to be less popular, many institutions continue to use them to reach older fan demographics. At James Madison University, the athletics marketing department places advertisements in local newspapers and magazines, rents billboards along the interstate, mails season-ticket brochures, places flyers in locations around the community, and creates commercials for local radio and television stations. Each of these types of advertising, of course, carries a purchase or rental cost.

These efforts notwithstanding, in recent years a majority of advertising has been shifted online to try to capture a portion of the 1.4 billion people using social media (Arno, 2012). In particular, many intercollegiate athletics programs use online advertising to appeal to their younger demographics. A 2012 survey revealed that 94 percent of marketers used social media for marketing (Miller, 2012). The same survey found that 92 percent of marketers used Facebook, 72 percent planned to increase their Facebook presence, and 69 percent intended to increase their activity on Twitter.

According to Fugere (2013), online advertising and social media are replacing traditional forms of advertising for a number of reasons.

- They are cost effective—unless you opt to pay for promotions, social media are free.
- They go viral.
- They live forever—what happens on the Internet stays on the Internet.
- They foster relationships—social media provide two-way communication channels.
- They generate leads—social media are trackable and make it possible to measure the exact impact that a social campaign has on a company's success.

The CBSSports.com College Network produces websites for approximately 150 athletics departments, including those at such prominent schools as the University of Notre Dame and the University of Southern California. The advantage for these institutions lies in the fact that CBSSports.com

---

The University of Michigan's Social Media and Online Presence

The University of Michigan athletics department maintains the following kinds of social media and online presence ("Follow the Wolverines," 2013):

- Facebook—each sport has its own page, and the football page has garnered more than a million "likes."
- Twitter—each sport has its own account, and football has well over 100,000 followers.
- YouTube—fans can watch videos from all of Michigan's varsity sports.
- Apps—options are provided for iPhone, Android, and iPad.
- Instagram—fans can view visually enhanced behind-the-scenes and game-day images.
- Foursquare—Wolverine fans can "check in" at any Michigan sport venue and become eligible for giveaways, unlock exclusive offers, and learn Michigan trivia while connecting with other fans.
- E-mail newsletter—A good way to collect e-mail addresses and provide fans with recent information about the sports program or specific team.

produces, manages, and hosts their athletics website, along with their e-commerce solutions, streaming products, and mobile services (CBS Sports, 2012). Other companies, including NeuLion and Sidearm Sports, also power websites for a number of athletics departments across the country.

Depending on the size of the college or university, as well as the particular needs of its athletics department, day-to-day management of a website may either be outsourced to a multimedia company or be handled in-house. When it is handled in-house, the marketing department often includes an employee responsible for maintaining the site. Increasingly, however, the trend is to outsource the function of producing and managing website content to multimedia companies. Many colleges and universities also realize the value of streaming content, which allows stakeholders such as students, fans, parents, and alumni to watch various sporting events that they would otherwise not be able to see in person. The cost for streaming video is relatively inexpensive for most colleges and universities, and it meets the needs of providing content to these numerous stakeholder groups.

One of the challenges of marketing in intercollegiate athletics is appealing to the many stakeholder groups. Consider for a moment how perceptions of athletics on campus can differ between faculty, administrators, students, student-athletes, coaches, parents, alumni, local fans, and corporate sponsors. For example, many faculty perceive athletics as an intrusion into the academic mission of the university and are therefore not interested in the success of the athletics program. In contrast, alumni often demand winning performance and view their affiliation with the university through the lens of the athletics program's level of success. For some students, their very choice of a university depends on the success of the athletics program.

With all of this in mind, athletics is sometimes viewed as the front porch of the university. As a result, the various social media platforms are used not only as a way to provide information about the athletics program but also to also extend the brand of the university. In fact, for many individuals, their first impression of a college or university comes through athletics. One example can be found at Florida Gulf Coast University, which received instant recognition on television and social media platforms after its success in the 2013 NCAA men's basketball tournament.

LICENSING

How often do you see someone wearing a shirt or cap bearing the name of a college or university? The answer is probably quite often. Colleges and universities use licensing as a way to extend their brand. More specifically, licensing is a contractual method that universities use to develop and exploit their intellectual property by transferring the rights of use to third parties without transferring ownership. For example, you can purchase a lamp and various other accessories bearing the UCLA Bruins logo that are manufactured by a company called CSI International in Niagara Falls, New York. In order to use a school's logo, the licensee (e.g., CSI International) may pay an initial licensing fee or a royalty fee, and it assumes the risks inherent in making the product. In turn, the licensor (e.g., UCLA) looks for potential licensees and polices the marketplace for anyone selling products bearing its name or marks without permission.

The advantage of licensing for most colleges and universities comes in the form of increased awareness of the institution's name. In some cases, licensing also allows the university to expand into new markets while assuming little risk. For example, a university that wants to enhance its image among high school students could put its name on a product that appeals to the high school market.

The potential disadvantage of licensing hinges on the fact that the school can lose control when another party makes a product bearing the university's name. To minimize problems, the Collegiate Licensing Company (CLC) was formed in 1981 to help schools protect and control the use of their logos through trademark licensing. CLC currently works with more than 200 colleges and universities, various bowl games, athletics conferences, the Heisman Trophy Trust, and the NCAA. CLC was purchased in 2007 by IMG Worldwide and operates as an affiliate of IMG College (Collegiate Licensing Company, 2014).

MARKETING AND ATMOSPHERICS

For students, alumni, and other fans, the atmosphere at a stadium or arena can offer an exciting escape from the worries of the day. In fact, game-day environments at various universities can be very interesting. For example, television cameras at Cameron Indoor Stadium in Durham, North Carolina, often capture Duke University students with painted faces, who are referred to by television announcers as the "Cameron Crazies." For many fans, the emotional appeal of being part of the game-day atmosphere is a motivational factor, and this motivation can be used as a tool through which collegiate sport marketers generate excitement.

Atmospheric management refers to intentional control and structure based on environmental cues, and it starts with an understanding of the target market (Schwarz, Hunter, & Lafleur, 2013). It is considered part of the promotional mix in sport, focusing in particular on the "place of purchase," and may include elements of the physical setting as well as sensory elements. Although a sport marketer has little if any control over the outcome of an athletic competition itself, he or she can exert influence on the physical setting of athletics facilities.

With this in mind, universities across the country spent roughly US$15 billion on new or improved sport facilities between 1995 and 2005 (Bennett, 2012). Both smaller and larger institutions are continuously revamping their facilities or building new stadiums, arenas, and practice facilities. For example, California University of Pennsylvania recently spent an estimated US$40 million on a new 142,000-square-foot (13,000-square-meter) convocation center, which it boasts is the largest indoor venue between Morgantown, West Virginia, and Pittsburgh, Pennsylvania. In addition, Cornell University recently renovated the Lynah Rink to add additional seating, expand the concourse, add luxury seating, and upgrade the locker facilities and lobby space ("College athletics," 2007).

Such upgrades allow sport administrators to exercise greater control over the physical environment and further expand various sensory elements—components of the game-day atmosphere that appeal to spectators' five senses of sight, hearing, touch, taste, and smell. Such components involve a wide range of factors, from the smells generated by concession stands, to seating for the band members who provide music at the event, to improved public address systems, along with numerous other amenities.

Sight

The core product on the court or field is the contest itself; therefore, much of what consumers watch are, of course, the athletes. Granted, most athletics programs at colleges and universities highlight the importance of academics and use the term "student-athlete" when referring to an athlete. The NCAA even runs a commercial noting that more than 400,000 student-athletes are "going pro in something other than sports." At the same time, athletics is a drawing card, and the athletics department at Ohio State University was one of the first to recognize the entertainment value of sport in its mission statement. Today, many intercollegiate sport events include some form of entertainment.

Universities recognize that athletes serve as entertainers on the court or field. With this entertainment function in mind, intercollegiate sport marketers also schedule various performers to entertain during intermissions, timeouts, and other breaks in the athletic action. Performers range from

---

Top Five Songs Played at Major League Sporting Events in 2009–2010 according to BMI

1. "We Will Rock You" by Queen
2. "Let It Rock" by Kevin Rudolf with Lil Wayne
3. "Burn It to the Ground" by Nickelback
4. "Boom Boom Pow" by the Black Eyed Peas
5. "Car Wash" by Christina Aguilera and Missy Elliot

From M. Rand, 2011, "The list of popular music is sure to depress you," *Minneapolis Star Tribune.* Available: www.startribune.com/sports/blogs/116873753.html.

mascots to impersonators of superstars (e.g., Michael Jackson or Elvis) to local acts (e.g., school rope-jumping teams, jugglers, and animal acts).

Hearing

Auditory elements, such as the public address system and music, are key factors in providing spectators with information and adding entertainment value. The public address announcer serves as the master of ceremonies and keeps the audience informed about the latest happenings during the event. Music is also used by sport marketers to excite the crowd and set the scene, and computer technology now gives event personnel access to hundreds of songs. What is so great about music is that it evokes memories and incites emotion in individual spectators.

In collegiate sport, of course, music is also played by marching bands and pep bands. Fight songs played by marching bands often appeal to the pride and emotion of university alumni. The alma mater is sung after football games at places like the University of Notre Dame and Ohio State University. Thus music can be used by collegiate sport marketers as a form of entertainment, but it also appeals to memories of days gone by and to the attachments that alumni and current students form to their college or university.

Touch

Perhaps the most difficult of the five senses for sport marketers to appeal to is the sense of touch. To engage this sense among its fans after winning the national championship in basketball, the University of Kentucky took the NCAA trophy on a statewide tour and allowed fans to touch it and have their photos taken with it ("Kentucky's NCAA trophy," 2012). Unlike the athletes, spectators are normally passive during the athletic contest itself. However, sport marketers can engage spectators through the sense of touch by using creative in-game promotions. Examples include shooting contests, dizzy-bat races, and football throws, as well as songs played over the public address system to promote coordinated clapping or stomping. This type of in-game promotion allows for hands-on involvement by spectators.

Taste and Smell

Taste and smell are widely used by marketers of intercollegiate sport. Of the five senses, smell is the most strongly connected to an individual's emotions and therefore is used to create lasting connections with fans. Key smells can include natural elements, such as newly cut grass in baseball or the smell of sweat in a gymnasium. The most notable smells, however, come from concession foods. For example, spectators attending a football game at Williams-Brice Stadium at the University of South Carolina can taste and smell Thai food. At Sanford Stadium at the University of Georgia, lemonade is a popular choice (Luther, 2012). Many athletics departments outsource their concession operations to companies such as Aramark and Levy Restaurants.

The sport industry is a service-related industry, and the experience that a fan undergoes at a sporting contest is intangible. In contrast, most consumer products (e.g., computers, automobiles, office products) are tangible in the sense that they can be touched. Despite the intangible nature of the sport product, however, atmospherics allow the sport consumer to have some tangible experiences in the process.

COMMUNITY RELATIONS

Athletics programs around the country are emphasizing the importance of community relations initiatives. Athletes in these programs are involved in initiatives such as reading to school groups, visiting hospitals, running youth league clinics, and coordinating canned food drives. The traditional idea of community relations is that an organization will "give back" and serve as a "good citizen" in its respective community. This notion derives from corporate public relations, which encompasses all non-sales-oriented public relations activities designed to reach target audiences (Irwin et al., 2008).

Waddock and Boyle (1995) suggest that although many companies want to support the community relations function, the pressure to become a global competitor and the shifting demands made on employees affect the ways in which companies define and work with their communities. Corporations are becoming more sophisticated in terms of developing strategies to deal with community issues, such as environmental degradation, educational problems, poverty, and crime. Thus, marketers of intercollegiate athletics must be aware of these issues and how they can be leveraged within their program.

Most athletics departments include at least one employee devoted to handling what is called community affairs or community outreach. For example, bilingual student-athletes at Ohio State have helped promote literacy by reading to primary school students at the Columbus Spanish Immersion Academy. The celebrity of athletes provides sport organizations with advantages over other businesses in providing inspiration in areas such as education, health care, environmental concerns, and other social or cultural issues.

Intercollegiate athletics programs recognize the need to partner with the community to enhance the relationship between "town and gown." For example, South Georgia State College in Douglas, Georgia, seeks to build relationships, encourage participation, and solicit the support of local civic groups, local businesses, community leaders, and local citizens through community relations efforts ("Mission Statement," 2013). In another example, community relations programs at UCLA are implemented in the marketing department through programs such as I'm Going to College, Athletics for Youth, Bruin School Days, youth football, Adopt a Classroom, and Reading Days. In the Adopt a Classroom program, a school registers a classroom, and UCLA officials assign it to a member of one of the participating teams. The student-athlete then corresponds with students in the designated classroom throughout the season. The program concludes with an opportunity for the students to visit UCLA to cheer on the team and meet their student-athlete after the event ("Programs," 2013).

Stanford University views community involvement as integral to developing both strong, well-rounded student-athletes and a unified athletics department. Stanford's community relations platform—Stand Tall, Stand Proud—is based on four principles: to teach, to lead, to win, and to serve. Community relations initiatives at Stanford include Commitment to Excellence on the Farm, Ronald

McDonald House, Habitat for Humanity, Cardinal for the Community, Haven House, and the Opportunity Center ("Community Relations," 2013).

Such programs highlight the fact that the college or university seeks to serve the local community. As athletics programs expand, institutions buy new land for building additional facilities, and local residents sometimes question the institution's motives. However, most institutions want to be perceived as contributing to the community. In a similar manner, the sponsor (e.g., McDonald's) wants to give back to the local community and form partnerships with those affiliated with the institution.

Community relations differs from marketing in important ways. Marketing involves an organization's efforts to meet the needs and wants of its consumers, whereas community relations involves more of an obligation on the part of the organization to give back to the local community. Therefore, students interested in cause-related initiatives should consider a career in community relations. Many sport organizations have departments dedicated to public and community relations. In intercollegiate sport, the majority of athletics departments carry out this function through the marketing department. Responsibilities in a community relations position may include coordinating charitable donation programs, athletes' appearances, and pregame and on-field activities. Most job descriptions for community relations positions require someone with excellent communication, organizational, and interpersonal skills.

NATIONAL ASSOCIATION OF COLLEGIATE MARKETING ADMINISTRATORS

As with many fields in the sport industry, sport marketing has its own professional development association. The National Association of Collegiate Marketing Administrators (NACMA) is home to more than 1,200 members and "provides educational and professional development opportunities for career advancement in marketing, revenue generation, and communication" ("NACMA Mission Statement," 2013). NACMA is an affiliate of the National Association of Collegiate Directors of Athletics (NACDA). Founded in 1965 and headquartered in Ohio, NACDA has more than 6,000

Industry Profile
Craig Pintens

University of Oregon, senior associate athletics director for marketing and public relations

How long have you been in this role at the University of Oregon?

I started in September 2011.

What are your current job responsibilities?

Oversee the marketing and communication departments, serve as department spokesperson, manage the IMG College relationship, and serve as the liaison with the Pac-12 Network.

Oregon is one of the social media leaders in collegiate athletics. How has the Oregon athletics department used social media, and how valuable are social media?

We utilize social media as a key component of our overall communication strategy. Social media is a great way to reach our fans and provide the type of interaction that helps further our brand initiatives. We place a lot of value on social media because it is a great way to instantly reach your fan base at a high frequency. It is a vital part of our communication mix.

How did you break into the sport industry?

My first job was with the Milwaukee Brewers answering phones to sell tickets in the call center during the summer of 1998. With the home run chase, the Brewers had a number of games down the stretch against the [St. Louis] Cardinals and [Chicago] Cubs. It was a lot of fun.

What has been your biggest professional accomplishment?

It still is yet to come. I don't spend too much time looking back at what has been accomplished, but instead look forward to what can be accomplished.

What has been the greatest challenge in your career?

Breaking into the industry is the hardest part, as once you get your foot in the door it is all downhill.

What is one story you are continuing to watch in the world of sport today?

How are we going to attract fans into our venues when we are competing with excellent television coverage?

What advice would you offer for people considering a career in this industry?

You need to have passion. Working in sports is a lifestyle, not a career. If you can't get excited about getting up every morning and doing this, then it isn't for you.

---

members from all kinds of colleges and universities in the NCAA, the National Association of Intercollegiate Athletics, and the National Junior College Athletic Association ("Infographic," 2013).

NACMA members share promotional ideas and marketing strategies with each other. NACMA offers membership to students and to active employees working for an athletics department, on-campus property, corporation, or outsourced marketing agency (e.g., Learfield Sports, IMG College). Benefits of a NACMA membership include the following:

- Members can register as mentees and mentors in NACMA's professional development mentoring program. Mentees are paired up with and given an opportunity to learn from veteran collegiate athletics administrators.

- Members can attend the annual convention at a discounted rate to learn about industry trends, participate in interactive breakout sessions, and network with peers across the country.

- Members enjoy access to an online library of resources and best practices for marketing, ticketing, and promotions.

- Discounted membership pricing is available for students.

SECONDARY TICKET MARKET

Tickets sales make up an important part of the overall revenue for athletics departments. According to NCAA statistics, schools in the Football Bowl Subdivision had over US$45.6 million in combined ticket sales in 2012 (National Collegiate Athletic Association, 2014). Traditionally, revenue sports (e.g., football, hockey) subsidize nonrevenue sports at most institutions. Though many fans get their tickets directly from the institution's athletics ticket office, athletics departments are increasingly realizing the importance of the secondary ticket market.

Individual athletics departments and their respective conferences, as well as the NCAA, have all recently started signing revenue-sharing deals with online secondary ticket companies such as StubHub (Cozart, 2010). Institutions such as Michigan State University, the University of Maryland, and the University of Pittsburgh work with StubHub to offer a place for fans to buy and sell tickets to their sporting events. In this way, athletics officials can refer ticketless fans to a website that helps ensure the legitimacy of the marketplace. The outsourced companies share their profit from resold tickets with the athletics department.

The secondary ticket market, also known as the resale market, exists between fans and brokers of event tickets after they have been purchased from the primary market (Burgess, 2012). The primary ticket market, on the other hand, involves tickets sold by a sport team, an outsourced ticket agency (e.g., Ticketmaster), or an artist. The secondary market includes the person-to-person resale market (e.g., buying from a friend); the scalper market, in which tickets are resold in the vicinity of the sport venue; and the secondary ticket websites (e.g., StubHub, Razorgator, and TicketsNow) that provide access to ticket deals and sold-out tickets.

Although the traditional marketplace for intercollegiate athletics departments has been the primary market, more institutions are realizing the value of the secondary market. Burgess (2012) notes the following benefits of the secondary ticket market:

- Exhaustive inventory (tickets generally available for whatever event you want to attend)
- Aggregate prices that provide consumers with a comprehensive picture of what is available
- Detailed analytics and price forecasts, which ensure that the consumer gets the best deal
- Possibility of purchasing tickets below face value
- Transparent fees

The secondary ticket market is estimated to account for billions of dollars in sales each year (Burgess, 2012). The leading website in the secondary ticket market is StubHub.com, a subsidiary of eBay that brought in estimated revenues of US$325 million for all sport events in 2010. As much as 65 percent of the total sales on such websites are conducted by individual or part-time sellers; the remaining 35 percent involve large sellers or brokers (Ozanian, 2011).

Secondary ticket websites are valuable to sport teams but have also been criticized. The secondary market does allow sport teams to offer additional value to season-ticket holders. For example, season-ticket holders at the University of Texas may find comfort in knowing that they can resell a ticket on StubHub if they are unable to attend a football game. Secondary ticket websites also offer consumers the option of buying or selling tickets and some offer loyalty programs along with guarantees that your tickets will arrive in time and be valid for entry at the event. The sites have been criticized, however, for underselling tickets and for allowing large brokers to purchase tickets in bulk, thus precluding individual sport consumers from buying them.

Within college football, secondary ticket markets have impacted supply and demand within Division I College Bowl Games. In particular, low prices charged by secondary ticketing sites have reduced the number of tickets that athletic departments have been able to sell. This ticketing dilemma is described further in the following case study.

DYNAMIC TICKET PRICING

The prices of season, mini-plan, and single-game tickets for intercollegiate sporting events are

The Impact of Secondary Ticket Markets on BCS Bowl Games: Virginia Tech Versus Rutgers in the Russell Athletic Bowl

The Russell Athletic Bowl is played at the Citrus Bowl stadium in Orlando, Florida, which seats more than 65,000 spectators. Russell Athletic signed an agreement in 2012 with Citrus Sports to be the title sponsor of the game through 2015. The Russell Athletic Bowl currently matches top teams from the Atlantic Coast Conference and the American Athletic Conference. However, in the BCS era it matched the top non-BCS (Bowl Championship Series) selection from the Big East with the second non-BCS selection from the ACC. The 2012 game was played on Friday, December 28, at 5:30 p.m. and featured a matchup between the ACC's Virginia Tech Hokies and the Big East's Rutgers Scarlet Knights. The game was broadcast on ESPN.

More generally, college football teams in 2012 played in 35 NCAA bowl games, for which more than US$290 million in payouts derived from television contracts and sponsors, such as Russell Athletic. Each team in the 2012 Russell Athletic Bowl received about US$1.5 million. This type of payout is divided between several shareholders. For example, the Big East shares all of its television and bowl money equally after paying expense allowances and mileage credits to those who qualify for the bowl on a tiered basis. Tiering refers to media rights. First-tier media rights normally refers to games picked up by national television media outlets, whereas a third-tier right may refer to a game televised regionally. Teams must also pay to bring players, coaches, bands, cheerleaders, boosters, and administrators. In addition, payments must be made to coaches who have an incentive clause built into their contract for appearing in a bowl game (Sherman & Renshaw, 2012).

The Ticketing Dilemma

To the average fan watching various bowl games on television, it may seem as if the schools are raking in the money. However, the NCAA reports that US$12.8 million in bowl tickets went unsold or were given away in 2011. At the same time, participating schools are asked to sell an allotment of tickets while competing against secondary ticket market websites such as StubHub. According to AD Jim Weaver, Virginia Tech was allotted 13,500 tickets to sell for the Russell Athletic Bowl. Virginia Tech was fully responsible for selling 6,000 of these tickets and partially responsible for another 2,000. Beyond those totals, the Atlantic Coast Conference would eat the cost of any unsold tickets. However, 17 days prior to the game, Virginia Tech had sold only about 3,000 of its allotted seats. As Virginia Tech was selling these tickets for $72 on its website, seats for the same game could be found on StubHub for as low as $4 per seat (Bitter, 2012). Meanwhile, Rutgers was allotted 12,500 tickets and had sold only 5,500 just days prior to the game (Sherman & Renshaw, 2012).

As you can see, a bowl game is not always the money-making proposition that many people believe it is. When Virginia Tech played Michigan in the Allstate Sugar Bowl on January 3, 2012, the school incurred US$3.18 million in expenses and US$954,770 in unsold tickets. Similarly, in West Virginia University's 2012 Orange Bowl victory over Clemson, it lost US$217,000 after tabulating all of its expenses. In another example, in 2008, Rutgers appeared in the PapaJohns.com Bowl in Birmingham, Alabama, and despite receiving US$1.2 million for its appearance still lost US$184,000 after spending money to send the band and cheerleaders with the team (Sherman & Renshaw, 2012).

Because of these costs, the difficulty of selling tickets to bowl games is of great concern to universities. In the case of Virginia Tech, it was difficult to sell tickets to the Russell Athletic Bowl in part because the team had been invited to prestigious BCS bowl games (e.g., the Sugar

Bowl) in past years. In addition, universities are trying to sell tickets to high-capacity stadiums and must compete against low-priced tickets sold on the secondary market.

Case Study Questions

1. What are some ways in which teams can minimize the impact of the secondary ticket market should they decide to accept a bid to a bowl such as the Russell Athletic Bowl?

2. If you had been a ticket representative at Virginia Tech, how would you have marketed tickets for the Russell Athletic Bowl to alumni, current students, and local fans in Orlando?

3. If you had been a ticket representative at Rutgers, how would you have marketed tickets for the Russell Athletic Bowl to alumni, current students, and local fans in Orlando?

typically set months before a team begins play. Preseason ticket sales for revenue sports are important to most athletics departments because they indicate expected attendance for the upcoming season. Ticket sales prior to the start of the season also help spur excitement about the upcoming season and build momentum for additional sales during the season. For ticket holders, buying tickets prior to the start of the season offers the advantage of reduced prices.

In recent years, however, teams have begun to realize that ticket prices have not truly reflected fair market value and that additional revenue could be made. As a result, institutions have been begun adopting the model of dynamic ticket pricing that has become increasingly popular in professional sport. At the forefront of this move in college sport have been such prominent institutions as the University of California, the University of Washington, and the University of South Florida. As perfected by the secondary ticket market, dynamic ticket pricing allows fan demand, or the lack thereof, to set the ticket prices for each sporting event. Specifically, dynamic pricing is defined as a "pricing strategy in which prices change either over time, across consumers, or across product/service bundles" (Kannan & Kopalle, 2001, p. 63). In the context of sport, ticket prices may change based on factors such as the day and time of the contest, the strength of the opponent, the weather, or overall demand for tickets.

One leader in dynamic ticket pricing software is Qcue, which has formed a partnership with the University of California athletics department, as well as many professional teams. The company's software "analyze[s] real-time sales data and other external factors to generate sales and revenue forecasts based on various pricing strategies" ("Qcue," 2012). External factors that can be considered in the analysis include the opponent, the team record, player performance, day of the week, time of the game, and weather conditions. Within minutes of evaluation, the team can recommend price changes, and Qcue's software will make the necessary adjustments on all ticketing platforms.

The athletics department at the University of California offers a good example of dynamic ticket pricing. Prior to the football season, athletics staff may deem their in-conference contest against the University of Oregon to be a premium game. Anticipating a sellout, the dynamic ticket pricing model allows ticket prices to increase as the game draws closer and ticket inventory decreases. In contrast, Cal staff might view the home game against unranked Colorado as one that will not draw as well. As a result, the dynamic ticket pricing model lowers prices below face value to drive attendance. The Cal staff will not, however, drop the price below the season-ticket holder price per ticket (University of California, 2013). The Cal athletics department also uses dynamic pricing to encourage fans to purchase early or become season-ticket holders. At the same time, fans who do hold season tickets are not affected by the school's dynamic pricing structure; they are still guaranteed to pay the best possible price.

The dynamic ticket pricing model provides many benefits. Digonex, another leader in the dynamic ticket pricing software industry, suggests the following benefits of dynamic ticket pricing ("Why Digonex?," 2011):

- Increases revenue with more accurate pricing over a unit's life cycle
- Increases attendance to increase sales of ancillary products
- Generates additional revenue during peak sales periods
- Stimulates sales when demand subsides to get people in seats
- Generates excitement and a sense of urgency to buy

Still, not all schools are prepared to endure the risks associated with dynamic ticket pricing. A survey conducted by Paciolan, maker of a software used widely by athletics ticket departments for managing ticket sales, found that 19 percent of institutions said they were moderately likely to adopt dynamic pricing within the next year (Smith, 2012). Why the reluctance? For one thing, since dynamic ticket prices fluctuate throughout the season, fans may become upset or feel alienated if they paid more per ticket than someone else sitting in the same section at the same game. To compensate, teams need to increase overall communication with fans and encourage preseason ticket sales. In addition, the process of moving to a dynamic ticketing solution can present challenges for an athletics departments in the form of adopting new technology, training employees, and educating consumers about how ticketing will change.

Here are some suggestions for athletics administrators who are considering the transition to dynamic ticketing. First, consult with other institutions that have adopted dynamic ticketing and take into account the strengths and weaknesses of implementing such a system at your institution. Second, contact software companies, such as Digonex and Qcue, to learn more about dynamic ticketing. Third, develop a plan and a timetable for launching dynamic ticketing. Once you have developed a plan, the athletics department should begin to educate its consumer base about the benefits of dynamic ticketing. It should also start the process of training employees about these benefits

and the technical aspects of using the dynamic ticketing software.

PROMOTION

Attending a sporting event provides a form of entertainment in exchange for an individual's time and money. Due to the large number of entertainment options available to potential consumers, sport marketers develop promotions to attract people to a game and provide entertainment throughout the event. With this context in mind, sport promotion is defined as "a fully integrated set of communication activities intended to persuade consumers toward a favorable belief or action as a tactical component of the overall marketing campaign" (Irwin et al., 2008, p. 3).

In-Game Promotion

Many institutions at every level of intercollegiate athletics implement some form of in-game promotional activity during sporting events. These promotions usually take place before play or during breaks in play—for example, in pregame and postgame time slots, at halftime, and during inning changes and timeouts. Some in-game promotions, such as tossing a t-shirt into the crowd when a baseball player hits a homerun, run for the entire length of a season. Others, such as Boy Scout Day or a performance by a celebrity musical act, take place at most a few times a year. Another popular promotion in may arenas is the scoreboard "kiss cam," which pans the crowd looking for a couple that will provide a "smooch" (Steinberg, 2013).

Since in-game entertainment is designed to incentivize people to become repeat buyers, most institutions include information about it on their athletics website and in collateral material. For example, George Mason University (GMU) describes its in-game promotional activities, and the respective sponsors, on its athletics website ("In-Game Promotions," 2012) in a sidebar titled GMU's In-Game Promotions.

In addition to running in-game contests, 94 percent of college marketing directors hire local and national acts to perform at games, usually during halftime (Martin, Miller, Elsisi, Bowers, & Hall, 2011). The following list gives a small sample of popular acts that travel the country every year to perform at professional and intercollegiate sporting events.

Leadership Lesson

Meetings and Movies

One of the most common problems in athletics departments is that of silos. Functional units accomplish the tasks they are charged to fulfill without realizing the synergistic potential of collaboration. In a recent study of the top 25 most followed NCAA Division I track and field Twitter accounts run by athletic sports information departments (Doran, 2013), not a single promotional tweet was found in the sample of over 4,000 tweets. A conclusion of the study was that many teams utilizing Twitter are not capitalizing on its promotional potential. The sports information account managers provide information to fans, but they do not appear to interface with those who might hope to market the programs. This chapter merges two units (ticketing and internal marketing) that in many universities run into problems when there is a lack of communication. In this leadership lesson we will focus on the effective use of meetings as an avenue to enhance departmental communication and combat the tendency for departmental silos.

In chapter 3 we presented traditional meetings best practices. These are helpful and can be relevant in many organizations. If meetings seem to be dragging, there is a lack of passionate debate, or if participants leave the meeting feeling bedraggled rather than energized, it might be time to take a different approach. Business consultant Patrick Lencioni has compared meetings to movies. He finds it baffling that most executives would rather spend two hours sitting in a movie that is inherently passive and irrelevant than sitting in a meeting that should be interactive and directly relevant to our lives (2004). He has urged executives to learn from screenwriters. In order for meetings to be captivating, there must be a hook, conflict that is nurtured so participants are engaged from action to credits, and clearly defined contextual structure.

The hook: Meeting participants should be given a reason to care; a reason to believe that what transpires within the meeting is critical to their lives. "The key to injecting drama into a meeting lies in setting up the plot from the outset. Participants need to be jolted a little during the first ten minutes of a meeting, so that they understand and appreciate what is at stake" (Lencioni, 2004, p. 228).

Nurtured conflict: Meetings exist to share information, discuss alternatives, and ultimately make decisions and action plans. When intelligent and vested people come together to discuss relevant issues, it is important and natural for disagreement to arise. As a meeting leader, this debate can be facilitated by expecting and encouraging conflict. In a moment of tension, for instance, a leader might interject, "Before you continue, and I definitely want you to continue, I just want to say that this is *exactly* the kind of thing I was talking about when I said we need to start engaging in more conflict..." (Lencioni, 2004, p. 231). When conflict is not addressed—when team members are not allowed or encouraged to advocate their positions and ideological passion—resentment can ensue and issues that could be resolved openly can fester and manifest themselves in political and interpersonal tension.

Defined contextual structure: One of the problems with agenda-driven weekly or monthly staff meetings is they often create "meeting stew" wherein issues are discussed, not necessarily in order of importance, jumping from strategic issues to tactical issues and everything in between. In order to avoid the lack of productivity associated with these stew-type meetings, Lencioni (2004) recommends four separate meetings:

1. **The daily check-in (or huddle):** The purpose of this meeting is for executive teams to report on their activities of the day, facilitate synergy, and avoid duplication of effort. This meeting is to be held for a maximum of five minutes with all participants standing.

2. **The weekly tactical:** The purpose of the regular weekly or biweekly tactical meeting is to discuss issues of immediate concern. It should last between 45 and 90 minutes progressing as follows:

    a. **The lightning round:** A quick reporting session in which each participant spends a maximum of 60 seconds reporting on two or three of their priorities for the week.

    b. **Progress review:** No more than five minutes is spent discussing progress toward key organizational metrics.

    c. **Real-time agenda:** Based on the issues raised in the lighting round and the progress review, the meeting's focus naturally evolves, acknowledging that only issues of immediate concern are discussed (long-term complex or policy-related discussions require additional preparation and can take the wind out of many real-time discussions).

3. **The monthly strategic meeting:** The purpose of the regular monthly strategic meeting is to wrestle with critical issues that determine the fundamental direction of the organization. The length of the meeting will vary depending on the number of topics considered, but at least two hours per topic should be allocated. Members should come prepared to discuss, defend, and challenge other perspectives about the issues.

4. **The quarterly off-site review:** The purpose of the quarterly review meeting is to step away from regular issues and routines to review the organization from a holistic perspective. Topics should include comprehensive strategy, team, personnel, and competitive or industry reviews.

Meetings should be viewed as a time-saver that can facilitate team-building and organizational synergy. The cohesive, proactive, passionate, and confrontational approach established in meetings will help to prevent politics and enhance productivity throughout the organization. To illustrate this, imagine the different outcomes of two athletic departments: One with a cohesive sports information, marketing, ticketing, media, and development team working together in constant communication with one another, and another where department heads meet, but very little cross-functional cooperation exists. In the first department, you can imagine the energy and creative approaches to facilitate fan involvement, and in the second department, you might find a sports information director generating a tremendous amount of tweets, but only communicating one perspective in a broad organizational mission.

The final step to maximize meeting productivity has been labeled *cascading communication* (Lencioni, 2004). Teams should take a moment to identify key messages that need to be communicated. It can be helpful to review the progress made throughout the meeting, clarify any confusion among the executive staff, and emphasize the information that should (or should not yet) be communicated to the lower levels of the organizational hierarchy. When executive teams are on the same page, other staff within the organization will sense and reflect that unity.

- Extreme Team (www.extremedunks.com)
- ZOOperstars (www.zooperstars.com)
- Red Panda (www.talentbookingusa.com/comedy/red-panda.htm)
- Tom Silver, Hypnotist (www.hypnosiswebcasts.com)
- AcroDunk (www.acrodunk.com)
- Quick Change (www.funny-business.com/quick-change)

The process of formulating a strategic promotional schedule begins several months before a season begins in order to ensure that all details can be carefully developed and implemented. To begin the brainstorming process, marketing teams examine the previous year's promotions and decide

GMU's In-Game Promotions

- **Chick-fil-A 80-Point Promotion**—When the men's basketball team scores 80 points during a home game, everyone in the crowd wins a free chicken sandwich.
- **Verizon Wireless Predict the Points**—Tweet @MasonMBB using the hashtag #mason-points with the number of points you think the Patriots will score in that night's men's game. One fan who guesses correctly will receive a special Verizon Wireless Pack.
- **Washington Post Post-Game Autographs and Free Throws**—After every weekend game, kids are invited to shoot postgame free throws on the floor of the Patriot Center and get autographs from selected Mason players.
- **University Mall Theatres Deal or No Deal**—One lucky contestant will be chosen to shoot for cash by making a layup, free throw, and three-pointer. The tricky part is risking the money you've earned to shoot for bigger prizes. If you miss, you go home with nothing. While in your seat, look to the sky for the falling bags of popcorn and movie passes from University Mall Theatres.
- **Apple Federal Credit Union T-Shirt Toss**—Get on your feet and make some noise. We will be launching free t-shirts at each home game to the loudest fans.
- **University Mall Lucky Row**—Grab a free Mason basketball program on your way into the Patriot Center each night, and if the inside cover is signed by the Patriot, then you and your entire row are winners.

which were popular enough to carry into a new season. Marketers can also research and observe peers' promotions and decide which would be enjoyable for their own fans. Once all promotions have been determined, marketers plug the information into the team's home schedule.

Some promotions, such as Girl Scout Day, are typically planned for a weekend game, when members of the target group are most likely to attend. Other promotions, such as ZOOperstars, might be scheduled for televised games or against nationally ranked opponents. Most national acts cost several thousand dollars per game, and sport marketers want to use these options for premium games. In fact, these performances often increase attendance at the event. They can also generate additional revenue, because many athletics marketing departments solicit corporate sponsorship to cover the cost of booking such acts.

There has been some debate among both professional and collegiate marketers about which games should be given increased promotion. Due to budget restraints, most teams cannot mount maximum promotions for every game and are therefore faced with a few options: focus on weekday games, which typically bring in lower attendance, or on weekend games when a larger crowd is expected. The idea behind using promotions for weekday games is to encourage fans to attend nonpremium games. Some marketers, however, would rather create the ultimate game-day experience when a nearly sold-out venue is anticipated. Fans at such games will have an enjoyable social experience and therefore will be motivated to attend more frequently. Either way, athletics marketers ultimately use promotion because of its potential to give them a return on their investment. Although a promotion adds to expenses, the cost is often outweighed by the additional revenues generated through corporate sales and the chance to incentivize new consumers and reach new markets.

To ensure the promotion runs smoothly, marketers of collegiate sporting events often use a timing sheet. A timing sheet simply provides the details as to what is happening on the field or court during the course of the event. The timing chart can be distributed to everyone involved in running the event and it helps to ensure that everyone knows what they are doing and when. A sample basketball timing sheet is shown below.

Sample Basketball Timing Sheet

James Madison University Basketball 2010–2011
Pregame/Halftime Format
James Madison Dukes vs. Duke Blue Devils
Tuesday, November 30, 2010 at 7:00 p.m.

Game Clock	EST	Activity
60:00	5:55 p.m.	Start countdown
55:00	6:00 p.m.	Court available for warm-up
30:00	6:25 p.m.	Teams leave floor
20:00	6:35 p.m.	Teams reenter arena
0:00	6:55 p.m.	National anthem by Brittany Young
		Recognition of Dawn Evans
		Team introductions
		DU (starters and coaches)
		JMU (starters and coaches)
	7:00 p.m.	Tip-off

First Half

There will be official media timeouts after the 16:00, 12:00, 8:00, and 4:00 minute marks, each with the duration of 105 seconds. Teams will each be entitled to four (4) 30-second timeouts and one (1) 60-second timeout for the game. Three (3) 30-second timeouts may be carried over to the second half. Two (2) 30-second timeouts may be called in succession but must be indicated by the coach or player when the timeout is called.

Halftime

15:00		Clear court
14:30		ZOOperstars!
6:00		PAs
5:00		Floor available for warm-up

Second Half

To allow for radio and television to run commercial advertisements without missing the action on the court, media timeouts are built into every game. There will be official media timeouts following a dead ball after the 16-, 12-, 8-, and 4-minute marks in both halves. In addition, the first called 30-second team timeout in the second half will automatically become a full-length media timeout and will not replace the next scheduled media timeout.

Top Giveaway Items

Here are the top giveaway items as ranked by Broughton (2012) in *SportsBusiness Journal*'s annual survey of Major League Baseball teams.

1. Bobblehead
2. T-shirt
3. Headwear
4. Backpack/bag
5. Magnet schedule

6. Photo
7. Toy
8. Poster
9. Jersey
10. Retail coupon

Sales Promotion

Whereas in-game promotions provide entertainment value during a game, sales promotion provides incentives to stimulate sales and increase attendance. According to Irwin et al. (2008), sales promotion seeks to influence buyers' behavior and generally comes in the form of reduced prices, premium giveaways, contests, free samples, and other add-ons.

The University of Iowa athletics department offers a variety of giveaway items and ticket discounts to entice people to attend home basketball games. Here is a sampling of Iowa's sales promotion offerings ("Iowa Men's Basketball," 2012).

- Family Four-Pack Night—$45 buys four tickets, four hot dogs, and four sodas
- Camper Reunion Day—free admission for all men's basketball campers
- UI faculty/staff appreciation night—free admission for faculty and staff
- Player, mascot, and coach bobbleheads
- Free pizza for Iowa students
- Dollar dog night—$1 buys a hot dog

Another form of sales promotion used to increase attendance is the student reward program, which has become an increasingly popular approach in recent years. It is important to most institutions that students attend athletic events. Student attendance enhances the game-day atmosphere and contributes to the pride that students take in the institution. As a result, in many cases, the athletics department allocates a certain number of tickets for student use. When these tickets are not claimed by students, however, they are often returned to inventory and in some cases go unsold. One way of addressing this issue is through student reward programs.

In 2008, the University of Tennessee athletics department established a student reward program as a way to increase awareness and attendance among its student population. Both undergraduate and graduate students are eligible to earn a certain number of points by attending selected sporting events. As students accumulate points, they rise to various prize levels at which they can receive premium items. The prizes range from t-shirts and hats to shorts and sweatpants ("Student Rewards," 2013). The results of Tennessee's student reward program are encouraging. Average student attendance has increased by 300 percent for nonrevenue sports and 177 percent for all sports combined ("University of Tennessee Student Rewards Program," 2010).

CONCLUSION

Intercollegiate athletics marketers can gain a competitive advantage by leveraging the newest technology in order to increase revenue from ticket sales and conduct promotional campaigns. Marketers now use various types of social media to connect with their fans. In addition, new and improved athletics facilities across the country continue to raise sport consumers' expectations. Sport marketers must be aware of these expectations and find ways to create a game-day atmosphere that meets them. Finally, intercollegiate athletics programs are increasingly looking for ways to connect with their community. Community relations programs should not only target the campus and community but also take into account the global nature of the sport product.

DISCUSSION QUESTIONS

1. How do the primary and secondary ticket markets differ?
2. What main factors affect ticket pricing for colleges and universities that use dynamic ticket pricing?
3. Describe the difference between in-game promotion and sales promotion.
4. How can a sport marketer use atmospherics to appeal to a spectator's sense of hearing?
5. Describe some ways in which athletics programs advertise their products and services.
6. Why do intercollegiate athletics programs emphasize community relations initiatives?

LEARNING ACTIVITIES

1. Secondary ticket market—First, view the website of your favorite college or university and see if it offers an opportunity for season-ticket holders to sell unused tickets. Second, choose a large Division I team and compare the price of a ticket purchased on its website with the price on StubHub.com. Write a one paragraph summary of your findings.
2. In-game promotion—Attend a local college or university athletic event and make a list of the in-game promotions during the event. Chart their purpose and when they occur (e.g., halftime, timeouts).
3. Community relations—Choose a social problem related to education, poverty, or the environment. Then develop a community relations program that addresses your chosen problem. Describe the program in detail.

Courtesy of Virginia Tech Athletics

CHAPTER 9

Corporate Sponsorship

Robert Zullo, Seton Hill University

In this chapter, you will explore

- various platforms that businesses can use to market themselves;

- different types of inventory available to businesses who become corporate partners;

- how the sales process operates, including some challenges specific to intercollegiate athletics; and

- how to assess sponsorship effectiveness, including strategies to offset ambush marketing efforts.

SUSTAINING SPONSORSHIP SUPPORT

After a highly successful basketball season that included capacity crowds and a postseason bid, the head coach just announced his plan to depart your program for a higher-paying job. Students, fans, and alumni are concerned about the effect of his departure because the program had been a long-standing doormat prior to his arrival. In addition, sponsors are concerned that the loss of the head coach will result in less attendance at games and therefore less exposure. As an account executive, how would you convince your sponsors to sustain or even increase their financial commitment to sporting events during this time? How can you save this vital revenue stream?

Depending on the size and scope of an institution's athletics department, a sport marketing director may handle a tremendous variety of responsibilities. In larger institutions, the position generally entails promoting the athletics department's brand to loyal patrons in an effort to drive ticket sales. This work often involves crafting and implementing promotional efforts and implementing exciting game-day experiences by coordinating a script detailing event progression and management of the music, cheerleaders, videoboard, announcers, officials, and everything in between. At a smaller school, the sport marketing director may also serve as the licensing liaison for organizations interested in using the school's athletics-related intellectual property, as well as the driving force behind community relations efforts and sponsorship sales. This chapter focuses on one of these responsibilities—the development of corporate partnerships.

The word *sponsor* can be used interchangeably in this context with *partner*, because businesses can support the athletics department either through financial support that enhances revenue or through in-kind gifts that reduce expenses. Either way, this support is offered in return for the opportunity for the sponsor to be affiliated with the department's teams in hopes of garnering support from the organization's fans (Donavan, Carlson, & Zimmerman, 2005). Viewing corporate sponsors as partners fits well with a relationship marketing mind-set, which is built on the idea that sport patrons themselves are more than consumers and should be viewed as partners for the long run rather than as a mere source of immediate financial gratification (Capulsky & Wolf, 1990). Relationship marketing can enhance a school's competitive advantage over its peers through sustainable partnerships that outlast negative developments such as losses or poor off-the-field behavior (Morgan & Hunt, 1999). Corporate partnerships offer the sport marketing director the chance to forge a long-term relationship based on interactive and personal communication built on the premise of an equal partnership (Shani, 1997).

PLATFORMS

Businesses can promote themselves to prospective customers in many ways. Chick-fil-A, for example, can use any of a variety of options for advertising or promoting its products, including direct mailing of coupons as well as advertising in newspapers or on radio, television, billboards, or the Internet. The company can also promote itself or its products through the formation of a corporate sponsorship or partnership. *Sponsorship* is a two-way exchange between a sport organization and a corporate partner. The business pays a rights fee or offers in-kind remuneration for the opportunity to promote itself. As the example of Chick-fil-A suggests, even a single business and a single sport organization can find a variety of avenues through which to engage in mutually beneficial exchanges. Indeed, using a variety of platforms can add complexity to the sponsorship process, and a business such as Chick-fil-A has many options for forming corporate partnerships in college sport alone (Irwin, Sutton, & McCarthy, 2008).

PROPERTY

For sponsorship purposes, the athletics department is known as the *property or rights holder,* which means that it controls its property and determines

Platforms Available in College Sport With Examples

School—Hardees sponsors Virginia Tech athletics.

Team—Great Atlantic Lacrosse Company sponsors University of North Carolina lacrosse.

Facility—Verizon sponsors the Verizon Center, home of the Georgetown Hoyas basketball team.

Conference—BB&T is a sponsor at the Corporate Champions level of the Atlantic Coast Conference.

Governance level—Coca-Cola is a sponsor at the Corporate Champion level of the National Collegiate Athletic Association (NCAA Corporate, 2013).

Coach—Stop In Food Stores sponsors Virginia Tech head football coach Frank Beamer and his BeamerBall website (www.beamerball.com).

Media—Home Depot is a partner with ESPN's College Gameday (http://espn.go.com/college-football/gameday).

Event—Wounded Warriors Project basketball tournament includes local sponsorship involvements—for example, a local physician sponsoring a game (Gazelle, 2014).

how it can be used (Lynde, 2007). An athletics department's property typically extends to include the website, radio broadcasts of games, coaches' shows, and facility signage. Some schools secure sponsors through their in-house staff, but many Division I schools outsource their media rights management to companies that specialize in forming corporate partnerships, such as IMG College, Learfield Sports, and Nelligan Sports Marketing (Johnson, 2005).

Whether this function is handled in-house or by an outside firm, the athletics department must identify its assets so that it can inform potential business partners about the inventory available to them for gaining exposure. Traditional inventory includes signage at athletics facilities (e.g. LED videoboards, scoreboards, ribbon boards and permanent signage) and videoboards), print options (e.g., media guides, ticket backs, and game programs), radio commercials during broadcasts of sporting events, television commercials during broadcasts of coaches' shows, website options (e.g., contests, rotating banners), game-day promotions, and premium item giveaways that include recognition of the corporate partner (Johnson, 2005).

In addition to the traditional properties used by corporate sponsors to promote their messages and products, a growing number of nontraditional inventory items are also being offered, including the use of a school's athletics logo (which is the school's intellectual property), naming rights (discussed later in this chapter), experiential marketing opportunities, and access to hospitality opportunities (Smith, 2011b). Though a sign at an athletics facility may promote a corporate partner's message, experiential marketing is based on the growing belief that consumers want to use their senses to engage firsthand with a brand, product, or service (Experiential, 2012).

For example, instead of a fitness facility promoting its massage service through a radio or television commercial, it might offer free massages to stressed fans at a home sporting event. At the conclusion of the massage, the company could offer a coupon designed to drive traffic to the fitness facility. Fans who join the facility could then receive a t-shirt bearing the athletics department's logo; this arrangement would also be an example of intellectual property use.

Providing hospitality-related inventory for corporate sponsors can range from simply offering tickets and parking privileges to providing access to a corporate village—or anything in between. Schools have expanded the concept of access assets to include sideline passes, postseason trips, and the opportunity to travel with the team on charter planes. Access options can also include allowing corporate partners greater time with the athletes

Evolution of the University of North Carolina's Limited On-Site Inventory

Until 2005, the University of North Carolina's (UNC's) athletics facilities contained limited signage for athletics sponsors. The approach did keep venues free of clutter, but the downside was felt in lost potential revenue from corporate partners as athletics officials waged a longtime debate with school officials and alumni (Steinbach, 2005). New LED scoreboards, coupled with the need for new revenue to offset the school's rising tuition costs, led the school to secure a seven-figure deal with a sponsor seeking exclusivity at the Dean Smith Center, where the men's basketball team competes. The move resulted from recommendations by a UNC task force on signage in athletics facilities that included students, alumni, university officials, and members of the school's athletics administration.

or head coaches of successful teams (Chelap, 2012).

A corporate village can enable businesses to offer food and beverages to invited guests in a relaxed environment before and after a game. To enhance the game-day experience of the corporate village, many hospitality areas are situated close to a football stadium, and they may host visits from the band, cheerleaders, or mascot. Some schools even hold a live pregame radio show from the site of the corporate village. These options give businesses access to premium assets that typical fans cannot enjoy.

Another nontraditional avenue of corporate partnership involves business-to-business exchanges (Lynde, 2007). For example, the upkeep of an athletic field, stadium, or arena may require the purchase of considerable quantities of improvement products from a local home improvement store. With this in mind, the sales team for the athletics department might form a partnership with the local store that gives the department lower prices if it pledges to make its purchases strictly from the sponsoring store (Smith, 2011a). The deal could include a performance-based renewal clause that depends on the athletics department to hit certain benchmarks in its purchases. For example, the corporate partnership deal could automatically renew annually at a certain level based on how much the department spends at the store. The corporate partner will be happy with this deal because of the guaranteed business; thus it will continue renewing its status as a partner of the athletics program.

COMPATIBILITY AND THE SALES PROCESS

Many businesses have a close affiliation with sport due to the relevance of their products to athletic endeavors (Lynde, 2007). Examples of products with this kind of endemic or natural relationship to sport include Gatorade, Powerade, Aquafina, and Dasani, all of which relate to sport because of their hydrating capacity for the student-athletes who compete. Other good fits include apparel and equipment providers (e.g., Nike, Adidas, and UnderArmour), as well as regional health care and sports medicine providers.

Some sponsor relationships, on the other hand, may not be obvious at first. Consider, for example, the possibility of a funeral home sponsoring an intercollegiate athletics department. In this case, the question of compatibility has to be raised. Does the business "fit" with the athletics department and its stakeholders? Are both the athletics department and the business pursuing the same target audience (Lynde, 2007)? As a matter of fact, the Old Dominion University athletics department has found a good fit with a local funeral home that views Monarchs athletics events as providing a positive and uplifting atmosphere in which to talk about something that can be uncomfortable for people to discuss (ODU Athletics, 2012). The funeral home sponsors pregame shows for football and basketball and also includes signage and in-game radio commercials in its partnership. Another good fit involves Werner Ladder, designated as the official

Determining Whether a Sponsorship F-I-T-S an Athletics Department

F—focus area. Where is the company located, and who does it want to affect? What advertising options in the area can help it create that effect?

I—intangibles. Is there a similarity of values and beliefs between the athletics department and the business? Is the product endemic to college sport? Are the sponsorship rates for this property affordable as compared with other options in sport? Are both the athletics department and the business interested in a comparable charitable or holiday-themed tie-in?

T—target audience. Who is the business trying to reach, and what is the makeup of the stakeholders of the athletics department (including fans, students, and alumni)?

S—seasonality. For example, do athletics events present the opportunity to promote gym memberships to the masses when people are making New Year's resolutions to lose weight?

Reprinted, by permission, from T. Lynde, 2007, *Sponsorships 101: An insider's guide to sponsorships in corporate America* (Southlake, TX: Lynde & Associates).

ladder sponsor of the NCAA basketball tournaments, where the iconic image of championship teams cutting down the nets atop a ladder offers the company great visibility for its products.

Brainstorming ideas for companies that might provide a good fit can be done during the initial stages of prospecting, which is simply the first stage of sales, wherein the sales team identifies organizations that are potential sponsors (Fullerton, 2007). Prospecting can be done in many ways. Members of the sales team can review current and past sponsors. They can also look at competitors' sponsors. They can examine sponsors of other events in the area, ranging from concerts, festivals, and fairs to sporting events, including professional sports, high school athletics, golf tournaments, races, and more (Fullerton, 2007). Sales team members can also prospect by joining the local chamber of commerce or simply perusing the regional telephone book.

In pursuing any of these strategies, the sales staff must consider compatibility in light of the fact that some schools place certain businesses off limits due to ethical concerns. The staff should also remember that the more compatible a business is with the athletics department, the easier it will be to leverage a potential sponsorship with that business. As a result, it is critical for the sales team to thoroughly research potential sponsors before visiting them (Chelap, 2012).

Potential sponsors can be grouped into *catego-ries,* and *exclusivity* can be given to those who are willing to pay more in order to ensure that their competitors will not be affiliated with the athletics department (Fullerton, 2007). For example, PepsiCo may be the exclusive pouring rights provider for an athletics department, thereby preventing Coca-Cola from being involved in sponsorship of that department's athletic events. Such categories can be either narrow or broad (Fullerton). Defining categories narrowly could mean, for example, putting McDonald's in the category of fast food, Subway in the category of sandwich shops, Pizza Hut in the category of sit-down pizza restaurants, Papa John's in the category of pizza delivery, and DiGiorno Pizza in the category of pizza available in the grocery store. Defining a category broadly, on the other hand, could involve creating a single category for insurance, rather than breaking it down into life insurance, car insurance, health insurance, and other forms of insurance.

It can be tempting to create narrow categories in an effort to secure a high volume of corporate partners, but doing so also runs the risk of generating *clutter* (Irwin et al., 2008). In this context, clutter refers to the process of inundating consumers with advertising messages, thereby rendering the messages ineffective. This mistake can lead corporate partners to spend their advertising dollars elsewhere instead of with your athletics department.

On the other hand, creating a category that

Special Considerations for Sponsorships

Sales can benefit athletics departments by providing revenue or in-kind remuneration that offsets a traditional expense. In-kind sponsorship might include a car provided by a local dealership for the head coach to use on recruiting trips, food and beverages for use in hospitality settings, or charter buses from a local transportation company. However, though it is important to generate revenue and minimize expenses, sponsorships that undermine university values should be avoided.

With this caveat in mind, the prospect of sponsorships involving alcohol-related partners, casinos, state lotteries, and the various branches of the U.S. military can raise great debate among stakeholders about their place (or lack thereof) on a college campus (Irwin et al., 2008). For example, given that binge drinking is a problem in U.S. higher education, some schools may embrace the philosophy that alcohol-related partners are to be shunned completely. Other schools may work with a beer partner provided that the partner's message focuses heavily on responsible drinking. The message might include urging consumers to adhere to the legal drinking age, turn the keys over to a designated driver, and know when they have consumed too much alcohol (Smith, 2011a).

State lotteries have frequently created a win-win approach to corporate partnership by promoting the fact that many of the funds generated from the lottery are used to help a state's educational system (Steinbach, 2011). Military branches use a similar approach in their sponsorships by stating that they are not advocates for or against war but merely protective forces for the nation's safety that provide many enrollees with structure, discipline, and even funds for further education (Steinbach, 2003). Additional types of sponsor that may face restrictions include those associated with tobacco, pharmaceutical sales, guns, and sensitive social topics such as religion, abortion, sexuality, and political matters. For example, the Hooters restaurant sponsorship of a Division I golf tournament in 2003 generated considerable attention as critics argued that the scantily clad female waitresses clashed with the principles and values of higher education ("Hooters," 2004).

is too broad in an effort to offer fewer sponsors more exposure runs the risk of losing potential sponsors and therefore leaving potential revenue untapped. A cost-benefit analysis can help the athletics department and the sales team decide which approach to take—narrower or broader. Some schools, such as the University of Michigan and the University of North Carolina, believe in the less-is-more philosophy and choose to minimize commercialization (Steinbach, 2005).

Prospecting is a continuous process, but the sales progression begins with the development of rate cards that include a description of the event, who attends it, available inventory, key benefits available to sponsors, and contact information for the salesperson (Irwin et al., 2008). Rate cards can also include current sponsors' testimonials or evaluative metrics demonstrating success in order to promote the effectiveness of corporate partnerships. After preparing its rate cards, the sales team begins to build relationships with businesses by setting up

meetings to discuss the value of a corporate sponsorship (O'Brien, 2012).

Many businesses designate a gatekeeper to slow down or stop a sales team. As a result, the sales process requires persistence and determination. Effective research can also be helpful by yielding insight into the best time to approach the business, the individuals who make the key decisions, the business's current marketing strategies and advertising outlets, and any other information that helps open the doors (Irwin et al., 2008).

Many people in sales invite decision makers from a potential business partner to a game in order to whet their appetite and demonstrate what options are available to the business as a corporate partner (O'Brien, 2012). Other sales strategies include the simple use of visual images or video recordings to bring the inventory directly to potential corporate partners in their own offices. Though some sponsorships may be secured on the first sales visit, most require both an introductory meeting

Red Flag in Sales

Head coaches frequently have their own relationships with area businesses as part of the team's operations or summer camps. Although this practice is acceptable, the sport marketing department should establish a clear written policy about the process for soliciting money or in-kind support from businesses. In the absence of such a policy, a coach may ask a restaurant or hotel for its support at a time when a member of the sales team is also approaching the business with a larger sponsorship proposal (Hoch, 2009). This lack of coordination is frequently referred to as nickel-and-diming a business, and it gives the impression that the athletics department is not communicating effectively (O'Brien, 2012). It may also reduce the financial magnitude of a potential partnership if the business is already spending money directly through a coach without the sport marketing director's knowledge or consent.

and follow-up meetings, in which the sales team presents detailed and personalized sponsorship options to effectively meet the needs and goals of the business (O'Brien, 2012). These options are frequently tiered, thereby enabling the salesperson to come in with a customized sponsorship package at one price but also showcase another more attractive option in hopes that the business is willing to spend more. Many sales team members earn a commission on their sales, which means that *upselling* or getting the business to spend a little more increases both the corporate partner's exposure and the salesperson's pay.

After the proposals have clearly been laid out and defined, the sales team should make an offer to the business and close the deal, thereby securing the partnership. Contracts detailing the specifics of the partnership are valuable requirements because they eliminate ambiguity about matters such as when payment is due or who covers which costs.

A corporate partner pays a *rights fee* for the opportunity to be a partner and to promote its business, brand, product, or service. But if the sponsor wants to leverage its sponsorship further, it should be willing to spend money on sponsorship *activation,* which means bringing the sponsorship to life (Chelap, 2012). Passive forms of sponsorship include, for example, hanging a banner or creating signage. For a business wanting to hang a banner at a soccer game, it could be noted in the contract that the business will incur the cost of producing the banner.

Sponsors may also seek more aggressive sponsorships that require more complexity and work. If, for instance, a sponsor wants to provide a premium giveaway at a sporting event, it would incur the cost of producing the giveaway item. Assistance would also be needed in distributing the giveaway. If the sponsor wants to provide a booth where fans can sample the product or engage in experiential marketing, the sponsor would pay that activation cost (Chelap, 2012). Costs may also be incurred through hospitality expenses. The process of "eduselling," or carefully walking corporate partners through every step of the partnership process, makes sponsors aware that for every dollar they spend on the right to promote themselves, they should be prepared to spend at least another dollar in activation, thus increasing the potential for measurable success (Irwin et al., 2008).

In closing a deal, therefore, salespeople should not focus only on earning their commission but should use eduselling to help their corporate partners see how best to use the partnership to the full advantage of both the business and the athletics department (Irwin et al., 2008). Salespeople should also be willing to blend in smaller, low-cost inventory items, such as public address announcements and program advertising, to provide *value added* to the partnership. Corporate sponsors can then truly view themselves as partners in supporting the athletics department.

MEASUREMENT AND AMBUSH MARKETING

Sponsorships may go unrenewed for many reasons, including a poor return on investment, a decision to go in a different corporate direction, budget cutbacks, poor execution by an event organizer, increased sponsorship costs, or conflict with an organizer (Copeland, Frisby, & McCarville, 1996). One additional reason is simple inability of a salesperson to prove quality aftermarketing efforts. After the contract is signed and the sponsorship is activated, sales team members are encouraged to continuously communicate with their business partners to ensure their happiness (Titlebaum & Watson, 2001). A happy corporate partner can yield renewals.

Because businesses have many options for their advertising dollars, sales staff must provide both tangible and intangible measurements of corporate partnership success with the athletics department. After an initial visit with a potential corporate partner, a salesperson develops ideas to best promote the business in a manner consistent with the inventory that the business wants to use. Both the inventory items and the ideas for using them should be in line with what the corporate partner is looking to spend. In delivering the idea, it is not enough for it to be tailored; it should also be measurable, so that it can evaluated in the end (Irwin et al., 2008).

Thus, in activating a sponsorship, the sales team needs to be prepared to provide evidence of fulfillment of the sponsorship. Did the sponsorship accomplish what it was intended to accomplish? If so, how? If not, why not? Examples of intangible measures include photo or video evidence of a partnership generating pride among participants competing in a halftime event or of students wearing premium giveaway t-shirts in the student section at a game. Such evidence illustrates for sponsors that they are reaching their target audience.

Quantitative measurements might include the attendance total at a sporting event, the number of people who purchased a game program and therefore might see the partner's ad, or the length of air time or the number of impressions that a sign at an athletics facility yields during the course of a sporting event or season. In fact, though these are all quantifiable measurements, today's sales teams strive to generate even greater detail in their sponsorship measurements (O'Brien, 2012). Examples

> *If you make a sale, you make a commission. If you make a friend, you make a fortune.*
>
> Jeffrey Gitomer, *The Little Red Book of Selling*

include the number of visitors to fan fests, as well as their demographics; the number of new e-mail addresses generated through a contest; and the number of coupons passed out at an event in order to drive traffic to the business partner.

Sponsors seek differentiation, because they want their brand, their business, their product, and their services to be remembered by the patrons supporting the athletics department. Although some corporate partners may prefer simple signage at the stadium or an ad placed in a game program, even these basic inventory options present the opportunity for differentiation. An ad in a game program can be turned into a coupon for fans to use, thereby making it more measureable. A videoboard commercial can be turned into a trivia contest in which fans text answers, thereby engaging the audience more actively while garnering a database of phone numbers.

Businesses have more advertising options than ever for developing high-quality, effective, and measurable returns on their investment, which of course heightens the likelihood of renewal. Creativity in activation design helps sponsors stand out as more traditional kinds of inventory grow outdated (Bynum, 2006). Today's sponsors are no longer impressed with a thank-you letter from a head coach. Instead, business decision makers need to demonstrate to their superiors that corporate sponsorship with athletics helps their bottom line (Chelap, 2012). In this environment, a banner recognizing the sponsor is less attractive than a creative opportunity such as a contest that puts a lucky fan on the field for the coin toss of a football game while also producing a database of names and contact information (generated through contest entries) and therefore yields a greater return on investment for the corporate partner.

Similarly, though college sport fans are passionate about their schools, simple affiliation is no longer enough for corporate partners to justify expenditures. However, continual assessment of sponsorship effectiveness helps renew sponsors' trust (O'Brien, 2012). Innovation and creativity in the differentiation process can also yield a larger rights fee for the sales team.

Throughout the entire sales process, attention must be given to the possibility of *ambush marketing,* in which a business tries to profit from the assets of an athletics department without paying a rights fee. This practice might take the form of a business passing out coupons or samples of its product in a parking lot where fans are tailgating or arriving for an event. It might also be implemented as fans exit an athletics facility after a sporting event.

To minimize ambush marketing, the sport marketing department must communicate to the entire athletics department the identity of the department's official corporate partners (Norcross, 2011). In this way, all members of the department will act as an enforcement team because they all realize the value of a corporate partner to the financial well-being of the athletics program (Irwin et al., 2008). Education enables each member of the marketing department to help protect corporate partners who have paid for the right to associate with the athletics program and its events.

> Simply knowing a sponsor has been on board for a number of years does not ensure the company's continued support.
>
> Titlebaum & Watson, 2001

FACILITY NAMING RIGHTS AND FAIR MARKET VALUE

Athletics departments may also use corporate sponsors to help with the cost of facility development or renovation through the purchase of corporate naming rights (Muret, 2011). Whether the naming right involves an entire facility or sections of it (e.g., parking lot, premium seating level, food court), this type of sponsorship offers corporate partners broader exposure, particularly at multipurpose facilities that also host events such as concerts, stage shows, speakers, and meetings. Naming rights can also broaden exposure for corporate partners through media coverage when the affiliated team plays on regional or national television. In determining a rights fee, the school should conduct sound market research to identify the *fair market value.* This research might include communicating with other schools in the conference or the region about comparable partnerships, exchanging infor-

mation at conferences and professional meetings, and reading industry publications, such as *Sports-Business Journal.*

As with other forms of sponsorship, the sales team must be able to measure the return on investment for naming rights. To do so, 21 Marketing, a firm that specializes in maximizing sponsorship activation, examines the following 11 key metrics ("Do Naming-Rights Deals," 2011):

1. National and international TV exposure
2. Exterior exposure (e.g., a facility located next to an interstate that results in exposure for anyone passing by)
3. On-site exposure for attendees
4. Ad campaigns
5. Local TV and radio broadcasts
6. Editorial coverage
7. Team publications
8. Collateral material
9. Direct mail, Internet, community, and partner promotions
10. Image association in ad campaigns
11. Hospitality

Though effective in revenue generation, corporate naming rights may not be an option on every campus, because some schools use a traditional naming-rights approach to honor individual donors or sizable contributors to the school itself. Affiliating with a corporate entity can also prompt greater public examination and even complaints about the corporate partner. This risk played out in recent years in the form of critics scrutinizing corporate naming-rights deals involving the banking industry at a time when the U.S. government was bailing out many of those businesses (Steinbach, 2009).

OUTSOURCING AND UBIT TAXES

Some schools use their in-house sport marketing staff to secure sponsorships. As mentioned earlier,

Students Protest Corporate Naming Right

Officials at Florida Atlantic University recently came under pressure from students after the school's president announced a 12-year naming rights deal worth US$6 million with the GEO Group, a private prison corporation. The students' protest stemmed from their belief that the company engaged in human rights violations at GEO Group facilities. The students were supported by the American Civil Liberties Union, which led to national media coverage of the school's naming-rights deal (Zinzer, 2013). Eventually the gift was rescinded and the naming rights deal was halted.

however, there is a growing trend at the Division I level to outsource the sales effort to companies such as Nelligan Sports Marketing, IMG College, Learfield Sports, and CBS Collegiate Sports Properties. Outsourced marketing firms traditionally work with Division I schools because their larger fan base enables the firm to generate greater revenue and thus a profit for the parent company.

The benefits of partnering with an outsourced marketing firm include expertise specific to sales and revenue generation (Johnson, 2005). This know-how enables the in-house sport marketing staff to focus on promoting ticket sales and enhancing the in-game atmosphere (McKindra, 2005). The outsourced firm can also provide financial support in purchasing new equipment, such as scoreboards, that the school might not otherwise be able to afford on its own.

Generally, the outsourced firm represents several schools; therefore, when its account executives represent the firm in talks with a potential sponsor, they can highlight the increased exposure that the sponsor would receive. For example, if an account executive from IMG College talks with Enterprise Rent-a-Car about a sponsorship that would affect all schools represented by IMG College, the executive

Industry Profile

Janeen Lalik

Senior vice president, IMG College

Janeen Lalik is senior vice president of business development for IMG College's business ventures division. In this role, Lalik is responsible for integrating new IMG College business offerings into current collegiate partner programs. She also analyzes potential new initiatives for implementation at IMG College, pursues new multimedia partnerships with collegiate properties, and collaborates to extend partnerships with existing collegiate multimedia partners. In addition, Lalik supports IMG's partnership with the Barclays Center in Brooklyn to develop college events.

Prior to assuming her current role with IMG College, Lalik was instrumental in the growth of ISP Sports before its acquisition by IMG in 2010. Her first role was director of the ISP MVP program. After being promoted to assistant vice president in 1998, she assumed responsibility for all research and development related to new business acquisitions, as well as employee recruitment. She was named a vice president in 2005 and a senior vice president in 2007.

A graduate of Central Michigan, Lalik worked previously with the Detroit Pistons and Palace Sports and Entertainment. She was named to the *SportsBusiness Journal* Forty Under 40 in 2009 and named as a *Triad Business Journal* Woman Extraordinaire in 2008.

Reprinted, by permission, IMG College. Available: www.imgcollege.com/about/leadership-team/team/janeen-lalik.

Leadership Lesson

Seek First to Understand, Then to Be Understood

As we prospect for and seek to confirm corporate partners, it is tempting to create a one-size-fits-all approach. Indeed, it certainly might save printing costs or pitch preparation time if each presentation were identical! The problem with this approach is that most corporate partners are very different from each other; as a result, prefabricated package deals are unlikely to maximize the potential benefits that can be achieved through a personalized partnership.

Even after you research a company and feel that you will be able to convince it to sign on, think again—dig a little deeper. Until you understand the organization's unique needs and goals, you won't be able to form an optimal partnership. "The amateur . . . sells products; the professional sells solutions to needs and problems" (Covey, 2004, p. 244). In order to find those solutions, you must first take the time to listen—to really understand the other party's goals. Once you understand those needs, it is much easier to craft a synergistic partnership.

This principle is as true and important in day-to-day interactions as it is in corporate sponsorship meetings. Communication experts estimate that only 10 percent of our communication is derived from the words that are spoken. The rest happens through body language (60 percent) and sounds and intonation (30 percent). (Covey, 2004)

Given the critical nature of communication in organizational and personal life, it is troubling that this skill is often taken for granted. Though most of us have the physical ability to hear, very few have taken the time to develop the transformative skill of listening. When you demonstrate a true desire to learn from and understand someone, you are able to communicate with him or her on a new level, and through this process you make the person feel incredibly valued. As Henry David Thoreau once stated, "The greatest compliment that was ever paid me was when one asked me what I thought, and attended to my answer" (qtd. in Rosenblum, 2000, p. 103).

To illustrate the point, Stephen Covey uses the example of going to the optometrist. After listening to you briefly, the doctor hands you his or her glasses and says, "Put these on. I've worn this pair of glasses for 10 years now and they've really helped me. I have an extra pair at home; you can wear these" (2004, p. 236). Once you put the glasses on, you can see even less—everything is a blur—because, of course, the glasses don't correct the vision impairments that *you* have. They might work well for the doctor, but not for you.

As in this illustration, when we listen to others we often prescribe before we diagnose. We judge before we truly understand. We see another's issues through our own paradigm rather than seeking first to understand his or her paradigm. It's a lot easier to hand someone a pair of glasses than to make time to understand his or her unique viewpoint. In conversation, most people listen with the intent of replying rather than the intent of understanding. We do this because we hope that others

> *The single biggest problem in communication is the illusion that it has taken place.*
>
> George Bernard Shaw
>
> *The most important thing in communication is to hear what isn't being said.*
>
> Peter F. Drucker
>
> *We have two ears and one mouth so that we can listen twice as much as we speak*
>
> Epictetus

(continued)

LEADERSHIP LESSON *(continued)*

will understand us; however, when little true listening takes place between parties, very little communication or understanding occurs.

So, what can we do? Seek first to understand, then to be understood. A good place to start is to practice active listening, in which you strive to understand the complete message being sent by the other person. Once this is mastered, Covey recommends empathic listening, in which you strive to look through another person's frame of reference and understand through his or her lens. Both of these skills start with actively determining to give the speaker your undivided attention. Look at the speaker directly, view his or her body language, block out distracting thoughts or environmental factors, and avoid forming a response until the speaker has finished his or her thought and your comprehension is complete.

Empathic listening involves four developmental stages.

1. Mimic the content to demonstrate that you heard what the other person said. This is the least effective technique but the easiest.

2. Rephrase the content to ensure your understanding of what you perceive the speaker to be saying. Sometimes clarifying questions might be needed before you are able to rephrase the content, but avoid the pitfall of asking too many questions and creating the feeling that you are "grilling" the speaker.

3. Reflect the feeling you observe. There is always emotion behind words, and understanding this emotion will help you understand the content more fully.

4. Rephrase the content and reflect the feeling. Once you have mastered stages 2

and 3 in a situation, you can reflect true understanding by interlacing both the core content and the feeling of the person with whom you're communicating. (Covey, 2004)

To solidify your gains, use the following ground rules for listening as you strive to develop this critical skill.

- Don't interrupt.
- Don't change the subject or move in a new direction.
- Don't rehearse in your own head.
- Don't interrogate.
- Don't teach.
- Don't give advice.
- Don't discount the speaker's feelings by using stock phrases such as "it's not that bad" or "you'll feel better tomorrow."
- *Do* reflect back to the speaker what you understand and how you think the speaker feels. (Burley-Allen, 1982; Salem, 2003)

As Covey (2004, p. 253) says, "As you learn to listen deeply to other people, you will discover tremendous differences in perception. You will also begin to appreciate the impact that these differences can have as people try to work together in interdependent situations. You see the young woman [in reference to a visual illusion shown in figure 1.4]; I see the old lady. And both of us can be right." Whether you are striving to close a multiyear, multimillion-dollar partnership agreement or resolve a disagreement with a coworker, seeking first to understand, and only then to be understood, will facilitate illuminating dialogue that can turn a difficult situation into a tremendous opportunity for relationship development.

might stress that the rental agency's services could be targeted to fans at schools across a certain part of the country. The downside of outsourcing the rights is that the school relinquishes the control that comes with keeping the sales effort in-house (Robinson, 2004). The school must also split the sponsorship

revenue with the outsourced firm.

Outsourced marketing firms, frequently known as third-party marketing firms, typically pay a school in one of three ways. The firm may pay a guaranteed fee to the school, the two parties may share the revenue generated, or the school and the firm may create a payment option that combines both the guaranteed fee and a revenue-sharing element beyond an established threshold (Smith, 2011b). A larger Division I school debating whether to keep its sales effort in-house or outsource it would typically send out a request for proposal inviting firms to bid on the opportunity to work with the athletics department.

If the athletics department chooses to use an outsourced firm, the firm then sells sponsorships as an extension of the department (McCarthy, 2006). This is a risk-for-reward proposition, because the firm needs to meet its financial obligations to its schools. In trying to meet its quota, an outsourced marketing firm sells aggressively, thereby requiring the school to be in continuous communication with the firm in order to maintain a sense of control (McKindra, 2005). In addition, because school presidents, fans, and alumni frequently disapprove of excessive commercialization at sporting events in higher education, it is important to clearly establish a win-win approach in the request-for-proposal stage of the process.

Because outsourced firms work with a multitude of schools in a region or even across the nation, they are more versed in the fair market value of various inventory offerings. Though rights fees may vary from region to region, the expertise and depth of an outsourced firm's research can bring to light the fact that some corporate partnerships have been financially undervalued. As a result, a change in the sales team can frequently yield "sticker shock" when an outsourced firm tells a corporate partner that the price of being a sponsor is going to increase (O'Brien, 2012). In such cases, the firm thoroughly details why the rights fee has increased, but the explanation is not likely to be well received by the business, regardless of how undervalued the previous contractual arrangements may have been for the athletics department.

Another value of using an outsourced marketing firm is the presence of UBIT taxes. UBIT stands for unrelated business income tax, which can be involved in sport sponsorships. Higher education institutions are mindful of their tax-exempt status and of the potential for losing this status through excessive UBIT taxes (Graham, Goldblatt, & Delpy, 1995). Through affiliation with an outsourced marketing firm, the school can shift that concern from itself to a third party.

CONCLUSION

Corporate partnerships can play a vital role in generating revenue or offsetting expenses in intercollegiate athletics. Businesses have many platforms for advertising and promoting themselves, including corporate sponsorships in intercollegiate athletics. In trying to maximize such opportunities, sport marketing staffs must exercise caution in light of concerns about overcommercialization in higher education. Athletics departments can promote their corporate partners in various ways through signage, multimedia options, hospitality, naming rights, and other options that can be sold either by in-house staffers or outside firms. The sales process begins with prospecting and stresses the fact that today's corporate partners seek robust measurable value and differentiation in their sponsorship activation.

DISCUSSION QUESTIONS

1. A new president takes over at the university and expresses concern about athletics facilities resembling a professional sport arena due to the heavy presence of sponsorships. The president wants a cleaner venue, but the athletics department needs the revenue. How would you create a win-win scenario?

2. A local business has sponsored the athletics department for decades. Recently, however, the department has outsourced its multimedia rights to a third-party firm, which, in light of fair market value, has raised the rates for certain inventory items, thus alienating the business. The owner of the business carries a great deal of clout in the community. How would you appease the business owner and try to retain the business as a sponsor?

3. Your athletics department has a partnership with a pizza delivery business. The pizza business's competitor learns that students are camping out for a highly anticipated game and delivers free pizza to the happy recipients. What concerns emerge in this situation?

4. A corporate sponsor calls at the last second and requests tickets for a sold-out event. The sponsor already has tickets but stresses the urgency of the matter. How would you handle this situation? Would your response change if the sponsor were deciding whether or not to renew his or her deal? Would your response depend on the level of financial support provided by the sponsor?

5. In building a new athletics facility, prominent alumni have indicated that they will contribute major gifts to begin the construction only if the venue is kept free of sponsorships. Knowing that this limitation will negatively affect annual revenue, how would you address this situation?

6. A potential sponsor is eager to support the athletics department but only if its product is carried in the dining hall in place of a competitor's product. How would you approach the dining services department about replacing one of its products with this potential sponsor's product?

LEARNING ACTIVITIES

1. The athletics department is building a new basketball arena. What opportunities exist for new inventory options that could benefit corporate partners? To find inventory ideas, visit athletics department websites and those of IMG College, Learfield Sports, and Nelligan Sports Marketing.

2. Fair market value dictates that sponsors pay a rights fee consistent with what the market will bear. Assume you are a business owner and call the following parties to ask for their advertising rates: a local newspaper, a local television station, a local radio station, a local direct mailer, and a local billboard manager.

3. A potential sponsor wants to support the athletics department but only if its sponsorship includes supporting a local nonprofit. Using online resources, identify local sport-related nonprofits that could be tied into the sponsorship proposal. Repeat the exercise assuming that the business wants the sponsorship to support cancer prevention and treatment, antibullying efforts, or the promotion of health and fitness among youth.

Photo courtesy of Dymphena Clark

Facility and Event Management

Robert Zullo, Seton Hill University

In this chapter, you will explore

- fundamentals of event management,

- safety measures and risk assessment,

- fans' increasing assertion of what they perceive as their rights at games,

- facility planning and funding, and

- current issues in facility and event management.

BALANCING STUDENT EXCITEMENT WITH SAFETY

In the final seconds of a highly contested basketball game, the home team is on the verge of upsetting the top-ranked team in the country, and the student section is eager to celebrate the momentous occasion on the court. The head coach of the visiting team has previously indicated his discontent with people storming the court due to his concern for his players' safety. However, keeping the students confined to the stands is going to be difficult, because those in the upper rows have started to move closer to the court, flooding into the aisles. With two minutes left in the game, what are your concerns about this situation, and how have you proactively addressed these concerns? How has your facility and event management staff prepared in advance for this moment? How will you assess the effectiveness of your game-day preparation?

In intercollegiate athletics, facility and event managers face the challenging if not daunting task of ensuring that facilities are prepared for a wide range of athletic and nonathletic events, each of which comes with its own facility needs. Whether hosting a tennis tournament or a football game, certain specifications need to be met in order to adhere to regulated standards. Facility and event staff must also meet the requirements of people working in sports information, development, and marketing in order to best service the media, donors, and corporate sponsors. Adequate staffing is essential, especially for large-scale events, which may require support in terms of parking, ticket taking, ushering, and concessions. Event managers must also accommodate staff in sports medicine and strength and conditioning who are there to meet the game-day needs of the athletes themselves (Steinbach, 2005e). These diverse challenges typically go unnoticed by casual fans, but meeting them is essential to game-day operations.

Facility management also entails working with senior athletics and university officials on short- and long-term strategic planning for capital needs and improvements. In addition, the increasing emphasis on naming rights and premium seating requires facility managers to collaborate with staff members involved in sponsorship, development, and ticket sales. Facility structure and use are also expected to comply with federal legislation, including the Americans With Disabilities Act and Title IX. Facilities may also be shared with professional sport teams or used for concerts and other special events, such as convocations.

On game days, fans' behaviors can present an escalating concern if unsporting activities get out of hand. In particular, concerns have grown about alcohol consumption during tailgating at or before intercollegiate athletic events. In addition, in the aftermath of the 9/11 tragedy, threats of terrorism are also a concern. Challenges are evident even on peaceful days with a number of unique facility and game day initiatives increasing including green initiatives and events held at nontraditional locations.

For most people who work in event operations, the duties require long hours, because most events are held on weekends, nights, and holidays. At the same time, administrators need balance in their lives in order to be able to meet the demands of the role (Meiser, Tucker, & Abaray, 2011; Steinbach, January 2005e). To efficiently meet this challenge, they must have a firm understanding of facility and event management.

EVENT MANAGEMENT AND OPERATIONS

When sport fans attend an event, they generally pay little regard to the tremendous behind-the-scenes effort that makes the event possible. Directors of facilities and events coordinate the logistics with little fanfare. This work includes scheduling facilities and ensuring that each detail is properly handled to enable a successful event (Palmero, Li, Lawrence, & Conley, 2011). The work involves three stages—preevent planning, event implementation, and postevent analysis—that address factors such as space usage, timing, and staffing to maximize

Industry Profile

Jenny Claypool

Director of championships, Stanford University

May 7, 2009
by Casey Lindberg, Stanford News Service

Having just earned a master's degree in sport management from the University of Massachusetts Amherst—and with joblessness just days away—Jenny Claypool walked up to the Stanford box office to buy a ticket for the first home game of the football season. In the ticket window was a help-wanted sign, so Claypool prudently inquired about the position.

"Well, how much help do you need?" Claypool asked.

"Well, how much can you do?" the ticket seller replied.

"I can do whatever you need," Claypool answered back.

That was 1990, and Claypool has worked for Stanford ever since—all along the way, doing just about whatever needed to get done. She has worked for the ticket office, for facilities and operations, as a secretary for sports teams, and as an assistant to the senior associate athletics director. She's now the director of championships for the athletics department.

In that position since 2000, Claypool's dedication and long hours ensure that conference and national championship events hosted by Stanford run smoothly. It is in recognition of these efforts that Claypool is a 2009 recipient of the Amy J. Blue Award, which is bestowed annually upon university staff members who exhibit exceptional passion and dedication.

Stanford may host up to 20 championships in a given year, and Claypool organizes and coordinates any activity related to those events. She does everything from making hotel reservations and coordinating banquets to working with coaches and volunteers to make sure that the events are received well by all of the teams and visitors.

"Repeatedly, I hear from colleagues at the NCAA and around the country how much they like having events at Stanford because they know we will run a first-class operation," said Beth Goode, senior associate athletics director. "And that is due in full to Jenny's efforts."

The amount of work it takes to pull off these events might overwhelm someone with less enthusiasm and commitment than Claypool. Recently, she worked nearly 100 hours in one week, organizing conference championships for lacrosse, volleyball, and golf. But Claypool doesn't see the heavy workload as a headache; for her it is a challenge and an opportunity to represent Stanford in the best light possible.

"If we're going to do it, we're going to do it right," Claypool said. "Anything that I do is a reflection not only of me but of the athletics department and the university. So we should always be putting our best foot forward."

Claypool's drive and work ethic are also a reflection of her dedication to the development of student-athletes at Stanford: "Ultimately, my job is to help our student-athletes become the best people that they can become, because they are our future."

In addition to overseeing championship events, Claypool interacts with student-athletes as the host of new student-athlete orientation every fall and as coordinator of the NCAA postgraduate scholarship program. Gathering interesting facts and details that incoming students include in their orientation RSVPs, Claypool reviews and remembers each one.

"When she meets with them at orientation," Goode said, "they are constantly amazed that she knows them, remembers them, and this connection helps students instantly feel welcomed."

As much as Claypool touches the lives of student-athletes, they have also touched hers. In 1995, Claypool's father passed away early on a Saturday morning. So, to take her mind off that, Claypool headed to the men's volleyball match that night, where she learned that the coaches had told the team what had happened. Claypool fought back tears last week,

(continued)

Industry Profile *(continued)*

as she recalled how the players came up to her, hugged her, and expressed their sympathy for her loss.

"To feel like I have a family, a second family, is just so very touching to me," Claypool said. "I'm grateful to have them in my life."

Claypool said she feels lucky to be at Stanford, and that she doesn't know what she did to deserve to be where she is. Claypool said that it is "just humbling and overwhelming to think that people think what I do is worthwhile and worthy of receiving this award."

Reprinted, by permission, from C. Lindberg, 2009, "Director of athletic championships scores one of Stanford's top staff awards," *Stanford Report.* Available: http://news.stanford.edu/news/2009/may6/amyjenny-050609.html.

efficiency, accountability, and fiscal responsibility. Events are detailed to the minute in order to ensure that they run smoothly for all stakeholders, including participants, officials, and spectators.

Facility Scheduling and Setup

The facility and events department works with each athletics program to schedule practice and game usage, including setup and breakdown. Multipurpose facilities may also require the staff to change the setup from one event to another—for example, converting a basketball arena from a basketball practice setup to a wrestling or volleyball venue. Space must be provided for such essentials as benches, coolers, and fitness equipment (Steinbach, January 2005e). However, equipment cannot be left in place; instead, it needs to be stored when not in use in order to lower the risk of injury (Borkowski, 2006).

Game-day needs may also include a variety of technological setups, including headsets for coaches, as well as specific scoreboard needs for sports such as wrestling and basketball. This factor can be complicated when an athletics program, such as the Georgetown University men's basketball team, competes at an off-campus venue, thus requiring communication with the staff of a separate facility. In Georgetown's case, the team plays at the Verizon Center, which is also home to a National Basketball Association team and a National Hockey League team, thus compounding scheduling and event management issues.

Game-Day Preparation

For game days, facility and event managers work with the sports information department to ensure that their colleagues can adequately support the

needs of members of the media. This aspect may include setting up the press box and issuing credentials to certified media members (Purvis, 2012). Credentials may be all-access or site-specific, the latter of which limits an individual to the press box, sideline, locker room, or interview room.

At large-scale events, game-day preparation also requires staff to have maintenance support available to repair scoreboards, elevators, escalators, heating and cooling units, refrigeration units, and power supplies (Purvis, 2012). At the conclusion of a sporting event, custodial services and cleaning crews are necessary to return the facility and its environs to their original state.

Game-day preparation must also put adequate staffing in place for concessions, ticket taking, and ushering. Personnel support extends to the premium seating areas, such as suites and club levels. Because many of these extended staff members are the first people to interact with fans, it is vital that they possess high-quality customer service skills. Toward this end, Arizona State University and Auburn University use Disney to educate and prepare their game-day staff members, including everyone from the vendors outside the stadium to the ushers inside (Steinbach, 2013). Disney uses the adage that everyone at its theme parks is a performer who helps make the venue the "happiest place in the world," and this philosophy includes those selling food and merchandise, as well as the custodial staff. Colleges can borrow this philosophy to good effect, since most fans do not interact with the athletics director (AD), the head coach, or student-athletes on game day, but they do interact with support staff (Steinbach, 2013).

Personnel needs vary by sport and game. Larger-scale sporting events require additional personnel, especially if fans have been eagerly anticipating the contest (Steinbach, 2006f). Students can overcrowd a seating area and present issues by sitting on the rails or in the aisles, thus drawing concern from police and fire marshals. Inadequate staffing in such situations not only leaves potential hazards unaddressed but also casts the school in a bad light (Steinbach, 2006f). First responders, including first-aid capabilities, need to be included in sufficient proportion to the crowd size.

Staff must also ensure that designated parking areas are kept available for important donors, which requires additional security officers who can also facilitate orderly tailgating. Campus and area police can help, but some schools or athletics departments are billed for the presence of this additional security support. Tailgating also creates a need for intensive trash clean-up, particularly after large-scale events (Johnston, 2009). Unlike a professional sport facility, an institution of higher education must return to its primary objective of educating and developing students immediately after the sporting event, and schools can incur tremendous costs and publicity concerns if the campus is littered or damaged (Diamond, 2009). Viable solutions include encouraging student organizations to pass out trash bags or employing them in the clean-up process. School and athletics officials, and those in public safety roles, must continue to evaluate, communicate, and adjust tailgating policies as needed (Gillentine, Miller, & Crow, 2010).

Staff Motivation

Some staffing needs may be met through positions that pay an hourly wage, but many support personnel are volunteers. Because events tend to involve long hours on nights, weekends, and holidays, facility and event managers need to incorporate planning specifically aimed at boosting the morale and customer-service focus of their game-day staff (Bang & Ross, 2009). Examples of employee moral boosters include knowing everyone's name, recognizing employees when they do something good (e.g., through a Wall of Fame or an employee of the month), arranging pep talks by coaches or student-athletes, setting up a suggestion box, hosting an end-of-year dinner, and implementing an incentive program with prizes (e.g., merchandise discounts, promotional giveaways, gift certificates).

Each staff member can affect a fan's experience at an event, and high-quality service maximizes repeat customers and boosts game-day revenues.

Parking

Large-scale sporting events held on campus can have a tremendous effect on the daily routine of many school constituents. Although college football games are traditionally held on Saturdays, some programs play home games during the week. In addition, more schools are embracing the idea of Saturday classes, which are held while games are being played. Thus solid partnership is needed among school officials to determine who is in charge of what areas and when (Palmero et al., 2011).

Campuses with larger stadiums must also arrange for ample parking or shuttle services, which requires collaboration between school and community officials to support the parking needs of students and fans alike. Many institutions use parking lots close to the stadium as benefits for donors, thus requiring students and staff to vacate the lots in the late hours on the day before a game (Purvis, 2012).

Consideration for persons with a disability can be challenging if spots usually reserved for such persons are converted into donor parking on game day. It is essential to comply with the Americans With Disabilities Act and maintain sufficient accessible parking for all patrons (Pate, Bemiller, & Hardin, 2010). Information about parking for persons with a disability should be included in ticket brochures and on the departmental website. In addition, staff members in the development, ticketing, and parking offices should be educated about accessible seating and parking. The Americans With Disabilities Act is discussed in further detail later in the chapter.

SAFETY AND RISK ASSESSMENTS

Facility and event managers have an obligation to protect the individuals who participate in, attend, and work at an event. Preserving the safety of everyone involved requires a high standard of care. Meeting this standard requires managers to conduct risk assessments to examine potential

Post-Katrina, College Athletics Departments Serve as Disaster Response Specialists

By Paul Steinbach

Amid hundreds of Walmart mattresses covering the floor of the Pete Maravich Assembly Center stood Louisiana State University's 6-foot-9 sophomore basketball star Glen Davis—his outstretched arms supporting intravenous medication drips for separate individuals who had, like thousands of others, sought refuge from the ravages of Hurricane Katrina in this campus sports arena turned triage unit. With proper equipment on which to hang the IV bags not yet available, in stepped "Big Baby," as Davis is known around campus, to quite literally shoulder the burden. It's just one vivid image among many that gave LSU athletics director Skip Bertman chills late in August 2005 during the first harrowing days of the evacuation of New Orleans, as the storm made landfall some 80 miles [130 kilometers] southeast of Baton Rouge.

It was a scene befitting a war zone. Helicopters carrying evacuees landed on LSU's outdoor track-and-field facility at a pace of one every 10 minutes. The university's Carl Maddox Field House opened its doors to the infirm. Ambulance sirens whined relentlessly. As volunteer doctors and nurses assumed around-the-clock control of the athletics department's facilities, Bertman briefed student-athletes—including 33 members of the football team who hailed from the New Orleans area but had no way of knowing the fate of family members once the phone systems there failed—about the situation. "The football players said, `Well, what can we do while we're waiting?'" Bertman recalls.

Soon those among LSU's 430 scholarship athletes who were on campus (classes had not yet begun and, in fact, would be delayed by the three-week-long disaster-relief effort) began visiting with evacuees and collecting supplies such as bed sheets and toiletries from within the Baton Rouge community. Coaches and strength coordinators unloaded food from semi trailers. Equipment managers laundered linens and clothing. "In the first three days, our athletics department sent over every bandage and every piece of gauze that we had," says Bertman, adding that the Maravich Center alone would treat some 27,000 evacuees. "I was very proud to be part of LSU when I saw what people had done. It was heroic stuff."

A year later, Hurricane Katrina—and its hastily arriving successors, Hurricanes Rita and Wilma—are rightly being viewed as watershed episodes on the time line of disaster recovery. For the first time in American history, civil authorities saw athletics facilities as indispensable destination points for the displaced and desperate. "Prior to these disasters, the concept of a megashelter was not heard of in our country," says Greg Davis, director of the University of Louisiana at Lafayette's Cajundome, which housed an estimated 18,500 evacuees in the four months following Katrina, including as many as 7,000 at a time. "The American Red Cross had not even thought of major facilities such as arenas, convention centers, and stadiums being used as megashelters. Prior to Hurricanes Katrina and Rita, the Red Cross served as the primary provider of shelter to disaster evacuees, using mostly schools and church halls, but the disasters that they had dealt with before were not even near the scale of those two events."

Moreover, college campuses proved particularly effective in dealing with the disasters' aftermath due to their concentrations of both large facilities and able personnel. Their successes were enough to either create or expedite movements within certain collegiate athletics conferences to draft disaster preparedness plans. Says Mike Slive, commissioner of the Southeastern Conference, which encompasses four states that sustained hurricane damage last year, "The way our presidents and chancellors thought about it, particularly after the experience at LSU, is that many of our institutions are uniquely equipped to assist civil authorities, for two reasons. One, we often have the facilities, as LSU did, to take care of large numbers of people. And secondly, athletics department staffs are trained and experienced in moving large numbers of people, because we have such huge crowds that attend our athletic events. Recognizing that, it's clear that athletics departments and major institutions with athletics facilities should be part of the first response."

Reprinted, by permission, from P. Steinbach, 2006, "Post-Katrina, college athletic departments serve as disaster response specialists," *Athletic Business*. Available: www.athleticbusiness.com/Emergency-Response/post-katrina-college-athletic-departments-serve-as-disaster-response-specialists.html.

sources of injury, from the moment someone arrives on campus to the moment he or she departs. The assessment should consider participants, spectators, staff, the facility itself, and equipment used at the event (Borkowski, 2010; Steinbach, 2005e). An organizational chart can be used to indicate who oversees what, thus increasing efficiency and accountability (Palmero et al., 2011).

Risk assessment is a continuous process in facility and event management, and it should address such areas as participant safety, terrorism threats, student behavior, alcohol consumption, and tailgating. The assessment process (Westerbeek et al., 2006) itself should include the following steps.

1. Identifying specific potential risks
2. Establishing policy and procedures
3. Documenting all incidents
4. Executing the policy and procedures
5. Evaluating continuously

Facilities that are not in use should be secured because if left unsecured they can result in lawsuits (Borkowski, 2006). When legal matters do arise, for this or any other reason, schools may use either in-house or third-party legal counsel to advise administrators (Scholand, 2011).

Participant Safety

A primary area of concern for event managers is ensuring participants' safety around the playing surface. Of course, an adequate standard of care must be provided to coaches and participants; the standard of care is what would be consistent at other athletic events as determined by a court of law. Close attention must be paid to the fact that participants' momentum can carry them off of the playing surface and into the stands. As a result, a buffer zone should be established around the playing area to protect student-athletes. Filling the buffer zone with extra seats or media tables invites an accident (Borkowski, 2006).

Care must also be taken regarding cheerleaders and photographers, who frequently surround the playing surface (Steinbach, 2008b). Even band equipment can be problematic, as was the case in a 2008 football game between Houston and Marshall in which a wide receiver suffered a broken leg after running into a band cart on the sidelines (Associated Press, 2010a; Dodd, 2009; "MU's tab," 2012). With such risks in mind, officials have the obligation to do a preevent inspection in and around the competition area, and any concerns should be addressed with the event manager and rectified.

Safety measures can extend into the event itself, as demonstrated by referees halting a 2001 basketball game in Richmond, Virginia, between the University of Virginia and Michigan State University. Despite the game being nationally televised on ESPN2, the officials, in consultation with event managers, determined that the court was too slippery and thus unsafe. The condition resulted from condensation due to the combination of an unseasonably warm winter day and the fact that facility's primary tenant was a minor league hockey team, whose ice rink sat below the basketball court (Phillips, 2013).

Protective measures must also be taken in the postgame phase of an event, as student-athletes, coaches, and referees frequently find themselves swarmed by fans who have rushed the playing surface (LaVetter & Choi, 2010; Steinbach, 2006a). Fans may be energized by a game being televised or seeing their school play a rival or nationally ranked opponent, thus requiring event managers to anticipate fans storming the playing surface. Public address announcements can be used to encourage fans to stay in their seats, but many will not listen to the messages. In some cases, public safety officials may simply be unable to hold the fans off the court or field, in which case it is vital to first secure the officials and the visiting team and escort them to their locker rooms (Steinbach, 2006a).

Tornado Interrupts SEC Basketball Tournament at the Georgia Dome

March 15, 2008

By ESPN with contributions from Mark Schlabach, Andy Katz, and the Associated Press
The National Weather Service on Saturday confirmed that a tornado struck downtown Atlanta on Friday night, damaging the Georgia Dome and forcing the Southeastern Conference tournament to move.

The weather service issued a tornado warning for the Atlanta area at 9:26 p.m. ET after radar indicated a storm capable of producing a tornado was located about six miles [10 kilometers] west of Atlanta. The storm ripped a hole in the roof of the Georgia Dome, delaying Mississippi State's 69-67 overtime win over Alabama for more than an hour and forcing the SEC to move the remainder of the tournament to the campus of Georgia Tech.

National Weather Service meteorologist Barry Gooden said the tornado in downtown Atlanta produced winds up to 110 miles [about 180 kilometers] an hour—making it a strength EF1 on the Enhanced Fujita scale—then grew into an EF2 tornado, which can produce winds up to 135 miles [about 220 kilometers] an hour.

As Mississippi State led 64–61 with 2:11 left in overtime, a loud blast was heard inside the dome. The girders near the dome's roof began to swing, and a gaping section of the north part of the roof was ripped open, dropping debris that included nuts and bolts.

Players and coaches from the Bulldogs and Crimson Tide were sent to the locker room, along with the coaches' wives and children, and stadium officials began to evacuate fans in the upper reaches of the stadium.

There was also damage at nearby Philips Arena, where the Atlanta Hawks were playing the Los Angeles Clippers. The storm blew out windows in the CNN Center and the Omni Hotel and caused property damage throughout downtown Atlanta. Georgia Power Company spokeswoman Consuela Monroe said about 10,000 customers had lost power in the Atlanta area.

The Georgia–Kentucky game, postponed from Friday night because of the storm, was played Saturday at Georgia Tech's Alexander Memorial Coliseum.

Because Georgia Tech's home gym holds 9,100 fans, thousands fewer than the Georgia Dome can accommodate for basketball, the SEC decided to play the games with only media, school pep bands, cheerleaders, and team family members in attendance.

Conference spokesman DeWayne Peevy told ESPN.com the league consulted with NCAA tournament selection committee chairman Tom O'Connor, the athletic director of George Mason, on the postponement decision. SEC commissioner Mike Slive is on the committee as well and was part of the decision process from Indianapolis.

Peevy said the league considered all possible scenarios—including having co-champions by playing one game Saturday and the semifinals Sunday—but was told that because the league gives its automatic qualifier to the NCAA tournament to its conference tournament winner, it would have to finish the conference tournament to secure that automatic bid.

Reprinted, by permission, from M. Schlabach and A. Katz, 2008, "Storm that damaged Georgia Dome, Atlanta was a tornado," *Associated Press* Available: http://sports.espn.go.com/ncb/champweek2008/news/story?id=3295046.

For the same reason, it is also advisable to use collapsible goalposts at football stadiums to help protect student-athletes, officials, coaches, and spectators (LaVetter & Choi, 2010). More generally, facility and event managers must adopt and strictly follow standard operating procedures consistent with the expectations of each respective sport. Given the numerous sports included in intercollegiate athletics, the many procedures are not addressed individually in this chapter, but they can be found by consulting with governing bodies at the conference and national levels. Following such standards reduces an institution's liability.

Terrorism Threats

Another area of concern centers on post-9/11 threats of terrorism. A large-scale sporting event gives terrorists a potential opportunity to attack at a time when sport fans are in a relaxed but highly visible state (Cohen, 2001; Hall, Marciani, Cooper, & Phillips, 2010; Miller & Dunn, 2011). To counter this risk, continuous education must be provided to facility and event management personnel in order to reinforce procedures, identify vulnerable areas, and foster ongoing evaluation of threat assessment (Hall et al.).

In fact, this area of concern is grave enough that the University of Southern Mississippi has created a research center focused on it. The center recommends the adoption of certain preevent strategies, including policies and procedures that address facility access, game-day activity monitoring, and video surveillance (Marciani & Hall, 2007). Tactics to lower the risk of terrorism include the use of bag checks, bomb-sniffing dogs, trained security, and barriers to keep vehicles at a distance from the facility (Steinbach, 2006b). Additional security practices can include the following:

- Central command to coordinate security responses
- Venue lockdown prior to any event
- Prohibition of concession deliveries within 90 minutes of the event
- Live on-premises security 24/7
- Restrictions on access to critical areas of the facility
- Photo identification and zone passes for employees
- Creation of a formal risk management plan
- Preevent training program for all event staff
- Coordination with local and state police agencies
- Preparation of a formal evacuation plan
- Awareness of potentially explosive or otherwise dangerous facilities nearby
- Undercover surveillance with radio equipment dispersed throughout the building
- No-fly zones over and around the building
- Mobile emergency room vehicle on standby
- One crowd observer per 250 people in all sections of the venue
- Security patrols in the parking lot
- Periodic broadcast to spectators regarding security practices and restricted items
- Ban on carry-in backpacks and other large bags
- Postevent debriefing for all personnel

These security practices are recommended in the Springfield College Security Study (Pantera, Accorsi, Winter, Gobeile, Grieveas, Queen, et al., 2003). In addition to preventive measures, facility and event managers should establish a security action plan to be activated if a terrorist attack does occur (Miller & Dunn, 2011). This type of plan is addressed in the University of Southern Mississippi sidebar.

Student Behavior

A third area of concern involves student behavior. Though most student sections provide a positive home-court or home-field advantage, it takes only a few individuals to cause concern with negative behavior (Steinbach, 2008a). Bad behavior can take place at any type of contest, as demonstrated by a December 2009 sporting event at which home fans chanted misogynistic and homophobic slurs at student-athletes. The event was a women's squash match hosted by Dartmouth College, and rival Harvard University was the target (Ulrich, 2010). Coaches can also be targeted, as when University of Wyoming students chanted "alcoholic" at Colorado State men's basketball coach Larry Eustachy despite his being sober for more than a decade (Chase, 2013).

Whether a problem involves chanting, clothing choices, or other behavior, facility and event managers should have a policy in place for addressing problematic situations when they arise. Often, a warning to the student is enough to stifle the issue, but ejection from the facility is another option when fans behave in a way that reflects poorly on the school and the athletics department. In fact, the Big Ten Conference retains the right to terminate entire student sections if a school is sanctioned

University of Southern Mississippi and Facility/Event Security

By Dr. Lou Marciani and Dr. Stacey Hall

Catastrophic events and elevated terrorist threat levels serve as constant reminders that sport venues, including collegiate and high school stadiums and arenas, are vulnerable to disasters. These events can result in significant property damage, personal injury, and loss of life. If that's not a good enough reason to take action, consider these arguments:

- Schools have a moral and legal responsibility to protect spectators, officials, competitors, employees, the community, and the environment to the highest degree possible.
- Athletics programs must comply with the contractual minimum security and safety obligations outlined by their athletics conference or state association and the regulatory requirements of municipal, county, state, and federal agencies.
- Having a plan in place will enhance one's ability to recover from financial losses, regulatory fines, lost market share, damage to equipment or products, and business interruptions if a crisis does occur.
- Preventive procedures reduce civil and criminal liability in the event of an incident.
- A proactive plan enhances an athletics department's image and credibility with spectators, competitors, employees, corporate sponsors, and the community.
- It may lead to reduced venue insurance premiums.
- If a disaster strikes and a school is not prepared, the resulting fear could irrevocably damage a program. If calamity occurs on a national scale, it could cripple a multibillion-dollar industry.

Any good spectator security plan must also have procedures for evacuation. Here is the command structure currently being used at the University of Southern Mississippi, as well as the guidelines for the process.

Command Post Team: The following personnel report to the Incident Command Post (ICP) upon learning of an emergency situation:

Incident Commander (IC): This is the on-site senior-ranking officer of the university police department who will be in command of all evacuation operations. The on-site senior-ranking officer of the local fire department will assume command of fire-related and hazardous material incidents.

Principal Evaluation Officer (PEO): This is the on-site senior ranking member of the athletics department or designee who will direct actual evacuation procedures.

Evacuation Operations Officer (EOO): The associate athletics director for facilities, this person will assist the PEO with evacuation procedures and replaces the PEO in case of his or her absence.

Police Supervisor: The major of operations or the next-highest-ranking member of the university police force will coordinate and direct the use of all sworn and nonsworn security on scene.

Other members of the command post team include a police supervisor, security supervisors, a medical supervisor, and a physical plant supervisor. We also identify a public information officer who is in charge of releasing information to the media.

The Plan

Upon notification of an emergency, the IC will contact the PEO and then other members of the command post team. The command post team will proceed to the ICP to assess the emergency. In the event that the emergency is unexpected and warrants immediate attention, the IC and the PEO may decide to proceed with the evacuation plan right away.

However, whenever possible, evacuations will be preceded by a preevacuation alert in order to allow personnel to prepare the facility for exit. This will include making sure all exits are open and communicating with the police dispatcher, coaches, officials, media, and all staff about the alert.

Upon receiving notification of a preevacuation alert, all employees will perform preevacuation duties, report to assigned areas, and await further instructions. If the IC determines that circumstances warrant ordering evacuation, he or she will

- authorize the press box to announce the appropriate predetermined message;
- instruct the ICP police dispatcher to announce over the two-way radio to proceed with the evacuation plan;
- instruct the assistant athletics director of operations to inform the referee and coaches that evacuation has been ordered and, with assistance of event staff, escort the teams and officials from the field to the appropriate location in the field house; and
- monitor reports from the field and make necessary changes as situations dictate.

Before any evacuation is declared completed, it must be established that all patrons have evacuated the facility. Before exiting the facility, the event staff assisting with the evacuation will sweep each area to make sure all patrons have vacated.

If time is not available to issue a preevacuation alert, the command post team should proceed to the ICP to immediately identify the emergency and make sure the evacuation plan is proceeding. Event staff must be prepared to respond quickly, without instruction if need be, to their assigned areas and proceed with the plan. If the emergency is not known, event staff in the field who are aware of what has occurred should report the incident to the ICP for evaluation by the command post team.

These instructions are also important:

- All patrons with disabilities are evacuated first.
- All athletics staff, contractual services, and event management staff are expected to become familiar with the plan and be prepared to follow direction as provided.
- To ensure an efficient flow of information to the ICP, all personnel must notify their supervisors of changes and developments in regard to the emergency. This will ensure that decisions made from the ICP are based on the most current and best information available.
- When any part of this plan is implemented, all nonessential radio traffic must cease. Only communications that relate to the emergency should be made.
- During the evacuation plan, all event staff should take the proper precautions to stay out of harm's way.

Personal safety is more important than the protection of facilities or material assets.

Reprinted, by permission, from L. Marciani and S. Hall, 2007, "Home-field security," *Athletic Management* Available: www.athleticmanagement.com/2007/08/13/home-field_security/index.php.

three times for chants targeted at specific opposing players (Steinbach, 2008a). Schools have also used their own coaches to encourage students to cheer loudly but tastefully (Steinbach, 2001). Failing to proactively curtail students' poor behavior can result in negative attention through the media and potential fines levied by governing bodies.

With such concerns in mind, athletics administrators at Virginia Tech have been proactive in their efforts to prevent poor behavior. The Hokies Respect program encourages all participants and supporters to display good sporting behavior at sporting events while still generating the lively home-field advantage that the Hokies enjoy.

Supported by former athletics director Jim Weaver and former university president Charles Steger, the program focuses on welcoming visiting fans and providing a generally welcoming game-day atmosphere, both inside and outside the football stadium and basketball arena ("Hokies Respect," 2013).

The campaign is prominently featured on the athletics website, along with video testimonials from fans, and is promoted in game-day programs and alumni magazines. In addition, prominent Virginia Tech athletics alumni start home football games by reciting a pledge reminding Virginia Tech fans that "Hokies respect the moment, the opponent, the game, themselves, and the competition" ("Hokies Respect," 2013). The program was initiated to curtail abusive chants, foul language, drunken behavior, taunting, and littering of the playing field.

Alcohol at Sporting Events

One highly debated question of risk is whether schools should serve alcohol at their sporting events. Among schools that do sell alcohol, many restrict alcohol consumption to their premium seating areas to foster greater contributions by donors in return for this benefit. The NCAA and other governing bodies have remained neutral on the issue, choosing to grant institutional control over pouring choices (Steinbach, 2004b).

Critics of alcohol sales during events note that binge drinking is a sizable problem on college campuses and argue that serving alcohol sends the wrong message to students (Popke, 2005). Indeed, excessive pregame drinking was so prominent at University of Wisconsin football games that the school implemented breathalyzer tests of students cited for alcohol violations as a deterrent (Steinbach, 2007b). Sanctioned students were tested at future events and denied admission if they had alcohol in their system.

Proponents of allowing alcohol consumption inside stadiums and arenas point out that it can generate considerable revenue. They also argue that many patrons will consume alcohol prior to the event while tailgating (Steinbach, 2005d). Indeed, West Virginia University came under scrutiny due to alcohol consumption during tailgating before home football games. For years, fans would

binge-drink before kickoff and try to sneak alcohol inside the facility. Season-ticket holders grew upset about the behavioral issues inside the stadium and threatened not to renew their tickets.

In an effort to combat the complaints, West Virginia took a different approach—it brought the alcohol inside the stadium. Specifically, for the 2011 season, West Virginia implemented two major changes at home football games. First, alcohol was sold inside Milan Puskar Stadium. Second, fans who exited the stadium during the game could no longer gain readmission (Novy-Williams, 2011; Steinbach, 2011; "WVU approves," 2011), because the athletics department believed that some fans were using halftime as a chance to return to their tailgating areas in order to binge-drink. The sale of alcohol inside the stadium includes several provisions:

- Strict enforcement of ID checks
- Purchase limits
- No alcohol point of sale near the student section
- No alcohol sales in seating areas
- No alcohol sales after the midpoint of the third quarter
- Designated driver program

The third-party concession group assumed responsibility for training its staff, managing intervention procedures, and procuring the alcohol license. The adoption of alcohol sales was implemented in conjunction with the TEAM (Techniques for Effective Alcohol Management) Coalition, a nonprofit organization that addresses alcohol consumption in stadiums and arenas. The Coalition works with beer distributors, traffic safety authorities, concessionaire groups, and facility managers to identify solutions for offering a more respectful, fan-friendly atmosphere at events in professional sport, entertainment, and intercollegiate athletics. For the 2011 season, West Virginia University earned US$700,000 in additional revenue through alcohol sales while also reducing alcohol-related police calls by 30 percent.

Alcohol-related safety measures can include restricting how early fans can tailgate, limiting the duration of tailgating, and banning kegs and other large alcohol containers (Steinbach, 2003b).

Fans can be educated in advance about alcohol policies through the athletics and school websites (Menaker & Connaughton, 2010). Some schools also designate certain drinking areas, and others clear the school's property of tailgaters once the game begins. Earlier kickoff times also reduce the amount of time available for alcohol consumption prior to the game.

"We're not hosting a bar," noted former University of Notre Dame associate vice president Bill Kirk. "People come for the game, and if they want to have a drink and a sandwich before and after, we'll accommodate that. But we're not a place where we open up our campus to folks just coming to party" (Steinbach, 2003b, para. 15).

Tailgating Concerns

For many fans, the game-day experience begins long before tipoff or kickoff with tailgating on campus. Setting up chairs, tables, grills, and tents increases the fans' time on campus but also comes with concerns. The possession and consumption of alcohol is difficult to monitor, but it needs to be addressed in order to ensure patrons' safety. In addition, donor parking spaces should be numbered to assign ownership to each space. Doing so prevents problems such as exceeding parking lot capacity or having fans tailgate in multiple parking spaces. Campus and local police officials can help prevent such problems through continuous presence, particularly at large-scale events.

With such issues in mind, event managers must foresee risks and oversee tailgate areas as potential liabilities. For a tailgating management plan to succeed, each of the following areas must be addressed and communicated to all constituents (Gillentine et al., 2010):

- Enforcement procedures
- Cooperative agreements
- Designated tailgating areas
- Tailgating hours

Sports is life with the volume turned up. People don't like to be told anything today. "I bought my ticket, and I can do whatever the hell I want to do. So what if a guy makes an announcement?"

Barry Mano, president, National Association of Sports Officials (qtd. in Steinbach, 2001, para. 11)

- Parking
- Grilling
- Glass containers
- Trash receptacles
- Stadium reentry
- Alcohol consumption
- Evaluation and monitoring

FAN RIGHTS

The back side of many tickets includes a statement that fans are subject to removal from the venue at the discretion of facility managers or the athletics department (Nagel, 2011). Event organizers do have the legal right to eject patrons due to the fact that tickets are revocable licenses (Nagel). Of course, ejecting fans is not a desirable outcome, but it can be difficult to know where to draw the line. Many fans attend college events to physically support and vocally cheer on their team. Some fans argue that they have the right to freedom of speech, but when speech crosses into vulgarity or profanity, facility managers seek ways to indulge the passion of the fan base in a clean format.

Examples of fans attempting to assert their rights have occurred at the University of Maryland, the University of Virginia, and San Jose State University. The University of Maryland tried to improve student behavior at home basketball games by creating a student task force designed to identify strategies for reducing offensive behavior. At the request of the state attorney general, the committee took care not to violate First Amendment rights, thus forcing it to seek other recommendations. The task force met 12 times over three months, held an open town hall forum, and surveyed more than 200 students. The task force ultimately recommended a number of initiatives to encourage voluntary compliance with guidelines for positive fan behavior:

- An accessible t-shirt exchange at athletics venues to provide free t-shirts to students who turn in profane ones

Compliance Education at Athletics Facilities

At the University of Colorado and Iowa State University, athletics facility bathrooms are used as locations for compliance tips educating fans about the dos and don'ts of behavior that can affect student-athletes' eligibility (Steinbach, 2008d). Specifically, spaces in stalls, above urinals, and near sinks are used to display educational messages to the schools' fans in order to facilitate greater compliance with NCAA rules and regulations.

- Head coaches addressing incoming first-year students during convocation at the beginning of each school year
- An open practice with the head basketball coach prior to a marquee game to discuss with students the value of good sporting behavior
- A lighthearted game-day newspaper (featuring nonprofane but creative, witty cheers created by students) for basketball fans to continue the tradition of shaking the papers while the opposing team is introduced
- A best-sign contest on the videoboard at football and basketball games to encourage creative and appropriate signs and banners
- Additional signage discouraging profanity at athletics venues

In 2008, the University of Virginia attempted to ban signs at its football stadium after a slow start to the season. Fans were critical of the head coach, and a fan had been ejected from a 2007 game for displaying a sign calling for the coach's firing (Miller, 2008). Students protested the ban, noting that the school's founder, Thomas Jefferson, was a proponent of free speech. Though the school's athletics director wanted a positive, game-day environment, the ban was overturned when it became too big a distraction.

Fans may complain about profanity, alcohol abuse, and violence at sporting events, but a March 2005 San Jose State home basketball game yielded another event management issue—provocative moves by the school's dance team (Steinbach, 2005a). When an elder alumnus and major donor called the dance team "trash," a member of the team approached him to address the issue. A heated confrontation ensued, and a parent of the dance team member sued the school because an athletics department official, in trying to intervene, had placed his hands on the young female student. Possible solutions to this situation might include screening the dancers' outfits, music selection, and performance routines. However, even such proactive steps will not necessarily restrain fans who believe that their purchase of a ticket entitles them to freely speak their mind at an event.

FACILITY PLANNING

Optimal facility planning involves all stakeholder groups that may use or be involved with the facility, including participants, administrators, sports medicine staff, strength and conditioning staff, members of the media, hospitality providers, concession providers, and other support groups (Browne, Briggs, & Strube, 2008; Bynum, 2007). Money is generally a primary consideration, and sharing space and choosing certain materials (e.g., turf rather than grass) can reduce both construction and operational costs (Steinbach, 2006e). At the same time, cost-saving measures should be balanced with administrative considerations, such as scheduling and fiscal oversight.

In the planning stages of facility development and renovation, project managers should invest the time and energy to identify specific facility needs. This process includes conducting thorough feasibility studies and benchmarking. In choosing a firm to serve as an architectural, engineering, or construction partner, managers should balance cost-efficiency with demonstrated success and testimonials from other schools to ensure timely construction.

Needs Assessment

A facility's stakeholders include not only coaches and student-athletes but also recruits, support staff, and fans. Athletics facilities may also be shared with the school's student body for recreational purposes. In addition, consideration must be given to the needs of the media, concession operators, and hospitality providers, which may call for premium seating. Including constituents from this wide range of stakeholders provides more robust dialogue to help with facility needs assessment early in the process (Westerbeek et al., 2006).

Feasibility Study

A feasibility study can help with facility renovation and construction by bringing objectivity to the process (Seifried, 2012). It includes an affordability analysis, steps to decrease the risk of failure, a best-fit examination of the facility in relation to users, an exploration of budget issues, and an initial game plan for marketing and public relations (Westerbeek et al., 2006). The study is conducted by thoroughly examining such considerations as the following:

- Historical issues
- Facts
- Goals
- Stakeholders
- Time lines
- Market research

This process enables objective scrutiny of proposed locations, weather implications for construction, legal issues, and financial concerns, especially hidden costs (Westerbeek et al., 2006).

Benchmarking

Benchmarking enables school officials to research other facilities in order to glean ideas and develop comparisons. Benchmarking can be done through initial on-campus research followed up by trips to other schools. These trips provide a firsthand perspective on new resources and technology, such as upgrades in LED scoreboards that can enhance the game-day experience and increase revenue (Dahlgren, 2000). Similarly, exposure to amenities such as banners, wall murals, floor graphics, and wall padding can stimulate ideas for visual additions to enhance the facility experience for staff, recruits, student-athletes, and patrons (Steinbach, 2005b). These trips can also foster discussion of program-

ming, structural systems, safety concerns, turf and flooring needs, and appropriate HVAC and lighting systems (Browne et al., 2008).

Requests for Proposals

After the needs assessment, feasibility study, and benchmarking steps have been completed, it is time to solicit proposals from architects, engineers, and construction firms (Westerbeek et al., 2006). Schools put out a request for proposal (often referred to by the acronym RFP) inviting firms to submit bids detailing their capabilities for consideration by the school after a set deadline. Some firms may be invited to campus for further discussion. The construction or renovation process can involve a large number of contractors and subcontractors, and checking references and examining their past facility projects can lower the risk of failure. The Virginia Tech sidebar demonstrates how problematic facility construction can be and thereby emphasizes the importance of establishing effective contracts.

Environmentally Friendly Facilities

Facilities are generally constructed with sustainability and multipurpose functionality in mind in order to maximize the investment. Sustainability emerges, for example, in the use of sensor-activated lights or natural lighting to reduce power usage, the inclusion of renewable energy sources, and the promotion of waste reduction programs, recycling, and other environmentally friendly programs. Schools can also reduce storm-water runoff or use the water for other purposes. In addition, facilities can recycle construction material or expect building materials to come from a regional supplier, thereby reducing carbon emissions from transportation (Funk, 2007). Some schools, such as Wartburg College, have even incorporated wind power to become more energy efficient (Cohen, 2007). The University of Mississippi pursues energy efficiency through the use of solar panels on selected athletics facilities (Cohen, 2000). Even bike racks and priority parking for carpoolers can help the environment (Funk, 2007)

Facilities can also earn LEED (Leadership in Energy and Environmental Design) certification if they meet certain criteria as evaluated by the

Legal Issues With Virginia Tech's Lane Stadium Expansion

Expansion of Virginia Tech's football stadium proved to be a lengthy process that resulted in multiple lawsuits between the university, contractors, and subcontractors. In addition, season-ticket holders were inconvenienced. All of these problems reinforced the need for effective legal counsel in contractual matters involving architects, engineers, and construction firms.

August 2003

The school's board of visitors approves the US$52.5 million plan. Initially, the blueprints embrace a plethora of new features, including professional stadium lighting, several lounges and suites, new indoor and outdoor club seats, and a new president's box.

February 2004

The Turner Construction group is awarded the bid to upgrade Lane Stadium. To design plans, Virginia Tech contracts the Moseley, Harris, and McClintock firm, which subcontracts Thornton Tomasetti to plan structural steel designs.

March 2004

This is the launch date, and the intended termination date is August 2005.

May 2004

Turner Construction alleges receiving design documents two months later than anticipated.

August 2005

The 2005 football season starts with a game against Marshall University, and the construction has not been completed. Season-ticket holders are displaced.

October 2005

Varney Inc. sues Turner Construction for breach of contract. Varney asks for US$3,694,984 from the construction group: US$889,810 for a withheld payment and US$2,805,174 for Varney's inability to manage other projects during the time. Turner had hired Varney for mechanical work, including plumbing, air conditioning, heating, and ventilation.

February 2006

The October 2005 case is settled for an undisclosed monetary amount.

May 2006

Gate Precast Co. sues Turner Construction for breach of contract, claiming entitlement to US$673,731. Gate also files suit against four insurance companies for a bond securing payment to Turner's subcontractors.

June 2006

Virginia Tech is awarded a certificate of occupancy, signifying project completion.

October 2006

Turner Construction group sues Virginia Tech for unfulfilled payment obligations.

Data from McConnell and Anderson 2006; Pieper 2006.

U.S. Green Building Council (Cohen, 2010). The four tiers of LEED certification are platinum, gold, silver, and certified. For example, the University of Florida's Heavener Football Complex earned platinum recognition, the University of Minnesota's TCF Bank Stadium earned silver certification, and Bowdoin College's ice rink and Penn State's baseball stadium are certified (Cohen, 2010). Many schools perceive efforts to go green as cost prohibitive, but these expenses are declining annually.

Americans With Disabilities Act

Facility and event managers also need to be knowledgeable about the Americans With Disabilities Act and how it affects not only spectators but also student-athletes who may be injured. This is especially true in regard to new facility construction (Dethlefs, 2007) and facility alterations (Steinbach, 2007a). Seating for persons with a disability should include a variety of options, provide sightlines comparable to those of other seats, and be easy to access from the parking area, concession stands, and restrooms (Grady, 2010). In addition, staff working in disability seating and parking areas need to be knowledgeable about the principle of accessibility in event management, thus ensuring high-quality customer service in an area that is frequently neglected (Grady).

Providing such options can entail additional construction costs but ensures compliance with the federal legislation requiring that 1 percent of seating be appropriate for persons with a disability (Steinbach, 2007a). Noncompliance can carry its own costs. The University of Michigan, for example, faced lawsuits and was the subject of protests about noncompliance from the state U.S. Office for Civil Rights during alterations of its football stadium in 2006 (Steinbach, 2007a).

Title IX

Title IX is another piece of federal legislation that requires adherence, in this case with respect to comparably scheduling events and practice times, determining locker room sizes, and providing resources for both men's and women's programs. Complaints regarding noncompliance, which can come from coaches or student-athletes, are handled by the U.S. Office for Civil Rights (Funk, 2010). For example, San Diego State University settled

with a former swimming coach at a cost of more than US$1 million due to shortcomings in providing equitable facilities and practice times (Cohen, 2008). In terms of facilities, administrators should foster equity in all areas of construction, upgrades, resources, and operations. Title IX is addressed in greater detail in chapter 4.

FACILITY BUDGETING

Despite the bleak financial realities faced by most intercollegiate athletics departments, administrators have escalated expenditures on facility construction and renovation in order to seek a competitive advantage in recruiting. This phenomenon has come to be known as the "arms race of expenditures." In this race, schools adopt the mentality that if they spend a bit more than their conference rival (e.g., on a practice facility, locker room, player lounge, weight room, coach's salary, or sports medicine facility), the investment should translate into better recruits and ultimately a higher winning percentage. However, because this competitive mentality is shared by many institutions, each school spends more and more in an effort simply to keep up with its rivals (Bennett, 2012; Bynum, 2007; Steinbach, 2003a). This tendency is most common at Division I schools found in the ACC, Big Ten, Big 12, Pac-12 and SEC conferences, where coaches particularly aspire to occupy facilities that are welcoming to recruits in terms of size, amenities, and personal touches (Mead, 2007).

Institutions that generate less revenue must plan strategically to assess their facility needs with a limited budget. Stressed budgets can cause adjustments in staffing, including split shifts, seasonal staffing, the use of contracting services, and a reliance on volunteers (Sports Turf Managers Association, 2011). When budgets are reduced, emphasis should also be placed on minimizing utility costs and maximizing the efficiency of staff (Gioglio, 2011; Palmero et al., 2011). Fiscal matters and budgeting are discussed further in chapter 7.

FACILITY FUNDING

Schools use a wide range of financing mechanisms for facilities, including naming rights, bonds, institutional support, student fees, and funding from local governments (Myers, 2008). This varied

Industry Profile

Jeremy Foley

Director of athletics, University of Florida

You rose from game operations to athletics director. What advice would you offer students who aspire to become an AD?

I think it is important to constantly set goals, track your progress toward them, and self-evaluate. Most people set goals and want to achieve them, but the successful ones are willing to look themselves in the mirror and ask, "How can I get better?" It's also very, very important to be loyal to your organization, your coworkers, and your boss. Without loyalty, it's hard for an organization to be successful. That said, there are many challenges and difficult decisions with any career, and the right decisions aren't always the easiest decisions. Sometimes you have to do what's best for your organization versus what's best for an individual.

What future trends do you anticipate in facilities and event management in intercollegiate athletics?

For various reasons that are well documented, attendance is down at all venues, and that is an area of concern for our industry. A current trend, which will continue to be a future trend, are the challenges all of us are facing in college and professional sports—to continue to find ways to serve our customers and make attending our events an attractive option for them now and in the future.

What is the best part of your job?

The best part of this job is the impact you have on young people's lives. I tell all of our prospective student-athletes that want to come to school here, "We want these to be the best years of your lives." We want them to graduate, win championships, and when it's all said and done, we want them to say, "I would do it all over again if I had the chance."

What books do you recommend for those aspiring to work in intercollegiate athletics?

Good to Great by Jim Collins, *The Leader-ship Secrets of Colin Powell* by Oren Harari, and *The 7 Habits of Highly Effective People* by Stephen Covey.

Jeremy N. Foley began his career with the University of Florida (UF) athletics department as an intern in the Gator ticket office in 1976. Within three years, he was the director of ticket and game operations. Throughout his rise to the director of athletics position, which he earned in 1992, he has managed virtually every aspect of the athletics program. Foley's philosophy involves the continued building of a comprehensive athletics program, with the goal of having the UF program ranked as the top overall athletics program in the nation.

As chief financial officer for the University Athletic Association (UAA), Foley has spearheaded a number of capital improvement projects in the athletics department. The project list includes two major expansions of the football stadium; a multipurpose athletics field house; and new facilities for tennis, track and field, soccer, baseball, golf, softball, swimming, and lacrosse. Foley also played a role in the academic advising center on the University of Florida campus, which serves both Gator student-athletes and other students, and assisted in funding the renovation of the Stephen C. O'Connell Center that serves as the home for the basketball, gymnastics, swimming and diving, and volleyball programs.

Also under his watch, the James W. "Bill" Heavener Football Complex—a project that enhanced the football experience for Gator student-athletes, staff, and visitors—was completed in July 2008 and received platinum LEED certification, the highest ranking available. It was the first building in Florida, and the first athletics facility in the nation, to achieve platinum status. Foley's most recent project was the lacrosse facility—a 1,500-seat stadium offering fans a great view of this fast-paced sport—which was completed prior to the inaugural season in the spring of 2010.

Professional Experience

- Athletics director (March 1992 to present)
- Senior associate athletics director (January 1987 to March 1992)
- Interim athletics director (September 1986 to January 1987)
- Associate athletics director for business affairs (June 1981 to September 1986)
- Assistant athletics director (May 1980 to June 1981)
- Director of ticket and game operations (March 1979 to May 1980)
- Ticket manager (February 1977 to March 1979)
- Intern (August 1976 to February 1977)

Reprinted, by permission, from GatorZone. Available: www.gatorzone.com/foley.

approach was demonstrated by the University of Minnesota in its financing of an on-campus football facility. In order to open the US$200 million stadium in time for the 2009 football season, the school needed both state support and other revenue streams. A naming rights deal drew some criticism about excessive commercialism but enabled the school to earn US$35 million toward the facility's cost ("Minn. banks," 2006; Steinbach, 2006c).

The three-year fundraising process was supplemented by student fees. Students agreed to the heightened fee in exchange for greater input on the facility's advisory board, benefits at other sporting events, and reduced green fees at the school's golf course. State funding contributed about US$10 million but required the school to give up some land to the state. Collectively, the funding streams enabled the school to better finance the construction project.

More generally, the selling of facility naming rights is becoming more prevalent in intercollegiate athletics but is still not as widely accepted as it is in professional sport (Chen & Zhang, 2012). At this point, it is a more common practice for schools to honor individuals affiliated with the school, including donors. In another area of difference with professional sport venues, despite the Minnesota arrangement, it is less common for institutions of higher learning to rely on taxpayers to help fund intercollegiate athletics facilities, as politicians face other pressing fiscal burdens in their regions (Brown & Nagel, 2010).

One trend in new facility construction in intercollegiate athletics that is growing, however, is the inclusion of premium seating (e.g., suites, club levels, and courtside bunkers) due to the considerable long-term revenue-generating capabilities of these amenities (Lawrence & Titlebaum, 2010; Steinbach, 2005c). Premium seating areas can provide an environment in which businesses want to host clients, reward employees, conduct business, and offer hospitality in a fun atmosphere (Lawrence, Kahler, & Contorno, 2009; Titlebaum, DeMange, & Davis, 2012). Through collaborative planning with targeted businesses, the development and ticketing offices can maximize funding capabilities, as these groups can best assess the market demand for various kinds of seating.

CURRENT ISSUES

Although the fundamental principles of facility and event management are consistent, new issues continue to arise or evolve, and administrators must be prepared to meet these challenges. Emerging issues include, for example, the process for bidding to host a postseason event, decisions about whether to outsource facility management to third-party firms, outsource concessions, or play neutral-site games; ways of thinking outside the box and preparing for the unexpected; and practices for preventing the spread of communicable diseases. Each of these areas is discussed in the following sections.

Purdue University Explains the Necessities of Premium Seating

At Purdue University, the installation of premium seating at Ross-Ade Stadium represented no more than US$18 million of a three-year US$70 million renovation completed in 2003, yet income from the premium seating pays US$4.3 million toward the entire project's US$4.7 million annual debt service. "This is the message that I've been trying to get out to the public from the get-go, because there was this presumption that we were spending $70 million to create upscale seating for rich ticket buyers," says Glenn Tompkins, Purdue's senior associate athletics director for business.

"In fact, of the $70 million, more than $50 million was for infrastructure that benefits the average fan sitting in the stands. It's more concession stands and restrooms, wider seats and concourses, and improved concrete and sound—I could go on and on. The income from the premium seating is what makes all the other benefits possible."

Reprinted, by permission, from P. Steinbach, 2005, "Honeymoon suites," *Athletic Business*. Available: www.athleticbusiness.com/stadium-arena/honeymoon-suites.html.

Bidding to Host NCAA Postseason Events

When a school bids to host a postseason event, it typically responds to a request for proposals in which the NCAA (or other governing organization) sets forth its minimum expectations. For example, the bidding process might require potential hosts to provide a specified number of seats in a facility, ample nearby hotels, experience in hosting comparable events, and a leadership team with demonstrated knowledge in this realm (Bilsky, 2007). Because many teams participate in postseason events, a school can enhance the attractiveness of its bid by forming partnerships with local hotels, restaurants, and transportation and sport commissions. In addition, they can analyze past hosted events to develop projected expenses and revenues, including an anticipated budget for providing the resources needed for media relations, sports medicine, and sport marketing (publicity).

In putting forth a bid, Steve Bilsky (2007, para. 27–29), athletics director at the University of Pennsylvania, challenges administrators to ask the following questions.

• First, do you have the support of the entire community? You should consider whether being a championship host would benefit only your institution or if the community would benefit through added tourism dollars and positive publicity. The easiest way to answer this question is to discuss your ideas with tourism officials and other local agencies. Do not hesitate to ask the mayor or even your state's governor for financial support.

• Second, can you put on a championship-caliber event? The student-athletes competing are the very best at their sport and deserve a venue worthy of the occasion. If you will not be hosting the event at your own site, make sure the event managers know what they are doing and have a proven record of accomplishment. Nothing spoils an event more than spectators spending an inordinate amount of time parking, waiting in line for tickets, and searching for concessions and restrooms, or teams arriving and not knowing where to be at what times.

• Third, can you make a competitive bid? Make sure that facilities are up to snuff and that the infrastructure is there to support the event. And be realistic about your customer base—large events like the lacrosse championships are highly sought after, and one of the criteria is whether a venue can offer the right amount of revenue.

Outsourcing Facility Operations

Many schools outsource facility operations to a third-party group in order to benefit from their expertise and maximize cost-efficiency. Such companies, including AIG, SMG, and Global Spectrum, help manage larger arenas in the areas of booking, sales, marketing, concessions, public relations, and risk management (Palmero et al., 2011; Steinbach, 2004a). In addition, schools can generate revenue by hosting nonathletic events booked by the company while also saving money, because the third-party firm receives a bulk discount on purchases of items needed for facility management. Hosting additional events can also add value in naming rights and sponsorship agreements for the venue.

Other third-party firms, such as Landmark Event Staffing, can help with crowd management, security, guest services, and event traffic and parking. Still others, such as the Colonnade Group, offer expertise in hospitality management and oversight of premium seating.

These potential benefits notwithstanding, using a third-party firm to manage a facility can also be problematic because the school exercises less control over the venue. For example, an athletic team would not be working directly with a school official in scheduling practices at the game-day facility, which could be in use for an outside event (Steinbach, 2004a).

The decision about whether to outsource facility management involves several factors. First, at some schools, there is no decision to make, because school policy requires in-house management. For schools without such a policy, the decision should be revisited periodically by examining the current level of satisfaction with the facility's management, as well as its staffing capabilities. Another consideration involves risk. Outsourcing management operations may not only enable a school to host more events and generate greater revenue but also transfer the financial and legal risks to the third-party company (Palmero et al., 2011). One way to determine an arena management model is to use the decision framework presented in figure 10.1.

Coordinating Concessions

More than half of Division I athletics departments outsource their concessions in order to take advan-

> We're not architects or builders. We are operators, so we look at design from a very practical point of view. Many of the facilities that we operate are university buildings with athletics as the prime tenant, but they also have a broader mandate to be public civic centers. They need to be programmatically capable of handling multiple types of events.
>
> Frank Russo, senior vice president, Global Spectrum (qtd. in Steinbach, 2004a, para. 5)

tage of specialized firms' expertise, enhance revenue opportunities, and stay current with industry trends (Steinbach, 2000). Schools choosing to keep concessions in-house tend to do so in the interest of greater control. Popular concessionaires used in the industry include Aramark, Sodexo, Centerplate, Levy Restaurants, and Cintas.

The benefits of outsourcing concessions have been summarized as follows by Jim Baker, former senior athletics administrator for the University of Texas: "It's not just one person you are calling on. You're calling on a company that can help you. That's their business. They're doing a better job than we could do, and we're making more money off the concessions than we ever did (Steinbach, 2000, para. 5). Some schools' concession contracts are tied into the school's dining service contract, whereas others are specific to athletics. The contract may also indicate whether the parent concession company can include vendors local to the area, such as Primanti Brothers in the Pittsburgh region (Steinbach, 2008c).

Planning Neutral-Site Games

In Division I college football, established neutral-site rivalries have led athletics administrators to ponder whether their schools should play in such a format. While the Georgia–Florida game (played in Jacksonville) and the Texas–Oklahoma game (played in Dallas) are staples for fans, other programs, such as Notre Dame, have also ventured into neutral-site games. These games can help coaches recruit a selected area or give the school a chance to play in an area with a heavy alumni presence.

However, they also have to make sense fiscally, as the host facility is traditionally responsible for assuming event management duties through contractual obligations (Dougherty, 2008). The host school may also have to educate the facility's staff and administrators about standards and expectations, particularly if the facility is not familiar with

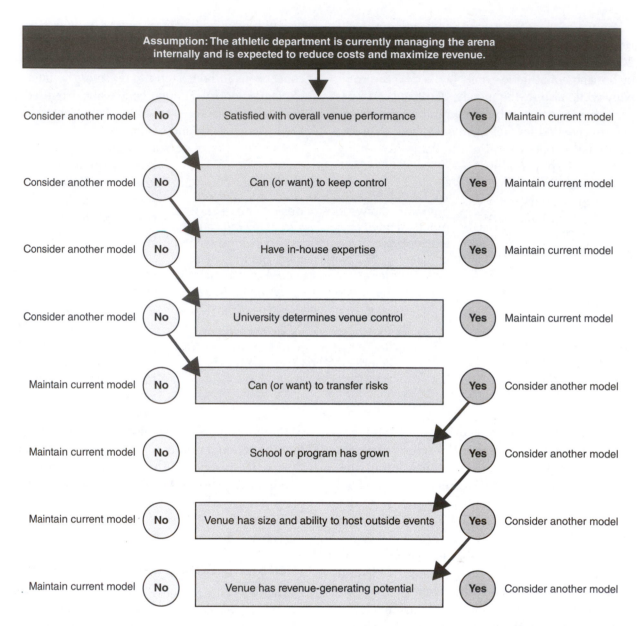

Figure 10.1 Decision framework for determining an arena management model.

Reprinted, by permission, from M. Palmero et al., 2011, "Who is in charge? An analysis of NCAA Division I arena management models," *Journal of Venue and Event Management* 3(2): 18-32.

hosting an event in a certain sport. In addition, coaches and student-athletes want a neutral-site game to feel like a home game in terms of scheduling practice, arranging transportation, and enjoying other resources comparable to those of their home facility. Fans also expect that the event should meet the same professional standards expected at an on-campus home event. These standards include high-quality ticketing, parking, security, concessions, and other aspects of the game-day experience.

Thinking Outside the Box

Creative thinking has taken more college sporting events outside. In one particularly dramatic example, Michigan State University played the University of North Carolina in men's basketball on a U.S. aircraft carrier (Moore, 2011). Though the crowd of just over 8,000 may seem small, it included the president of the United States and members of the active military. Roy Williams, head coach of the Tar Heels, said, "I could coach another 10 or 15 years, and it would be hard to top this, unless it's the Final Four" (Bishop, 2011, para. 6).

Of course, outdoor games can be affected by the weather, including low temperature, low visibility, and high wind, but adaptations can be made in the playing surface, the lighting, the stands, and the locker rooms. A provisional facility can also be made available. For the game on the aircraft carrier, contingency plans included a second basketball court belowdecks in case of inclement weather (Bishop, 2011).

Another example of an indoor-turned-outdoor event is a women's basketball game between Arizona State and the University of Tennessee (Associated Press, 2006). The game, which benefited the fight against breast cancer, was attended by more than 16,000 fans. In yet another example, Michigan State University hosted the University of Michigan in a men's hockey match played at Michigan State's football stadium and attended by more than 74,000 fans (Associated Press, 2010b).

Expecting the Unexpected

In October 2010, a University of Notre Dame student videographer ascended into the air on a hydraulic lift in high winds to videotape the football team's practice (Associated Press, 2011). When the lift toppled, the student fell to his death. In response, the Indiana Occupational Safety and Health Administration fined the school US$77,500 for putting an employee in an unsafe work environment. Though the lifts were not supposed to be used in wind over 28 miles (45 kilometers) per hour, the machine toppled in winds over 50 miles (80 kilometers) per hour.

Because school officials did not have the on-field capability to measure the wind speed, they referred to weather reports from earlier in the day (Zinser, 2011). The athletics director was present at practice that day, and the head coach made the decision to practice outside despite the unsettling conditions (Bishop, 2012). The lifts are used in many sports and band practices, and people who supervise the use of the machines need to be fully educated about proper usage, inspection regulations, and equipment limitations in order to keep employees safe.

Preventing the Spread of Communicable Diseases

Student-athletes, coaches, administrators, and custodial crews also need to be aware of the threat of transferable diseases that lurk in athletics facilities. For example, methicillin-resistant Staphylococcus aureus (MRSA) is a potentially deadly problem in facility management because it can be resistant to antibiotics and can spread quickly within the confines of a locker room, weight room, or sports medicine facility. MRSA killed a college football player in Pennsylvania in 2003 (Kimmel, 2006), and Stanford University's football team was hit with an outbreak in 2006 (Scholand, 2007). Sports that involve heavy body-to-body contact are more prone to the transfer of the infection, which can also spread quickly beyond the playing field.

Facility managers work diligently to avoid this type of problem. Specifically, they work with sports medicine staff to take precautionary measures such as the following:

- Eliminate shared towels, which can transfer MRSA.

- Use antimicrobial soaps in showers and bathrooms because MRSA can be present on traditional bar soap.

- Sanitize locker rooms and bathrooms on a weekly basis.

- Use antimicrobial additives in the laundry because MRSA can withstand traditional laundry detergents.

- Regularly sanitize strength and conditioning equipment and areas, including floors and carpets.

- Use antimicrobial hand wipes and sanitizers in athletics training rooms when working with all student-athletes.

- Test health care providers for MRSA regularly because they can be carriers of the infection.

- Continuously educate everyone involved about the dangers of the infection and how quickly it can spread.

The risk of infection can also be lowered by identifying high-risk areas and raising awareness among student-athletes and coaches through posters and other visual aids (Scholand, 2008). In addition, individuals who clean athletics facilities must understand the dire nature of the infection and do their part to be proactively diligent and aggressive in the fight.

COLLEGIATE EVENT AND FACILITY MANAGEMENT ASSOCIATION

In order to succeed, facility and event administrators need to take advantage of professional development opportunities to grow while also providing the best and most up-to-date service to their school. They can do so by joining an organization such as the Collegiate Event and Facility Management Association (CEFMA). CEFMA provides educational programs, professional development and networking opportunities, and best practices to enhance event and facility management. In conjunction with the National Association of Collegiate Directors of Athletics (NACDA), CEFMA promotes the growth, leadership, integrity, and success of administrators and professional staff involved in collegiate athletics. Student rates are available for membership and for the professional conference held each summer. Benefits of CEFMA include the following:

- Complimentary copy of NACDA's magazine, *Athletics Administration*, published eight times a year and featuring the CEFMA Corner, which highlights current information about intercollegiate facility and event management submitted by CEFMA members
- Reduced registration rates for the annual CEFMA convention, which is held in conjunction with the NACDA convention
- Opportunity to belong to the CEFMA electronic mailing list to communicate directly with CEFMA members
- Opportunity to receive the NACDA Daily Review e-mail, which compiles web links to articles related to intercollegiate athletics
- Opportunities to receive shared expertise from Homeland Security, the Spectator Sports

Security Management Group, and other federal and state agencies through programs sponsored at CEFMA's annual meeting and in other continuing education formats
- Opportunities for networking and resource sharing with the diverse group of professionals who make up CEFMA and NACDA's other affiliate associations
- Additional benefits received through a partnership between CEFMA and the International Association of Venue Managers (IAVM):
  - Access at the IAVM member cost to events, meetings, and schools, including subject-specific webinars and educational programming for individuals from entry level to executive level
  - Access to IAVM's social media platform VenueNet, which provides immediate access to the 3,500 IAVM members to discuss topics and best practices and share information with our peers in the broader facility and event management industry
  - Electronic copy of the quarterly publication *Facility Manager*, a dedicated public assembly building magazine that tackles subjects of interest in our industry, identifies trends, introduces readers to other professionals in the industry, and covers new developments

CONCLUSION

This chapter examines the foundation of facility and event management. Athletics administrators in this area help ensure that coaches, student-athletes, fans, media, sponsors, sports medicine practitioners, donors, and others have what is needed in order to succeed, whether in practice or on game day. Facility management involves handling both short-term and long-term planning, budgeting, and funding while striving to meet the standards required by such legislation as the Americans With Disabilities Act and Title IX. Facility managers are also responsible for facility schedules, setup, and staffing, including everyone from custodians to ushers to workers overseeing the parking lots.

Game-day preparation and management are detailed processes that ensure the safety not only

Leadership Lesson
Motivation 3.0

Event operations staff are those who organize experiences, coordinate vendors, greet visitors, welcome longtime supporters, and provide hospitality for fierce competitors. If collegiate athletics is the front porch of the university, facility and event operations staff are the friendly neighbors who wave on the front lawn. During the course of conference tournaments, summer camps, simultaneous home competitions, and back-to-back-to-back-to-back late nights and early mornings, these jobs can be physiologically draining. There are units throughout the country, however, that have mastered the art of hosting—units that maintain a staff full of people eager to go out of their way to facilitate optimal experiences for their guests and who find great fulfillment in completing their jobs well. They do this through what Daniel Pink refers to as the societal operating system Motivation 3.0.

According to Pink, at one point, humans were driven by biological needs (Motivation 1.0), but they evolved to respond to rewards and punishments—the carrot-and-stick method of motivation. This was Motivation 2.0, and it can still be an effective extrinsic motivator, particularly for algorithmic or repetitive tasks (those that follow a set of established instructions toward a single conclusion) and for activity that brings a baseline reward (for instance, a salary). However, for heuristic tasks—those that require experimentation, creativity, artistry, and novel solutions—extrinsic "if-then" rewards can actually foster negative behavior. Specifically, they can

- extinguish intrinsic motivation;

- diminish performance;
- crush creativity;
- crowd out good behavior;
- encourage cheating, shortcuts, and unethical behavior;
- become addictive; and
- foster short-term thinking. (Pink, 2009, p. 59)

Throughout my athletics career, the overall goal was always to be a better athlete than I was at the moment—whether next week, next month, or next year. The improvement was the goal. The medal was simply the ultimate reward for achieving that goal.

Sebastian Coe, Olympic silver-medalist, British politician, and successful sport administrator (London 2012 Olympic Games, FIFA)

Pink argues that it is time for a societal upgrade to Motivation 3.0—an approach founded on three elements that facilitate intrinsic motivation: autonomy, mastery, and purpose. These three elements must work in concert in order to encourage professional success and foster personal fulfillment in ourselves and in our colleagues.

Autonomy

We are innately self-directed, but this internal drive is often suppressed by outdated notions of "management." Several studies have demonstrated that companies outperform their competitors when they foster an autonomous work environment (Baard, Deci, & Ryan, 2004; Deci & Ryan, 2008). One way to foster autonomy is by creating a "results-only" work environment. In this approach, individuals are accountable for their work, but what they do (task), when they do it (time), who they do it with (team), and how they do it (technique) are all up to them.

Mastery

Autonomy alone cannot breed motivation, but it helps. Whereas earlier management methods led to compliance through control, autonomy can lead to mastery, which is the second element necessary to foster intrinsic motivation. Mastery abides by three rules (Pink, 2009):

(continued)

Leadership Lesson *(continued)*

1. Mastery is a mind-set: It requires believing that one's abilities are infinitely improvable and that learning goals are valued over performance goals.
2. Mastery is pain: It demands relentless effort, steady perseverance, and disciplined practice.
3. Mastery is an asymptote: It can never be fully realized, which makes its pursuit alluring, joyful, and frustrating.

In order to facilitate mastery in your team members, give them tasks that continually challenge and stretch their skill set. In addition, emphasize collaboration. Facilitate task shifting and cross-training, and allow diverse groups to work with one another to stimulate new ideas and processes.

Purpose

The final element of the three-part formula for Motivation 3.0 is purpose, which provides an overarching context within which people can pursue mastery through autonomous means. As emphasized throughout the leadership lessons in this book, "the most deeply motivated people—not to mention those who are most productive and satisfied—hitch their desires to a cause larger than themselves" (Pink, 2009, p. 133). Within this mind-set, purpose maximization and profit maximization are equally important.

The University of North Carolina at Chapel Hill (UNC) has become known for its event operations. Walk into any event, and you will likely be greeted by a smile from a helpful staff member who takes pride in the particular element of the event operations plan with which he or she is currently tasked. Much of this success derives from the work of Ellen Culler, the director of event operations. She leads and trains her team with care and passion, allows them autonomy in execution, facilitates an environment that fosters mastery, and above all emphasizes that it is a privilege to play a part in hosting events at Carolina. She empowers those around her to strive to do better, continually challenges them, and reminds them that they are part of something great. In other words, the event operations unit at UNC is fueled by Motivation 3.0.

> *One cannot lead a life that is truly excellent without feeling that one belongs to something greater and more permanent than oneself.*
>
> Mihaly Csikszentmihalyi, psychology professor and researcher (most famous for *Flow: The psychology of optimal experience*)
>
> *The desire to do something because you find it deeply satisfying and personally challenging inspires the highest levels of creativity, whether it's in the arts, sciences, or business.*
>
> Teresa Amabile, Harvard business school professor and researcher (best known for research on creativity)

of event participants but also of spectators. Administrators continuously assess risks while trying to respect the rights of fans, including students. Continuous education is required as administrators strive to implement best practices regarding diverse issues, including the threat of terrorism, alcohol-related concerns, rowdy fan behavior, environmental concerns, concession offerings, decisions about outsourcing facility management, decisions about playing at neutral-site contests, and handling the various other expected and unexpected issues that arise in this line of work.

DISCUSSION QUESTIONS

1. Your school is set to play a bitter rival in a televised Saturday night game at your home court. Coaches and student-athletes have played up the rivalry in recent years through unflattering comments about each other in the media. In addition, there is no love lost between the two schools' fans (students and alumni). At past games, objects have been thrown onto the court, and profanity has been chanted at the visiting team. The president of your institution wants to know what steps you are taking to ensure the safety of everyone at the game. She does not want an embarrassment on national television. What is your answer?

2. The board of trustees has asked for a report identifying the pros and cons of permitting alcohol sales at home sporting events. What schools would you consult with to address this request? What pros and cons would you point out?

3. At a nationally televised season-opening football game, weather has affected play as a result of multiple storms in the area. What factors need to be considering in deciding whether to continue the game, reschedule it, or cancel it?

4. Your athletics facility is booked for two sporting events on one day. A basketball game will take place at noon, followed by wrestling at 7:00. What needs to be done to ensure that both events are mounted successfully? What are your concerns?

5. Your facility is hosting a conference basketball championship over the span of several days. The last game on one particular day extends to eight overtime periods, sending your support staff home well after midnight. The staff, including ticket takers, ushers, and security officers, must return the next morning to continue operating the tournament. Given their lack of sufficient sleep, how would you boost their morale?

6. Your school is hosting an NCAA tennis championship that features a team championship, singles championship, and doubles championship for both men and women. Weather has affected play, leaving you to determine the options for ensuring that the tournament is completed in good time. Assuming that you have an indoor facility, explore all of your options, identifying the pros and cons of each scenario.

LEARNING ACTIVITIES

1. Examine the NCAA's website for postseason bid specifications. Pick a Division I sport and determine what facilities in your area meet the NCAA's expectations. Repeat the exercise for various sports and at the Division II and Division III levels.

2. Draft a game-day time line and a checklist of what is needed to host a sporting event at your school. Invite an athletics administrator to class and compare your time line and checklist with those used by the school.

3. Go to an on-campus athletics facility and conduct a risk assessment of it. Repeat the assignment with other athletics facilities on campus. Repeat the assignment again during live sporting events.

4. Go to an on-campus athletics facility and identify ways in which it could be upgraded to benefit student-athletes, coaches, administrators, and fans. Discuss which is more feasible—renovation or new construction. Repeat the assignment with other facilities on campus.

5. Use online resources (e.g., YouTube) to examine new facilities, including locker rooms, practice facilities, and game-day venues. Identify trends resulting from the arms race and discuss what amenities could be seen in the near future.

6. The baseball team has done very well, and its ranking indicates that is should play a game at home in the opening rounds of the postseason tournament. However, the NCAA requires schools to bid if they have an interest in hosting. Find the NCAA postseason bid specifications and identify a particular school's strengths for putting a bid forward.

Photo courtesy of Mississippi State Athletic Department Media Relations

CHAPTER **11**

Alumni Relations and Athletics Development

Robert Zullo, Seton Hill University

In this chapter, you will explore

- the importance of fundraising in intercollegiate athletics;
- how to identify, cultivate, and steward donors;
- ways in which donors can contribute to intercollegiate athletics departments;
- ways to thank donors for their support; and
- concerns that can arise with fundraising.

WHO IS IN CHARGE?

Your iconic football coach is retiring, and as the athletic director (AD), you are ready to form a search committee to identify his replacement. The retiring coach would like his longtime assistant to become the new head coach. At the same time, the biggest donor to your athletics department has created a short list of candidates that she would like you to consider. The candidates include NFL head coaches who are paid at a substantially higher level than the retiring coach. Your experience with agents tells you that new hires also tend to bring additional expenses in the form of facility upgrades and assistant personnel salaries.

Your short list of candidates does not include any of your donor's candidates. However, the donor has indicated that either the next head coach comes from her list or her contributions to the athletics department and the university come to an end. How do you find a solution that identifies the best candidate for your school while retaining the support of your top donor?

As discussed in chapter 7, athletics departments build the revenue portion of their budget through a variety of sources, which can include (to name a few) ticket sales, sponsorship revenue, allocations from conferences and governing bodies, state appropriations, student fees, and concessions. For the vast majority of institutions, however, expenses heavily outpace revenues ("NCAA Revenues," 2012). Therefore, in order to meet the growing financial demands of athletics administration, it is imperative for most institutions to seek financial support from athletics donors through fundraising efforts.

In intercollegiate athletics, fundraising is frequently referred to as development. As Bobby Purcell (2009), executive director of the Wolfpack Club at North Carolina State University athletics, says, "With the rising costs of college athletics and the continued race to have the best facilities, development work is going to be more important than ever. Raising money for scholarship and operating endowments is going to become imperative. Planned giving will be a major focus for all of us. The pressure to raise more money and to find new sources of revenue will be greater than ever."

Donors' contributions help offset, for example, the expense of scholarships, facilities, and salaries. Thus fundraising is a priority of for all athletics directors today. In fact, Doug Knuth, director of athletics at the University of Nevada, emphasizes the importance of fundraising by noting that "everyone's a fundraiser," which means that the development skill set is needed in each athletics staff member (Knuth, 2010).

Fundraising involves identifying, cultivating, and stewarding donors. Lu Merritt (2009), head of the Hokie Club at Virginia Tech athletics, believes that people working in development need to possess "the ability to listen to your donor/prospect when you are interacting with them. Listen carefully to what they tell you, as often they provide much helpful information." He also adds that "development officers should construct their questions well in order to draw out the hoped-for information." In other words, skillful execution is needed in order to build relationships, make an ask and gain a donor's financial support.

Development work also requires flexibility. As described by Gene Smith, athletics director at Ohio State University, "Fundraising is critical in today's business model within athletics departments. Great organizations are able to be agile and innovative with their development planning and solicitations" ("Convention Preview," 2010).

With expenses in intercollegiate athletics escalating, robust donor support is critical. Cultivating lifelong donors helps offset annual costs over the long term. Personalized cultivation and stewardship enable donors to feel that they are part of the athletics department's success, both on the playing surface and in the classroom.

CULTIVATING DONORS: CLUBS, ASSOCIATIONS, FOUNDATIONS, AND SOCIETIES

Fundraising successfully requires support from many people. As Tsiotsou (2007) notes, development entails establishing long-term relationships

Industry Profile

Dirk Katstra

Executive director of the Virginia Athletics Foundation and associate athletics director for external affairs, University of Virginia

This interview was conducted on October 26, 2012, by the National Association of Athletic Development Directors (NAADD).

You have been involved with Virginia athletics for over 20 years and have been serving as the executive director of the University of Virginia Athletics Foundation for the past 16 years. What is the main difference in how you fundraise from when you began as director to how you operate now?

I take a much longer view now. I don't get caught too much in the immediate reaction by donors to wins, losses, coaches, etc. I try to focus more on building the long-term relationship and trust building than I did many years ago.

The Virginia Athletics Foundation is currently under way on two large capital projects, an indoor practice facility and Lannigan Track. Can you please discuss both of these projects and the progress on them?

We recently announced that we will name the indoor practice facility for George Welsh, who is a legendary football coach at Virginia. We are in the final stage of the fundraising for this project and hope to finish the fundraising by the end of 2012. It will open in time for spring football practice in 2013. We completed the first phase of our track facility and are working on identifying prospects to help with the second phase. We have not done any improvements to the track facility since it opened in 1971 and knew it was time to renovate. Thankfully, we received a $5 million lead gift from a former volleyball player to help with the initial phase. The second phase will be much harder.

The University of Virginia set a very high fundraising goal of $14,525,000 for the 2012 year. Can you explain the thought process behind how you set your goals and some of the challenges you face?

In the past, our annual fund goal was set based on what it took to fund all of our scholarship costs and other annual budget obligations. Over the past several years, the economy has taken its toll on our annual fund. Now we set our goals based on what we think we can achieve given the current conditions. Our goal for this year was based on a growth rate of approximately 5 percent over where we finished in 2011, which may have still been a little aggressive, given the success of our revenue sports. Until our annual fund recovers, we are using cash reserves from past years' successes to balance our funding obligations.

You manage a 21-person foundation staff and serve as the associate AD for external affairs. With such large responsibilities, how do you manage your time to be an effective leader?

The balance of time has been the biggest challenge. Over the past year, I have tried to focus more on investing in our people—assessing what they need in order to be successful, quick check-ins to see how they are doing, and responding as quickly as I can to their needs and questions. I have good people who help to manage various parts of the organization, and I have tried to give them opportunities to lead and manage as well.

Previously, you served as an NAADD conference rep, and now you are a member of the executive committee for NAADD. What does it mean to you to be part of the executive committee?

I have always been an advocate of NAADD and our profession in general. We can learn so much from each other, and our profession fosters an environment of sharing. We have enjoyed a great network within the ACC and being able to be a part of connecting that to NAADD was very fulfilling and beneficial. Serving on the executive committee of NAADD just took it to the next level. There are so many talented people in our profession, and I feel fortunate to have the opportunity to interact with them on a national level.

(continued)

INDUSTRY PROFILE *(continued)*

October and November is the time of the year for development professionals to start a new basketball season while football is in full swing. How do you balance your personal life and professional life during this time?

This is a hard one. I have an unbelievable wife and family. We have three active kids who have their own sporting events on Saturdays and throughout the winter. Like many others, we do the best we can to balance everything. One of the best things about college athletics is that it is a family-friendly environment, and our kids can participate by going to games. They love getting to know the student-athletes. Finding the downtime can be difficult, but it is important to find it, to keep everything in perspective. I often say to donors that their outlet is college sports, but it is our life, and sometimes it is hard to separate the two. But it is a good life, and I wouldn't trade it.

If you could provide advice to a person looking to climb the ladder in the development profession, what would it be?

Spend time really getting to know people—whether it is coaches, student-athletes,

colleagues in your athletics department, conference, nationally, etc. Do it because you genuinely care, not because you are just trying to network for networking's sake. Find a mentor. It may be someone in your athletics department or on your campus or within NAADD or NACDA [the National Association of Collegiate Directors of Athletics]. Use them as a resource. People in our profession genuinely care about others who are in our business.

When it comes time for the NAADD convention in June, what do you most look forward to? And what do you take away with you?

I always look at the convention as an opportunity to learn something new. None of us have mastered the art of fundraising, and I always come back from the convention with one new nugget of information or a reminder of something that I need to do better. The relationships that I have made over time at the convention have been invaluable to my growth in the profession and personally. It is really good to get away from our campus to see what others are doing. So many people are doing innovative things.

Reprinted, by permission, from NAADD, 2012, *Q&A with Dirk Katstra, Executive Director of the Virginia Athletics Foundation/Associate Athletic Director for External Affairs, University of Virginia.* (National Association of Athletic Development Directors). Available: www.nacda.com/sports/naadd/spec-rel/102612aaa.html.

with both current and prospective donors. This goal is achieved in part by forming clubs, foundations, associations, and societies in conjunction with the athletics department. Such groups make it easier to identify more donors, establish contact with them, and solicit them for donations (Humphreys & Mondello, 2007).

The solicitation message can even be communicated in the name of the organization, as demonstrated by Clemson University. Supporters of the Clemson Tigers belong to IPTAY, which stands for "I pay ten dollars a year." It can also be helpful to identify inspirational key words, such as *champion, legacy, innovation, rebrand, initiative,* and *team* to create an optimistic atmosphere of success in pursuing a fundraising goal.

One of the appealing aspects of fundraising is the fact that the sky is the limit. As noted by

Tim McMurray, associate athletics director for development at Southern Methodist University, "there are only so many tickets that you can sell and only so many sodas that you can pour. But the one area in our profession where there's no ceiling is the number of private dollars you can bring into your program" (qtd. in Steinbach, 2009). In contrast, other sources of funding may be limited. Businesses, for example, allocate only a certain amount of funds to corporate sponsorship; they may also pursue other promotional options. Similarly, facilities have set seating capacities, thus putting a firm limit on the number of people who can attend an event. But individual donors may be willing to contribute for various reasons, in varying forms and amounts, to support an athletics department.

By joining an athletics-related club, donors can obtain various benefits based on their level of giving. Depending on the institution, benefits may include tax breaks, priority seating and parking, professional and social contacts, invitations to members-only functions, access to coaches and student-athletes, hospitality, publications (e.g., media guides, programs), decals, tickets to away games and postseason competition, and travel with the team. For example, when the University of Alaska Anchorage created the Seawolf Athletic Association to carry out fundraising for its athletics department (Northcutt, 2010), the department reaped the following benefits.

- Fundraising for athletics as a whole versus sport-specific donations
- Streamlined fundraising process
- Collective growth of volunteer support
- Conversion of sport-specific fans into Seawolf athletics fans
- Creation of a scholarship endowment program
- Establishment of a database of potential donors, particularly alumni
- Engagement with alumni through season recaps, newsletters, and special events
- Development of a phonathon with participation by student-athletes

A development club should not single out graduates but should be open to both alumni and nonalumni, because both groups are invaluable to athletics fundraising efforts. Indeed, Tsiotsou (2007) found that alumni and nonalumni donors do not differ in their motivation, involvement, income, or contributions. Instead, research has found that the level of a donor's contribution depends on income and on the donor's involvement with the athletics program (Tsiotsou, 2004).

A donor's giving behavior can also be affected by demographic factors, such as age, gender, residency, and education (Tsiotsou, 2004). Solicitation of donors should include such previously ignored groups of women and minorities (Robinson, 1998; Shapiro & Ridinger, 2011; Staurowsky, 1996; Tsiotsou, 2006). Great prospects can also be found

All donors want to think they're the only donor you have. Whether they're $50-a-year donors or $50,000-a-year donors, they think they're just as important as everybody else.

Kevin Hansen, development manager, Lutz Software (qtd. in Steinbach, 2003)

in the fan base of nonrevenue sports (Bernat, 2010).

Relationship building helps increase trust, and when donors have confidence in the reliability and integrity of the university, they are likely to be more motivated to give. In these conditions, they believe the leadership and want to be involved (Tsiotsou, 2007). Toward this end, development officers can help donors learn about the athletics department by conducting social events where speeches are given by campus and athletics leaders (Tsiotsou, 2007). For example, Marquette University hosts five fall luncheons at which the athletics director communicates vision and new ideas to prospective donors (Szelc, 2011). In addition, many schools, including Michigan State University, offer donors the first opportunity to see newly completed facilities or renovated projects (Steinbach, 2005c). And the University of Missouri athletics department hosts an annual student-athlete awards dinner, called the ROARS program (the mascot is a tiger), to which donors are invited (Baumgartner, 2009).

It is also important, as emphasized by Bill Ring (2010b), director of development for athletics at Boston University, to find the right voice in which to talk with donors. Sometimes this effort means having student-athletes personalize the experience by sharing their success stories. This is especially true in Division II and lower levels, where donors can better appreciate the effect they have on a student-athlete's education (Gardiner, 2009). Donors can also be informed through e-mails, traditional mailings, newsletters, and publications. Such materials provide opportunities to indicate donor contributions via narratives or lists (Tsiotsou, 2007).

Personnel resources in athletics development vary by the school. At a larger Division I school, the department may include senior staff, major gift facilitators, support staff, gift processing personnel, interns, and graduate assistants (Kirinovic & Milliron, 2009). Smaller schools may require personnel to perform many of these roles by themselves.

Think of a development office as a baseball team. One star player does not win a game;

instead, it is a collaborative effort by many team members. On a baseball team, the first batter in the lineup is expected to get on base. The second batter is expected to advance the runner into scoring position, whereupon the third and fourth batters can drive in the run. Development works in the same way, as one development officer might begin the conversation with a donor, after which another staff member might advance the relationship in creative ways. Still other development staff members may be more skilled at making the ask itself and securing the donation (Stallman & Mankenberg, 2008).

> To accomplish longitudinal bonds, athletic fundraising needs to keep donors motivated, build trust, enhance their loyalty, and increase their involvement with the athletic programs of the university.
>
> Tsiotsou, 2007, p. 87

Fundraising is relationship driven, and in some cases a particular development staffer has an exceptionally strong one-on-one relationship with a donor. Even these relationships, however, need support in the stewardship process. This is particularly true as development offices strive to maintain relationships with donors regardless of changes in personnel. Thus fundraising always requires skillful collaboration as a TEAM, which serves as a useful acronym to remind us that "together everyone accomplishes more."

For all schools, but especially those with a smaller development staff, volunteers are also vital in the cultivation and stewardship process (Hall, 2009). For example, the University of California Riverside has found that good structure, proper recruitment, and continuous communication enables a smaller staff to garner additional support in its fundraising efforts (Hall, 2009). In turn, a volunteer board, complete with bylaws, enables volunteers to have a say in fundraising. In another example, the University of Arizona Wildcat Club has a volunteer force of 112 people deployed in Arizona, California, Kansas, Illinois, Colorado, and Oregon to spearhead grassroots efforts as an extension of the club (Pascoe, 2011). Similarly, Southern Methodist University relies on 31 volunteers in 21 regions of the United States to serve as an extension of the Mustang Club (Steinbach, 2012).

BROADENING THE DONOR BASE

Broadening the donor base can be as simple as pursuing referrals from current donors, but it also entails researching alumni databases, former letter winners, parents, ticket holders, and members of the community (Barber, 2007). In 2011, the University of Arizona Wildcat Club consisted of 7,200 members. Led by athletic director Greg Byrne, the club set a goal of increasing membership to 12,000 within two years (Pascoe, 2011). With an annual membership fee of $100, that increase (of nearly 5,000 members) would increase annual giving by about US$500,000 per year. More important, it would deepen the pool of donors who might be solicited for larger contributions.

Young Alumni

Complications arise when premium seating for donors is limited, thus creating the need for a waiting list. A similar problem can arise when students graduate and no longer have access to sold-out sporting events. One option, of course, is to expand premium seating areas, thus enabling greater contributions. In another approach, some schools have enabled students to earn priority points for attendance at sporting events during their undergraduate years. For example, after noticing a trend of decreased demand for student tickets for home football games, the University of Georgia pulled 2,000 tickets and allocated them to young alumni who previously would not have had access to seats (King, 2013). This move heightened their affinity with the program and built their point level as recent graduates so that they did not have to make a substantial contribution to gain access while their earning power was still low.

Former Student-Athletes

Great prospects can also be found among former student-athletes (Bernat, 2010). Giving by former student-athletes is influenced by the potential

University of Minnesota Athletics Development Website

GoldenGopherFund.com is a full-service athletics development website that emphasizes the importance of donor support in maintaining a world-class academic and athletic environment for Gopher student-athletes. "Our mission in developing GoldenGopherFund.com is to allow donors to access information and understand why their gift is important while providing a connection to our organization," said associate athletics director David Crum. "I believe we've raised the bar with GoldenGopherFund.com as we use this website as a communication and customer-service platform for all of our donors and inspire them to support Gopher athletics."

The Golden Gopher Fund provides opportunities for more than 750 student-athletes across 25 sport programs. As a key tool for increasing support, GoldenGopherFund.com provides visitors with comprehensive information regarding the various ways to support student-athletes. The website is a destination for all current and potential members, and is designed to provide up-to-date, accurate, and detailed information for any individual or entity interested in supporting Gopher athletics.

GoldenGopherFund.com focuses on important details related to the annual fund, capital campaigns, preferred and premium seating, parking, endowments, and various donor events, as well as ways to get involved in supporting Gopher student-athletes. Other special features include interactive benefits, charts, in-depth stories covering donors and the positive impact they have had on the lives of Minnesota's student-athletes, and photo and video galleries.

"We have told our personal Gopher story in the hopes that others will be inspired to support our fine student-athletes, exciting initiatives, and future dreams," said Nancy Lindahl, who, along with her husband John, is currently featured on the website. "It has been rewarding and inspiring to be part of the Gopher team. We are very proud of the University of Minnesota's reputation in intercollegiate athletics. We have a great legacy and a bright future."

Reprinted, by permission, from D. Crum, 2011, *University of Minnesota launches athletic development website.* (National Association of Athletic Development Directors). Available: www.nacda.com/sports/naadd/spec-rel/031511aae.html.

donor's importance to, connection with, knowledge of, and experience with the athletics program (Brown, Clayborn, Hays, & Pritchard, 2008; Shapiro, Giannoulakis, Drayer, & Wang, 2010). Strategies for engaging former student-athletes in giving include inviting them to serve on volunteer committees, hosting reunions and alumni weekends, and communicating actively with former student-athletes, especially when changes are made in the coaching staff (Gimbl, 2010b; LaPlante, 2011). Many schools also create a letter-winner's club specifically for former student-athletes and managers.

MOTIVATING DONORS

As ample research indicates, donors give for a variety of reasons (Billing, Holt, & Smith, 1985; Gladden, Mahony, & Apostolopoulou, 2005; Mahony, Gladden, & Funk, 2003; Staurowsky, Parkhouse, & Sachs, 1999; Strode & Fink, 2009; Tsiotsou, 1998). For example, they may want to receive personal recognition, memorialize a friend or family member, influence decisions, socialize or affiliate with the university or other supporters (e.g., attend sport events with friends and family members), receive tangible benefits (e.g., priority ticketing, parking, and access), satisfy their philanthropic motives, or enhance the program's athletics success. Indeed, Strode (2009) found that donors believe their support of an athletics department could yield success for a team. In turn, such success heightens a donor's affiliation with the program.

Development staff members should consider these various motivations. Simply providing access to premium tickets is not sufficient. In a cautionary example, Arizona State University's Sun Devil Club consisted of 12,500 active donors in 2008. By 2010, however, membership was down to 4,000, and the drop cost the organization almost US$4 million (Steinbach, 2012). Self-analysis by the organization found that the group had relied too heavily on premium seating as its primary means for raising funds.

To achieve healthy department–donor relations, it is crucial to understanding the motives that drive giving. Tim McMurray, associate athletics director for development at Southern Methodist University, indicates that "what really separates a good development officer is if you can get to the root of the no. Is it no to timing? Is it no to the amount? Or is it no to the cause? If it's one of the first two, that's forgivable. We can work around that—we can get into payment plans or we can lower the amount of the ask. If it's no to the cause, then we've got work to do internally. People have to feel good about your cause" (Steinbach, 2009).

In addition, the cause itself can vary. For some donors, the cause is team success, whereas for others it is helping student-athletes achieve an education. Therefore, it is vital to listen to donors, because giving is not a one-size-fits-all endeavor. More specifically, segmenting donors based on motivation can benefit fundraisers in the following ways (Tsiotsou, 2007):

- Provides the base for targeted fundraising
- Helps develop more effective marketing mixes in order to motivate specific donor segments
- Facilitates cause differentiation
- Enables marketing strategies targeted toward specific motivational groups
- Enables shaping of fundraising tactics to optimize results
- Provides easier identification of fundraising opportunities and threats

BENEFITS OF GIVING: PRIORITY SEATING AND PARKING

Ideally, demand for premium seating is greater than availability, thus creating a "tough ticket"

Sitting courtside at University of Georgia basketball is the closest thing to being a part of the game without playing or coaching in it. Unless you are sitting on the bench with the team, it is the best way to feel and see all the energies, efforts, and emotions of the players and coaches before, during, and after each game.

Frank Beltran, men's basketball courtside seat holder (qtd. in Center, 2010)

and enhancing the urgency that donors feel to contribute (Steinbach, 2005c). With this potential motivation in mind, athletics departments often tie giving to the privilege to purchase premium seating (or any seating). For example, to gain the opportunity to purchase two tickets to an Ohio State football game, it is necessary to donate at least $1,500 to the Buckeye Club.

Supporters of the athletics department also have the opportunity to make contributions to the department that provide them with other benefits, including premium seating. Benefit points can be based on the contribution amount and on the number of years for which a contributor has given, thus rewarding loyalty (Berman, 2011). Development software can be used to help development officers and donors evaluate the benefits that accompany various levels of donation while also preserving the integrity of the process such that it becomes more transparent to staffers and donors alike (Steinbach, 2003).

Donors frequently ask, "Who gets better seats—those who give more or those who give longer?" It is vital for development offices to remember the long-term value of a season-ticket holder who contributes annually but not substantially (Mahony et al., 2003). Annual contributions from such donors opens the door to continuous revenue through ticket sales, parking fees, and concession and merchandise sales at sporting events. Thus it is important for athletics departments to recognize not only amount but also longevity in annual giving.

Fans who desire better seating or premium seats can be encouraged to donate at a higher level and to keep giving annually in order to retain their premium seating benefits. Contributions for premium seating (e.g., suite, club level) may also give donors access to areas that allow alcohol consumption at sporting events and invitations to closed dinners with team and staff members (Center, 2010).

Contributions also offer tax benefits, because institutions of higher education are considered nonprofits, which means that donations are fully

Ten Ways to Blow the Ask

By Marija Pientka, associate athletics director for development, University of Wisconsin–Madison

If you've been in this profession for long, you've probably stumbled your way through an ask or two—and have learned lessons to improve for the next time. Prior to your next prospect meeting, check to see if you're committing any of these common mistakes before you blow the ask.

Mistake 1: You don't present the "right" project.

We've all been there. The athletics director sets a "priority," and there's pressure to meet the fundraising goal.

This might seem obvious, but you must do your homework on every prospect to ensure that the project you're presenting really speaks to that individual. If a prospect gets excited about programmatic support, presenting a bricks-and-mortar facility project—even if it's the priority of your athletics department—can really be off-putting to the prospect. It shows you haven't taken the time to get to know him or her. Be sure that the project you're presenting is something the prospect has a genuine interest in, and you'll be much more likely to secure a commitment.

Mistake 2: You don't ask for the right amount.

Asking for the right amount is just as important as finding the right project.

Prospects rarely get offended if you ask for too much. Most people are flattered that you think they're capable of such a gift. And a high ask can raise someone's sights. But asking for too little shows you haven't prepared properly, which can derail the development process.

Mistake 3: You didn't sufficiently prepare the prospect for the ask.

No one likes to be caught off guard by someone making an unexpected request—and that goes double for solicitations.

Be sure to lead your prospects to a point where they know you're going to ask for a significant gift. Make sure they're ready to seriously consider such a request. When the time for the solicitation comes, you might not even have to ask for the gift; the prospect will understand why you are there, what size gift you are seeking, and what the gift will support.

Mistake 4: You exclude important people from the ask.

Although you might be more comfortable making an ask during a one-on-one meeting—less of an audience, right?!?—be sure that you don't exclude someone who might play an important role in the donor's decision-making process.

Does your prospect consult with a spouse, an attorney, or an accountant? If so, ask if that individual might be included in the meeting. It can be very frustrating to finish a solicitation only to learn that someone who'll be part of the decision was not present.

Mistake 5: You "wing it" during the solicitation meeting.

When you, your athletics director, and the prospect get together and start talking, you hope the ask might just "naturally" happen. But there's a good chance it won't, especially if the dollar amount is very significant.

Before the meeting, be sure to map out a plan for how the conversation will unfold. Determine in advance who will state the need, put the ask on the table, and outline next steps at the end of the meeting.

Mistake 6: You waffle when making the ask.

You've put a great deal of time and energy into developing a positive relationship with the prospect. When the time comes for an ask, don't back down. If you don't ask, the prospect won't give.

Think of it this way: you're offering the prospect an opportunity to invest in your program. Prospects often appreciate having interesting ideas brought to them for their consideration. So move forward with confidence and conviction—seasoned with humility—and you'll see positive results.

(continued)

TEN WAYS TO BLOW THE ASK *(continued)*

Mistake 7: You stick blindly to your agenda.

Despite your best preparations, sometimes the ask meeting will veer in an unexpected direction. If you're thrown a curve ball, be flexible and try to salvage the meeting as best you can.

But don't be so determined that you steamroll past the issue at hand, potentially offending your prospect and damaging the chance of a gift in the future. If you can't get back on track, you might say to the prospect, "You know, I came here today to discuss a significant commitment to the athletics department. Why don't I address (the immediate concern) today, and then we can schedule a time to talk further about the campaign."

Mistake 8: You pressure the donor for a commitment.

When you make an ask, know when to stop talking and patiently wait for a response.

Your prospects are successful, educated people. They gather information, process it, and make careful decisions. When you ask for a significant investment in your institution, they're going to need time to think it over. If you insist on walking out the door with a signed pledge agreement, you may find yourself leaving empty-handed. Instead, put a proposal on the table and give the prospect time to mull it over. This approach might even yield a greater gift than one he or she can agree upon immediately.

Mistake 9: You promise donors things you can't deliver.

It's easy to get carried away when describing the recognition or special treatment a donor might receive in appreciation for a gift. If you can't get the donor on the team plane for the Rose Bowl, don't offer it. It's better to under-promise and over-deliver.

Mistake 10: You announce the gift prematurely.

You've just received a commitment, and you're bursting with excitement! But be sure everything is in place before you announce the gift, lest the news travel back to the prospect prematurely. This could not only upset the prospect and jeopardize his or her commitment; it could also create a problem for the campus if for some reason the gift does not materialize.

Reprinted, by permission, from M. Pientka, 2009, *Best practices: 10 ways to blow the ask* (National Association of Athletic Development Directors). Available: www.nacda.com/sports/naadd/spec-rel/101609aak.html.

deductible at their fair-market value (Howard & Crompton, 2003). Deductions can total up to 30 percent of an individual's adjusted gross income, and donations beyond that level can be allocated to the individual's adjusted gross income over the next five years (Howard & Crompton).

Donors who give at higher levels can also earn premium parking close to the athletics facility. Such parking allows fans to tailgate close to the event and to arrive closer to the starting time of a game since their space is reserved. Thus it is another premium benefit that can be used with priority ticketing to catalyze fundraising.

WAYS TO GIVE

When donors think about supporting athletics, they may initially believe that cash is the only way to contribute. In fact, however, donors can support

athletics in various ways, including donations of real estate, investments, employee donations, and more. Contributions can be part of a major gift, a capital campaign effort to raise a substantial amount of funds, or an endowment program that funds a scholarship or other expense item. Additional forms of giving include deferred giving and matching gifts. Smaller forms of giving include purchasing a brick toward a building project, participating in a silent auction, or even taking part in a camp held by an athletic team. Development officers should work diligently to ensure that all types of contribution are encouraged.

Major Gifts

Fundraising involves relationship building with donors who believe in a cause; as a result, it takes time and involves an extensive process (Lindahl,

Ticket Holder Sues

When Mississippi State University adopted a point system to reward donors while assigning seats for basketball season-ticket holders prior to the 2006-2007 basketball season, it likely envisioned a boost for its fundraising coffers. But what it got was a lawsuit.

Matthew Wiggins, a season-ticket holder since 1975, sued the university after his tickets were redistributed to another donor. Because Wiggins's seats were behind the bench, the coveted spot was transferred to a donor who gave more to the Bulldog Club. Wiggins claims that he has a right to the tickets, which he has renewed for the past 21 years. In October 2006, he was granted a legal injunction that prevents the university from redistributing his tickets until the case is heard by a Hinds County judge, and he continues to occupy his usual seats this season.

The MSU athletics department says that changing to the point-based system was a necessity in order to compete with other Southeastern Conference teams, nine of which have already adopted a similar system. In 2004, Mississippi State's athletics budget ranked last among SEC schools.

University officials could not comment on the ongoing lawsuit, but Michael Younger, an attorney representing the Bulldog Club, said the right to make final decisions on season tickets belongs to the university. "The University . . . has complete and full authority to allocate seating to best maximize the amount of money generated for and on behalf of the athletics department," Younger said in a written statement.

Mississippi State isn't the first university to face a legal challenge over its point-based system, and it appears that the school has precedent on its side. When the University of Kansas announced that it would use a similar program in 2003, two longtime season-ticket holders who were asked to donate $5,000 in order to keep their seats sued the university, claiming that it was "unlawful taking of property by a state agency." The plaintiffs were among 121 season-ticket holders who did not donate to the school's Williams Fund or had fallen behind on their contributions and were asked to contribute the money or be assigned less desirable seats.

As in Mississippi State's case, the plaintiffs suing KU also sought a court-ordered delay to the redistribution program while their lawsuit played out. However, they were denied by a Douglas County district judge, who cited a 2001 case against Wichita State University, in which the court ruled that a university controls the license of its season tickets.

To explain the system and respond to questions and complaints, Kansas administrators set up a number of open meetings, which they say were pivotal in addressing fans' grievances. "We met with as many people as we could here on campus and around the state and we listened and explained and took notes about what they had to say," says Jim Marchiony, associate athletics director at KU. "We communicated as openly about the system as we could before it was put into place.

"There were some people happy about this system because they were finally being rewarded for their contributions to Kansas athletics over the years," he continues. "And there were people who were not happy because they had been sitting in prime seats for years without contributing."

In the KU program's first two months, during which double points were awarded for all money donated, Kansas set a fundraising record of US$7 million. Marchiony said much of the initial resistance has now died down as the system is up and running smoothly.

"I think the misconception of a points system was that ticket holders were being forced to donate thousands of dollars to go to an event, and that is not the case," Marchiony says. "There are many people who donate $100 a year and have season tickets."

"But if you want to sit courtside, you're going to be in competition with people who give a lot to Kansas athletics," he continues. "It's the same concept as plane tickets, where you have to pay more to sit in first class."

1995). By cultivating a relationship with a donor, the development office can gauge whether the donor wants to support a specific athletics program or athletics in general. In other words, donors have the option of contributing either restricted or unrestricted gifts. Unrestricted giving, which is preferred by a development staff, enables the school to use the funds for any purpose (Humphreys & Mondello, 2007). Restricted gifts, on the other hand, are earmarked for a specific purpose.

Major gifts can be used to reduce the expenses associated with facility construction or renovation. For example, the University of Virginia built a new track-and-field facility thanks in large part to a lead major gift of US$5 million (Troudt, 2011); similarly, Southern Methodist University used two lead gifts to enable renovation of its coliseum (Leonard, 2011). With renovation expenses expected to reach US$40 million, the project was funded largely through the two gifts—a US$20 million gift from a foundation and a US$10 million gift from a former student-athlete (Leonard).

Stadium and arena construction and renovation provide the most visible projects, but major gifts can also be used to facilitate work on other projects, such as locker rooms and premium seating areas. The same University of Virginia donor who contributed to the track-and-field facility also contributed US$1 million to facilitate the renovation and improvement of the women's volleyball locker room and training facility. Major gifts can also facilitate enhancement of weight rooms, training tables, and academic facilities, thus supporting student-athletes in their wellness and their studies. In other examples, a US$3 million lead gift enabled Northern Illinois University to start construction on an indoor practice facility (Scissors, 2011), and a lead gift enabled Indiana University to open a modern academic learning center for student-athletes (Dolson & Bomba, 2011).

Endowment Programs

Endowment programs enable development offices to cultivate funds from donors, invest the principle, and use the interest to cover annual operating expenses in perpetuity (forever). Given a 5 percent interest rate, an endowment donation of $250,000 would yield an average of $12,500 per year. Endowment funds can grow more quickly in a bull market, thus providing considerable interest. Covered expenses can include, for example, the cost of scholarships, coaches' salaries, facility upkeep, and operational budgets. In return for the donation, the donor may be recognized in various ways, depending on the expectation set by the school, but it often includes a naming opportunity for the endowment.

One example of a successful scholarship endowment program can be found at Boston College, where the cost of an athletics scholarship was US$53,500 in 2011. With 272 scholarships committed to student-athletes, the school needs to generate funds targeted for this considerable expense (Foley, 2011). To meet this need, Boston College uses an endowment fund supported by an annual donor luncheon on a home football weekend where student-athletes, coaches, and school administrators meet the donors who support them. The personal interaction continues with thank-you notes and updates from student-athletes coordinated through the development office. The program enabled Boston College to increase its total of endowed scholarships from 31 in 2005 to 162 by 2011 (Foley).

Stanford University has used the endowment model to generate a substantial revenue stream when the economy is sound. Because endowment investments are prone to the same volatility that characterizes investments in general, they can be affected by an economic downturn. Stanford was no exception during a downturn a few years ago, when an athletic endowment of US$520 million was reduced to US$410 million in the course of one fiscal year (Schlabach, 2009). Oklahoma State athletics suffered a similar loss when a gift of US$165 million from T. Boone Pickens peaked at US$400 million but collapsed to US$125 million in a bear market (Steinbach, 2009).

Another issue that arises in endowment programs hinges on the fact that donors tend to support highly visible sports, such as football and men's basketball, which offer a widely desired affiliation with high-profile athletes and coaches. Even so, targeted cultivation and stewardship can yield positive fundraising results across all sport teams. At Boston University, Clifford and Jill Viner offered their financial support for two athletics scholarships, including one in swimming and diving. They described their thinking in this way: "We believe

Boston College Endowed Athletics Scholarships

Endowed athletics scholarships provide a way for Boston College athletics to work toward the long-term success of the department by ensuring that there will be sufficient income to support student-athletes long into the future. These funds are invested in the university's endowment, and approximately 5 percent of the value of a fund supports the scholarship for the designated recipient each year.

Endowed funds can be established with a gift of $250,000. You would have the opportunity to name the fund according to your wishes—this can be in honor or memory of a loved one or to establish a family legacy. You may also personalize your fund to match your interests, perhaps to a specific sport or for a student-athlete enrolled in a particular major. The fund would live in perpetuity at BC and provide support to a student-athlete. You would have the opportunity to meet the recipient of your fund each year and watch him or her grow as a student and athlete at BC.

Endowed funds established at the $1 million level provide the opportunity to restrict, in perpetuity, to a specific position on a team. For instance, one may choose to support the starting running back on the football team.

By agreeing to enrich our athletes in this way, you would be invited to our annual gathering of student-athletes to kick off the year and meet your recipient. You would also receive periodic updates on the performance of the fund, its history, and detailed biographical information about your recipient from the athletics director.

Athletics Financial Aid Fund

A named endowed fund may also be established with a commitment of $100,000. The difference is that you would not be able to restrict the fund to a specific sport and the fund would not be assigned to a specific student-athlete. Instead, it would be a part of the general athletics endowment in support of scholarships.

Support Operating Endowment

Funds in support of operating expenses may be established with a commitment of $100,000 or more and can be designated for operating expenses associated with any of our 31 varsity sports. For instance, a football operating fund could enhance the annual support of this program.

Facilities Enhancement Fund

For future projects, we want to have funds immediately available. This may include a myriad of options, such as expanding, renovating, or updating specific areas in Conte Forum or renovating spaces in the Yawkey Center. It would be important to demonstrate that funds are readily available when we embark on any number of facility projects for the department.

Reprinted, by permission, from *Ways to give: Endowed scholarships*. (Chestnut Hill, MA: Boston College). Available: www.bceagles.com/boosters/bc-endowment-current-winners.html.

in offering support to anyone whose lives we can touch. Athletics builds teamwork, camaraderie, discipline, and commitment. All of those characteristics will serve a person well throughout life, in business, in pleasure, and in learning how to work together" (qtd. in Ring, 2010a).

Capital Campaigns

Athletics departments work with their academic counterparts via capital campaigns to address the school's capital, operating, and endowment efforts over a limited time frame. The establishment of a board of supportive donors initiates the process, which also includes the recruitment of other donors in a private or "silent" phase. For example, the University of New Mexico athletics department was charged with raising US$75 million as part of an institutionwide fundraising effort based on the theme of a Lobo Leap to Excellence. Lead gifts from NBA player Danny Granger and NFL player

Brian Urlacher, both alumni, enabled the campaign to start with US$1 million (Ryan, 2010). This silent phase allows time to solicit major financial commitments in order to build fundraising momentum for a more public phase.

Penn State initiated a capital campaign titled For the Future: The Campaign for Penn State Students as part of a concerted effort to create a prosperous future from an operational and competitive standpoint. Although the campaign targets overall enhancement of the university, the fundraising arm of the school's athletics department was expected to raise US$225 million as part of the larger campaign. The athletics funds will be allocated in the following manner (Gimbl, 2010a).

- Scholarships—$140 million
- Coaching endowments—$10 million
- Facilities—$70 million
- Program endowments—$5 million

As Tsiotsou (2007) has stressed, campaigns centered on increasing a university's prestige can help build donors' motivation. Prestige can be measured both quantitatively (e.g., in terms of winning percentages, championships, and graduation rates) and qualitatively (e.g., through placement of alumni and other personal success stories) (Tsiotsou, 2007). Campaign themes should also emphasize the fact that donors' gifts help the school build resources that are comparable to, if not better than, those featured by their counterparts—both academically and athletically (Ford, 2009; McGinniss, 2011; O'Brien, 2010; Stanley, 2009).

To enhance a campaign's chance of success, a school can divide it into phases (Terrell, 2010). Doing so enables the school to prioritize its needs and reassess the level of contributions. At the University of North Carolina, for example, phase I of a football stadium renovation focused on the Kenan Football Center, which affected the program's daily operations. Phase II emphasized the stadium enclosure, the addition of premium seating, and the updating of concourse amenities (Terrell, 2010).

Matching Gifts and Employee Giving

The process of employee giving can be simplified through payroll deduction, and employees who give can be recognized at an annual luncheon. Many employers will match an employee's charitable donation, though certain employers will not match a donation to an athletics department; some of these, however, can be persuaded to match donations earmarked strictly for scholarship purposes (Howard & Crompton, 2003). In one example of successful employee giving, Monmouth University strives for 100 percent participation in its employee giving campaign, meaning that every employee contributes to the athletics fund. Indeed, in 2009 the school achieved a 100 percent participation rate among 81 part-time and full-time employees, yielding US$28,000 for the annual fund (Wulfekotte, 2010).

Real Estate and Investments

Donations of real estate and investments offer the donor relief from long-term capital gains taxes (Howard & Crompton, 2003). The tax reduction depends on how long the donor held the asset before donating it. The maximum capital gains tax rate is 20 percent of the increase in the value of the real estate or investment from the point of original purchase to the point of selling it (Howard & Crompton). The tax rate decreases if the asset is held longer than a year and decreases further if the asset is held longer than five years. However, by donating the asset rather than selling it, the donor eliminates the tax completely

Deferred and Planned Giving

Deferred giving, accomplished through contributions that take effect after one's death, may sound morbid, but it is a common form of donation, particularly among passionate supporters who want to leave a lasting legacy (Kegler, 2010). Planned giving can include wills, trusts, insurance policies, and annuities. Because the athletics department, a nonprofit entity, is named as the recipient, the donor's estate does not have to pay state or federal inheritance taxes on the donated assets (Howard & Crompton, 2003). Life insurance policy gifts also offer value to an athletics department provided that the premiums are paid in full and the athletics department is listed as the sole beneficiary. Trusts can be used to provide a fixed annuity to the donor until his or her death, at which time the remainder of the trust benefits the athletics department.

Auctions, Bricks, and Camps

Smaller contributions can also be garnered through targeted events or campaigns, including auctions, building bricks, and camps. Auctions, either online or in-person, can feature such items as access to special events, coaches, and game-worn apparel. The University of Indianapolis also includes merchandise from sponsors, ranging from oil changes to condo rentals, to deepen its online auction offerings (Riley, 2010). Some athletics departments outsource auctions to a third-party firm, which may charge a fee for its services, take a portion of the generated revenues, sell banner advertising around the auction, or implement an entry fee for donors who want to participate (Popke, 2008).

Brick campaigns draw funding by enabling donors to personalize a brick for a walkway or plaza to commemorate their contribution. Louisiana State University uses a brick campaign in which donors' bricks are placed near the home of Mike the Tiger, the school's mascot, a Bengal tiger that lives on campus (Mike the Tiger, 2013). In this way, a brick that costs the school $10 or $20 can be marked up in value, thus earning the school considerable revenue through a cost-effective commemoration (Bynum, 2004).

Additional revenue can be generated through special events, such as fantasy camps for both men and women. Many fans will pay to play side by side with past greats or to be coached by a well-known head coach. Offerings include football camps for women, parent-and-child camps, and alumni outings such as golf tournaments (Zullo, 2011).

GROWING AFFINITY: CLUBS AND ORGANIZATIONS BEYOND CAMPUS

For larger athletics departments with a significant fan base, local chapters of booster clubs can be formed throughout a state or geographic region. These organizations give fans a place to share their passion while enhancing the regional, national, and, in some cases, global reach of the athletics department. Groups may gather to watch nationally televised games, arrange outings to home sporting events, and develop other social activities, including golf tournaments. During the summer, an athletics department can have its coaches travel to meet fans

in a given region, knowing that the local chapters can arrange the facility and food for the event.

One downside of local chapters is that their operational expenses are passed on to the area fan base, which can dilute development efforts focused on major gifts. For example, a donor paying for a local membership may construe that contribution as focusing on athletics development, whereas in fact membership dues may be used to offset operational expenses for the local chapter's events. Thus the development staff needs to communicate regularly with local chapters to avoid donor confusion regarding local contributions perceived to be earmarked for the athletic development office.

Concerns can also arise about control between the athletics department and any outside organization supporting athletics. For example, a representative of a Quarterback Club backing the Notre Dame football team embezzled more than US$1 million (Morant, 1999). The funds were spent on lavish gifts and trips for members of the football team. The NCAA determined that the club was affiliated with the University of Notre Dame, effectively making club members representatives of the school. As a result, gifts from the members constituted impermissible extra benefits, and the school was sanctioned with scholarship losses and probation (Dufresne, 1999). With these issues in mind, proactive education about rules and regulations should extend to all clubs and organizations associated with the athletics department in order to maintain compliance with governing body requirements.

CONCERNS WITH FUNDRAISING

Although fundraising provides an athletics department with a crucial revenue source, working with donors can also create issues of concern. For one thing, each institution must prioritize whether academic needs or athletic needs come first in fundraising. In addition, an economic downturn affects all giving, including fundraising efforts in intercollegiate athletics (Brown, 2011a). Another potential issue involves donor influence, which can affect both the operations and the image of an athletics department, as in the case of rogue boosters who hinder an athletics department's compliance with NCAA rules and regulations.

Industry Profile

Ross Bjork

Athletic director, The University of Mississippi

Ross Bjork was announced as the seventh full-time director of athletics at Ole Miss on March 21, 2012. Bjork, 40, arrived in Oxford as the youngest AD among Bowl Championship Series schools, coming off a successful stint in that post at Western Kentucky University.

Bjork's first full week at the post was spent on the Rebel Road Trip, a six-day, 16-stop tour of the region that served to unite the Rebel fan base. He carried that momentum into the launch of a major sales campaign for football season tickets, which included television and radio advertising, billboards, Internet marketing, and a new outbound telemarketing call center.

Professional Conduct Dictates Your Future

By Ross Bjork

In the world of collegiate athletics, our job is to interact with a cross-section of people on a daily, almost minute-by-minute basis. From student-athletes, to professors, to coaches, to donors, to alumni and fans, all of us have to use our communication skills on a regular basis in order to get the job done. In addition, if you have aspirations to advance your career, your conduct in this realm will dictate your future. Here are a few best-practice tips I try to live by.

- **First impressions.** The old saying "you never get a second chance to make a first impression" is absolutely true—meaning you have to be on "your game" at all times and be ready for the first moment of interaction with someone. Typically, you have four to six seconds to make your first impression last. Be ready.

- **Professional conduct.** Integrity and honesty are essential to your success, so always be mindful that your personal code of conduct will dictate your future, no matter what. Are you the social butterfly of the department, always looking for a good time? It is okay to have fun socially, but be mindful of your surroundings and who is watching. In the end, all we have is the character by which we live, and our actions speak louder than words.

- **Looking good and speaking well.** Every day we are placed in a position to speak to a group of people or in one-on-one settings. You should always dress appropriately for the situation and speak with clarity. Give examples and tell stories to make your point about what is important. Know your audience in advance and relax for the big moment. Practice makes perfect, so act like you have been there before and you will do great. Don't be afraid to put yourself out there and seek out speaking engagements in your community. The public likes to hear about your athletics program and your student-athletes.

- **Presentation skills.** When you do get that big moment to speak, make sure to follow a few simple techniques so you make a lasting impression. Stand up straight and look people in the eye. Always have a smile when you are speaking—it makes you and the audience feel at ease. Smiling can not be emphasized enough. Overall, be yourself and talk passionately about your program.

- **Running a meeting.** Nothing can prepare you for speaking in public, and for your next career move, better than running and organizing meetings. Effective meeting skills will absolutely advance your career in so many ways. If you don't have a chance to run a meeting, ask your supervisor if you can lead the next staff meeting in order to gain experience. Or if you are a manager, rotate the staff meetings between your team members so that each person can gain the experience. I have seen this in action, and believe me, it works. Put yourself in decision-making situations during the meetings so that no one is wasting their time. Don't just meet to meet.

- **Professional etiquette.** Etiquette also applies to our daily routine of how we conduct ourselves. Be aware of your physical proximity to other people—know their personal space and stay out of it. Watch out for too many accessories, like bracelets and flashy rings. Less is more. Always—this cannot be emphasized enough—say please and thank you. You will be amazed at the results.

- **Your next professional move.** If you are seeking out your next move, the easiest way to the top is to reach maximum production in your current job. No one will recruit you unless you are doing a great job at your current employer. When you decide to network among your professional contacts, be cautious about nagging versus networking. If someone writes me a three-page e-mail asking for professional advice, most likely it will sit there for a while before I respond. Keep all of your messages short and to the point, and ask for something specific like a few minutes to speak on the phone. Create a personal advisory group and maintain frequent contact in order to discuss career opportunities and your next move. We have chosen collegiate athletics for a reason, so please keep our interactions professional in all aspects.

Bjork's Career Time Line

2012–present: Ole Miss, director of athletics

2010–2012: Western Kentucky University, director of intercollegiate athletics

2005–2010: UCLA, senior associate athletics director for external relations

2003–2005: University of Miami, associate athletics director for external operations

2001–2003: University of Missouri, assistant athletics director for development

1997–2001: University of Missouri, athletics development officer

1996–1997: Western Kentucky University, assistant development coordinator

1995–1996: Western Illinois University, campus recreation graduate assistant and athletics department volunteer

1995: University of Tulsa, marketing intern

1994: Albuquerque Dukes, front office intern

Reprinted, by permission, from R. Bjork, 2010, *Best practices: Professional conduct dictates your future* (National Association of Athletic Development Directors). Available: www.nacda.com/sports/naadd/spec-rel/020810aab.html.

Although a successful athletics program can increase a school's visibility, some observers initially believed that athletics success was detrimental to collective fundraising efforts because of a negative effect on the academic mission of the institution (Stinson & Howard, 2004). However, as Stinson and Howard (2008) later found, donors who contribute to both academics and athletics give larger gifts than athletics-only donors and are retained longer than academics-only donors. Still, faculty members express concern when fundraising efforts appear to be misaligned with the mission of the institution.

In this context, development offices have to prioritize the projects that need donor support. This process has drawn scrutiny, as reform groups—including the Drake Group, the Coalition on Intercollegiate Athletics, and the Knight Commission on Intercollegiate Athletics—have offered recommendations for quelling the "arms race" of spending that exists in NCAA Division I athletics.

Institutions have to decide what approach they will take to the greater fundraising efforts typically resulting in a centralized approach or decentralized approach between the institution development and athletics development (King et al, 2010). Some of the benefits of having a centralized approach between the institution and athletics include the potential for more development staff fundraising in a clear and coordinated effort. There is a unified effort in working with the donors. The con of this approach is that, depending on the institution, athletics may believe that they are not a priority in the greater fundraising goals. However, at some institutions, the opposite may be true—in that the perception may be that athletic fundraising trumps academic fundraising (King et al, 2010).

In a decentralized approach, athletics development staff focus solely on fundraising for athletics; the university development staff is concentrated on fundraising for academics. However, this can lead to issue of a lack of coordinated efforts in prioritizing who approaches donors (King et al, 2010). The institution can suffer if its fundraising goals are not clearly stated and tensions develop between athletics development and fundraising for academics.

Donor Influence

Fundraising enables the athletics department to find additional revenue, but that revenue can come with outside influence. Donors sometimes feel that substantial contributions give them the right to weigh in on the hiring and firing of coaches and other issues affecting the department (Staurowsky et al., 1999). For example, T. Boone Pickens (Oklahoma State University), Phil Knight (University of Oregon), and Bobby Lowder (Auburn University) have donated substantially to their schools and are heavily influential in personnel-related decision making (Evans, 2009; Greenhouse, 2000; Thamel & Whitmire, 2011).

In addition, financial conditions can change quickly in intercollegiate athletics due to factors such as dwindling attendance or a lack of faith in a revenue sport's future. In such cases, head coaches can be bought out of their contracts to change the direction of a program, but doing so often requires the support of donors (Doughty, 2011). When donors provide funds to remove a coach, they may also want to influence the hiring of the new coach. In one dramatic case, the University of Connecticut parted ways with an athletics director after an unhappy donor—who disagreed with recent personnel decisions regarding the football program—asked for his contributions to be returned (Associated Press, 2011).

Donors can also influence a department's philosophy in other ways. At the University of North Carolina at Chapel Hill, key donors long believed that the Dean Smith Center, home of the basketball program, should not feature sponsor advertising (Steinbach, 2005a). As a result, the donors' decision to support the facility honoring the coach came at the price of lost sponsorship revenue for decades. On a very different matter, donors at San Jose State University voiced their collective opinion about in-game dance performances being too provocative, thus leading the school to modify the performances to suit supporters' wishes (Steinbach, 2005b). Development officers need to be mindful of the fact that, in addition to these case studies, research reiterates the reality that donors' contributions may be accompanied by their desire to exert influence and psychological commitment (Gladden et al., 2005; Mahony et al. 2003; Staurowsky et al., 1999).

The University of Notre Dame uses two policies to preclude issues from arising about donors' expectations regarding influence, as well as premium seating. The first policy hinges on the establishment of an athletics affairs committee. Acting on behalf of the school's board of trustees, the committee enables fans, including big donors, to voice their opinions (Rovell, 2013). It also enables the director of athletics to act on issues without undue influence from a major donor's opinion. In regard to seating, donors have to enter a lottery for seats at prominent events, and this requirement even applied to the 2013 Bowl Championship Series national title game (Rovell,

---

University of Connecticut Donor Displeasure

In a five-page letter to then–athletics director Jeff Hathaway, donor Robert Burton expressed his displeasure at not being consulted on the hiring of a new football coach at the University of Connecticut.

"I made two things very clear to you, as the largest donor in the UConn football program," said Burton, in one of no fewer than seven instances in which he implied that his donations had earned him the right to be a major voice in the coaching search. "I told you I wanted to be involved in the hiring process for the new coach. I also gave you my insight about who would be a good fit for the head coaching position as well as who would not. For someone who has given over $7 million to the football program/university, I do not feel as though these requests were asking too much" (Brown, 2011b).

2013). As a result, Kevin Compton, an alumnus of Notre Dame and substantial donor to the school's new hockey arena, had to secure his tickets through the lottery like everyone else.

Naming Rights

Concerns can also arise when naming rights are implemented to recognize donors and their contributions (Chen & Zhang, 2012). Individuals interested in the naming rights for a facility can expect to cover one-third to one-half of the funds for the facility's construction (Steinbach, 2004). This form of naming rights differs from corporate naming rights, in that there is no marketing relationship between the school and a business entity. As a result, naming a facility after an individual donor eliminates the factor of commercialism that accompanies corporate naming rights, but it can still present problems. Unlike a corporate naming-rights deal, naming a facility after a donor or a donor's request comes with no expiration date. Yet there is no guarantee that the association will remain a positive one.

In one dramatic example, Villanova University had planned to use the name du Pont Pavilion for its basketball arena to recognize John Eleuthère du Pont, a major donor to the facility. However, du Pont suffered from schizophrenia and later murdered Olympic wrestling gold medalist David Schultz (Crompton & Howard, 2003). In the aftermath, the school dropped the du Pont name.

In a less dire example, the University of Missouri opened a new basketball arena named the Paige Sports Arena in honor of the daughter of two prominent donors who contributed US$25 million to the project. Supporters of the university were disappointed to learn, however, that Paige Laurie did not attend the University of Missouri but rather the University of Southern California (Associated Press, 2004). The scandal grew larger when media outlets reported that she had paid college roommates US$20,000 to do her coursework. The facility was renamed.

NCAA Compliance

Other potential problems involve donors who break NCAA rules. In bringing donors close to the athletics department for their support, the department may become vulnerable to rogue donors who make

payments or provide other benefits to influence recruits or reward current student-athletes (Steinbach, 2002). Staff can use continuing education forums and up-to-date online information to instruct donors about what is permitted and what is not allowed in their interaction with prospective or current student-athletes. The vital theme of compliance can also be emphasized in media guides and game programs.

In an example of what can go wrong, the University of Miami athletics department engaged with a negligent football booster who jeopardized student-athletes' eligibility, teams' eligibility for championships and bowl games, and recruiting efforts by providing improper benefits to student-athletes (Robinson, 2011). Specifically, the donor provided meals, nightclub outings, yacht trips, Miami Heat tickets, cash, travel, and other items. When asked why he did so even though he knew it could jeopardize the football program, he said, "I did it because I could. And because nobody stepped in to stop me" (Robinson, 2011).

Coaches Fundraising Without Direction

It is a traditional fundraising tool to have coaches share their enthusiasm and vision for an athletics program with donors. Problems can arise, however, if coaches solicit donations without communicating with the development office. This practice is problematic because the development staff may be simultaneously building a relationship in preparation for asking a donor to make a substantial contribution. That preparatory work can go to waste if a coach asks for a smaller donation to cover a program-specific need and the donor then refuses the development office's request because he or she has already contributed to the coach. To avoid working at cross-purposes and leaving money on the table, coaches and development offices need to communicate continuously about program needs, prospective donors, and planned asks so that a coach does not undercut or limit the process (Thornburg, 2012).

CURRENT ISSUES

As budgets have gotten tighter and tighter, some schools have eliminated sports in order to reduce expenses. This practice creates a tremendous amount of stress and negative publicity for an athletics department. At the same time, development offices are trying to identify tomorrow's donors and encourage them to become supporters of athletics at an earlier age than was typical in the past. This focus means that development offices are tapping into the student body to build students' awareness of the importance of long-term giving. These competing trends—pressure to cut expenses and pressure to increase fundraising—mean that people working in development must carefully manage relationships amid the reality that some stakeholders may face disappointment when their sport is cut.

Eliminating Sports

In recent years, athletics programs have been cut at a number of schools, including the University of California, Arizona State University, the University of Maryland, and James Madison University. The elimination of a sport can lead student-athletes, coaches, and supporters to feel that their sport is not viewed as important. Supporters may feel alienated by the school and conclude that the eliminated program is given less priority than the school's revenue sports (Rheenan, Minjares, McNeil, & Atwood, 2011). To minimize such occurrences, administrators must work with coaches of nonrevenue sports early on to identify donors. Proactive efforts to procure private donations can help coaches and student-athletes understand that cutting sports is a last resort due to budgetary issues and is not related to such issues as Title IX, academics, or other concerns (Weight & Cooper, 2011).

In some cases, a certain sport—for example, the baseball team at the University of California—is asked to be self-funded, meaning that the school does not assist in fundraising (Phelps, 2012). In the case of Cal baseball, a nonprofit organization called the Cal Baseball Foundation was responsible for fundraising as an all-volunteer group that reported to the school's officials to ensure communication, efficiency, and sustainability (Phelps). For such sports, administrators must continuously educate coaches to help them understand that their fundraising role may be crucial to the long-term viability of their program (Berkowitz, 2011).

Creating Student Donors

McClung (2010) emphasizes the fact that solicitation of donors can start as early as students' undergraduate years. This type of fundraising can be carried out through the creation of a student support group. Students who attend more sporting events and already display great affinity for their athletics program may require less marketing in order to appreciate the benefits of joining such an organization, whereas their peers who are not active athletics supporters may require more persuading (McClung). Such nonsupporters will need greater education about the value and perks of being a student booster, including stronger school allegiance, affordability, and social contacts.

Missouri Western State University created a Max Experience program in which students gave their input about how to enhance the game-day atmosphere and facilities (Lau, 2010). The students' inclusion helped enhance the school's relationship with these prospective donors. In addition to giving input on facility upgrades, student supporters enjoyed various perks, such as the following:

- Free admission to all athletics contests
- Free admission for immediate family members
- Free concession items at home football and basketball contests
- Summer fee waiver at the fitness center
- Enhanced pep band and cheer squad
- Free promotional events and items
- Shuttle bus between dorms and the arena for home basketball games
- Free transportation to one away football game and one away basketball game
- Priority parking for off-campus students
- Babysitting service for young children of students

Preserving Continuous Trust

The University of Kansas suffered through a damaging scandal surrounding its priority seating plan centered on tickets to its sold-out home men's basketball games. In the scandal, five former staff members were sentenced for their involvement in a scheme in which basketball and football tickets allocated for donors were instead sold to ticket brokers. In addition, two staff members were sentenced to probation for failure to report a crime (Fagan, 2011). The US$2 million scheme included 17,000 basketball tickets and 2,000 football tickets over a five-year period.

The scandal forced school officials to welcome auditors and heighten the transparency of the priority seating program. Then–interim athletics director Sean Lester noted, "I think our donors appreciate the enhancements we have made in transparency, accountability, and the fact that so many of their seating locations have improved. We are unwavering in our continued commitment to our student-athletes, donors, and fans" (Fagan, 2010). To restore confidence, the university made changes in the athletics department's leadership—on the athletics board, among senior administrators, and in the director of athletics position. The school also hired an independent auditor. In an effort to prevent such problems, some schools, such as the University of Washington and the University of Texas, rely on internal auditors, risk management assessors, and external auditors to preserve trust in their ticket sales and distribution policies (Associated Press, 2010).

NATIONAL ASSOCIATION OF ATHLETIC DEVELOPMENT DIRECTORS (NAADD)

NAADD provides professional development through an annual conference and online resources.

Membership facilitates networking and provides access to educational sessions, such as best practices education and roundtables at the summer conference. Officers and committees steer the group and select annual award winners and keynote speakers. The leadership also facilitates question-and-answer sessions and fosters the demographic diversification of professionals working in the industry. Online resources available throughout the year address current events, explore new strategies, and provide educational webinars. Reduced-price memberships are available to help students engage in professional development early in their career.

CONCLUSION

Athletics departments use fundraising as a revenue stream to supplement funds earned through other means, such as ticket sales, sponsorship revenue, allocations from conferences and governing bodies, state appropriations, student fees, and concessions. Funds raised can be used to support scholarships, facilities, salaries, operating costs, and other rapidly growing expenses. Donors have to be identified and cultivated so that relationships can be built to garner the donor's financial support over the long term. Motivated donors provide support through such varied means as major gifts, endowment programs, capital campaigns, and planned giving. Despite its benefits, fundraising can create problems when donors become overzealous or coaches attempt to solicit funds without proper direction. Scandals and crises can also affect the credibility of fundraising efforts.

The Athletics Department—Front Porch or Window to the World

When an athletics department is flourishing on the field, it can build excitement among alumni and fans. Home sporting events and extensive media coverage of athletics can offer uplifting experiences and memories to many supporters. Replicating this success on the academic side of campus can prove more difficult despite the quality of research, education, and job placement.

T.K. Wetherell, former president of Florida State University, has referred to athletics as a school's "window to the world" (Hyland, 2010). Other leaders, including University of North Texas president Neal Smatresk and former University of Central Arkansas president Allen Meadors, have suggested that athletics can be viewed as the front porch of an institution, thus implying that athletics is the first thing that people see at the school (McCollum, 2009; Smatresk, 2011). When the athletics momentum is positive, the school's donors and supporters can embrace the excitement. Those moments can be fleeting, however, in times of crisis, especially a crisis that threatens to harm the reputation of a great academic institution.

Leadership Lesson

Your Authentic Leadership Style

Imagine sitting across from a donor who has deep pockets and an affinity for your women's soccer program. If you can convince her to donate, you will make a name for yourself in the department and make the soccer coach very happy. For a moment, you feel a twinge of self-doubt—you've never been in this situation before. You watched your predecessor close deals in his charismatic and somewhat brash style, and you concluded that his approach must be what donors like. He was worshiped in the department and brought in millions. So you do your best to channel his style, even though it's not entirely natural for you. The lunch ends early, you don't get the donation, and the potential donor reports back to the department that she just didn't trust you and doesn't feel comfortable giving at this time.

So often, we believe that in order to fit the mold of a leader, we must act in a certain way. In this leadership lesson, we will debunk that myth and help you discover your own authentic leadership style.

During the last 50 years, more than a thousand studies have been conducted by leadership scholars seeking to pin down the profile of a leader. So far, no one has identified definitive characteristics. Some overarching conclusions, however, have been drawn. Leadership is not about charisma, personality, or even talent. Instead, it is about vision, principles, passion, discipline, and purpose (Collins & Porras 1994; Covey, 2004; Drucker, 2005; George & Sims, 2007; Goleman, 2000; Kotter, 2001). A leader is not someone who gets by on quick-fix personality alterations learned at the latest seminar but a person who is genuine and authentic—who has what Covey calls the "character ethic" (2004). Indeed, George, Sims, McLean, and Mayer (2007) have argued

People trust you when you are genuine and authentic, not a replica of someone else.

George et al., 2007, p. 129

that authentic leadership emerges through our individual life stories.

As a result, as you continue your journey toward becoming a leader in the industry of intercollegiate athletics, it is important for you to gauge where you have been, where you are, who you are, where you hope to go, and who you hope to be. As you do so, George et al. (2007) suggest that you ask yourself the following questions.

- Which people and experiences in your early life had the greatest effect on you?

- What tools do you use to become self-aware? What are the moments when you say to yourself "this is the real me"?

- What are your most deeply held values? Where did they come from? How do your values inform your actions?

- What motivates you extrinsically? What are your intrinsic motivations? How do you balance extrinsic and intrinsic motivation in your life?

- What kind of support team do you have? How can your support team make you a more authentic leader? How should you diversify your team to broaden your perspective?

- Is your life integrated? Are you able to be the same person in all aspects of your life—personal, work, family, and community? If not, what is holding you back?

- What does being authentic mean in your life? Are you more effective as a leader when you behave authentically? Have you ever paid a price for your authenticity as a leader? Was it worth it?

- What steps can you take today, tomorrow, and over the next year to develop your authentic leadership?

One of the most dangerous myths that can trap you in your professional progression is that of the "complete leader"—the idea that in order to be credible you must be flawless and know everything. This notion can lead you to present yourself as a contrived version of what you think a leader should look like. However, a growing body of literature supports doing the opposite of this cookie-cutter approach. Specifically, scholars have urged leaders to do the following.

- Accept that you're human, with strengths and weaknesses (Ancona, Malone, Orlikowski, & Senge, 2007).

- Blend deep personal humility with intense professional will (Collins, 2005).

- Show that you're human, capitalize on your uniqueness, and care passionately about your employees (Goffee & Jones, 2000).

- Be self-aware—know your strengths, weaknesses, drives, and values (Goleman, 2005)

DISCUSSION QUESTIONS

1. Why do people give money to worthy causes? What are some reasons for which people might give specifically to intercollegiate athletics?

2. A very generous donor is willing to contribute at a level that surpasses any other donor. However, this donor wants significant influence in personnel decisions, especially with respect to the hiring and firing of head coaches. Identify the pros and cons of accepting the donor's contribution.

3. A prospective donor is very excited about supporting the athletics department and very interested in securing naming rights for a proposed facility. The naming rights would honor a deceased family member who graduated from the school. However, the donor's intended level of giving is not consistent with the standards set by the development office for receiving the naming rights. How would you handle this situation?

4. The president of the school has made it very clear that the capital campaign is to focus on enhancing academic programs. However, donors continue to indicate an interest in making athletics-specific contributions in order to support the continuing success of the school's football program. The school's development office is growing more resentful of the athletics development office. How would you rectify the situation?

5. The head coaches of certain sports want to engage in their own fundraising efforts, separate from the efforts of the development office. The coaches perceive that their sports are viewed as unimportant as compared with revenue-generating sports. How would you address their concerns and work toward an amicable solution?

6. After much scrutiny and consideration, the school's governing body has accepted a recommendation to move forward with eliminating certain sport programs. Donors are furious about the decision. How would you address their concerns by using the school's decision as an opportunity to educate people about the finances of intercollegiate athletics?

LEARNING ACTIVITIES

1. A new donor is very excited about supporting the athletics department and believes that his contributions should entitle him to greater benefits. Pick one of the five major athletics conference (ACC, Big Ten, Big Twelve, Pac Twelve, SEC) at the Division I level and examine each school's website to find information about benefits provided to big donors. Share your findings with the class. Do the assignment again with a Division I conference outside of the big five, a conference at the Division I FCS level, or a Division II conference.

2. After much scrutiny and consideration, the school's governing body has accepted a recommendation to move forward with eliminating certain sport programs. Students, especially student-athletes, are furious about the decision. Using your research skills find examples of where this has occurred and how schools dealt with the negativity from students and the backlash from alumni, especially lettermen. Share your examples with the class.

3. Your athletics department is moving up to a new level of competition, and greater expenses are anticipated with the move to a new conference. As a result, the donor base needs to be increased, starting with current students. Examine athletics department websites and use your findings to formulate a student support group that balances a focus on home-team spirit with creating future athletics donors.

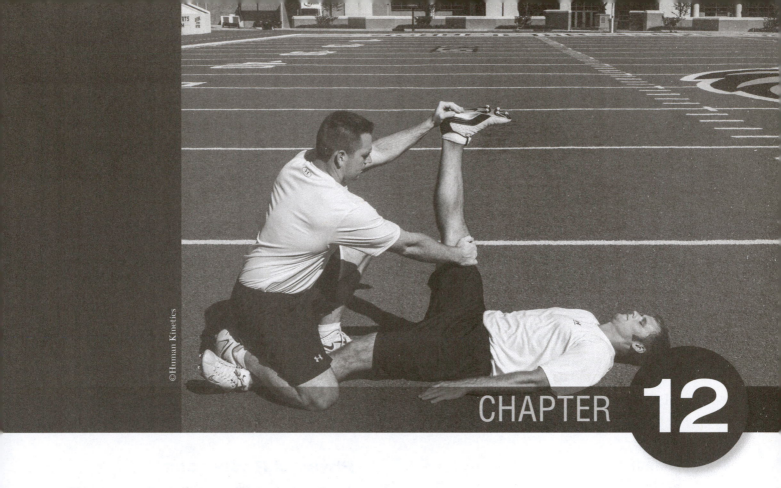

CHAPTER **12**

Support Services

Landon T. Huffman, Guilford College

Coyte G. Cooper, University of North Carolina at Chapel Hill

In this chapter, you will explore

- the operations of support services, including sports medicine, digital media services, equipment staff, and holistic development personnel; and
- challenges associated with resource allocation in support services.

A DAY IN THE LIFE OF AN INTERCOLLEGIATE ATHLETE

As an intercollegiate varsity athlete currently in season, your next contest is a few days away, and you're settling into your weekly routine. Last night you spent the evening at study hall until 10:00 p.m., so it's especially difficult this morning to wake up for your 6:00 a.m. workout and lift. After your training session with the strength and conditioning staff you make time to eat a hearty breakfast before sitting in your first lecture class beginning at 8:00 a.m. Once classes conclude in the early afternoon you report for practice. You dress according to the equipment provided and go to the athletic training room to have your ankles and wrists taped in preparation for practice.

After practice, you're on your way back to the locker room when your team's sports information director approaches and asks you to take part in a new video that will be highlighted on the athletics department's website and broadcast during your next home game. You take time to shower, then get ice wrapped on your elbow before heading to the cafeteria, where you're scheduled to meet with the sport nutritionist to discuss weight management strategies. You have a five-page paper due tomorrow, so you plan to go to study hall tonight, but that will have to wait until after you watch 30 minutes of film from practice, 30 minutes from your previous competition, and an hour of your upcoming opponent.

In reading the opening scenario, you may have noticed that a collegiate student-athlete comes into contact with a variety of athletics department staff members. As an aspiring intercollegiate administrator, it is important for you to understand the various ancillary groups that play a vital role in an athletics department's operation—and in a student-athlete's daily pursuit of excellence.

HOLISTIC DEVELOPMENT STAFF AND SERVICES

Student-athletes are the center of athletics departments, and it is necessary to consider the ancillary services provided to optimize their holistic—physical, mental, spiritual, social, and emotional—development (Hirko, 2009; Howard-Hamilton & Sina, 2001; Pascarella & Blimling, 1996; Watson & Kissinger, 2007). In the not-too-distant past, the head coach was the individual responsible both for student-athletes' physical development and for their health and safety—for example, a coach might supervise weight lifting, tape ankles and wrists, and provide first aid. However, at most institutions, these duties have evolved, and the resources provided have become more specialized in order to address the various dimensions of student-athletes' development.

Physical Resources

The services provided to care for athletes' physical development are arguably the most familiar because of their history in athletics and their obvious implications for performance, health, and safety (Dzikus, Hardin, & Waller, 2012; Powers, 2007). For instance, the introductory scenario shows the student-athlete beginning the morning with a workout supervised by strength and conditioning staff. Whether in season or out of season, student-athletes must maintain or improve their conditioning and strength. With this need in mind, the strength and conditioning staff may structure their sport-specific programs to push athletes to be bigger, faster, and stronger for the sake of athletic competition.

A well-planned strength and conditioning program also reduces the likelihood of sport-related injury (Nadelen, 2012; Thacker, Gilchrist, Stroup, & Kimsey, 2004). As a result, athletics administrators hiring strength and conditioning professionals would be wise to recruit individuals who possess a background in academic disciplines such as physiology, kinesiology, and exercise science.

Another ancillary resource offered to optimize physical development is sport nutrition. From the perspective of athletic performance, specialized instruction from a sport nutritionist is appropriate for diet management strategies and for meeting goals such as losing weight, gaining muscle mass, and trimming body fat (American College of Sports Medicine, American Dietetic Association, & Dieticians of Canada, 2000; Rodriguez, DiMarco, & Langley, 2009). However, the sport nutritionist and the strength and conditioning coach should not operate independently of each other. Instead, they should collaborate to construct individualized, comprehensive programs that help athletes reach their weight management goals.

Sport nutritionists also advise athletes about eating a balanced, nutritionally efficient diet. Student-athletes live in a unique environment in which they are subjected to strenuous athletic, academic, and social demands. Like other college students, however, they may be tempted to skip breakfast, rely on convenient fast foods, or replace water with unhealthy beverages. If their diet is consistently deficient in vitamins, minerals, proteins, fats, and carbohydrates, they will not have the necessary nutrients, energy, and hydration to allow them to meet their responsibilities.

Arguably the most prominent ancillary resource catering to the physical needs of student-athletes is that of sports medicine. However, due to the complexities and legal implications of sports medicine in an athletics department, it is addressed after the following discussion of other types of holistic care personnel.

Mental Resources

First and foremost, student-athletes are students in a higher education setting. Still, as they pursue their education, they are challenged to juggle the demands of athletics as a prominent component of their daily schedule. In light of the considerable time they invest in their practice, competition, and travel schedules, they may benefit from specialized academic support services. Academic support services for student-athletes can vary slightly from university to university; generally, however, they may include subject tutors, academic mentors, study groups, learning specialists, and academic advisors (Broughton & Neyer, 2001; Comeaux, 2013; Covell & Barr, 2010; Wolverton, 2008). Academic support personnel for student-athletes are critically important because they help these uniquely situated students navigate their educational experience, balance the demands of academics and athletics,

and prepare themselves for life after their playing career ends. These personnel also help student-athletes meet academic eligibility requirements.

There is another dimension of the mental aspect of the student-athlete experience, and this one goes beyond the pursuit of an academic skill set. This dimension is addressed by sport psychology, which focuses primarily on enhancing performance by equipping athletes with strategies to help their mental self-talk work for them rather than against them (Weinberg & Gould, 2011). An athletics administrator may hire a sport psychology consultant (SPC) as a part-time or full-time member of the holistic care team.

For example, let's imagine that the student-athlete described in the introductory scenario consistently experiences extreme frustration or anxiety upon perceiving that he or she has made a mistake. An SPC is trained to help the student-athlete manage such feelings through appropriately individualized measures. The consultation can extend to helping the student-athlete manage mental self-talk relating to technique. Thus, when a student-athlete experiences a slump in performance, an SPC can provide an alternate perspective and voice that may help the student-athlete internalize the situation more effectively in order reach to his or her athletic performance potential.

The sport psychology profession entails much more than what is briefly mentioned here. It is, in fact, an academic discipline with strenuous professional standards and credentialing (Association for Applied Sport Psychology, 2013a, 2013b). The current trend is to integrate sport psychology professionals into intercollegiate athletics departments to facilitate holistic care for student-athletes.

Spiritual Resources

Whereas many people are comfortable with the more tangible outcomes of physical and mental development, spiritual care for student-athletes seems more likely to be questioned. However, as discussed in this chapter's leadership lesson, many leadership experts advocate caring for the spiritual dimension of our lives. Spiritual care in this sense does not necessarily refer to anything religious; rather, it involves value clarification, value commitment, study, and meditation.

Although students are encouraged to engage

in self-reflection during their college years, this broader sense of spirituality (which can manifest itself through adhering to a particular faith tradition) (Astin, Astin, & Lindholm, 2011; Delaney & Madigan, 2009; Galli & Reel, 2012; Hales, 2007; Koenig, 2009; Koenig, Parkerson, & Meador, 1997; Shaw, Joseph, & Linley, 2005) is often ignored. In order to address this important element of holistic development, some athletics departments partner with a sport chaplain to help student-athletes engage their spirituality. Although the broader profession of chaplaincy promulgates professional standards, the specialized nature of sport chaplaincy is continuing to emerge. In fact, no standardized model for sport chaplaincy exists in intercollegiate athletics departments, which makes this ancillary service a challenge to implement (Dzikus et al., 2012). Nonetheless, aspiring athletics administrators should be aware of the trends and challenges, because these ancillary resources continue to grow and evolve in order to better serve student-athletes holistically.

Social and Emotional Resources

Have you ever noticed a student-athlete development coordinator in an athletics department's staff directory and wondered about his or her job duties? Broadly, the responsibilities of this position include planning, organizing, and implementing leadership, interpersonal, and life skills initiatives for student-athletes. Examples include community service projects, ropes course challenges, résumé and interview workshops, dinner etiquette sessions, and motivational and leadership seminars (Covell & Barr, 2010; Wolverton, 2008). These events are structured to foster social and emotional competences by exposing student-athletes to culturally diverse programs.

In light of increased occurrences of mental and emotional health issues among active and retired athletes, athletics departments have begun integrating licensed social workers and licensed mental health professionals into their holistic care team (Hayden, Kornspan, Bruback, Parent, & Rodgers, 2013). These individuals can be employed either part-time or full-time to assess, diagnose, and treat psychological and emotional issues and disorders. These relatively new developments in intercolle-

giate athletics promise to address the social and emotional dimension of human beings as framed by Covey (2004) in this chapter's leadership lesson.

As you may have observed, the holistic services discussed here are not exclusive to a single dimension of personhood—that is, physical, mental, spiritual, social, or emotional. Rather, the dimensions are interconnected. Consequently, the staff members who make up the holistic care team should recognize the value of each other's area of expertise and collaborate to best promote student-athletes' holistic personal development.

Before shifting gears to discuss additional prominent support services outside of the holistic care team, we focus now on the role of sports medicine. Athletics administrators must have a working knowledge of the complexities involved in sports medicine so that they can proactively serve student-athletes, operate in a fiscally sound manner, and avoid negligence claims.

SPORTS MEDICINE

Given the increasingly high financial stakes of intercollegiate athletics, emphasis in sports medicine units is placed on providing exemplary physical care to athletes to get them back to optimal performance as soon as possible without compromising their health and safety. In addition, the presence of performance-enhancing drugs and the increase in knowledge about concussions and other head injuries have put a spotlight on the personnel who confront these controversial issues. Sports medicine personnel are capable of providing exceptional care, but they face challenges that athletics administrators should be aware of—for example, resource allocation, facility management, liability mitigation, and organizational structure, which all affect the treatment that student-athletes receive.

Athletic Training

Although you may have heard the terms *sports medicine* and *athletic training* used interchangeably, the first step in better comprehending this ancillary service is to understand the difference between these terms. Sports medicine involves all members of the sports medicine staff, which can include athletic trainers, physicians, orthopedic surgeons, physical therapists, dentists, and masseuses, to name a few. Athletic training, in particular, involves personnel who are certified according to professional standards set forth by the National Athletic Trainers' Association (NATA) (2014a), Board of Certification for the Athletic Trainer (BOC), and the individual state in which they practice. Please note also that the professional title of these individuals is not simply "trainer" but "athletic trainer."

Of the various members of the sports medicine team, athletic trainers have the most interaction with student-athletes and are the most likely to be full-time employees of a college or university. Therefore, this section primarily addresses issues regarding their role in the athletics department. It is understandable that athletics administrators may not be familiar with all of the specific standards required to become an athletic trainer; however, it is critical that administrators appreciate the daily role that athletic trainers play in virtually every student-athlete's life.

Daily Operations of a Certified Athletic Trainer

As with any occupation, certified athletic trainers' daily operations in collegiate athletics can vary widely, both from sport to sport and from institution to institution. Duties can also vary depending on the athletics department's organizational structure and its ratio of athletic trainers to student-athletes. Amid these variations, however, intercollegiate athletic trainers share common responsibilities.

In a broad sense, a typical day for a certified athletic trainer (ATC) involves administrative duties, rehabilitation and treatment, staff and coach meetings, prepractice preparation and treatment, practice responsibilities, and postpractice treatment. These duties can include, but are not limited to, injury prevention, clinical evaluation, diagnosis, immediate care of injuries, and rehabilitation of injuries. ATCs may also be involved in reconditioning an athlete after an injury to ensure that he or she successfully returns to preinjury levels without rushing the rehabilitation (S.D. Halverson & K. King, personal communication, January 2013).

In addition, each of these obligations includes its own list of responsibilities. For example, administrative duties include maintaining health records, complying with safety and sanitation standards, managing inventory, budgeting, organizing the

facility, cleaning, and maintaining equipment. Providing this level of detail for all areas of the job, however, goes beyond the scope of this chapter. Therefore, we now turn our attention to understanding the critical decisions that an athletics administrator must make regarding the commitment to sports medicine at his or her institution (S.D. Halverson & K. King, personal communication, January 2013).

Resource Allocation

As with operating any organization, budgeting and resource allocation deserve much attention. At an NCAA Division I Football Bowl Subdivision (FBS) institution, the budget for sports medicine could be greater than US$1,000,000 annually, as compared with a couple hundred thousand dollars at NCAA Division III schools. This budget line item includes ATCs' salaries, compensation for student assistants, facility debt service, purchase and maintenance of equipment, insurance premiums, and outsourced medical treatment (e.g., from physicians, orthopedic surgeons, chiropractors, physical therapists, optometrists, cardiologists, neurologists, dentists, and dermatologists) (S.D. Halverson & K. King, personal communication, January 2013).

The majority of the dollars allocated to sports medicine in athletics departments depends largely on athletics administrators' commitment to injury prevention. For example, athletics administrators must decide how many ATCs and student assistants to hire for appropriate sport coverage. They must also decide whether or not to invest in modern equipment intended to reduce the likelihood of sport injuries. Hiring more ATCs and acquiring state-of-the-art equipment are calculated investments that may decrease liability, health care bills, and rehabilitation time increase the performance of student-athletes (S.D. Halverson & K. King, personal communication, January 2013).

These are just a few of the considerations that an administrator must ponder when allocating resources for sports medicine. The NATA document *Recommendations and Guidelines for Appropriate Medical Coverage of Intercollegiate Athletics* (NATA, 2014b) offers universities a well-developed tool for evaluating their current level of coverage for student-athletes (S.D. Halverson & K. King, personal communication, January 2013).

Facility Management

Also in the interest of injury prevention, administrators and ATCs are wise to thoroughly discuss facility management. Facility space on college campuses comes at a premium, and it can be a challenge to acquire or construct the square footage necessary to effectively meet the needs of hundreds of student-athletes. In addition, if possible, it is logical for the athletic training room to be near the strength and conditioning area for the following reasons: medical staff may use strength-training and agility equipment in this area, proximity between the two facilitates collaboration between ATCs and strength and conditioning staff, and proximity enables a quick medical response in an emergency situation. To ensure that such concerns are understood and addressed, athletics administrators should seek advice from sports medicine staff regarding how to make the facility as practical and functional as possible before attempting to secure space (S.D. Halverson & K. King, personal communication, January 2013).

As an aspiring athletics administrator, you should be aware that there is an "arms race" in collegiate athletics regarding sports medicine facilities and equipment. For example, athletic training facilities at major NCAA Division I FBS institutions can range from "dated" 1,000-square-foot (93-square-meter) facilities constructed in the mid-1990s to modern 8,000+ square-foot (740-square-meter) facilities (S.D. Halverson & K. King, personal communication, January 2013).

The arms race also involves state-of-the-art equipment used by ATCs, which, on the high end, can include an underwater treadmill (e.g., HydroWorx) that costs approximately US$100,000 and requires thousands of dollars' worth of annual maintenance! For example, figure 12.1 provides a glimpse inside the hydrotherapy room in the newly constructed athletic training facility at the University of Tennessee. In this context, spending millions of dollars to provide superior treatment may be justified not only for the sake of the health, safety, and welfare of student-athletes but also for attracting prospective student-athletes (S.D. Halverson & K. King, personal communication, January 2013).

Photo courtesy of University of Tennessee.

Figure 12.1. **A hydrotherapy room at the University of Tennessee contains two HydroWorx underwater treadmills equipped with six underwater cameras for motion analysis.**

Liability Mitigation

Because we live in litigious times, it is critical to briefly discuss liability and risk management in relation to sports medicine. Once again, resource allocation plays a role here. For example, if an athlete suffers a traumatic injury, who is responsible for paying for the medical services—the student-athlete's health insurance provider or the university's insurance provider? What if the student-athlete does not have health insurance?

The answer will depend on decisions that have been made by the school's athletics administrators. Some universities require student-athletes to be 100 percent responsible for their health insurance—or lack thereof. In that case, paying for surgery caused by a sport injury would fall on the student-athlete's shoulders. On the other end of the spectrum, an athletics department may commit to covering 100 percent of the costs of medical treatment for injuries sustained during sport participation. This approach, of course, results in increased insurance premiums and medical expenses for the athletics department. In order to avoid potential grievances, it is vital for athletics administrators to have discussions with the sports medicine staff and with student-athletes and their families to clearly outline policies and procedures (i.e., financial liability) should an injury occur (S. D. Halverson & K. King, personal communication, January 2013).

Another common concern for athletics administrators in liability management relates directly to human resources. If an athletics department has fifteen sport teams but only four full-time ATCs, where does the additional needed support come from? The answer usually involves undergraduate students aspiring to be ATCs and sometimes graduate students who may or may not already have their ATC certification. Student assistants may be eligible to receive compensation in the form of tuition reimbursement, room and board, free meals, and free gear, which constitutes another budget consideration (S.D. Halverson & K. King, personal communication, January 2013).

Student assistants provide much-needed support for ATCs and are allowed to perform limited athletic training duties at the discretion of their supervising ATC. They must not, however, practice any athletic training duties outside of the direct supervision of an ATC. Student assistants who overstep their permitted responsibilities, whether intentionally or unintentionally, could cause harm or trouble for a student-athlete, a supervising ATC, the student assistant himself or herself, or the athletics department overall. Consequently, it is important for athletics administrators to communicate clearly with ATCs, students, and legal counsel to ensure that everyone is aware of, and held accountable for, ensuring that student assistants stay within their proper role in athletic training settings (S.D. Halverson & K. King, personal communication, January 2013).

Another legal consideration involving the health and safety of intercollegiate athletes focuses on traumatic head injuries, such as concussions. Sports medicine professionals are often the first line of defense in diagnosing and properly treating athletes who may have suffered head trauma. If the proper standard of care is neglected, legal consequences can result.

Organizational Structure

Another important issue directly related to resource allocation and liability management involves the organizational and reporting structure of a sports medicine unit in an athletics department. Ancillary staff are housed in a variety of functional areas in athletics departments across the county, but sports medicine is unique. Athletics administrators are wise to deliberate on the reporting lines involving sports medicine professionals because strict legal standards apply to medical reporting and decision making. Therefore, special attention is devoted here to the organizational structure of sports medicine in athletics departments; in particular, we focus on two prominent models, which are referred to as model A and model B.

Model A

The majority of institutions assume this model, in which sports medicine is housed in the athletics department like any other functional area (e.g., media relations, sport marketing, compliance). In this model, the director of sports medicine is a full-time employee of the athletics department and may be a physician or ATC. He or she oversees all ATCs involved with the athletics department and reports to the athletics director.

Those instituting this model are likely to use

relatively more outsourced medical personnel (e.g., physicians, orthopedic surgeons, chiropractors, physical therapists, dentists). As a result, athletics administrators need to be prepared to pay private clinic fees to secure these services. Although outsourcing may be expensive, one advantage is that the arrangement protects the athletics department from a liability standpoint since the burden falls on the contracted third party (S.D. Halverson & K. King, personal communication, January 2013).

Another concern with this model is a possible conflict of interest in decision making by the sports medicine staff. Since the director of sports medicine and ATCs can be hired and fired at will by the athletics director, these personnel must, unfortunately, manage the expectations of coaches. This possibility raises ethical considerations because it makes the health and safety of student-athletes more likely to be put in jeopardy. For instance, an ATC may feel pressured to appease a coach by clearing a player to return to competition prematurely rather than making a medically sound decision in favor of the student-athlete's well-being. The pressure derives from the fact that in this model of the reporting lines of authority, the athletics director signs the payroll checks, and ATCs may feel that if they anger a powerful coach they

may be fired (S.D. Halverson & K. King, personal communication, January 2013).

With this potential pitfall in mind, athletics administrators must foster an environment that allows sports medicine staff to feel comfortable making decisions in the best interest of the welfare of student-athletes instead of the outcome of a competition. Figure 12.2 outlines a hypothetical organizational chart structured according to model A (S.D. Halverson & K. King, personal communication, January 2013).

Model B

The main difference between model A and model B is that model B situates sports medicine outside of the athletics department, most likely as a division of campus health. Therefore, the director of sports medicine reports to the director of campus health, who subsequently reports to the chancellor or vice chancellor—not the athletics director. In this model, the director of sports medicine still hires and supervises all ATCs but under the guidance of the director of campus health. As a result, ATCs in this model are technically employed by campus health rather than by the athletics department; however, the athletics department reimburses campus health to distribute the salaries (S.D.

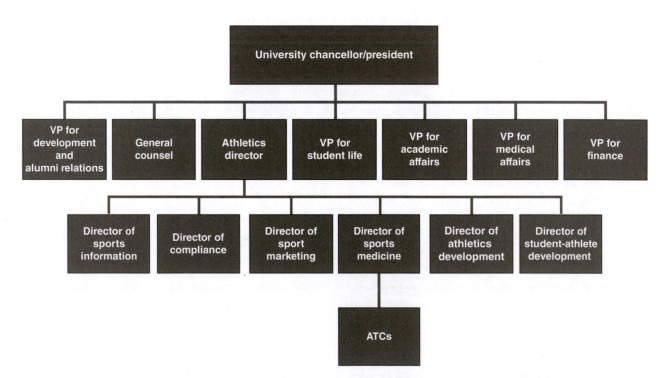

Figure 12.2. **Hypothetical university organizational structure—model A.**

Halverson & K. King, personal communication, January 2013).

As you may have deduced, this structure of reporting buffers ATCs from potential pressure exerted by coaches, since accountability is dictated by campus health rather than the athletics department. In addition, sports medicine units that operate according to this model are more likely than those in model A to use the services of other campus health employees (e.g., physicians, surgeons, physical therapists) instead of outsourcing to professionals in private practice (S.D. Halverson & K. King, personal communication, January 2013). Figure 12.3 outlines a hypothetical organizational chart structured according to model B. Notice the difference in reporting lines between model A and model B.

As you can see, sports medicine's role in an athletics department involves many moving parts. In addition, sports medicine personnel, particularly ATCs, have daily interaction with student-athletes and coaches. Therefore, gaining a better understanding of their daily operations and decision-making processes can help administrators make informed decisions to prevent litigation and practice fiscally sound resource allocation. In pursuing the profession of athletics administration, you take on the obligation of protecting the holistic wellness, health, safety, welfare, and integrity of student-athletes. Comprehending the sports medicine support group is a critical step toward meeting that responsibility.

The ancillary groups discussed thus far engage in considerable direct interaction with student-athletes on a day-to-day basis, particularly regarding their personal holistic wellness. Athletics departments also include other support services that bear less responsibility for student-athletes' wellness but still have a substantial effect on the student-athlete experience. A few of these prominent support services are discussed in the following sections.

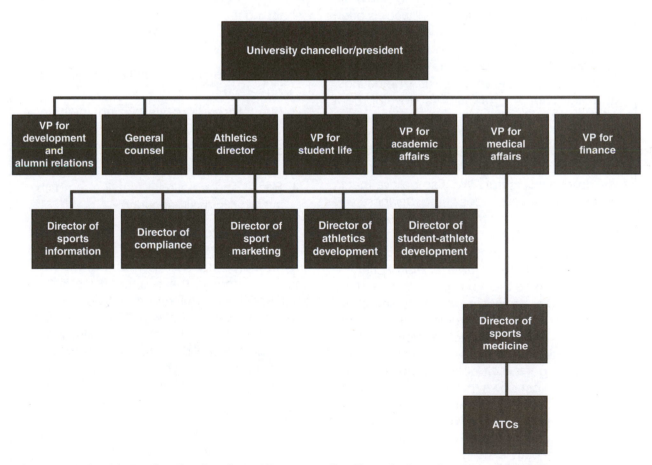

Figure 12.3 **Hypothetical university organizational structure—model B.**

Leadership Lesson

Sharpen the Saw

This chapter explores daily operations and challenges associated with a variety of functional areas that work in concert with the other units discussed throughout this book. It is critical to take a step back to review each of the working parts that function independently to facilitate optimal athletics department operations. Now that we have discussed the complex issues, processes, and oversight needed in the administration of intercollegiate athletics, it may not surprise you to hear of the 80-hour work week that many athletics department staff members commonly work.

Indeed, the typical 8-to-5 work week is often just the beginning of an administrator's schedule. The evening fundraising events, matchups, and awards ceremonies pile up, in addition to road trips, conference or NCAA meetings, and occasional professional development conferences. As a result, it is often said that working in athletics is not a job but a lifestyle and that in order to succeed you must have a passion for the industry and the work you do. We believe this is true. We also believe that in order to achieve success *and balance,* you must proactively do what Stephen Covey calls "sharpening the saw."

Covey (2004) shares an example illustrating this principle in *The 7 Habits of Highly Effective People.* Imagine that you see someone in the woods who is zealously working to saw down a tree. You can see the tremendous effort the person is putting into each movement of the saw, but little progress is being made. You comment to the person, "It looks like you're working very hard to cut down this tree! Why don't you take a few minutes to sharpen the saw?!" The person responds "Yes, I've been working for five hours, but I don't have time to sharpen the saw. I'm too busy sawing!"

> *Show me a man who cannot bother to do little things, and I'll show you a man who cannot be trusted to do big things.*
>
> Lawrence D. Bell, founder of Bell Aircraft Corporation (manufacturer of first supersonic aircraft)

A few minutes spent refining the instrument could have saved a lot of time, but instead the determined worker chose to pour all energy into feverishly extending and retracting a dull blade. How many times have you sat down to get something done and, because you were feeling a bit hazy, you ended up reading the same paragraph over and over or you were sidetracked from the task you initially set out to accomplish? These outcomes might be symptomatic of trying to work with a dull saw.

Sharpening the saw, according to Covey (2004, p. 288), involves "preserving and enhancing the greatest asset you have—you." Covey outlines four dimensions that need attention.

1. Physical (exercise, nutrition, stress management)
2. Mental (reading, visualizing, planning, writing)
3. Spiritual (value clarification and commitment, study, meditation)
4. Social and emotional (service, empathy, synergy, intrinsic security)

Taking time to renew and refresh yourself is critical. There will always be something that seems more important or more urgent, but spending time on these dimensions is "the single most powerful investment we can ever make in life" (Covey, 2004, p. 289). Take time to work out, read, ponder, pack a healthy lunch, attend professional development conferences, and spend time with your family. Take time to sharpen your saw. If you question the time spent on any of these investments, just think of the hours wasted by the person in the woods!

This concept offers many applications for organizational renewal. We would like to focus here on the importance of feedback. Eliciting feedback from those you work with can help you focus your self-improvement efforts—and sharpening the saw is all about self-improvement. Arguably the most effective method of feedback is 360-degree (or multi-rater) feedback because of its comprehensive nature. In essence, you receive feedback from everyone you work with (from 360 degrees around you), including your peers, your boss, any direct reports, yourself, and sometimes even your customers. Generally, the feedback should be relatively simple, allowing those participating in the process to share their perceptions of your strengths and "developmental needs" or "opportunities for improvement." The most effective 360-degree feedback programs are confidential, constructive, and part of a developmental plan wherein feedback is supported with follow-up and coaching.

As you manage the variety of tasks and issues discussed in this chapter and throughout this book, you will inevitably learn and grow. Each on-the-job experience can bring unique insights and can contribute to your skill set, thus enhancing your competences and marketability. When you also choose to proactively develop your greatest asset—yourself—your abilities increase exponentially. Time will pass, you will get older, and the job will get done. But whether you enjoy the journey, and whether you squeeze everything you can out of your experiences, is up to you.

> *It's the little things that make the big things possible. Only close attention to the fine details of any operation makes the operation first class.*
>
> J. Willard Marriott, founder of the Marriott Corporation & Marriott International (one of the largest hotel companies in the world)

DIGITAL MEDIA SERVICES

Digital media services, which generate products such as graphics and videos, have become an essential element of athletics departments' branding and operations. As discussed in various other chapters, websites have become an essential technological medium for brand-building initiatives (Wallace, Wilson, & Miloch, 2011). When websites are crafted properly and filled with creative content, they provide a unique opportunity to house informational and promotional materials in a manner that enhances the athletics department's brand (Cooper & Weight, 2011). Websites provide a platform to market the personnel and programs housed in the department. In fact, they often include a themed video section offering innovative feature stories, highlight clips, coach and player interviews, and other promotional pieces.

In terms of staying on the cutting edge of marketing endeavors, the creation of unique digital content also provides innovative materials to be circulated via social media. This is a primary reason for the trend of athletics departments investing in digital media. High-quality digital media make it likely that revenues will increase because more visitors to the site provide an enticing sponsorship opportunity. At a minimum, an increase in web visitors allows athletics departments to build and publicize their brand in a manner of their choosing. Therefore, it is critical to become aware of the personnel who contribute to digital media services.

The demand for multimedia services is increasing in our society in general, and, as illustrated in the scenario at the beginning of the chapter, the demands of video services routinely affect student-athletes' schedules. Consequently, athletics departments are allocating more resources to video technology and management that extends beyond traditional website content. To better understand how video technology is managed and integrated into athletics departments, it is helpful to approach this ancillary group from two perspectives—external production and internal services. These two groups share similar tasks, technology, equipment, and footage, but their job responsibilities and operations differ.

External Video Production

One of the first things that many spectators notice upon entering a stadium or arena is the animation on a videoboard (e.g., jumbotron, LED ribbon board). This content is managed by dedicated ancillary staff, and due to its high visibility it is vital to understand how these services operate and function.

Video and multimedia services can be housed in a variety of functional areas in an athletics department. For instance, staff who produce video content intended for the public (e.g., for website, videoboard, or ribbon board use) could be directly supervised by the media relations staff, the sport marketing staff, or the multimedia and new media staff. These roles could also be outsourced to an organization outside of the athletics department. Video produced for these functions is intended to be professional and stimulating to the audience, and staff members hired to produce content for external presentation must have expertise in video editing and video production (C. Luke, personal communication, January 2013).

Although an employee or student assistant may be trained in the use of video editing software, this work often involves negotiating a learning curve in order to properly operate videoboards and ribbon boards due to their unique graphic user interface. For example, one of the most common manufacturers of videoboards, scoreboards, and ribbon boards is Daktronics. Therefore, external video staff are generally trained to use Daktronics equipment and software, and they are the ancillary group who communicates with Daktronics to address questions about this technology (C. Luke, personal communication, January 2013).

Challenges for administrators related to external production include resource allocation and infrastructure. As demand increases for multimedia across a variety of platforms and devices, administrators must reflect on their mission, vision, goals, and objectives to determine the amount of resources to invest in external multimedia production. For example, external video presentation services can be outsourced, but doing so creates a new set of challenges, including access to coaches, student-athletes, and facilities, as well as integration and compatibility with the athletics department's hardware and software. However, if administrators decide to keep external video presentation in-house, they must make a substantial financial investment to hire full-time staff and secure the needed infrastructure to produce high-quality multimedia content.

In addition, there is no consistent framework for positioning external video production in the athletics department organizational chart. In other words, there is no blueprint for its place in an athletics department. The trend is to place external video presentation in media relations, but some departments place it in sport marketing. Another alternative is to create a new functional area for this digital service, commonly referred to as digital media, which can also oversee social media initiatives. With all of this in mind, it is critical for you as an aspiring administrator to reflect on the technology and management challenges inherent in external video production in an intercollegiate athletics department.

Internal Video Services

In contrast to external video production, internal video services manage video and digital media not shown to the public. This work primarily involves managing video from competition, video from practice, and video used in team meetings. Internal video operations also help coaching staffs with game analysis software. A secondary responsibility is to produce digital media that can be used for team enhancement (e.g., game highlights, pregame motivational segments) and for recruiting purposes (C. Luke, personal communication, January 2013).

Most athletics departments include an individual who serves as the video coordinator and works closely with coaching staffs. This person may also double as an assistant coach or graduate student assistant. The video coordinator's job responsibilities vary from team to team and school to school, but they most likely focus primarily on coordinating internal digital media services for the football and basketball teams. To help you learn about internal digital media services in their most complex setting, the following discussion uses the scenario of a major NCAA Division I FBS institution.

Daily Operations

The fundamental purpose of internal digital media services is to capture, edit, catalog, and maintain a video library from practices, competitions, and opponents' competitions. The purpose of this extensive library is to provide the coaching staff with tools to evaluate and analyze their team and their opponents. In many programs, staff members film every practice throughout the season, using multiple cameras to film from a variety of angles (C. Luke, personal communication, January 2013).

In football, for example, cameras may be used at the following angles: (a) high, wide, sideline-to-sideline view of the full field for both offense and defense, (b) angle from the end zone from hash mark to hash mark for both offense and defense, (c) individual camera(s) to film position drills, and (d) any other perspectives the coaches desire. This variety of angles requires the staff to shoot from a variety of heights, as well as on the ground. Not all practice fields have a press box, so teams may use a scissor lift or scaffolding for filming. Due to liability and risk management issues, however, new game analysis technology offers remote filming to avoid requiring individuals to climb to these heights (C. Luke, personal communication, January 2013).

Each play is shot from these multiple angles with the intent of providing as much information as possible for performance analysis. Thanks to advancements in technology, the process of editing and cataloging clips and getting them ready to view takes only 45 to 60 minutes once practice ends. Now that you are aware of the many cameras and angles used on a daily basis, the next step is to understand how the technology is used to construct and maintain the robust digital media library.

Technology

Collegiate athletic teams use several brands of game analysis technology, including DVSport, LRS Sports, and XOS Digital. The differences between these brands resemble the differences between car manufacturers (e.g., Ford, Chevrolet, Toyota). Each brand has its strengths and weaknesses, but they all serve the same basic purpose. Ultimately, a team chooses a technology provider based on the coaching staff's preferences about aspects such as the user interface. The financial investment for these services—including the initial cost of hardware, software, training, and support—can run to about US$250,000, and the annual cost of maintenance and support can reach about US$40,000. It is con-

sidered worth the cost because it facilitates game analysis by enabling staff to log and catalog the tens of thousands of clips accrued throughout the season, thus aiding both organization and efficiency (C. Luke, personal communication, January 2013).

With this technology, each recorded play can be assigned any combination of attributes and codes according to the coaches' preferences. In football, for example, each clip can be assigned any of about 40 attributes, such as down, distance, yard line, run or pass, play-action, motion, offensive or defense formation, personnel, time, or hash mark. The coaching staff can then use the software to create a series of clips (often referred to as "cut-ups") filtered for any combination of the attributes (C. Luke, personal communication, January 2013).

For instance, a coaching staff or defensive player might want to prepare for the next opponent by analyzing the opponent's passing tendencies with a two-tight-end formation inside the 20-yard line on second or third down in the fourth quarter. Since the video coordinator has already uploaded the opponent's game films (previously acquired through the conference's exchange policy) and tagged each play, a few simple commands will compile a collection of clips from the entire season that meet all of the selected criteria. The coaching staff or player can then quickly evaluate those plays and prepare for the opponent's tendencies in that specific game situation before moving on to the next chosen situation (C. Luke, personal communication, January 2013).

As you might imagine, the chosen attributes vary from sport to sport, and different software companies may target different sports. In addition, a given brand may offer particular versions of software (just as Ford has offered various models, such as the Focus, the Mustang, and the Explorer) to meet the particular needs and preferences of a given sport or coaching staff. For instance, in track and field, it is more appropriate to analyze and improve one's personal performance than to analyze an opponent's performance. Therefore, a coach or athlete might call for cut-ups of personal acceleration out of the blocks (C. Luke, personal communication, January 2013).

Other options offered by digital media technology providers include resources such as recruiting databases, mobile apps, and replay services.

Altogether, this powerful capability to sort and filter video on demand for efficient game analysis helps justify the fiscal investment in ancillary staff and resources in the high-stakes world of elite intercollegiate athletics (C. Luke, personal communication, January 2013).

Personnel and Staff

The operating budget for internal digital media services varies from school to school, depending on the overall athletics department budget, but a typical budget for internal video services at a major NCAA Division I FBS football program is approximately US$250,000 per year. The number of full-time staff, part-time staff, and student assistants who work with internal video services varies, but the salary pool for staff is approximately US$170,000. Student assistants can be compensated through a salary, an hourly wage, tuition reimbursement, free equipment, or free meals (C. Luke, personal communication, January 2013).

For individuals interested in pursuing internal video management, no specific academic program or credential is required. Many video coordinators pursue a major in sport management, sport communication, communication, or journalism. However, the primary qualification is experience in working with a video staff. It is also helpful to become a member of the Collegiate Sports Video Association and attend the group's annual conference, where professionals and aspiring professionals network and participate in sessions to learn improved techniques for capturing, editing, and securing film for their databases. Ultimately, internal digital media services strive to enable the coaching staff and student-athletes to improve their performance through film analysis (C. Luke, personal communication, January 2013).

Digital media services are more prominent than ever in intercollegiate athletics departments. In fact, Jon Gilbert, who has prolific experience in managing various areas of collegiate athletics departments, emphasizes the necessity of digital media services in today's athletics environment (see the Industry Profile). Whether digital media products are generated to entertain fans or edited to serve as teaching and learning tools for coaches and players, athletics administrators need to familiarize themselves with video management and technology in order to more efficiently serve their internal and external stakeholders.

EQUIPMENT SERVICES

Another ancillary area that directly affects the student-athlete experience is equipment services. The role of equipment in intercollegiate athletics has recently come to be epitomized in the University of Oregon's athletics department, particularly its football program. Oregon's decisiveness in embracing innovative graphics and apparel has garnered its teams national visibility in the media. As Oregon's approach illustrates, equipment's role in a collegiate athletics department goes beyond outfitting student-athletes to include marketing and revenue generation (J. Freeman, personal communication, January 2013).

The dominant official equipment providers in collegiate athletics are Adidas, Nike, and UnderArmour, but each school is free to enter into contract negotiations with any equipment provider. Furthermore, each sport is likely given some latitude to negotiate with multiple brands regarding sport-specific equipment for its teams. For example, brand A may provide equipment for the football and basketball teams but be unable to provide soccer balls, swimwear, wrestling shoes, or field hockey equipment. As an athletics administrator, you will be tasked with negotiating equipment contracts, which have implications for virtually every member of the athletics department and for external stakeholders as well!

Equipment Contracts

Contracts with equipment providers can take a variety of forms. One element they typically include involves value-in-kind (VIK), which means that the company agrees to provide a certain amount of equipment for student-athletes, coaches, and staff; in return, the apparel company's brand receives exposure in the local, regional, or national media. Once the maximum VIK is reached, the contract usually provides for more equipment to be purchased at a fraction of the wholesale price. The company may also agree to pay a dollar amount to the athletics department. It is not uncommon to funnel this subsidy to supplement head coaches' base salaries, which can affect the quality of head coach that an athletics director can hire.

Industry Profile
Jon Gilbert

Executive senior associate athletics director, University of Tennessee

As you have no doubt noticed, athletics administrators juggle a wide variety of roles and responsibilities. No one knows this better than Jon Gilbert, who oversees the daily comprehensive operations at the University of Tennessee. Throughout his career, Gilbert has gained leadership experience by working in external operations, athletics development, facility and event management, ticketing, and sport supervision.

Recently Gilbert was kind enough to offer wisdom regarding resource allocation in contemporary intercollegiate athletics. Specifically, his insights were directly related to the vital role of support services in athletics departments. During the dialogue, Gilbert was asked, "If you were given the funds to hire one additional employee for any of the functional areas in the

University of Tennessee's athletics department, where would it be allocated?" Gilbert responded that the additional employee would be hired in technology—in particular, in digital media services.

The emphasis on technology management is a reflection of both external and internal stakeholders' demand for multimedia services. Given the growing popularity of social media, as well as creative graphic and video services, this emphasis makes sense because athletics administrators are constantly trying to gain an edge in positioning their department. With this goal in mind, assembling a competent staff that can effectively manage technology and digital media has far-reaching implications for the daily routines of student-athletes, coaches, staff members, and fans.

So how does millions of dollars' worth of athletics apparel and equipment get distributed to hundreds of athletes, dozens of coaches, and athletics department staff members? Enter equipment managers.

Equipment Managers

As you might imagine, it can be overwhelming for a coach to meet the inventory requirements of managing equipment shipments and distributions. Therefore, full-time equipment managers are hired to handle these needs in virtually every athletics department. There may be four to six full-time equipment managers in a major NCAA Division I FBS athletics department, and one-half to two-thirds of them likely work with football, whereas the others are responsible for all other sports. In fact, some major FBS athletics departments have only one full-time equipment manager outside of the football program (J. Freeman, personal communication, January 2013).

Full-time equipment managers are primarily responsible for inventory and for communicating

with apparel company representatives. It is critical to store, organize, and document incoming and distributed equipment in an efficient manner so that no NCAA rules are violated in the form of extra benefits for student-athletes. Full-time equipment managers are also responsible for communicating with an individual team's equipment representatives in order to distribute each team's gear and equipment (J. Freeman, personal communication, January 2013).

The method of equipment distribution differs for football teams as compared with virtually every other kind of team because football teams have large roster sizes, complex equipment requirements, and large budgets. In sports other than football, coaches likely receive equipment from the equipment manager and then distribute it to their student-athletes. There has, however, been a recent trend toward streamlining the inventory and equipment distribution processes. For example, student-athletes will go to the equipment storeroom, and the full-time equipment manager will scan the equipment and the student-athlete's identification card to keep accurate records of who receives what gear. Nonetheless, in sports other than football, coaches and student-athletes assume the primary responsibility of managing equipment for both practice and competition, including laundering and transporting equipment. Football, however, requires a great deal of attention to equipment management, and the following sections are more pertinent to football programs than to other sports.

Since there are relatively few full-time equipment managers, athletics departments enlist the help of student equipment managers to help with the day-to-day operations of individual sport teams. Not surprisingly, football programs employ the most student assistants. As with student video assistants, student equipment managers can receive compensation in the form of an hourly wage, a salary, tuition reimbursement, free meals, or free equipment (J. Freeman, personal communication, January 2013).

Student equipment managers are often responsible for preparing equipment for practices and competitions. On a daily basis, this work entails providing athletes and coaches with their practice gear (i.e., setting it up in their individual lockers), getting equipment ready on the practice field per the coaches' requests, storing equipment after practice, and washing laundry to prepare for the next day. On game day, student equipment managers' roles are similar. They set game equipment in lockers for athletes and coaches and organize equipment near the competition site so that replacement pieces are readily available and players miss as little playing time as possible (J. Freeman, personal communication, January 2013).

Equipment managers or student assistants are also responsible for packing equipment to be transported to away games. Athletics administrators are also likely to be involved in this process, because transporting equipment can be costly and time consuming. For example, do you invest in buying a tractor trailer or lease a truck for each road game to haul equipment? Can the equipment be transported by plane on a commercial flight? These are just a few of the relevant considerations, and though they may seem minor in the grand scheme of the decisions faced by athletics administrators, they are essential nonetheless.

Equipment can easily be taken for granted, but dozens of individuals help operate this multimillion-dollar ancillary group. Can you imagine competing for a national championship with your star player's shoe randomly breaking down or a key piece of equipment malfunctioning? Individuals probably do not pack two pairs of shoes, but equipment managers are proficient at handling inventory and organization so that spare equipment is close by to ensure that athletes and coaches can perform at their optimal level.

CONCLUSION

As an athletics administrator, you will find that various functional areas in an athletics department demand your time and attention. Among these areas are a number of seemingly minor ancillary groups that actually play a major role in the day-to-day operations of an athletics department. To be a successful administrator, you must be familiar with the details of these groups' operations. To that end, this chapter outlines a few of the ancillary groups commonly found in athletics departments, and it is now your responsibility to continue to develop your awareness and educate yourself about these groups' functions so that you can make informed, efficient, effective decisions that ultimately benefit hundreds of individuals.

DISCUSSION QUESTIONS

1. The athletics department's operating budget has been cut 10 percent from last year's level, and you are charged with making recommendations about which services and personnel on the holistic care team should be retained. What recommendations do you make?

2. The athletics department in which you work is restructuring its sports medicine unit. Describe three or four considerations that are critical to efficiently integrating sports medicine services in an athletics department.

3. As an administrator, what key areas of digital media should you consider when evaluating your digital presence?

4. Digital media services, including creative graphics and video production, can be housed in a variety of functional areas in an athletics department. What do you think is the best strategy for efficiently integrating these services into an athletics department?

5. Discuss the direct and indirect effects that a partnership with an apparel equipment provider can have on an athletics department.

LEARNING ACTIVITIES

1. Determine who makes up the holistic care team at your institution. Are there any gaps in your opinion?

2. Interview a video coordinator at your university's athletics department and discuss daily operations.

3. Conduct an internet search to review equipment contracts at a variety of institutions and compare their similarities and differences.

References and Resources

Chapter 1

About ND. (2013). University of Notre Dame. www.nd.edu/about/.

Allmendinger, D.F. (1973). The dangers of ante-bellum student life. *Journal of Social History* 7(1), 75–85.

Barr, C.A. (1998). *The faculty athletics representative: A survey of the membership.* Overland Park, KS: National Collegiate Athletic Association.

Bear, C. (2008, May 12). American Indian boarding schools haunt many. National Public Radio. www.npr.org/templates/story/story.php?storyId=16516865.

Birdseye, C.F. (1907). *Individual training in our colleges.* New York: MacMillan. http://books.google.com/books?id=B-v7ZFGz9MCYC&printsec=frontcover&source=gbs_ge_summary_r&cad=0#v=onepage&q&f=false.

Brady, E., Berkowitz, S., & Upton, J. (2012, November 20). College football coaches continue to see salary explosion. *USA Today.* www.usatoday.com/story/sports/ncaaf/2012/11/19/college-football-coaches-contracts-analysis-pay-increase/1715435/.

Buckeye Biography. (2013). Urban Meyer. Ohio State Buckeyes. www.ohiostatebuckeyes.com/sports/m-footbl/mtt/meyer_urban00.html.

Byers, W. (1995). *Unsportsmanlike conduct.* Ann Arbor: University of Michigan Press.

Carlson, S. (2013, January 28). What's the payoff for the "country club" college? *Chronicle of Higher Education.* http://chronicle.com/blogs/buildings/whats-the-payoff-for-the-country-club-college/32477.

Chu, D. (1989). *The character of American higher education and intercollegiate sport.* Albany, NY: SUNY Press.

Crowley, C. (2006). *In the arena: The NCAA's first century.* Indianapolis: National Collegiate Athletic Association.

Desrochers, D. (2013). *Academic spending versus athletic spending: Who wins?* Washington, DC: American Institutes for Research.

Dober, R.P. (2007). *Old Main.* Ann Arbor, MI: Society for College and University Planning.

Dunnavant, K. (2004). *The 50-year seduction: How television manipulated college football, from the birth of the modern NCAA to the creation of the BCS.* New York: St. Martin's Press.

Elfman, L. (2012, December 9). Football is king. *Inside Higher Education.* http://diverseeducation.com/article/50011/.

ESPN. (2012, August 28). Chat: 25 hours of college football. http://espn.go.com/sportsnation/chat/_/id/17020.

Gerber, E. W., Felshin, J., Berlin, P., & Wyrick, W. (1974). *The American woman in sport.* Reading, MA: Addison-Wesley Publishing Company.

Grant, C. (1981). Statement opposing the NCAA motion to offer women's championships in Division I. Statement presented at the NCAA Convention, Miami, FL. Courtesy of the Sharon Taylor Association for Intercollegiate Athletics for Women (AIAW) Archives in the Department of Sport Management at Drexel University.

Grundy, P. (2001). *Learning to win: Sports, education, and social change in the twentieth century.* Chapel Hill, NC: University of North Carolina Press.

Harris, R. (1932). *King football: The vulgarization of the American college.* New York: Vanguard Press.

Holland, J. (1974). AIAW handbook of policies and operating procedures. Washington, DC: American Alliance for Health, Physical Education, Recreation, and Dance.

Hosick, M. (2011, February 2). Equal opportunity knocks. *NCAA News.* www.ncaa.com/news/ncaa/2011-02-02/equal-opportunity-knocks.

Ingrassia, B. (2012). *The rise of gridiron university: Higher education's uneasy alliance with big-time football.* Lawrence: University of Kansas Press.

Intercollegiate Athletic Association of the United States. (1906). *Proceedings from the first annual meeting.* New York, NY. https://archive.org/details/proceedingsannu-14assogoog.

Ireland, C. (2012, April 19). Harvard's long-ago student risings. *Harvard Gazette.* http://news.harvard.edu/gazette/story/2012/04/harvards-long-ago-student-risings.

Jenkins, S. (2007). *The real Americans: The team that changed a game, a people, a nation.* New York: Random House.

Jordan, D.S. (1905, December 9). The Future of Football. *Collier's Weekly. 36:* 19–20.

Kiernan, J. (1932, November 13). King football: Racket or sport? *New York Times,* p. BR3.

McQuilkin, S.A., & Smith, R. (1993, Spring). The rise and fall of the flying wedge: Football's most controversial play. *Journal of Sport History,* 20(1), 57–64.

Mendenhall, T. C. (1993). *The Harvard-Yale boat race and the coming of sport to the American College: 18521924.* Mystic, CT: Mystic Seaport Museum.

National Collegiate Athletic Association. (1916, December 28). Proceedings from the Eleventh Annual Convention. New York: National Collegiate Athletic Association.

National Collegiate Athletic Association. (2013, January 21). Chronology of enforcement. Indianapolis: Author. http://archive.today/Ea1B

O'Neil, D. (2012, April 17). NCAA again tackles academic reform. ESPN. http://espn.go.com/mens-college-basketball/story/_/id/7823800/ncaa-takes-academic-reform-again-college-basketball.

Oriard, M. (2001). *King football: Sport and spectacle in the golden age of radio and newsreels, movies and magazines, the weekly and daily press.* Chapel Hill: University of North Carolina Press.

Oriard, M. (2009). *Bowled over: Big-time college football from the sixties to the BCS era.* Chapel Hill: University of North Carolina Press.

Oxendine, J. (1988). *American Indian sports heritage.* Lincoln, NE: University of Nebraska Press.

Pickeral, R. (2012, December 20). UNC probe reveals academic fraud. ESPN. http://espn.go.com/college-sports/story/_/id/8765672/north-carolina-tar-heels-investigation-reveals-academic-scandal-african-american-studies-department.

Rittenberg, A. (2013, February 20). Spartans blended race in 1960s. ESPN. http://espn.go.com/espn/print?id=8970293&type=story.

Robinson, C. (2011, August 16). Renegade Miami booster spells out illicit benefits to players. Yahoo Sports. http://sports.yahoo.com/investigations/news?slug=cr-renegade_miami_booster_details_illicit_benefits_081611.

Rudolph, F. (1990). *The American college and university: A history* (Rev. ed.). Athens: University of Georgia Press.

Sack, A. L., & Staurowsky, E. J. (1998). *College athletes for hire: The evolution and legacy of the NCAA amateur myth.* Westport, CT: Praeger Press.

Savage, H. (1929). *American college athletics, Bulletin no. 23.* New York: Carnegie Foundation for the Advancement of Teaching.

Seidentop, D., & Vandermars, H. (2011). *Introduction to physical fitness and sport.* East Windsor, NJ: McGraw-Hill.

Smith, R. (1988). *Sports and freedom: The rise of big-time college athletics.* New York: Oxford University Press.

Smith, R. (1994). *Big-time football at Harvard, 1905: The diary of coach Bill Reid.* Champaign, IL: University of Illinois Press.

Smith, R. (2001). *Play-by-play: Radio, television, and big-time college sport.* Baltimore: Johns Hopkins University Press.

Soares, W.G. (1979). *A history from 1820 to 1890 of two theories of physical training: The collegiate gymnastics movement and the rise of intercollegiate athletic teams at Amherst, Harvard, Princeton, and Yale.* Unpublished doctoral dissertation. New York: Teachers College, Columbia University.

Sperber, M. (1993). *Shake down the thunder: The creation of Notre Dame football.* New York: Henry Holt.

Staurowsky, E.J. (2011, December 1). Urban and me: We're almost twins . . . except for that six-year $26.6 million contract. *College Sports Business News.*

Staurowsky, E. J. (2012). A radical proposal: Title IX has no place in college sport pay-for-play discussions. *Marquette Sports Law Review 22* (2), 575–595.

Stevens, M. (2007). *Creating a class: College admissions and the education of elites.* Cambridge, MA: Harvard University Press.

Suggs, W. (2005). *A place on the team: The triumph and tragedy of Title IX.* Princeton, NJ: Princeton University Press.

Sweet, W. (2011, August 29). 150 years ago: Amherst established nation's first college health program. Amherst News. www.amherst.edu/aboutamherst/news/news_releases/2011/08/node/337711/.

Tucker, T. (2004). *Notre Dame vs. the Klan: How the Fighting Irish defeated the Ku Klux Klan.* Chicago: Loyola Press.

UPI (1973, January 13). Dramatic move by NCAA gives women 20 national title events. *Lodi News-Sentinel.* http://news.google.com/newspapers?nid=2245&dat=19810113&id=ReMzAAAAIBAJ&sjid=ajIHAAAAIBAJ&pg=6996,1427102.

Vecsey, G. (2011, November 8). The dangerous cocoon of King Football. *New York Times,* p. B16.

Watterson, J.S. (2000). *College football: History, spectacle, controversy.* Baltimore: Johns Hopkins University Press.

Whiton, J. (1901, June). The first intercollegiate regatta. *The Outlook, 18*(5), 286–289.

Wilson, W. (1909, November).What is a college for? *Scribner's,* 570–577. www.unz.org/Pub/Scribners-1909nov-00570.

Chapter 2

Big Ten Conference. (2013). www.bigten.org/genrel/071311aaa.html.

Coalition on Intercollegiate Athletics. (2013). http://blogs.comm.psu.edu/thecoia/.

Covey, S.R. (2004). *The 7 habits of highly effective people: Restoring the character ethic.* New York: Free Press.

Drake Group. www.thedrakegroup.org/.

Duderstadt, J. J. (2003). *Intercollegiate athletics and the American university: A university president's perspective.* Ann Arbor, MI: University of Michigan Press.

Elmore, T. (2010). *Habitudes: Images that form leadership habits and attitudes.* . Duluth, GA: Growing Leaders, Inc.

Faculty Athletics Representatives Association. (n.d.). Faculty athletics representative Minor, J.T., & Perry, L. (2010). Faculty involvement in athletic decision making: A review of three athletic major conferences. Academia.edu. www.academia.edu/1119307/Faculty_Involvement_in_Athletic_Decision_Making_A_Review_of_Three_Athletic_Major_Conferences.

Forde, P. (2010, June 13). Swarbrick focused on ND's interests. ESPN. http://sports.espn.go.com/ncf/columns/story?columnist=forde_pat&id=5267138.

Frankl, V.E. (1963). *Man's search for meaning.* New York: Washington Square Press.

Knight Commission on Intercollegiate Athletics. (2009). Quantitative and qualitative research with Football Bowl Subdivision university presidents on the costs and financing of intercollegiate athletics: Report of findings and implications. www.knightcommissionmedia.org/images/President_Survey_FINAL.pdf.

Maxwell, J.C. (2011). Leading a life of intentional influence. www.johnmaxwell.com/cms/images/uploads/ads/Leading_a_Life_of_Intentional_Influence.pdf.

National Association of Intercollegiate Athletics. (2013). About the NAIA. www.naia.org.

National Christian College Athletic Association. (2013). About us. www.thenccaa.org/sports/2012/6/20/GEN_0620123640.aspx.

National Junior College Athletic Association. (2013). Today's NJCAA. www.njcaa.org.

National Collegiate Athletics Association. (2013). NCAA 2013-2014 Division I Manual. www.ncaapublications.com.

National Collegiate Athletics Association. (2011). NCAA Revenues and Expenses Report. www.ncaapublications.com.

National Collegiate Athletics Association. (2009). NCAA 2008-2009 Membership Report. www.ncaapublications.com.

National Collegiate Athletics Association Core Purpose and Values (2014). www.ncaa.org/about/ncaa-core-purpose-and-values.

National Collegiate Athletics Association Finances. (2014). www.ncaa.org/about/resources/finances.

O'Neil, D. (2012, May 11). The trickle-down effect of realignment. ESPN. http://espn.go.com/mens-college-basketball/story/_/id/7916050/a-look-realiignment-perspective-smaller-basketball-conferences-college-basketball.

Peter, J. (2007, January 5). Playoff plunderer. Yahoo! Sports. http://rivals.yahoo.com/ncaa/football/news?slug=jo-delany010507.

Schlabach, M. (2011, July 12). NCAA: Where does the money go? ESPN. http://espn.go.com/college-sports/story/_/id/6756472/following-ncaa-money.

Smith, C. (2012, March 14). March Madness: A trip to the Final Four is worth $9.5 million. Forbes. www.forbes.com/sites/chrissmith/2012/03/14/march-madness-a-trip-to-the-final-four-is-worth-9-5-million.

Stancill, J. (2013, April 18). Holden Thorp says athletics 'can overwhelm' chancellor. Raleigh News and Observer. www.newsobserver.com/2013/04/18/2834890/holden-thorp-says-athletics-can.html.

United States Collegiate Athletic Association. (2013). www.theuscaa.com.

Weight, E., Weight, M., Schneider, R. (2013). Confronting the arms race: Conference commissioner perspectives on spending within intercollegiate athletics. The International Journal of Sport Management. 14(4), 1–21.

Chapter 3

Abreu, A., Macedo, P., & Camarinha-Matos, L.M. (2009). Elements of a methodology to assess the alignment of core-values in collaborative networks. International Journal of Production Research, 47(17), 4709–4934.

Ammons, D., & Glass, J. (1988, May). Headhunters in local government: Use of executive search firms in managerial selections. Public Administration Review, 48(3), 687–693.

Bass, B. M. (1985). Leadership and performance beyond expectations. New York: The Free Press.

Bennis, W.G. (1984). Good managers and good leaders. Across the Board, 21(10), 7–11.

Berings, D., De Fruyt, F., & Bouwen, R. (2004). Work values and personality traits as predictors of enterprising and social vocational interests. Personality and Individual Differences, 36, 349–364.

Berkowitz, S., & Upton, J. (2011, October 6). Demands on college ADs resemble CEO challenges. USA Today. www.usatoday.com/sports/college/story/2011-10-18/athletic-director-salaries-cover/50671214/1.

Berry, L.L. (1999). Discovering the soul of service: The nine drivers of sustainable business success. New York: Harper Business.

Bjorn, T. http://twitter.com/thorrbjorn.

Bolon, D.S. (2005). Comparing mission statement content in for-profit and not-for-profit hospitals: Does mission really matter? Hospital Topics, 83, 2–9.

Bradshaw, B. (2011, October). [Web blog message]. From the AD's desk: A column from Temple University director of athletics Bill Bradshaw. Owlsports.com. www.owlsports.com/sports/2011/10/26/GEN_1026110048.aspx.

Branch, T. (October, 2011). The shame of college sports. The Atlantic. www.theatlantic.com/magazine/archive/2011/10/the-shame-of-college-sports/308643/.

Brandon, D. (2014, June 28). [Web blog message]. Brandon's blog: Preparing Student-Athletes for More Than the NBA. MGoBlue.com. www.mgoblue.com/brandon/.

Brown, W.A., & Yoshioka, C.F. (2003). Mission attachment and satisfaction as factors in employee retention. Nonprofit Management Leadership, 14, 5–18.

Burns, J. M. (1978). Leadership. New York: Harper and Row.

Byrne, G. [@Greg_Byrne]. (2014, June 28). Flying back to Tucson from Chicago. One hour left...anyone have any @AZATHLETICS questions to ask? Mention @Greg_Byrne [Tweet]. https://twitter.com/Greg_Byrne.

Byrne, G. [@Greg_Byrne]. (2011, Nov 22). And the new Arizona football coach and his family is . . .PICTURE. http://campl.us/gRvK [Tweet]. https://twitter.com/Greg_Byrne.

Castiglione, J. [@soonerad]. (2014, June 25). Thanks to so many #Sooners who have & will continue to support our student-athletes as they strive for greatness! #Boomer [Tweet]. https://twitter.com/soonerad.

Castiglione, J. [@soonerad]. (2014, May 20). Very proud of the fight in our @OU_MTennis team. Fell a little short tonight but played like champions. Gr8 yrs ahead #lessons4futuresuccess [Tweet]. https://twitter.com/soonerad.

Collins, D. (2009, July 5). Big man on campus: Ron Wellman refuses to let the size of the school inhibit the size of its dreams. Winston-Salem Journal. www2.journalnow.com/sports/2009/jul/05/campus-ron-wellman-refuses-to-let-the-size-of-the--ar-156459/.

Collins, J. (2001). Good to great: Why some companies make the leap . . . and others don't. New York: Harper Business.

Collins, J.C., & Porras, J.I. (1994). Built to last: Successful habits of visionary companies. London: Random House.

Conger, J. A., & Kanungo, R. N. (1987). Toward a behavioral theory of charismatic leadership in organizational settings. Academy of Management Review, 12, 637–647.

Cooper, C.G., & Weight, E.A. (nd). Division I, II, & III administrator values. Unpublished manuscript.

Cooper, C.G., & Weight, E.A. (2012). Maximizing organizational effectiveness: NCAA Division III administrator core values and departmental culturization. *Journal of Issues in Intercollegiate Athletics*. 5, 339–353.

Cooper, C.G., Weight, E.A., & Pierce, D. (2014). The leader–value continuum: NCAA Division I core values and transformational leadership. *The International Journal of Sport Management*. 15(2) 151–171.

Covey, S.R. (1989). *The 7 habits of highly effective people*. New York: Simon & Schuster.

Currie, J. http://twitter.com/John_Currie.

Deford, F. (2011, September 14). The NCAA and the so-called student-athlete. National Public Radio. www.npr.org/2011/09/14/140433661/the-ncaa-and-the-so-called-student-athlete.

Earnest, G.W., & Cugliari, C.W. (2009). Making meetings manageable. Ohio State Leadership Center. http://ohioline.osu.edu/lc-fact/0001.html.

Easterbrook, G. (2010, December 7). Why are athletic departments so big? ESPN. http://sports.espn.go.com/espn/page2/story?page=easterbrook/101207_tuesday_morning_quarterback&sportCat=nfl.

Earley, P.C., & Mosakowski, E. (2000). Creating hybrid team cultures: An empirical test of transnational team functioning. *Academy of Management Journal*, 43, 26-49.

Ely, R. J., & Thomas, D. A. (2001). Cultural diversity at work: The effects of diversity perspectives on work group processes and outcomes. *Administrative Science Quarterly*, 46, 229–273.

Ferguson, J., & Milliman, J. (2008). Creating effective core organizational values: A spiritual leadership approach. *International Journal of Public Administration, 31*, 439–459.

Frenette, G. (2010, December 11). Florida AD Jeremy Foley makes gutsy call by hiring Will Muschamp. *Florida Times-Union*. http://jacksonville.com/opinion/blog/400617/gene-frenette/2010-12-11/gene-frenette-florida-ad-jeremy-foley-makes-gutsy-call.

Gatorzone.com. (2011). Athletics director Jeremy Foley. www.gatorzone.com/foley/.

Gordon, J. (2009, July 27). Get the right people on the bus. Jon Gordon blog. www.jongordon.com/blog/2009/07/27/get-the-right-people-on-the-bus-2/.

"Graduation Rates" (2014). The National Collegiate Athletics Association. www.ncaa.org/about/resources/research/graduation-rates.

Graeff, C. L. (1983). The Situational Leadership Theory: A Critical View. *Academy of Management Review, 8*, 285–291.

Harmon, F.G. (1996). *Playing for keeps*. New York: Wiley.

House, R. J. (1971). A Path-Goal Theory of Leader Effectiveness. *Administrative Science Quarterly, 16*, 321–339.

Ind, N. (2007). *Living the brand* (3rd ed.). London, UK: Kogan Page.

Kotter, J.P. (1996). *Leading change*. Boston: Harvard Business School.

Lencioni, P.M. (2002, July). Make your values mean something. *Harvard Business Review*, 113–117.

Lencioni, P. (2006). *Silos, politics, and turf wars: A leadership fable about destroying the barriers that turn colleagues into competitors*. San Francisco, CA: Jossey-Bass.

Maxwell, J. (2005). *Developing the leader within you* (Rev. ed.). Nashville: Thomas Nelson.

McCoy, K. (2010, February 22). Domino's CEO David Brandon returns to his alma mater. *USA Today*. www.usatoday.com/money/companies/management/profile/2010-02-22-brandon22_CV_N.htm.

Meyer, J.D. (2008). *Scoring points online: College athletics departments' brand positioning through communications on the World Wide Web*. Unpublished master's thesis, University of North Carolina at Chapel Hill.

Milliman, J., & Clair, J. (1995). Environmental HRM best practices in the USA: A review of the literature. *Greener Management International, 10*, 34–48.

Mondello, M. (1997, February). Meet Jeremy Foley: Athletic director, University of Florida. *Coach and Athletic Director*. www.thefreelibrary.com/Meet+Jeremy+-Foley%3A+Athletic+Director,+University+of+Florida.-a019266603.

National Collegiate Athletics Association (2013). NCAA 2013-2014 Division I Manual. www.ncaapublications.com

National Collegiate Athletics Association Strategic Plan. (2004, April). Indianapolis, IN.

Newell, K. (2008, February 1). The best in the business: University of Florida athletic director Jeremy Foley. *Coach and Athletic Director*. www.highbeam.com/doc/1G1-175526847.html.

Ouchi, W.G. (1979). A conceptual framework for the design of organizational control mechanisms. *Management Science, 25*, 933–948.

Pattakos, A.N. (2004). The search for meaning in government service. *Public Administration Review, 64*(1), 106–112.

Ridpath, D., Yiamouyiannis, A., Lawrence, H., & Galles, K. (2008, December). Changing sides: The failure of the wrestling community's challenges to Title IX and new strategies for saving NCAA sport teams. *Journal of Intercollegiate Sport, 1*(2), 255–283.

Roby, P. (2012). *Values-driven leadership in the 21st century*. Presentation given at the 2012 NCAA Convention, Indianapolis, IN.

Schein, E.H. (2010). *Organizational culture and leadership*. San Francisco: Jossey-Bass.

SECSports.com. (2006, June 19). Street and Smith's names UF's Foley national AD of the year. www.secdigitalnetwork.com/NEWS/tabid/473/Article/126411/street-and-smiths-names-ufs-foley-national-ad-of-the-year.aspx.

Simon, H.A. (1977). *The new science of managerial decision making*. Englewood Cliffs, NJ: Prentice Hall.

Smith, M. (2011, December 5). Help with high-stakes hires: Colleges turn to search firms to find coaching, AD candidates.

Street & Smith's SportsBusiness Journal. www.sports-businessdaily.com/Journal/Issues/2011/12/05/In-Depth/Lead.aspx.

Splitt, F.G. (2011, March 8). "Academically adrift" in a sea of sports. *Chronicle of Higher Education.* http://chronicle.com/article/article-content/126643.

Sull, D. (2010, March). Are you ready to rebound? *Harvard Business Review,* 71–74.

Sull, D.N., & Spinosa, C. (2007). Promise-based management. *Harvard Business Review, 85,* 79–86.

Swann, W. B., Jr., Kwan, V. S. Y., Polzer, J. T., & Milton, L. P. (2003). Fostering group identification and creativity in diverse groups: The role of individuation and self-verification.

Personality and Social Psychology Bulletin, 29, 1396–1406.

The Happy Manager. (2012). *Rational decision making model.* www.the-happy-manager.com/rational-decision-making-model.html.

Tichy, N., & Charan, R. (1989, September–October). Speed, simplicity, and self-confidence. *Harvard Business Review,* 171–222.

Van Rekom, J., Van Riel, C.B., Wierenga, B. (2006). A methodology for assessing organizational core values. *Journal of Management Studies, 43*(2), 175–201.

Vedder, R. (2011, August 29). Intercollegiate sports: Have they no shame? *Chronicle of Higher Education.* http://chronicle.com/blogs/innovations/intercollegiate-sports-have-they-noshame/30217?sid=pm&utm_source=pm&utm_medium=en.

Vroom, V. H., & Yetton, P. W. (1973). *Leadership and Decision Making.* Pittsburgh, PA: University of Pittsburgh Press.

Ward, Jr., R.E., & Hux, R.K. (2011). Intercollegiate athletic purposes expressed in mission statements: A content analysis. *Journal for the Study of Sports and Athletes in Education, 5,* 177–200.

Welch, J., & Welch, S. (2005). *Winning.* New York: Harper Collins.

Yiamouyiannis, A., & Lawrence, H.J. (2009, May 29). *Sport opportunities in intercollegiate athletics: Using ethical theory and structured models to assist in responsible decision making.* Presentation for the North American Society for Sport Management Conference, Columbia, SC.

Yukl, G. (1989). Managerial leadership: a review of theory and research. *Journal of Management, 15*(2), 251–289.

Chapter 4

Acosta, V. & Carpenter, L.J. (2014). Women in intercollegiate sport. A longitudinal, national study, thirty seven year update. 1977–2014. Unpublished manuscript. www.acostacarpenter.org.

Barnhart, T. (2011, July 18). ADs, consider this a warning: NCAA isn't playing nice anymore. CBSSports.com. www.cbssports.com/collegefootball/story/15330179/ads-consider-this-a-warning-ncaa-isnt-playing-nice-anymore.

Brown, G. (2010, September 14). NC State AD Debbie Yow has a simple philosophy on sports sponsorship. NCAA.org. www.allstudentathletes.com/Blogs/DebbieYowNCSU.

Carpenter, L.J., & Acosta, V. (2005). *Title IX.* Champaign, IL: Human Kinetics.

Carroll, Lewis. *Alice's Adventures in Wonderland,* New York:MacMillan. (1865)

Collins, J.C., & Porras, J.I. (1994). *Built to last: Successful habits of visionary companies.* London: Random House.

Cook, S.G. (2010, December). Most college coaches don't understand Title IX. *Women in Higher Education, 19*(12), 31.

Covey, S.R. (2004). *The 7 habits of highly effective people.* New York: Simon & Schuster.

DeJulio, M., Grant, C., Judge, J., Morrison, K., O'Brien, T., & Sweet, J. (2008). Teaching Title IX facilitator's guide. The NCAA Title IX Resource Center. www.ncaa.org/gender_equity.

Drucker, P. (1967). *The effective executive.* New York: Harper & Row.

Feldman, B. (2007). *Meat market: Inside the smash-mouth world of college football recruiting.* New York: ESPN Books.

Hemminger, A., & Bensch, D. (2007). *Destination basketball: A once in a lifetime adventure to meet the best coaches in college hoops.* Oak Harbor, OH: Oak Town United.

Hosick, M.B. (2013, January 19). *Division I streamlines rulebook.* www.ncaa.org/about/resources/media-center/news/division-i-streamlines-rulebook.

Infante, J. (2011, July 10). Ohio State, Oregon, and West Virginia plotting the future of compliance. NCAA Bylaw Blog.

Kotter, J.P. (1996). *Leading change.* Boston: Harvard Business School.

Ludlow, R. (2011, June 23). Trustees may change how Ohio State oversees athletics. *The Columbus Dispatch.* www.dispatch.com/content/stories/local/2011/06/23/ohio-state-trustees-athletics.html.

McKee, S. (2004, March 25). Sweat, "soffies," and scholarships. *Baltimore Sun.* http://articles.baltimoresun.com/2004-03-25/sports/0403250083_1_competitive-cheerleading-title-ix-university-of-maryland.

National Collegiate Athletic Association. (2014). Gender equity. www.ncaa.org/about/resources/inclusion/gender-equity.

National Collegiate Athletic Association . (2013a). *2013–2014 NCAA Division I manual.* Indianapolis, IN.

National Collegiate Athletic Association. (2013b). *2013-14 Guide for the college-bound student-athlete.* Indianapolis, IN.

National Collegiate Athletic Association. (2011b). *2011–2012 Division I practice exam.* http://web1.ncaa.org/coachesTest/exec/practiceexam?division=1.

NCAA Education Services. (2003). *SWA: How to strengthen your athletics management team.* Indianapolis, IN.

NCAA Rules Enforcement: For the Good of the Game (2014). The National Collegiate Athletics Association. www.ncaa.org/about/resources/media-center/ncaa-rules-enforcement-good-game.

Peeler, T. (n.d.). Bio: Deborah Yow. Wolfpack athletics. www.gopack.com/genrel/yow_deboraha.01.html.

Rhoden, W.C. (2009, April 11). University compliance officers: Good cop, bad cop. *New York Times*, p. D2.

Samuels, J. (n.d.). Current Title IX policies are essential to implement Title IX's guarantee of equal opportunity. North Carolina Public Schools. www.ncpublicschools.org/federalprograms/titleIX/resources/brief?&print=true.

Staurowsky, E., & Weight, E.A. (2011). Title IX literacy: What coaches don't know and need to find out. *Journal of Intercollegiate Sport*, 4(2), 190–209.

Staurowsky, E.J., Weight, E.A. (2013). Discovering Dysfunction in Title IX Implementation – NCAA administrator literacy, responsibility, and fear. *The Journal of Applied Sport Management*. 5(1), 1–33.

The National Coalition for Women and Girls in Education. (2008). *Title IX at 35: Beyond the headlines*. www.ncwge.org/PDF/TitleIXat35.pdf.

Tiell, B., & Dixon, M.A. (2008). Roles and tasks of the senior woman administrator (SWA) in intercollegiate athletics. *Journal for the Study of Sports and Athletes in Education*, 2(3), 339–361.

Title IX of the Education Amendments of 1972, 20 U.S.C. Sections 1681–1688.

U.S. Department of Education, Office for Civil Rights. (1996, January 16). *Clarification of intercollegiate athletics policy guidance: The three-part test*. www.ed.gov/about/offices/list/ocr/docs/clarific.html.

U.S. Department of Education, Office for Civil Rights. (2005, March 17). *Additional clarification of intercollegiate athletics policy: Three-part test—part three*.

U.S. Department of Education, Office for Civil Rights. (2010, April 20). *Dear Colleague*. www2.ed.gov/about/offices/list/ocr/letters/colleague-20100420.pdf.

U.S. Department of Health, Education, and Welfare, Office for Civil Rights. (1979, December 11). *A Policy Interpretation: Title IX and Intercollegiate Athletics*. Federal Register, Vol. 44, No. 239. Rules and Regulations.

Weight, E.A., Staurowsky, E.J. (2014). Title IX literacy among NCAA administrators and coaches: A critical communications approach. *The International Journal of Sport Management*. 15(3) 1–29.

Women's Sports Foundation (2014). Title IX Legislative Chronology. https://www.womenssportsfoundation.org/en/sitecore/content/home/advocate/title-ix-and-issues/history-of-title-ix/history-of-title-ix.aspx.

Chapter 5

"About SAAC" (2014). The National Collegiate Athletics Association. www.ncaa.org/student-athletes/about-saac.

Adler, P., & Adler, P. (1987). Role conflict and identity salience: College athletics and the academic role. *Social Science Journal*, 24(2), 443–450.

Baille, P.H.F., & Danish, S.J. (1992). Understanding the career transition of athletes. *Sport Psychologist, 6*, 77–98.

Beland, J. (2004, September). NCAA board approves athletic reforms. *Academe, 90*, 13.

Bilas, J. (2012, March 14). Players should be compensated. *New York Times*. www.nytimes.com/roomfordebate/2012/03/13/ncaa-and-the-interests-of-student-athletes/college-athletes-should-be-compensated.

Branch, T. (2011). The shame of college sports. *The Atlantic*. www.theatlantic.com/magazine/archive/2011/10/the-shame-of-college-sports/8643/.

Case, B., Greer, S., & Brown, J. (1987). Academic clustering in athletics: Myth or reality? *Arena Review, 11*(2), 48–56.

Castle, J., & Myers, L. (2012, April 19). *Football academic advisors' perceptions of the "9 credit rule."* Presentation for the College Sport Research Institute, Chapel Hill, NC.

Chartrand, J.M., & Lent, R.W. (1987). Sports counseling: Enhancing the development of the student-athlete. *Journal of Counseling and Development, 66*(4), 164–167.

Covey, S.R. (1989). *The 7 habits of highly effective people.* New York: Simon & Schuster.

Covey, S.R. (2004). *The 7 habits of highly effective people.* New York: Simon & Schuster.

Danish, S.J., Petitpas, A.J., & Hale, B.D. (1993). Life development intervention for athletes: Life skills through sports. *Counseling Psychologist, 21*(3), 352–385.

Fountain, J.J., & Finley, P.S. (2009). Academic majors of upperclassmen football players in the Atlantic Coast Conference: An analysis of academic clustering comparing white and minority players. *Journal of Issues in Intercollegiate Athletics, 2*, 1–13.

Fountain, J.J., & Finley, P.S. (2011). Academic clustering: A longitudinal analysis of Division I football programs. *Journal of Issues in Intercollegiate Athletics, 4*, 24–41.

Gaines, C. (2013, February 7). Some schools are spending an incredible amount of money wooing high school football players. *Business Insider*. www.businessinsider.com/some-schools-are-spending-an-incredible-amount-of-money-wooing-high-school-football-players-2013-2?nr_email_referer=1&utm_source=Triggermail&utm_medium=email&utm_term=Sports%20Page%20Chart%20Of%20The%20Day&utm_campaign=Sportspage_COTD_020713.

Goleman, D. (1995). *Emotional intelligence: Why it can matter more than IQ.* New York: Bantum Books.

GoHeels.com. (2013). Richard A. Baddour Carolina Leadership Academy: Student-athlete leadership development. www.goheels.com/ViewArticle.dbml?DB_OEM_ID=3350&ATCLID=205498281.

Grasgreen, A. (2012, May 9). Tough choices for athletes' advisers. *Inside Higher Ed*. www.insidehighered.com/news/2012/05/09/ncaa-academic-rules-frustrate-advisers-athletes.

Gurney, G., & Southall, R.M. (2013, February 14). NCAA reform gone wrong. *Inside Higher Ed*. www.insidehighered.com/views/2013/02/14/ncaa-academic-reform-has-hurt-higher-eds-integrity-essay.

Hosick, M.B. (2011, February 2). History of the national letter of intent. NCAA. www.ncaa.com/news/ncaa/2011-02-02/history-national-letter-intent.

Huma, R., & Staurowsky, E.J. (2011). *The price of poverty in big time college sport.* Riverside, CA: National College Players Association.

Infante, J. (2012, August 27). Why it's time to get rid of unofficial visits. Athleticscholarships.net. www.athletic-scholarships.net/2012/08/27/why-time-get-rid-unofficial-visits.htm.

Lopiano, D. (2008). Key elements and best practices in the development of academic support programs. Sports Management Resources. www.sportsmanagementresources.com/library/key-elements-academic-support-programs.

National Association of Academic Advisors for Athletics. (2013). www.nfoura.org/.

National Association of Intercollegiate Athletics. (2013). NAIA eligibility. www.playnaia.org/page/eligibility.php.

National Collegiate Athletic Association. (2008). CHAMPS/Life Skills Program [Brochure]. Indianapolis, IN.

National Collegiate Athletics Association. (2013). NCAA 2013-2014 Division I Manual. www.ncaapublications.com

National Collegiate Athletics Association. (2014a). NCAA core purpose. www.ncaa.org/about/ncaa-core-purpose-and-values.

National Collegiate Athletic Association. (2014b). Remaining eligible: Amateurism. NCAA. www.ncaa.org/amateurism.

National Letter of Intent. (2013). www.nationalletter.org.

Nocera, J. (2013, January 25). The NCAA's ethics problem. *New York Times.* www.nytimes.com/2013/01/26/opinion/nocera-the-ncaas-ethics-problem.html?ref=joenocera&_r=0.

Olson, M. (2012, August 18). Unofficials mean—and cost—more than ever. ESPN. http://espn.go.com/college-sports/football/recruiting/notebook/_/page/unofficialvisits.

Parham, W.D. (1993). The intercollegiate athlete: A 1990s profile. *Counseling Psychologist,* 21(3), 411–429.

Renick, J. (1974). The use and misuse of college athletics. *Journal of Higher Education,* 45(7), 545–552.

Richards, C. (2011, November 10). Leadership forum fosters student-athlete development. *NCAA News.*

Sack, A.L., & Staurowsky, E.J. (1998). *College athletes for hire: The evolution and legacy of the NCAA's amateur myth.* Praeger: Westport, CT.

Savickas, M.L. (2005). The theory and practice of career construction. In S.D. Brown & R.W. Lent (Eds.), *Career development and counseling: Putting theory and research to work* (pp. 42–70). Hoboken, NJ: Wiley.

Steeg, J.L., Upton, J., Bohn, P., & Berkowitz, S. (2008, November 18). College athletes studies guided toward "major in eligibility." *USA Today.* http://usatoday30.usatoday.com/sports/college/2008-11-18-majors-cover_N.htm.

Thamel, P. (2011, October 2). Unofficial visits draw concern, not scrutiny. *New York Times,* p. D2.

Thaler, L.K., Koval, R. (2001). *The power of nice: How to conquer the business world with kindness.* New York: Random House.

The University of North Carolina at Chapel Hill Office of Faculty Governance. (2014). Committee on special talent. http://faccoun.unc.edu/committees-2/appointed-committees/undergraduate-admissions-committee/committee-on-special-talent/.

University of Washington. (2009, February 19). *Report to the Advisory Committee on Intercollegiate Athletics: Survey of SAAS reporting structures.* www.washington.edu/faculty/facsen/acia/saas_reporting_structure.pdf.

Whitlock, J. (2012, August 7). Admit amateurism is a sham. *New York Times.* www.nytimes.com/roomfordebate/2012/03/13/ncaa-and-the-interests-of-student-athletes/admit-amateurism-is-a-sham-2.

Winters, C.A., & Gurney, G.S. (2013). Academic preparation of specially-admitted student-athletes: A question of basic skills. *College and University,* 88(2), 2–9.

Zimbalist, A. (1999). *Unpaid professionals: Commercialization and conflict in big-time college sports.* Princeton, NJ: Princeton University Press.

Zola, W.K. (2013, February 13). The illusion of amateurism in college athletics. *Huffington Post.* www.huffingtonpost.com/warren-k-zola/college-athletes-pay-to-play_b_2663003.html.

Chapter 6

Adkison, J.M., associate athletics director, Embry-Riddle University. (2012). Interview by R. Zullo.

Anderson, T., assistant athletics director, media relations, University of North Carolina Pembroke. (2012). Interview by R. Zullo.

Andrews, P. (2005). *Sports journalism: A practical introduction.* Thousand Oaks, CA: Sage.

Associated Press. (2003, April 29). Pictures show Larry Eustachy at party. KCCI News. www.kcci.com/Pictures-Show-Larry-Eustachy-At-Party/-/9357770/7327770/-/rjwafuz/-/index.html.

Associated Press. (2006, May 26). Court upholds firing of Arkansas coach Nolan Richardson. *USA Today.* www.usatoday.com/sports/college/mensbasketball/sec/2006-05-26-arkansas-richardson-appeal_x.htm.

Associated Press. (2007, April 18). Hogs' Nutt addresses text scandal. *Lubbock Avalanche-Journal.* http://lubbockonline.com/stories/041807/col_041807011.shtml.

Ballouli, K., & Hutchinson, M. (2010). Digital-branding and social-media strategies for professional athletes, sports teams, and leagues: An interview with Digital Royalty's Amy Martin. *International Journal of Sport Communication,* 3, 395–401.

Barrow, L., associate sport communication director, University of Georgia. (2012). Interview by R. Zullo.

Battenfield, F.L., & Kent, A. (2007). The culture of communication among intercollegiate sport information professionals. *International Journal of Sport Management and Marketing,* 2(3), 236–251.

Benko, J., athletics business manager, University of Arkansas. (2012). Interview by R. Zullo.

Blaine, J., former assistant director, media relations, Mississippi State University Athletics. (2012). Interview by R. Zullo.

Bratton, T., director of baseball operations, Mississippi State University. (2012). Interview by R. Zullo.

Braun, A., executive senior associate director of athletics, Northeastern University. (2012). Interview by R. Zullo.

Bruno, R., & Whitlock, K. (2000). Nothin' but net. In M. Helitzer (Ed.), *The dream job: $port$ publicity, promotion and marketing* (3rd ed., pp. 429–441). Athens, OH: University Sports Press.

Butler, B., & Sagas, M. (2008). Making room in the lineup: Newspaper web sites face growing competition for sports fans' attention. *International Journal of Sport Communication, 1,* 17–25.

Carpenter, L.J., & Acosta, R.V. (2010). Women in intercollegiate sport: A longitudinal study—Thirty-three-year update. A report from the Smith College Project on Women and Social Change and Brooklyn College of the City University of New York. http://webpages.charter.net/womeninsport/.

Clavio, G. (2008). Demographics and usage profiles of users of college sport message boards. *International Journal of Sport Communication, 1,* 434–443.

Cone, J. (2011). The Penn State scandal: Crisis as opportunity. http://businessofcollegesports.com/2011/12/07/the-penn-state-scandal-crisis-as-opportunity/.

Connaughton, D., Spengler, J.O., & Bennett, G. (2001). Crisis management for physical-activity programs. *Journal of Physical Education, Recreation & Dance, 72*(7), 27–29.

Cooper, C.G. (2008). NCAA website coverage: An analysis of similar sport team gender coverage on athletic department home web pages. *Journal of Intercollegiate Sport, 1,* 227–241.

Cooper, C.G., & Cooper, B.D. (2009). NCAA website coverage: Do athletic departments provide equitable gender coverage on their athletic home web pages? *The Sport Journal, 12*(2). http://thesportjournal.org/article/ncaa-website-coverage-do-athletic-departments-provide-equitable-gender-coverage-on-their-athletic-home-web-pages/.

Cooper, C.G., Eagleman, A., & Laucella, P.M. (2009). NCAA March Madness: An investigation of gender coverage in *USA Today* during the NCAA basketball tournament. *Journal of Intercollegiate Sport, 2,* 299–311.

Cooper, C.G., & Pierce, D. (2011). The role of divisional affiliation in athletic department web site coverage. *International Journal of Sport Communication, 4,* 70–81.

Covey, S. R. (2004). *The 7 habits of highly effective people.* New York, NY: Simon & Schuster.

Cunningham, G.B., Sagas, M., Sartore, M.L., Amsden, M.L., & Schellhase, A. (2004). Gender representation in the NCAA News: Is the glass half full or half empty? *Sex Roles, 50,* 861–870.

Cutlip, S.M., Center, A.H., & Broom, G.M. (2000). *Effective public relations* (8th ed.). Englewood Cliffs, NJ: Prentice Hall.

Earnheardt, A.C. (2010). Exploring sports television viewers' judgments of athletes' antisocial behaviors. *International Journal of Sport Communication, 3,* 167–189.

Fisher, E. (2011, September 19). Miami story reset bar for investigative work online, Fuch says. *SportsBusiness Journal.* www.sportsbusinessdaily.com/Journal/Issues/2011/09/19/Media/Fuchs.aspx.

Fisher, R. & Ury, W. (2011). *Getting to YES: Negotiationg agreement without giving in.* New York, NY: Penguin Books.

Fombrun, C., Gardberg, N., & Sever, J. (2000). The reputation quotient: A multi-stakeholder measure of corporate reputation. *Journal of Brand Management, 7*(4), 241–255.

Gale, D., director of sales, Old Dominion University Sports Properties at CBS Collegiate Sports Properties. (2012). Interview by R. Zullo.

Gregory, S. (2009, June 5). Twitter craze is rapidly changing the face of sports. *Sports Illustrated.* http://sportsillustrated.cnn.com/2009/writers/the_bonus/06/05/twitter.sports/index.html?eref=sihpT1.

Harrison, C.K., Lawrence, S.M., Plecha, M., Bukstein, S.J., & Janson, N.K. (2009). Stereotypes and stigmas in college athletes in Tank McNamara's cartoon script: Fact or fiction. *Journal of Issues in Intercollegiate Athletics* [Special issue], 1–18.

Helitzer, M. (2000). *The dream job: $port$ publicity, promotion and marketing* (3rd ed.). Athens, OH: University Sports Press.

Howard, C.M., & Mathews, W.K. (2000). *On deadline: Managing media relations.* Long Grove, IL: Waveland Press.

Hubbard, R., associate director of health and wellness, Louisiana State University Athletics. (2012). Interview by R. Zullo.

Jackowski, M. (2007). Conceptualizing an improved public relations strategy: A case for stakeholder relationship marketing in Division I-A intercollegiate athletics. *Journal of Business and Public Affairs, 1*(1). www.scientificjournals.org/journals2007/articles/1016.htm.

Johnston, B., associate sport communication director, Virginia Tech. (2012). Interview by R. Zullo.

Lewis, E., senior associate athletics director, University of North Florida. (2012). Interview by R. Zullo.

Lovings, M., assistant football coach, University of Louisiana at Lafayette. (2012). Interview by R. Zullo.

Mandel, S. (2010, July 19). NCAA turning up heat on agent-player relations with more probes. *Sports Illustrated.* http://sportsillustrated.cnn.com/2010/writers/stewart_mandel/07/19/ncaa.agents/index.html?eref=sihp.

Masteralexis, L.P., Barr, C.A., & Hums, M. (2008). *Principles and practice of sport management* (3rd ed.). Burlington, MA: Jones & Bartlett.

Mathews, W. (2004, May–June). What should I tell them? Why every organization should have an official policy for communicating. *Communication World, 21*(3), 46–60.

Menaker, B.E., & Connaughton, D.P. (2010). Stadium alcohol policies: A comparison of policies available on college athletic department web sites. *International Journal of Sport Communication, 3,* 151–162.

Miller, R., Parsons, K., & Lifer, D. (2010). Students and social networking sites: The posting paradox. *Behaviour & Information Technology, 29,* 377–382.

Montoro, M., director of football communications, West Virginia University. (2012). Interview by R. Zullo.

Mullin, B.J., Hardy, S., & Sutton, W.A. (2007). *Sport marketing* (3rd ed.). Champaign, IL: Human Kinetics.

Panella, A., publications director, Virginia Tech Athletics. (2012). Interview by R. Zullo.

Pegoraro, A. (2010). Look who's talking—Athletes on Twitter: A case study. *International Journal of Sport Communication, 3,* 501–514.

Phua, J.J. (2010). Sports fans and media use: Influence on sports fan identification and collective self-esteem. *International Journal of Sport Communication, 3,* 190–206.

Public Relations Society of America (PRSA). (2000). Tips and techniques: Crisis planning and management. *PPC Online.* www.prsa.org/ppc/68001.html.

Record, K., director of athletics, University of North Carolina at Greensboro. (2012). Interview by R. Zullo.

Reichart-Smith, L. (2011). The less you say: An initial study of gender coverage in sports on Twitter. In A. Billings (Ed.), *Sports media: Transformation, integration, consumption* (pp. 146–161). New York: Routledge.

Ries, A., & Ries, L. (2002). *The fall of advertising and the rise of PR.* New York: Harper Collins.

Ruihley, B.J., & Fall, L.T. (2009). Assessment on and off the field: Examining athletic directors' perceptions of public relations in college athletics. *International Journal of Sport Communication, 2,* 398–410.

Salas, D., director of Internet services and webmaster, Virginia Tech Athletics. (2012). Interview by R. Zullo.

Sanderson, J. (2009). Professional athletes' shrinking privacy boundaries: Fans, information and communication technologies, and athlete monitoring. *International Journal of Sport Communication, 2,* 240–256.

Sanderson, J. (2011). To tweet or not to tweet: Exploring Division I athletic departments' social-media policies. *International Journal of Sport Communication, 4,* 492–513.

Satter, D., senior associate director of athletics for external relations, Akron University. (2012). Interview by R. Zullo.

Schmidt, T., assistant sports information director, Jacksonville State University. (2012). Interview by R. Zullo.

Schultz, B. (2005). *Sports media: Reporting, producing and planning* (2nd ed.). Brentwood, TN: Focus Press.

Schultz, B., & Sheffer, M.L. (2010). An exploratory study of how Twitter is affecting sports journalism. *International Journal of Sport Communication, 3,* 226–239.

Seitel, F. (2010). *The practice of public relations* (11th ed.). Upper Saddle River, NJ: Prentice Hall.

Smith, C., former athletics director, Western Carolina University. (2012). Interview by R. Zullo.

Smith, R.D. (2002). *Strategic planning for public relations.* Mahwah, NJ: Erlbaum.

Staples, A. (2011, March 21). Harrellson emerged from doghouse to become UK's steadiest player. *Sports Illustrated.* http://sportsillustrated.cnn.com/2011/writers/andy_staples/03/19/Kentucky.west.virginia.harrellson.

Stoldt, G. (2000). Current and ideal roles of NCAA Division I-A sports information professionals. *Cyber-Journal of Sport Marketing, 4*(1). http://fulltext.ausport.gov.au/fulltext/2000/cjsm/v4n1/stoldt41.htm.

Stoldt, G.C. (2008). Interview with John Humenik, executive director of the College Sports Information Directors of America. *International Journal of Sport Communication, 9,* 458–464.

Stoldt, G.C., Dittmore, S., & Branvold, S. (2006). *Sport public relations: Managing organizational communication.* Champaign, IL: Human Kinetics.

Stoldt, G.C., Miller, L.K., Ayres, T., & Comfort, P.G. (2000). Crisis management planning: A necessity for sport managers. *International Journal of Sport Management, 1*(4), 253–266.

Stoldt, G.C., Miller, L.K., & Comfort, P.G. (2001). Through the eyes of athletic directors: Perceptions of sports information directors and other PR issues. *Sports Marketing Quarterly, 10*(3), 164–172.

Stoldt, G.C., & Narasimhan, V. (2005). Self-assessments of collegiate sports information professionals regarding their public relations task expertise. *International Journal of Sport Management, 6*(3), 252–269.

Syme, C. (2012, March 11). The state of crisis communications in college athletics [Survey]. http://cksyme.org/the-state-of-crisis-communications-in-college-athletics-survey.

Thamel, P. (2011, May 31). Buckeyes' trials with Tressel are test for NCAA. *New York Times.* www.nytimes.com/2011/05/31/sports/ncaafootball/buckeyes-trials-with-tressel-are-test-for-ncaa.html.

Thompson, J., head coach, men's tennis, Virginia Tech. (2012). Interview by R. Zullo.

Thompson, W. (1996). *Targeting the message: A receiver-centered process for public relations writing.* White Plains, NY: Longman.

Wallace, L., Wilson, J., & Miloch, K. (2011). Sporting Facebook: A content analysis of NCAA organizational sport pages and Big 12 Conference athletic department pages. *International Journal of Sport Communication, 4,* 422–444.

Whisenant, W.A., & Mullane, S.P. (2007). Sports information directors and homologous reproduction. *International Journal of Sport Management and Marketing, 2*(3), 252–263.

Whiteside, E., & Hardin, M. (2011). Negotiating differences, identity and the glass ceiling in sports information. *Journal of Intercollegiate Sport, 4*, 210–226.

Whiteside, E., & Hardin, M. (2012a). Consequences of being the "team mom." Women in sports info and the friendliness trap. *Journal of Sport Management, 26*(4), 309-321.

Whiteside, E., & Hardin, M. (2012b). On being a "good sport" in the workplace: Women, the glass ceiling, and negotiated resignation in sports information. *International Journal of Sport Communication, 5*, 51–68.

Wigley, S., & Meirick, P.C. (2008). Interactive media and sports journalists: The impact of interactive media on sports journalists. *Journal of Sports Media, 3*(1), 1–25.

Williams, J., & Chinn, S.J. (2010). Meeting relationship-marketing goals through social media: A conceptual model for sport marketers. *International Journal of Sport Communication, 3*, 422–437.

Yanity, M., & Edmondson, A.C. (2011). Ethics of online coverage of recruiting high school athletes. *International Journal of Sport Communication, 4*, 403–421.

Chapter 7

About the NCAA. (2012). National Collegiate Athletic Association. www.ncaa.org/about/who-we-are/membership.

Allstate. (2012, September 6). Allstate's "Good Hands" field goal net program rewards Trojans' field goals, extra points with scholarship donations. Allstate Digital Newsroom. www.allstatenewsroom.com/releases/allstate-s-good-hands-field-goal-net-program-rewards-trojans-field-goals-extra-points-with-scholarship-donations.

Armstrong, K. (2009, December 3). Hofstra eliminates 72-year-old program. *New York Times.* www.nytimes.com/2009/12/04/sports/ncaafootball/04hofstra.html?_r=0.

Bachman, R. (2012, April 20). Cal's football-stadium gamble. *Wall Street Journal.* http://online.wsj.com/news/articles/SB10001424052702304432704577350214257041598.

Bachman, R., & Futterman, M. (2012, December 9). College football's big-money, big-risk business model. *Wall Street Journal.* http://online.wsj.com/news/articles/SB10001424127887324024004578169472607407806.

Bennett, B. (2012, June 14). Arms race proves recession-proof. ESPN. http://espn.go.com/college-football/story/_/id/8047787/college-football-facilities-arms-race-proves-recession-proof.

Bergeron, P.G. (2002). *Finance: Essentials for the successful professional.* Mason, OH: Thompson Education.

Besley, S., & Brigham, E.F. (2006). *Principles of finance* (3rd ed.). Mason, OH: Thompson Education.

Bowen, H.R. (1970). Financial needs of the campus. In R.H. Connery (Ed.), *The corporation and the campus.* New York: Academy of Political Science.

Bowen, H.R. (1980). *The costs of higher education.* San Francisco: Jossey-Bass.Brown, M.T., Rascher, D.A., Nagel, M.S., & McEvoy, C.D. (2010). *Financial management in the sport industry.* Scottsdale, AZ: Holcomb Hathaway.

Brady, E., Upton, J., & Berkowitz, S. (2012, March 29). Even small schools pay big for hot NCAA coaches. *USA Today.* http://usatoday30.usatoday.com/sports/college/mens-basketball/story/2012-03-29/salaries-continue-rise-shaka-smart-vcu/53828414/1.

Bryce, H.J. (2000). *Financial & strategic management for nonprofit organizations: A comprehensive reference to legal, financial, management, and operations rules and guidelines for nonprofits.* San Francisco: Jossey-Bass.

Collins, J., & Porras, J. (2002). *Built to last: Successful habits of visionary companies.* New York: HarperBusiness.

Columbo, J.D. (2010). The NCAA, tax exemption, and college athletics. *University of Illinois Law Review, 2010*(1), 109–163.

Congressional Budget Office. (2009). *Tax preferences for collegiate sports.* United States Congress. www.cbo.gov/sites/default/files/cbofiles/ftpdocs/100xx/doc10055/05-19-collegiatesports.pdf.

Covey, S.R. (2004). *The 7 habits of highly effective people.* New York: Simon & Schuster.

Differences among the three divisions: Division I. (2012). National Collegiate Athletic Association. www.ncaa.org/about/who-we-are/membership/divisional-differences-and-history-multidivision-classification.

Distributions. (2013). National Collegiate Athletic Association. www.ncaa.org/about/resources/finances/distributions.

Dosh, K. (2011, April 4). The college athletics programs most reliant on student activity fees. *Forbes.* www.forbes.com/sites/sportsmoney/2011/04/24/the-college-athletics-programs-most-reliant-on-student-activity-fees/.

Dosh, K. (2012a, May 11). College TV rights undergo makeovers. ESPN. http://espn.go.com/blog/ncfnation/post/_/id/61236/college-tv-rights-deals-undergo-makeovers-2.

Dosh, K. (2012b, August 4). What kind of debt do athletic departments carry for facilities? The Business of College Sports. http://businessofcollegesports.com/2011/08/04/what-kind-of-debt-do-athletic-departments-carry-for-facilities/.

Expenses. (2013). National Collegiate Athletic Association. www.ncaa.org/about/resources/finances/expenses.

Fornelli, T. (2011, August 8). Longhorn Network contract emerges. CBSSports.com. www.cbssports.com/mcc/blogs/entry/24156338/31192274.

Fulks, D.L. (2012). *Revenues & expenses: 2004–2011 NCAA Division I intercollegiate athletic programs report.* Indianapolis: National Collegiate Athletic Association.

Gerstner, J.C. (2012, July 3). Seven sports are eliminated at Maryland. *New York Times.* http://thequad.blogs.nytimes.com/2012/07/03/seven-sports-are-eliminated-at-maryland/.

Green, A. (2013, January 26). Athletic department cuts over $150,000 from budget enrollment numbers thrash UM athletic departments' budget. *Montana Kaimin.* www.montanakaimin.com/news/article_17362212-67f1-11e2-a81e-001a4bcf6878.html.

Gregoire, C., & Kohl-Welles, J. (2012, June 22). Title IX: Undeniable progress for women (and men), but challenges remain. *Seattle Times*. http://seattletimes.com/html/opinion/2018504862_guest23gregoire.html.

Hagel, J. (2014). How to better connect planning, forecasting, and budgeting. *Journal of Accountancy*. www.journalofaccountancy.com/Issues/2014/ Apr/forecasting-budgeting-cgma-magazine-20149480.htm.

Internal Revenue Service. (2011). Life cycle of a public charity/private foundation. www.irs.gov/charities/charitable/article/0,,id=136459,00.html.

Jessop, A. (2011, October 26). Louisville concession data. The Business of College Sports. http://businessofcollegesports.com/2011/10/26/1006/.

Kerkoff, B. (2012, July 7). An inside look at athletic budget growth at KU, K-State, and MU. *Kansas City Star*. www.kansascity.com/2012/07/07/3695045/an-inside-look-at-athletic-budget.html.

Kotter, J.P. (1999). *John P. Kotter on what leaders really do.* Boston, MA: Harvard Business Review Press.

Krammer, A. (2012, April 10). Pay to play: U shelled out $645,000 for nonconference games in '11–12: Programs are paying more money to bring in smaller schools for nonconference games. *Minnesota Daily*. www.mndaily.com/2012/04/10/pay-play-u-shelled-out-645000-nonconference-games-%E2%80%9911-12.

Lencioni, P. (2000). *The four obsessions of an extraordinary executive: A leadership fable.* New York: Jossey-Bass.

Lorenzen, M. (2012, March 26). Who really pays to play? The role of student fees. The Business of College Sports. http://businessofcollegesports.com/2012/03/28/who-really-pays-to-play-the-role-of-student-fees/.

Martin, R.E. (2009). The revenue-to-cost spiral in higher education. The John W. Pope Center for Higher Education Policy. www.popecenter.org/acrobat/revenue-to-cost-spiral.pdf.

Mincer, J. (2012, July 19). U.S. recession's other victim: Public universities. Reuters. www.reuters.com/article/2012/07/19/us-funding-state-idUSBRE86I04V20120719.

NCAA consolidated financial statements. (2013). National Collegiate Athletic Association. www.ncaa.org/sites/default/files/NCAA_FS_2012-13_V1%20DOC1006715.pdf.

Ourand, J., & Smith, M. (2012, November 9). ESPN homes in on 12-year BCS package. *SportsBusiness Journal*. www.sportsbusinessdaily.com/Special-Content/News/2012/BCS-ESPN.aspx.

Pac 12 2012–2013 handbook. (2012). Pac 12. http://compliance.pac-12.org/thetools/1314hbv1.pdf.

Peterson, K. (2009, July 15). College athletes stuck with the bill after injuries. *New York Times*. www.nytimes.com/2009/07/16/sports/16athletes.html?pagewanted=all&_r=0.

Reider, R. (2001). *Improving the economy, efficiency, and effectiveness of not-for-profits: Conducting operational reviews.* New York: Wiley.

Revenues. (2014). National Collegiate Athletic Association. www.ncaa.org/about/resources/finances/revenue.

Schnaars, C., Upton, J., Mosemak, J., & DeRamus, K. (2012). USA Today Sports' college athletics finances. *USA Today.* http://usatoday30.usatoday.com/sports/ college/story/2012-05-14/ncaa-college-athletics-finances-database/54955804/1.

Segal, G., & Summers, A. (2002, March 1). Citizen's budget reports: Improving performance and accountability in government. *Reason Foundation*. http://reason.org/news/show/citizens-budget-reports#sthash.hwS2uQ22.dpuf.

Smith, C. (2012, September 19). ACC's new exit fee: Punitive or par for the course? *Forbes*. www.forbes.com/sites/chrissmith/2012/09/19/accs-new-exit-fee-punitive-or-par-for-the-course/.

Smith, M. (2012, December 3). Master planners. *Sport Business Journal, 15*(33), 30.

Steinbach, P. (2012, July). Athletics development success hinges on broadening the donor base. *Athletic Business*. www.athleticbusiness.com/Fundraising/athletics-development-success-hinges-on-broadening-the-donor-base.html.

Suggs, W. (2009). Making money—or not—on college sports. *New Directions for Institutional Research, 144*, 19–31.

Texas' $150 million revenue the largest in college athletics. (2012, May 15). *Sporting News*. http://aol.sportingnews.com/ncaa-football/story/2012-05-15/texas-150-million-revenue-the-largest-in-college-athletics.

Thamel, P. (2011, September 19). With big paydays at stake, college teams scramble for a spot. *New York Times*. www.nytimes.com/2011/09/20/sports/ncaafootball/in-conference-realignment-colleges-run-to-paydaylight.html?pagewanted=all&_r=0.

USA Today Sports' college athletics finances. (2012). *USA Today.* http://usatoday30.usatoday.com/sports/college/story/2012-05-14/ncaa-college-athletics-finances-database/54955804/1.

U.S. Department of Education. (2012). Equity in Athletics Disclosure Act. www2.ed.gov/finaid/prof/resources/athletics/eada.html.

Vosgerchian, J. (2007, July 15). Adidas just did it. *Michigan Daily*. www.michigandaily.com/content/adidas-just-did-it.

Wetzel, D. (2012, April 24). Bowls' extravagant revenues are closely examined as the NCAA mulls a playoff system. *Yahoo! Sports*. http://sports.yahoo.com/news/ncaaf--bowls--extravagant-revenues-are-closely-examined-as-the-ncaa-mulls-a-playoff-system.html.

Chapter 8

Arno, C. (2012). Worldwide social media usage trends in 2012. Search Engine Watch. http://searchenginewatch.com/article/2167518/Worldwide-Social-Media-Usage-Trends-in-2012.

Bennett, B. (2012). Arms race proves recession-proof. ESPN. http://espn.go.com/college-football/story/_/id/8047787/college-football-facilities-arms-race-proves-recession-proof.

Bitter, A. (2012). Russell Athletic Bowl ticket sales sluggish at Virginia Tech, plus some other odds and ends. *HamptonRoads.com.* http://hamptonroads.com/2012/12/russell-athletic-bowl-ticket-sales-sluggish-virginia-tech-plus-some-other-odds-and-ends.

Broughton, D. (2012, November 12). Everybody loves bobbleheads. *Street & Smith's SportsBusiness Journal*, p. 9.

Burgess, C. (2012). The expert series: Guide to the secondary ticketing market. SeatGeek. http://tba.seatgeek.com/articles/secondary-ticket-market-and-resellers.

CBS Sports. (2012, March 28). CBSSports.com College Network. http://collegenetwork.cbssports.com/genre-l/032812aaa.html.

College athletics: Renovation, new construction remain on the rise. (2007, December 3). *Street & Smith's SportsBusiness Journal*, pp. 51–61.

Collegiate Licensing Company. (2014). About CLC. www.clc.com/About-CLC.aspx.

Community relations. (2013). Stanford Athletics. www.gostanford.com/community.

Cozart, E.S. (2010). *The relationship between the online secondary ticket market and college athletics.* Unpublished master's thesis, University of North Carolina at Chapel Hill.

Doran, A. J. (2013). *A content analysis of NCAA division I track & field teams' Twitter usage: Defining best practices in social media marketing.* The University of North Carolina at Chapel Hill, ProQuest, UMI Dissertations Publishing, 1538022.

Follow the Wolverines. (2013). Michigan Athletics. www.mgoblue.com/multimedia/twitter-facebook.html.

Fugere, L. (2013). 5 reasons social media marketing has replaced traditional advertising. Social Selling University. www.socialsellingu.com/blog/5-reasons-social-media-marketing-has-replaced-traditional-advertising/.

Infographic: NACMA soars to new heights. (2013). National Association of Collegiate Marketing Administrators. www.nacda.com/sports/nacma/spec-rel/052912aae.html.

In-game promotions—Basketball. (2012). George Mason Athletics. www.gomason.com/ViewArticle.dbml?DB_OEM_ID=25200&ATCLID=205360471.

Iowa men's basketball. (2012). Iowa Hawkeyes. www.hawkeyesports.com/tickets/iowa-tickets-m-baskbl.html.

Irwin, R.L., Sutton, W.A., & McCarthy, L.M. (2008). *Sport promotion and sales management.* Champaign, IL: Human Kinetics.

Kannan, P.K., & Kopalle, P.K. (2001). Dynamic princing on the Internet: Importance and implications for consumer behavior. *International Journal of Electronic Commerce, 5*(3), 63–83.

[Associated Press] Kentucky's NCAA trophy goes on statewide tour; Calipari to meet fans. (2012, April 11). *Courier-Journal.* http://archive.courier-journal.com/article/20120411/SPORTS03/304110071/Kentucky-NCAA-trophy.

Lencioni, P. (2004). *Death by Meeting.* Jossey-Bass: San Francisco, CA.

Luther, D. (2012). The coolest food item at the top 25 college football stadiums. Bleacher Report. http://bleacherreport.com/articles/1094021-the-coolest-food-item-at-the-top-25-college-football-stadiums#/articles/1094021-the-coolest-food-item-at-the-top-25-college-football-stadiums/page/11.

Martin, C.L.L., Miller, L.L., Elsisi, R., Bowers, A., & Hall, S. (2011). An analysis of collegiate athletic marketing strategies and evaluation processes. *Journal of Issues in Intercollegiate Athletics, 4,* 42–54.

Miller, M. (2012). The 5 Ws of social media marketing: Industry survey and insights. Search Engine Watch. http://searchenginewatch.com/article/2166552/The-5-Ws-of-Social-Media-Marketing-Industry-Survey-Insights-Study.

Mission statement. (2013). South Georgia State College. http://168.20.183.97/athletics/mission.html.

NACMA mission statement. (2013). National Association of Collegiate Marketing Administrators. www.nacda.com/nacma/nacma-overview.html.

National Collegiate Athletic Association. (2014). Revenues and expenses 2004–2012: NCAA Division I intercollegiate athletics programs report. www.ncaapublications.com/productdownloads/2012RevExp.pdf.

Ozanian, M. (2011). Why StubHub dominates the secondary ticket market. *Forbes.* www.forbes.com/sites/mikeozanian/2011/08/05/stubhub-dominates-the-secondary-ticket-market/.

Programs. (2013). University of California, Los Angeles. www.uclabruins.com/ViewArticle.dbml?&DB_OEM_ID=30500&ATCLID=208178341.

Qcue—how it works. (2012). Qcue. www.qcue.net/howit-works.php.

Schwarz, E.C., Hunter, J.D., & Lafleur, A. (2013). *Advanced theory and practice in sport marketing* (2nd ed.). New York: Routledge.

Sherman, T., & Renshaw, J. (2012). Bowl or bust? Rutgers facing thousands of dollars in unsold postseason tickets. NJ.com. www.nj.com/news/index.ssf/2012/12/bowl_or_bust_rutgers_facing_th.html.

Smith, M. (2012, July 30). Cal joins South Florida in dynamic ticket pricing as more colleges consider wading in. *Street & Smith's SportsBusiness Journal.* www.sportsbusinessdaily.com/Journal/Issues/2012/07/30/Colleges/Cal.aspx?hl=qcue&sc=0.

Steinberg, D. (2013, February 13). Kiss cam and unscripted close-ups usually make for a perfect match. *Washington Post.* www.washingtonpost.com/sports/kiss-cam-and-unscripted-close-ups-usually-make-for-a-perfect-match/2013/02/13/76b6fb68-7600-11e2-8f84-3e4b513b1a13_story.html?tid=pm_labs_sports_pop.

Student rewards. (2013). Tennessee Volunteers. www.utsports.com/fans/student-rewards/.

University of California. (2013). Cal introduces dynamic pricing for football, basketball. www.calbears.com/sports/m-footbl/spec-rel/072312aac.html.

University of Tennessee Student Rewards Program. (2010). Tennessee Volunteers. http://grfx.cstv.com/confs/nacda/

graphics/nacma/stp/TennesseeStudentRewardsProgram.pdf.

Waddock, S.A., & Boyle, M.E. (1995). The dynamics of change in corporate community relations. *California Management Review, 37*(4), 125–137.

Why Digonex? (2011). Digonex Technologies. www.digonex.com/why.shtml.

Chapter 9

Burley-Allen, M. (1982). *Listening: The forgotten skill.* New York: Wiley.

Bynum, M. (2006, October). Marketing—Three keys to attracting sponsorships. *Athletic Business.* www.athleticbusiness.com/three-keys-to-attracting-sponsorships.html.

Capulsky, R.J., & Wolf, J.M. (1990). Relationship marketing: Positioning for the future. *Journal of Business Strategy, 11*(4), 16–26.

Chelap, M., of Octagon. (2012). Interview by R. Zullo.

Copeland, R., Frisby, W., & McCarville, R. (1996). Understanding the sport sponsorship process. *Journal of Sport Management, 10*(1), 32–48.

Covey, S. R. (2004). *The 7 habits of highly effective people.* New York: Simon & Schuster.

Do naming-rights deals pay off? Measuring ROI in naming-rights deals. (2011, September 19). *SportsBusiness Journal.* www.sportsbusinessdaily.com/Journal/Issues/2011/09/19/In-Depth/ROI-chart.aspx.

Donavan, D.T., Carlson, B.D., & Zimmerman, M. (2005). The influence of personality traits on sports fan identification. *Sports Marketing Quarterly, 14*(1), 31–42.

Experiential Marketing Forum. (2012). www.experientialforum.com/.

Fullerton, S. (2007). *Sports marketing.* New York: McGraw-Hill/Irwin.

Gazelle Group. (2014). 2K Classic Supporting Wounded Wariors Project sponsors. www.gazellegroup.com/events/wwp/sponsor.htm.

Graham, S., Goldblatt, J.J., & Delpy, L. (1995). *The ultimate guide to sport event management and marketing.* Chicago: Irwin.

Hoch, D. (2009, May). How to solicit sponsorships. *Athletic Business.* www.athleticbusiness.com/fundraising/how-to-solicit-sponsorships.html.

Hooters sponsorship sparks debate. (2004, February/March). *Athletic Management.* www.athleticmanagement.com/2007/05/17/hooters_sponsorship_sparks_debate/index.php.

Irwin, R.L., Sutton, W., & McCarthy, L. (2008). *Sport promotion and sales management* (2nd ed.). Champaign, IL: Human Kinetics.

Johnson, K. (2005, February 21). A marketing slam dunk, *SportsBusiness Journal.* www.sportsbusinessdaily.com/Journal/Issues/2005/02/20050221/SBJ-In-Depth/Amarketing-Slam-Dunk.aspx.

Lynde, T. (2007). *Sponsorships 101: An insider's guide to sponsorships in corporate America.* Mableton, GA: Lynde & Associates.

McCarthy, M. (2006, November 16). Schools, coaches cash in on lucrative media deals. *USA Today.* www.usatoday.com/sports/college/football/2006-11-16-cover-coaches-media_x.htm.

McKindra, L. (2005, November 7). Marketing the mission. NCAA News. http://fs.ncaa.org/Docs/NCAANewsArchive/2005/Division+I/marketing%2Bthe%2Bmission%2B-%2B11-07-05%2Bncaa%2Bnews.html.

Morgan, R.M., & Hunt, S. (1999). Relationship-based competitive advantage: The role of relationship marketing in marketing strategy. *Journal of Business Research, 46*(3), 281–290.

Muret, D. (2011, October 10). Illini offer naming rights to finance arena renovation. *SportsBusiness Journal.* www.sportsbusinessdaily.com/Journal/Issues/2011/10/10/Facilities/Illinois.aspx.

NCAA Corporate Champions and Corporate Partners. (2013). National Collegiate Athletic Association. www.ncaa.org/championships/marketing/ncaa-corporate-relationships?division=d1

Norcross, L. (2011, February 28). Best defense against ambush marketing is a good offense. *SportsBusiness Journal.* www.sportsbusinessdaily.com/Journal/Issues/2011/02/28/Opinion/From-The-Field.aspx.

O'Brien, D., of IMG College. (2012). Interview by R. Zullo.

ODU Athletics. (2012, October 4). Funeral home finds football games are a solid marketing venue. www.odusports.com/ViewArticle.dbml?DB_OEM_ID=31100&ATCLID=208376391.

Robinson, M. (2004, February/March). Ready for a handoff? *Athletic Management, 16*(2).

Rosenblum, N.L. (2000). *Thoreau: Political writings.* Cambridge, UK: Cambridge University Press.

Salem, R. (2003). Empathic listening. In G. Burgess & H. Burgess (Eds.), *Conflict information consortium,* University of Colorado, Boulder. www.beyondintractability.org/essay/empathic-listening

Shani, D. (1997). A framework for implementing relationship in the sport industry. *Sports Marketing Quarterly, 6*(2), 9–15.

Smith, M. (2011a, August 29). UPS, MillerCoors go in—and go big—on campus. *SportsBusiness Journal.* www.sportsbusinessdaily.com/Journal/Issues/2011/08/29/Marketing-and-Sponsorship/UPS-MillerCoors.aspx.

Smith. M. (2011b, September 5). IMG's reach creates big college platform for UPS. *SportsBusiness Journal.* www.sportsbusinessdaily.com/Journal/Issues/2011/09/05/Marketing-and-Sponsorship/IMG-UPS.aspx.

Steinbach, P. (2003, September). Marketing—Attention! *Athletic Business.* www.athleticbusiness.com/attention.html.

Steinbach, P. (2005, May 1). Marketing—Signs of the times. *Athletic Business.* www.athleticbusiness.com/marketing/signs-of-the-times.html.

Steinbach, P. (2009, February). Fundraising—Naming rights deals scrutinized by private and public sectors alike. *Athletic Business*. www.athleticbusiness.com/Fundraising/naming-rights-deals-scrutinized-by-private-and-public-sectors-alike.html.

Steinbach, P. (2011, September). More college athletic departments partnering with state lotteries. *Athletic Business*. www.athleticbusiness.com/more-college-athletic-departments-partn.

Titlebaum, P., & Watson, S. (2001, January 1). After tackling a sponsorship, don't leave sponsors in the dirt. *Athletic Business*. http://athleticbusiness.com/articles/article.aspx?articleid=141&zoneid=35.

Zinzer, L. (2013, February 27). Florida Atlantic students protest GEO deal. *New York Times*. http://thequad.blogs.nytimes.com/2013/02/27/florida-atlantic-students-protest-owlcatraz/?ref=sports.

Chapter 10

Associated Press. (2006, September 12). Arizona State coach expects fun when Lady Raiders visit for outdoor game. *Lubbock Avalanche-Journal*. http://lubbockonline.com/stories/091206/col_4115836.shtml.

Associated Press. (2010a, August 31). Houston wide receiver Patrick Edwards sues Marshall, Conference USA over injury. ESPN. http://sports.espn.go.com/ncf/news/story?id=5516879.

Associated Press. (2010b, December 9). Michigan–Michigan State outdoor hockey game should set attendance mark. ESPN. http://sports.espn.go.com/ncaa/news/story?id=5903608.

Associated Press. (2011, March 16). Notre Dame cited for violations in Declan Sullivan's death. *USA Today*. http://usatoday30.usatoday.com/sports/college/football/2011-03-15-notre-dame-declan-sullivan-investigation_N.htm.

Baard, P.P., Deci, E.L., & Ryan, R.M. (2004). Intrinsic need satisfaction: A motivational basis of performance and well-being in two work settings. *Journal of Applied Social Psychology, 34*, 2045-2068.

Bang, H., & Ross, S.D. (2009). Volunteer motivation and satisfaction. *Journal of Venue and Event Management, 1*(1), 61–77.

Bennett, B. (2012, June 14). Arms race proves recession-proof. ESPN. http://espn.go.com/college-football/story/_/id/8047787/college-football-facilities-arms-race-proves-recession-proof.

Bilsky, S. (2007, April/May). The scoop on hosting. *Athletic Management*. www.athleticmanagement.com/2007/05/08/the_scoop_on_hosting/index.php.

Bishop, G. (2011, November 11). Season tips off in location unlike any other. *New York Times*. www.nytimes.com/2011/11/12/sports/ncaabasketball/unc-and-michigan-state-tip-off-on-an-aircraft-carrier.html?_r=0.

Bishop, G. (2012, December 29). In next scene: A dark cloud lifts. *New York Times*. www.nytimes.com/2012/12/30/sports/ncaafootball/declan-sullivans-family-responds-to-death-by-not-pointing-fingers.html?pagewanted=all.

Borkowski, R. (2006, October/November). When good facilities go bad. *Athletic Management*. www.athleticmanagement.com/2007/01/15/when_good_facilities_go_bad/index.php.

Borkowski, R. (2010, April/May). A closer look. *Athletic Management*. www.athleticmanagement.com/2010/04/04/a_closer_look/index.php.

Brown, M.T., & Nagel, M.S. (2010). Public recreation financing trends: Taxpayer backlash causes new models to emerge. *Journal of Venue and Event Management, 2*(1), 30–36.

Browne, W.A., Briggs, J., & Strube, B. (2008, August). Non-revenue sports gaining access to sophisticated practice facilities. *Athletic Business*. www.athleticbusiness.com/Locker-Room/non-revenue-sports-gaining-access-to-sophisticated-practice-facilities.html.

Bynum, M. (2007, March). Basketball and football practice facility design. *Athletic Business*. www.athleticbusiness.com/gym-fieldhouse/basketball-and-football-practice-facility-design.html.

Chase, C. (2013, March 7). Wyoming students chant "alcoholic" at Larry Eustachy. *USA Today*. www.usatoday.com/story/gameon/2013/03/07/larry-eustachy-alcoholic-wyoming-fans/1970217/.

Chen, K.K., & Zhang, J.J. (2012). To name it or not name it: Consumer perspectives on facility naming rights in collegiate athletics. *Journal of Issues in Intercollegiate Athletics, 5*, 119–148.

Cohen, A. (2000, April). Solar panels installed at Vaught-Hemingway Stadium at Ole Miss. *Athletic Business*. www.athleticbusiness.com/solar-panels-installed-at-vaught-hemingway-stadium-at-ole-miss.html.

Cohen, A. (2001, October). Securing sports facilities, post-9/11. *Athletic Business*. www.athleticbusiness.com/securing-sports-facilities-post-9-11.html.

Cohen, A. (2007, March). College and universities committing to wind power. *Athletic Business*. www.athleticbusiness.com/college/colleges-and-universities-committing-to-wind-power.html.

Cohen, A. (2008, October). Title IX rumblings in San Diego. *Athletic Business*. www.athleticbusiness.com/title-ix-rumblings-in-san-diego.html.

Cohen, A. (2010, February). Who cares what building was the first to receive LEED certification. *Athletic Business*. www.athleticbusiness.com/rec-center/who-cares-what-building-was-the-first-to-receive-leed-certification.html.

Dahlgren, S. (2000, August). LED technology brings fans closer than ever to the action. *Athletic Business*. www.athleticbusiness.com/Stadium-Arena/led-technology-brings-fans-closer-than-ever-to-the-action.html.

Deci, E.L., & Ryan, R.M. (2008). Facilitating optimal motivation and psychological well-being across life's domains. *Canadian Psychology, 49*(1), 14-23.

Dethlefs, D. (2007, September). Championship-caliber seating configurations for spectator facilities. *Athletic Business*. www.athleticbusiness.com/stadium-arena/

championship-caliber-seating-configurations-for-spectator-facilities.html.

Diamond, L. (2009, September 17). UGA news conference to detail tailgaters' destruction. *Atlanta Journal-Constitution*. www.ajc.com/news/news/local/uga-news-conference-to-detail-tailgaters-destructi/nQSjn/.

Dodd, D. (2009, June 11). Placing blame for Edwards injury a pain in itself. www.cbssports.com/collegefootball/story/11844867.

Dougherty, N. (2008, June/July). Home away from home. *Athletic Management*. www.athleticmanagement.com/2008/06/01/home_away_from_home/index.php.

Funk, A. (2007, October/November). It's easy being green. *Athletic Management*. www.athleticmanagement.com/2007/11/03/its_easy_being_green/index.php.

Funk, A. (2010, November). Learning from Title IX. *Athletic Management*. www.athleticmanagement.com/2010/11/29/learning_from_title_ix/index.php.

Gillentine, A., Miller, J., & Crow, B. (2010). Essential components of a "best practice" model for tailgating events. *Journal of Venue and Event Management, 2*(2), 54–68.

Gioglio, T. (2011, October/November). Bringing out the axe. *Athletic Management*. www.athleticmanagement.com/2011/10/20/bringing_out_the_axe/index.php.

Grady, J. (2010). Accessibility doesn't happen by itself: An interview with Betty Siegel, J.D., director of the Kennedy Center Accessibility Program. *Journal of Venue and Event Management, 2*(2), 69–74.

Hall, S., Marciani, L., Cooper, W., & Phillips, J. (2010). Needs, concerns and future challenges in security management of NCAA division I football events: An intercollegiate facility management perspective. *Journal of Venue and Event Management, 1*(2), 1–16.

"Hokies Respect." (2014). Virginia Tech. www.alumni.vt.edu/chapters/respect.html/.

Johnston, L. (2009, September 26). More Georgia fans put their trash away. *Atlanta Journal-Constitution*. www.ajc.com/news/sports/college/more-georgia-fans-put-their-trash-away/nQXDC/.

Kimmel, C. (2006, February/March). Handling MRSA. *Athletic Management*. www.athleticmanagement.com/2007/02/20/handling_mrsa/index.php.

LaVetter, D., & Choi, Y.S. (2010). Implications of toppling goal posts in college football: Managing institutional risk. *Journal of Sport Administration & Supervision, 2*(1), 52–62.

Lawrence, H., & Titlebaum, P. (2010). Luxury suite administrators: Essential to success. *Journal of Venue and Event Management, 2*(2), 42–52.

Lawrence, H.J., Kahler, J., & Contorno, R.T. (2009). An examination of luxury suite ownership in professional sports. *Journal of Venue and Event Management, 1*(1), 1–18.

Marciani, L., & Hall, S. (2007, August/September). Home-field security. *Athletic Management*. www.athleticmanagement.com/2007/08/13/home-field_security/index.php.

McConnell, R., & Anderson, K. (2006, October 24). Stadium construction company files lawsuit against Tech. *Collegiate Times*. www.collegiatetimes.com/stories/7808/stadium-construction-company-files-law-suit-against-tech.

Mead, D. (2007, August/September). Personalizing locker rooms. *Athletic Management*. www.athleticmanagement.com/2008/08/20/personalizing_locker_rooms/index.php.

Meiser, P., Tucker, T., & Abaray, C. (2011). Where the heart is. *Athletic Management*. www.athleticmanagement.com/2011/04/03/where_the_heart_is/index.php.

Menaker, B.E., & Connaughton, D.P. (2010). Stadium alcohol policies: A comparison of policies available on college athletic department web sites. *International Journal of Sport Communication, 3*(2), 151–162.

Miller, E. (2008, October 3). U.Va. repeals ban on signs, banners at football games. *Virginian-Pilot*. http://hamptonroads.com/2008/10/uva-repeals-ban-signs-banners-football-games.

Miller, J., & Dunn, A. (2011). Perceptions of terrorist threat: Implication for intercollegiate basketball venue managers. *Journal of Venue and Event Management, 3*(1), 2–10.

Minn. banks on stadium deal. (2006, October/November). *Athletic Management*. www.athleticmanagement.com/2007/01/15/minn_banks_on_stadium_deal/index.php.

Moore, D. (2011, November 12). UNC, Michigan State on flight deck. *USA Today*. http://usatoday30.usatoday.com/sports/college/mensbasketball/story/2011-11-11/Carrier-Classic-11/51171104/1.

MU's tab $250,300 in Houston WR suit. (2012, April 27). *Charleston Gazette*. http://wvgazette.com/Sports/201204270163.

Myers, J. (2008, February/March). Connecting the dollar signs. *Athletic Management*. www.athleticmanagement.com/2008/03/05/connecting_the_dollar_signs/index.php.

Nagel, M. (2011). Changing attitudes regarding ticket "rights." *Journal of Venue and Event Management, 3*(2), 34–38.

Novy-Williams, E. (2011, December 9). Football beer taps add safety, $700,000 to West Virginia University sports. Bloomberg News. www.bloomberg.com/news/2011-12-09/football-beer-taps-add-safety-700-000-to-west-virginia-university-sports.html.

Palmero, M., Li, M., Lawrence, H., & Conley, V.M. (2011). Who is in charge? An analysis of NCAA Division I arena management models. *Journal of Venue and Event Management, 3*(2), 18–32.

Pantera, M. J., III, Accorsi, R., Winter, C., Gobeille, R., Griveas, S., Queen, D., et al. (2003, Fall). Best practices for game day security at athletic & sport venues. *Sport Journal, 6* [Online]. www.thesportjournal.org.

Pate, J.R., Bemiller, J., & Hardin, R. (2010). Reserved: Best practices for on-campus football parking for people with physical disabilities. *Journal of Venue and Event Management, 2*(1), 2–13.

Phillips, M. (2013, January 3). U.Va. returns to Coliseum for the first time since ice game. *Richmond Times-Dispatch*. www.timesdispatch.com/sports/college/basketball/u-va-returns-to-coliseum-for-the-first-time-since/article_25702f6b-01ff-51e2-8a61-ff0a42042a84.html.

Pieper, L. (2006, July 5). Second contractor sues Turner Construction over Lane Stadium delays. *Collegiate Times.* www.collegiatetimes.com/stories/7170/second-contractor-sues-turner-construction-over-lane-stadium-delays.

Pink, D.H. (2009). *Drive: The surprising truth about what motivates us.* New York: Riverhead Books.

Popke, M. (2005, September). Drying agents. *Athletic Business.* www.athleticbusiness.com/drying-agents.html.

Purvis, B., assistant director, Pete Hanna Center, Samford University. (2012). Interview by R. Zullo.

Scholand, G. (2007, February/March). Blocking an outbreak. *Athletic Management.* www.athleticmanagement.com/2007/03/19/blocking_an_outbreak/index.php.

Scholand, G. (2008, February/March). Step by step. *Athletic Management.* www.athleticmanagement.com/2008/03/06/step_by_step/index.php.

Scholand, G. (2011, April/May). A solid defense. *Athletic Management.* www.athleticmanagement.com/2011/04/03/a_solid_defense/index.php.

Seifried, C. (2012). The historic structure report: A tool for the renovation, reconstruction, restoration and rehabilitation of sport facilities. *Journal of Venue and Event Management, 4*(1), 14–28.

Sports Turf Managers Association. (2011, January 10). Weathering the economic downturn. *Athletic Management.* www.athleticmanagement.com/2011/01/10/weathering_the_economic_downturn/index.php.

Steinbach, P. (2000, March). The benefits of outsourcing concessions. *Athletic Business.* www.athleticbusiness.com/Marketing/the-benefits-of-outsourcing-concessions.html.

Steinbach, P. (2001, April). Fan's mind-set fostered by rivalries can translate into acts of aggression. *Athletic Business.* www.athleticbusiness.com/fan-s-mind-set-fostered-by-rivalries-can-translate-into-acts-of-aggression.html.

Steinbach, P. (2003a, February). Locker room & laundry—Locked and loaded. *Athletic Business.* www.athleticbusiness.com/Locker-Room/locked-and-loaded.html.

Steinbach, P. (2003b, July). Party lines. *Athletic Business.* www.athleticbusiness.com/party-lines.html.

Steinbach, P. (2004a, July). Special operations. *Athletic Business.* www.athleticbusiness.com/special-operations.html.

Steinbach, P. (2004b, August). Sporting events and booze a volatile mix. *Athletic Business.* www.athleticbusiness.com/drugs-alcohol/drinking-games.html.

Steinbach, P. (2005a, May). Dance fever. *Athletic Business.* www.athleticbusiness.com/College/dance-fever.html.

Steinbach, P. (2005b, July). Venue visuals. *Athletic Business.* www.athleticbusiness.com/Marketing/venue-visuals.html.

Steinbach, P. (2005c, August). Honeymoon suites. *Athletic Business.* www.athleticbusiness.com/stadium-arena/honeymoon-suites.html.

Steinbach, P. (2005d, December). Last call. *Athletic Business.* www.athleticbusiness.com/Stadium-Arena/last-call.html.

Steinbach, P. (2005e, December). Sideline supplies. *Athletic Business.* www.athleticbusiness.com/Stadium-Arena/sideline-supplies.html.

Steinbach, P. (2006a, March). Storm fronts. *Athletic Business.* www.athleticbusiness.com/athlete-safety/storm-fronts.html.

Steinbach, P. (2006b, April). Enemy at the gates. *Athletic Business.* www.athleticbusiness.com/Facility-Security/enemy-at-the-gates.html.

Steinbach, P. (2006c, June). The University of Minnesota will get its on-campus stadium. *Athletic Business.* www.athleticbusiness.com/the-university-of-minnesota-will-get-its-on-campus-stadium.html.

Steinbach, P. (2006d, August). Post-Katrina, college athletic departments serve as disaster response specialists. *Athletic Business.* www.athleticbusiness.com/Emergency-Response/post-katrina-college-athletic-departments-serve-as-disaster-response-specialists.html.

Steinbach, P. (2006e, October). A majority of Division I-A football programs now use synthetic turf. *Athletic Business.* www.athleticbusiness.com/Outdoor/a-majority-of-division-i-a-football-programs-now-use-synthetic-turf.html.

Steinbach, P. (2006f, November). Sectional healing. *Athletic Business.* www.athleticbusiness.com/sectional-healing.html.

Steinbach, P. (2007a, March). Michigan Stadium is at the center of pending ADA litigation. *Athletic Business.* www.athleticbusiness.com/Stadium-Arena/michigan-stadium-is-at-the-center-of-pending-ada-litigation.html.

Steinbach, P. (2007b, November). At Wisconsin, past stadium alcohol policy violators must pass breathalyzer. *Athletic Business.* www.athleticbusiness.com/Spectator-Safety/at-wisconsin-past-stadium-alcohol-policy-violators-must-pass-breathalyzer.html.

Steinbach, P. (2008a, April). Abusive student sections drawing attention from outside the arena. *Athletic Business.* www.athleticbusiness.com/Spectator-Safety/abusive-student-sections-drawing-attention-from-outside-the-arena.html.

Steinbach, P. (2008b, April). Can sidelines be made safer for athletes who tread out of bounds? *Athletic Business.* www.athleticbusiness.com/Outdoor/can-sidelines-be-made-safer-for-athletes-who-tread-out-of-bounds.html.

Steinbach, P. (2008c, July). Concession contracts capitalizing on consumers' brand loyalty. *Athletic Business.* www.athleticbusiness.com/Marketing/concessions-contracts-capitalizing-on-consumers-brand-loyalty.html.

Steinbach, P. (2008d, November). Compliance primers adorn restroom walls at some universities. *Athletic Business.* www.athleticbusiness.com/compliance-primers-adorn-restroom-walls-at-some-universities.html.

Steinbach, P. (2011, May). Selling alcohol to fight alcohol abuse. *Athletic Business.* www.athleticbusiness.com/Drugs-Alcohol/selling-alcohol-to-fight-alcohol-abuse.html.

Steinbach, P. (2013, January). Athletic departments apply Disney principles to game day. *Athletic Business.* www.athleticbusiness.com/staffing/athletic-departments-apply-disney-principles-to-game-day.html.

Storm that damaged Georgia Dome, Atlanta was a tornado. (2008, March 15). ESPN. http://sports.espn.go.com/ncb/champweek2008/news/story?id=3295046.

Titlebaum, R., DeMange, C., & Davis, R. (2012). Professional versus collegiate facilities: Perceived motivations for luxury suite ownership. *Journal of Venue and Event Management, 4*(1), 2–12.

Ulrich, L. (2010, April/May). Ready or not. *Athletic Management*. www.athleticmanagement.com/2010/04/04/ready_or_not/index.php.

Westerbeek, H., Smith, A., Turner, P., Emery, P., Green, C., & van Leeuwen, L. (2006). *Managing sport facilities and major events.* New York: Routledge.

WVU approves alcohol sales in football stadium. (2011, June 3). *Pittsburgh Post-Gazette.* www.post-gazette.com/stories/local/region/wvu-approves-alcohol-sales-in-football-stadium-300506/.

Zinser, L. (2011, April 18). Notre Dame report spreads responsibility in Declan Sullivan's death. *New York Times.* www.nytimes.com/2011/04/19/sports/ncaafootball/19irish.html?_r=1&.

Chapter 11

Ancona, D., Malone, T.W., Orlikowski, W.J., & Senge, P.M. (2007). In praise of the incomplete leader. *Harvard Business Review, 85*(2), 92–100.

Associated Press. (2004, November 24). College removes name of Wal-mart heiress on area. *USA Today.* http://usatoday30.usatoday.com/money/industries/retail/2004-11-24-walmart-heiress-arena_x.htm.

Associated Press. (2010, May 28). KU scandal prompts universities to look at ticket rules. KUSports.com. www2.kusports.com/news/2010/may/28/ku-scandal-prompts-universities-look-ticket-rules/.

Associated Press. (2011, January 26). Connecticut donor wants $3 million back after athletic director dispute. *USA Today.* http://usatoday30.usatoday.com/sports/college/football/bigeast/2011-01-25-connecticut-donor_N.htm.

Barber, A. (2007, February/March). Pass go: Collect new donor. *Athletic Management.* www.athleticmanagement.com/2007/03/19/pass_go_collect_new_donor/index.php.

Baumgartner, S. (2009, December 10). University of Missouri's ROARS program. National Association of Athletic Development Directors. www.nacda.com/sports/naadd/spec-rel/121009aaa.html.

Berkowitz, S. (2011, April 18). Program-specific donations at Cal may alter fundraising practices. *USA Today.* http://usatoday30.usatoday.com/sports/college/2011-04-18-college-sports-funding-california_N.htm.

Berman, M. (2011, March 3). Virginia Tech will reward donors with new seating assignments. *Roanoke Times.* http://roanoke-times.vlex.com/vid/virginia-tech-will-new-seating-assignments-255754926.

Bernat, J. (2010, June). *NCAA Division I athletic development: A model for donor management in non-revenue-generating sports.* Poster session presented at the North American Society for Sport Management Conference, Tampa, Florida.

Billing, J.E., Holt, D., & Smith, J. (1985). Athletic fundraising: Exploring the motives behind donations. Chapel Hill: University of North Carolina Press.

Bjork, R. (2010, February 8). Best practices: Professional conduct dictates your future. National Association of Athletic Development Directors. www.nacda.com/sports/naadd/spec-rel/020810aab.html.

Brown, C., Clayborn, K., Hays, B., & Pritchard, Z. (2008). *Former collegiate athlete donor motivation study.* Paper presented at the College Sport Research Institute, Memphis, TN.

Brown, N. (2011a, March). Economy affects fundraising for college athletic facilities. *Athletic Business.* www.athleticbusiness.com/fundraising/economy-affects-fundraising-for-college-athletic-facilities.html.

Brown, N. (2011b, March). UConn drama shows a darker side of donor relations. *Athletic Business.* www.athleticbusiness.com/uconn-drama-shows-a-darker-side-of-donor-relations.html.

Bynum, M. (2004, July). Paving the way. *Athletic Business.* www.athleticbusiness.com/paving-the-way.html.

Center, C. (2010, November 16). Premium seating at the University of Georgia. National Association of Athletic Development Directors. www.nacda.com/sports/naadd/spec-rel/111610aaa.html.

Chen, K., & Zhang, J. (2012). To name it or not name it: Consumer perspectives on facility naming rights sponsorship in collegiate athletics. *Journal of Issues in Intercollegiate Athletics, 5,* 119–148.

Collins, J. (2005, July). Level 5 leadership: The triumph of humility and fierce resolve. *Harvard Business Review,* 136–146.

Collins, J.C., & Porras, J.I. (1994). *Built to last: Successful habits of visionary companies.* London: Random House.

Convention preview: Future of athletic development. (2010, March 1). National Association of Athletic Development Directors. www.nacda.com/sports/naadd/spec-rel/030110aag.html.

Covey, S. R. (2004). *The 7 habits of highly effective people.* New York: Simon & Schuster.

Crompton, J., & Howard, D. (2003). The American experience with facility naming rights: Opportunities for English professional football teams. *Managing Leisure, 8,* 212–226.

Crum, D. (2011, March 15). University of Minnesota launches athletic development website. National Association of Athletic Development Directors. www.nacda.com/sports/naadd/spec-rel/031511aae.html.

Dolson, S., & Bomba, K. (2011, October 28). IU highlights D. Ames Shuel Academic Center campaign. National Association of Athletic Development Directors. www.nacda.com/sports/naadd/spec-rel/102811aad.html.

Doughty, D. (2011, March 11). Coaching changes possible for some ACC also-rans. *Roanoke Times.* ww2.roanoke.com/sports/notebookplus/wb/279735.

Drucker, P.F. (2005, January). Managing oneself. *Harvard Business Review,* 100–109.

Dufresne, C. (1999, December 17). Notre Dame penalty is deemed "major." *Los Angeles Times.* http://articles.latimes.com/1999/dec/17/sports/sp-44956.

Evans, T. (2009, September 4). A playbook underwritten by deep pockets. *New York Times*. www.nytimes.com/2009/09/05/sports/ncaafootball/05okstate.html.

Fagan, M. (2010, November 18). Federal charges filed against five former Kansas Athletics officials accused of stealing tickets from KU. *Lawrence Journal-World*. www2.kusports.com/news/2010/nov/18/federal-charges-filed-against-five-former-kansas-a/.

Fagan, M. (2011, March 30). Former manager of KU athletics ticket office Kassie Liebsch sentenced to 37 months in federal prison. *Lawrence Journal-World*. www2.ljworld.com/news/2011/mar/30/former-manager-ku-athletics-ticket-office-sentence/?breaking.

Foley, J. (2011, February 24). Boston College's scholarship luncheon reiterates the importance of good stewardship. National Association of Athletic Development Directors. www.nacda.com/sports/naadd/spec-rel/022411aaa.html.

Ford, T. (2009, October 16). Capital campaigns in focus: Yale tomorrow. National Association of Athletic Development Directors. www.nacda.com/sports/naadd/spec-rel/101609aae.html.

Gardiner, J. (2009, August/September). A strong drive. *Athletic Management*. www.athleticmanagement.com/2009/08/16/a_strong_drive/index.php.

George, B. & Sims, P. (2007). *True north: Discovering your authentic leadership*. San Francisco, CA: Jossey-Bass.

George, W., Sims, P., McLean, A., & Mayer, D. (2007). Discovering your authentic leadership. *Harvard Business Review, 85*(2), 129–138.

Gimbl, R. (2010a, June 4). Capital campaigns in focus: Penn State University. National Association of Athletic Development Directors. www.nacda.com/sports/naadd/spec-rel/060410aaa.html.

Gimbl, R. (2010b, October 26). Engaging alumni athletes. National Association of Athletic Development Directors. www.nacda.com/sports/naadd/spec-rel/102610aab.html.

Gladden, J.M., Mahony, D.F., & Apostolopoulou, A. (2005). Toward a better understanding of college athletic donors: What are the primary motives? *Sport Marketing Quarterly, 14*(1), 18–30.

Goffee, R., & Jones, G. (2000, September). Why should anyone be led by you? *Harvard Business Review,* 63–70.

Goleman, D. (2000, March). Leadership that gets results. *Harvard Business Review,* 78–90.

Greenhouse, S. (2000, April 25). Nike's chief cancels a gift over monitor of sweatshops. *New York Times*. www.nytimes.com/2000/04/25/us/nike-s-chief-cancels-a-gift-over-monitor-of-sweatshops.html.

Hall, J. (2009, June/July). Up with volunteers. *Athletic Management*. www.athleticmanagement.com/2009/06/10/up_with_volunteers/index.php.

Howard, D.R., & Crompton, J.L. (2003). *Financing sport* (2nd ed.). Morgantown, West Virginia. Fitness Information Technology.

Humphreys, B.R., & Mondello, M. (2007). Intercollegiate athletic success and donations at NCAA Division I institutions. *Journal of Sport Management, 21*(2), 265-280.

Hyland, A. (2010, May 26). Biggest, longest-lasting impact of ticket scandal at Kansas University may have very little to do with tickets. *Lawrence Journal-World*. www2.kusports.com/news/2010/may/26/biggest-longest-lasting-impact-ticket-scandal-kans/.

Katstra, D. (2012, October 26). Interview by the National Association of Athletic Development Directors. www.nacda.com/sports/naadd/spec-rel/102612aaa.html.

Kegler, B. (2010, December 15). New deferred giving program leverages power of gifts. National Association of Athletic Development Directors. www.nacda.com/sports/naadd/spec-rel/121510aaa.html.

King, B. (2013, May 1). UGA students could see more football tickets taken away from them. *Atlanta Journal-Constitution*. http://blogs.ajc.com/junkyard-blawg/2013/05/10/uga-students-could-see-more-football-seats-taken-away-from-them/.

King, E.H., Sexton, E.L., & Rhatigan, J.J. (2010). Balancing fundraising in academic programs and intercollegiate athletics. *New Directions for Higher Education, 2010*(149), 65–71.

Kirinovic, M., & Milliron, M. (2009, June 25). OU best practices and peer comparison analysis. National Association of Athletic Development Directors. www.nacda.com/sports/naadd/spec-rel/062509aac.html.

Kotter, J.P. (2001, December). What leaders really do. *Harvard Business Review,* 85–96.

Knuth, D. (2010, December 17). Everyone's a fundraiser. National Association of Athletic Development Directors. www.nacda.com/sports/naadd/spec-rel/121710aam.html.

LaPlante, M. (2011, February 28). Colorado State looks to create a culture of giving among its student-athletes. National Association of Athletic Development Directors. www.nacda.com/sports/naadd/spec-rel/022811aac.html.

Lau, D. (2010, January 5). Missouri Western State gives students Max Experience. National Association of Athletic Development Directors. www.nacda.com/sports/naadd/spec-rel/010510aad.html.

Leonard, T. (2011, May 25). SMU to renovate Moody Coliseum through two lead gifts. National Association of Athletic Development Directors. www.nacda.com/sports/naadd/spec-rel/052511aab.html.

Lindahl, W.E. (1995). The major gift donor relationship: An analysis of donors and contributions. *Nonprofit Management and Leadership, 5,* 411–432.

Mahony, D.F., Gladden, J.M., & Funk, D.C. (2003). Examining athletic donors at NCAA Division I institutions. *International Journal of Sport Management, 7*(1), 9–27.

McClung, S. (2010, October 26–29). *Student booster programs: Marketing communication for the non-believers*. Presentation at the 8th annual conference of the Sport Marketing Association, New Orleans, LA.

McCollum, D. (2009, July 25). New UC president taking front-porch philosophy with athletics. *Log Cabin Democrat*. http://thecabin.net/news/local/2009-07-25/new-uca-president-taking-front-porch-philosophy-athletics#.UxnzUV5-Ufo.

McGinniss, K. (2011, January 25). University of Rhode Island's first athletics capital campaign proves to be a success. National Association of Athletic Development Directors. www.nacda.com/sports/naadd/spec-rel/012511aab.html.

Merritt, L. (2009, April 24). Questions and answers with NAADD past president Lu Merritt. National Association of Athletic Development Directors. www.nacda.com/sports/naadd/spec-rel/092409aab.html.

Mike the Tiger. (2013). Donate a brick. www.mikethetiger.com/bricks.php.

Morant, M. (1999, June 4). Tawdry, twisted tale. *Chicago Tribune*. http://articles.chicagotribune.com/1999-06-04/sports/9906050005_1_kim-dunbar-notre-dame-institutional-control.

NCAA revenues and expenses report. (2012). National Collegiate Athletic Association. http://ncaapublications.com/p-4306-revenues-and-expenses-2004-2012-ncaa-division-i-intercollegiate-athletics-programs-report.aspx.

Northcutt, T. (2010, December 15). Creation of Seawolf Athletic Association allows Alaska Anchorage to achieve success through streamlined structure. National Association of Athletic Development Directors. www.nacda.com/sports/naadd/spec-rel/121510aan.html.

O'Brien, S. (2010, February 1). Capital campaigns in focus: University of California, Santa Barbara. National Association of Athletic Development Directors. www.nacda.com/sports/naadd/spec-rel/020110aaa.html.

Pascoe, B. (2011, April 7). Arizona athletics: Fundraising objectives involve football suites, Miller's contract. *Arizona Daily Star*. http://azstarnet.com/sports/college/wildcats/arizona-athletics-fundraising-objectives-involve-football-suites-miller-s-contract/article_7f4ca69b-4248-59ae-b90d-e7c76bc5be10.html.

Phelps, M. (2012, April/May). A pitch for survival. *Athletic Management*. www.athleticmanagement.com/2012/03/31/a_pitch_for_survival/index.php.

Pientka, M. (2009, October 16). Best practices: 10 ways to blow the ask. National Association of Athletic Development Directors. www.nacda.com/sports/naadd/spec-rel/101609aak.html.

Popke, M. (2008, October). Online tools becoming popular in fundraising. *Athletic Business*. www.athleticbusiness.com/Fundraising/online-tools-becoming-popular-in-fundraising.html.

Purcell, B. (2009, December 4). Interview by the National Association of Athletic Development Directors. www.nacda.com/sports/naadd/spec-rel/120409aad.html.

Rheenan, D.V., Minjares, V., McNeil, N., & Atwood, J.R. (2011). The elimination of varsity sports at a Division I institution. *Journal for the Study of Sports and Athletes in Education, 5*(3), 161–180.

Riley, E. (2010, June 4). University of Indianapolis' Greyhound Club online auction. National Association of Athletic Development Directors. www.nacda.com/sports/naadd/spec-rel/060410aaf.html.

Ring, B. (2010a, May 4). Boston University scholarship program growing strong during economic downturn. National Association of Athletic Development Directors. www.nacda.com/sports/naadd/spec-rel/050410aae.html.

Ring, B. (2010b, December 19). Reforming practices essential as profession evolves. National Association of Athletic Development Directors. www.nacda.com/sports/naadd/spec-rel/121910aad.html.

Robinson, C. (2011, August 16). Renegade Miami football booster spells out illicit benefits to players. Yahoo Sports. http://sports.yahoo.com/investigations/news?slug=cr-renegade_miami_booster_details_illicit_benefits_081611.

Robinson, M. (1998, March). An untapped market. *Athletic Management*. www.momentummedia.com/articles/am/am1002/untapped.htm.

Rovell, D. (2013, January 7). Fighting influence. *ESPN The Magazine*, 32.

Ryan, L. (2010, May 4). Capital campaigns in focus: University of New Mexico. National Association of Athletic Development Directors. www.nacda.com/sports/naadd/spec-rel/050410aaj.html.

Schlabach, M. (2009, July 13). Financial difficulties making it hard for athletic departments to balance budgets. ESPN. http://sports.espn.go.com/ncaa/columns/story?columnist=schlabach_mark&id=4314195.

Scissors, A. (2011, September 28). NIU athletics receives largest gift in history. National Association of Athletic Development Directors. www.nacda.com/sports/naadd/spec-rel/092811aaj.html.

Shapiro, S.L., Giannoulakis, C., Drayer, J., & Wang, C. (2010). An examination of athletic alumni giving behavior: Development of the former student-athlete donor constraint scale. *Sport Management Review, 13*(3), 283–295.

Shapiro, S.L., & Ridinger, L.L. (2011). An analysis of donor involvement, gender, and giving in college athletics. *Sport Marketing Quarterly, 20,* 22–32.

Smatresk, N. (2011, November 11). A successful sports program benefits both the university and our community. *Las Vegas Sun*. www.lasvegassun.com/news/2011/nov/11/successful-sports-program-benefits-both-university/.

Stallman, R., & Mankenberg, C. (2008, April/May). It takes a team. *Athletic Management*. www.athleticmanagement.com/2008/04/28/it_takes_a_team/index.php.

Stanley, K. (2009, November 16). Capital campaigns in focus: Utah State University. National Association of Athletic Development Directors. www.nacda.com/sports/naadd/spec-rel/111309aaa.html.

Staurowsky, E.J. (1996). Women and athletic fundraising: Exploring the connection between gender and giving. *Journal of Sport Management, 10*(4), 401–416.

Staurowsky, E.J., Parkhouse, B., & Sachs, M. (1999). Developing an instrument to measure athletic donor behavior and motivation. *Journal of Sport Management, 10*(3), 262–277.

Steinbach, P. (2002, September). Booster shots. *Athletic Business*. www.athleticbusiness.com/booster-shots.html.

Steinbach, P. (2003, October). New development. *Athletic Business*. www.athleticbusiness.com/new-development.html.

Steinbach, P. (2004, April). Open market. *Athletic Business*. www.athleticbusiness.com/open-market.html.

Steinbach, P. (2005a, April). Signs of the time. *Athletic Business*. www.athleticbusiness.com/marketing/signs-of-the-times.html.

Steinbach, P. (2005b, May). Dance fever. *Athletic Business*. www.athleticbusiness.com/College/dance-fever.html.

Steinbach, P. (2005c, August). Honeymoon suites. *Athletic Business*. www.athleticbusiness.com/stadium-arena/honeymoon-suites.html.

Steinbach, P. (2009, November). In uncertain economy, athletics development more critical than ever. *Athletic Business*. www.athleticbusiness.com/College/in-uncertain-economy-athletics-development-more-critical-than-ever.html.

Steinbach, P. (2012, June). Athletics development success hinges on broadening the donor base. *Athletic Business*. www.athleticbusiness.com/Fundraising/athletics-development-success-hinges-on-broadening-the-donor-base.html.

Stinson, J.L., & Howard, D.R. (2004). Scoreboards vs. mortarboards: Major donor behavior and intercollegiate athletics. *Sport Marketing Quarterly, 13*(2), 129–140.

Stinson, J.L., & Howard, D.R. (2008). Winning does matter: Patterns in private giving to athletic and academic programs at NCAA Division I-AA and I-AAA institutions. *Sport Management Review, 11*(1), 1–20.

Strode, J., & Fink, J. (2009). Using motivational theory to develop a donor profile scale for intercollegiate athletics. *Journal for the Study of Sports and Athletes in Education, 3*(3), 335–354.

Szelc, J. (2011, January 4). Marquette University's athletic director luncheons. National Association of Athletic Development Directors. www.nacda.com/sports/naadd/spec-rel/060410aah.html.

Terrell, M. (2010, January 5). Capital campaigns in focus: New Kenan Stadium. National Association of Athletic Development Directors. www.nacda.com/sports/naadd/spec-rel/010510aaa.html.

Thamel, P., & Whitmire, K. (2011, January 8). Auburn's kingmaker isn't sharing in the moment. *New York Times*. www.nytimes.com/2011/01/09/sports/ncaafootball/09boosters.html?pagewanted=all&_r=0.

Thornburg, B., of Virginia Tech Athletics Hokie Club. (2012). Interview by R. Zullo.

Ticket holder sues. (2007, April/May). *Athletic Management*. www.athleticmanagement.com/2007/05/08/ticket_holder_sues/index.php.

Troudt, H. (2011, April 25). $5 million gift allows the University of Virginia to begin construction on new track and field facility. National Association of Athletic Development Directors. www.nacda.com/sports/naadd/spec-rel/042511aaa.html.

Tsiotsou, R. (1998). Motivation for donations to athletic programs. *Cyber Journal of Sport Marketing 2*(2).

Tsiotsou, R. (2004). The role of involvement and income in predicting small and large donations to college athletics. *International Journal of Sports Marketing & Sponsorship, 6*(2), 117–123.

Tsiotsou, R. (2006). Investigating differences between female and male athletic donors: A comparative study. *International Journal of Nonprofit and Voluntary Sector Marketing, 11*(3), 209–223.

Tsiotsou, R. (2007). An empirically based typology of intercollegiate athletic donors: High and low motivation scenarios. *Journal of Targeting, Measurement, and Analysis for Marketing, 15*, 79–92.

Weight, E.A., & Cooper, C.G. (2011). Bridging the gap: The perceptions of athletic directors and coaches regarding nonrevenue program discontinuation decisions. *Journal of Sport Administration & Supervision, 3*(1), 61–73.

Wulfekotte, C. (2010, February 5). Monmouth University's employee giving campaign. National Association of Athletic Development Directors. www.nacda.com/sports/naadd/spec-rel/020510aag.html.

Zullo, R. (2011, February/March). On-field fantasy: Athletic departments looking to bring in new money and deepen connections with fans are turning to a fun new idea—fantasy camps. *Athletic Management*. www.athleticmanagement.com/2011/02/26/on-field_fantasy/index.php.

Chapter 12

American College of Sports Medicine, American Dietetic Association, and Dieticians of Canada. (2000). Joint position statement: Nutrition and athletic performance. *Medicine and Science in Sports and Exercise, 32*(12), 2130–2145.

Association for Applied Sport Psychology. (2013a). About AASP. www.appliedsportpsych.org/about/.

Association for Applied Sport Psychology. (2013b). Become a certified consultant. www.appliedsportpsych.org/certified-consultants/become-a-certified-consultant/

Astin, A.W., Astin, H.S., & Lindholm, J.A. (2011). *Cultivating the spirit: How college can enhance students' inner lives.* San Francisco: Jossey-Bass.

Broughton, E., & Neyer, M. (2001). Advising and counseling student-athletes. *New Directions for Student Services, 93*, 47–53.

Comeaux, E. (2013). Rethinking academic reform and encouraging organizational innovation: Implications for stakeholder management in college sports. *Innovative Higher Education, 38*(4), 281–293.

Cooper, C.G., & Weight, E.A. (2011). Participation rates and gross revenue vs. promotion and exposure: Advertisement and multimedia coverage of 18 sports within NCAA Division I athletic department websites. *Sport Management Review, 14*(4), 399–408.

Covell, D., & Barr, C.A. (2010). *Managing intercollegiate athletics.* Scottsdale, AZ: Holcomb Hathaway.

Covey, S. R. (2004). *The 7 habits of highly effective people.* New York: Simon & Schuster.

Delaney, T., & Madigan, T. (2009). *The sociology of sports: An introduction.* Jefferson, NC: McFarland.

Dzikus, L., Hardin, R., & Waller, S.N. (2012). Case studies of collegiate sport chaplains. *Journal of Sport & Social Issues, 36*(3), 268–294.

Galli, N., & Reel, J.J. (2012). "It was hard, but it was good": A qualitative exploration of stress-related growth in Division I intercollegiate athletes. *Qualitative Research in Sport, Exercise, and Health, 4*(3), 297–319.

Hales, D. (2007). *An invitation to wellness: Making healthy choices.* Belmont, CA: Thomson Wadsworth.

Hayden, E.W., Kornspan, A.S., Bruback, Z.T., Parent, M.C., & Rodgers, M. (2013). The existence of sport psychology services among NCAA Division I FBS university athletic departments and counseling centers. *The Sport Psychologist, 27*(3), 296–304.

Hirko, S. (2009). Intercollegiate athletics and modeling multiculturalism. *New Directions for Higher Education, 2009*(148), 91–100.

Howard-Hamilton, M.F., & Sina, J.A. (2001). How college affects student athletes. *New Directions for Student Services, 2001*(93), 35–45.

Koenig, H.G. (2009). Research on religion, spirituality, and mental health: A review. *Canadian Journal of Psychiatry, 54*(5), 283–291.

Koenig, H.G., Parkerson, G.R., & Meador, K.G. (1997). Religion index for psychiatric research. *American Journal of Psychiatry, 154*(6), 885–886.

Nadelen, M. D. (2012, January 10). *Basic injury prevention concepts.* American College of Sports Medicine. www.acsm.org/access-public-information/articles/2012/01/10/basic-injury-prevention-concepts.

National Athletic Trainers' Association. (2014a). Get certified. www.nata.org/get-certified.

National Athletic Trainers' Association. (2014b). Recommendations and Guidelines for Appropriate Medical Coverage of Intercollegiate Athletics. www.nata.org/appropriate-medical-coverage-intercollegiate-athletics.

Pascarella, E.T., & Blimling, G.S. (1996). Students' out-of-class experiences and their influence on learning and cognitive development: A literature review. *Journal of College Student Development, 37*(2), 149–162.

Powers, E. (2007, June 28). When prayer reaches the locker room. *Inside Higher Ed.* www.insidehighered.com/news/2007/06/28/faith.

Rodriguez, N.R., DiMarco, N.M., & Langley, S. (2009). Position of the American Dietetic Association, Dietitians of Canada, and the American College of Sports Medicine: Nutrition and athletic performance. *Journal of the American Dietetic Association, 109*(3), 509–527.

Shaw, A., Joseph, S., & Linley, P.A. (2005). Religion, spirituality, and posttraumatic growth: A systematic review. *Mental Health, Religion, and Culture, 8*(1), 1–11.

Thacker, S.B., Gilchrist, J., Stroup, D.F., & Kimsey, C.D., Jr. (2004). The impact of stretching on sports injury risk: A systematic review of the literature. *Medicine & Science in Sports & Exercise, 36*(3), 371–378.

Wallace, L., Wilson, J., & Miloch, K. (2011). Sporting Facebook: A content analysis of NCAA organizational sport pages and Big 12 Conference athletic department pages. *International Journal of Sport Communication, 4*(4), 422–444.

Watson, J.C., & Kissinger, D.B. (2007). Athletic participation and wellness: Implications for counseling college student-athletes. *Journal of College Counseling, 10*(2), 153–163.

Weinberg, R.S., & Gould, D. (2011). *Foundations of sport and exercise psychology* (5th ed.). Champaign, IL: Human Kinetics.

Wolverton, B. (2008, September 5). Rise in fancy academic centers for athletes raises questions of fairness. *Chronicle of Higher Education.* http://chronicle.com/article/Rise-in-Fancy-Academic-Centers/13493/.

Index

Page numbers followed by an *f* or a *t* indicate a figure or table, respectively.

About the Editors

Erianne A. Weight, PhD, is the director of the prestigious Center for Research in Intercollegiate Athletics and a member of the sport administration faculty at the University of North Carolina at Chapel Hill. She is involved in a variety of Division I athletics consultancies through her role as a research consultant for Collegiate Sports Associates. It is her hope that through research, there will be an increase in the quantity and quality of opportunities for athletic participation and education for young people throughout North America. As a former NCAA Division I heptathlete, she has firsthand insight on the tremendous potential of education through athletics.

Robert H. Zullo, PhD, is the head of the sports management program at Seton Hill University in Greensburg, Pennsylvania. He taught previously at James Madison University and Mississippi State University. He has worked in intercollegiate athletics at the University of Georgia, Virginia Tech, and the University of North Carolina. He started his career in intercollegiate athletics administration through experiences with the University of Virginia athletics department and the Virginia Military Institute. He is a member of North American Society of Sport Management (NASSM), National Association of Collegiate Marketing Administrators (NACMA), and NIRSA: Leaders in Collegiate Recreation.

Contributors

Alyssa T. Bosley, MS
James Madison University

Coyte G. Cooper, PhD
University of North Carolina at Chapel Hill

Brendan Dwyer, PhD
Virginia Commonwealth University

Landon T. Huffman, PhD
Guilford College

Barbara Osborne, JD
University of North Carolina at Chapel Hill

Sally R. Ross, PhD
Grand Valley State University

Stephen L. Shapiro, PhD
Old Dominion University

David J. Shonk, PhD
James Madison University

Ellen J. Staurowsky, EdD
Drexel University